Center for Basque Studies
Basque Classics Series, No. 1

# The Old Law of Bizkaia (1452)

## Introductory Study
## and
## Critical Edition

by

Gregorio Monreal Zia

Translated by
William A. Douglass and Linda White

Preface by
William A. Douglass

Center for Basque Studies
University of Nevada, Reno
Reno, Nevada

This book was published with generous financial support from the Provincial Government of Bizkaia.

Center for Basque Studies
Basque Classics Series, No. 1
Series Editors: William A. Douglass, Gregorio Monreal and Pello Salaburu

Center for Basque Studies
University of Nevada, Reno
Reno, Nevada 89557
http://basque.unr.edu

Cover and series design © 2005 by Jose Luis Agote.
Cover illustration: Fragment of the painting *La jura de los Fueros de Vizcaya por Fernando el Católico* (1476). The work was painted by Francisco de Mendieta at the end of the sixteenth century.

Library of Congress Cataloging-in-Publication Data

The Old Law of Bizkaia (1452) : introductory study and critical edition / compiled, edited, and annotated by Gregorio Monreal Zia ; translated by William A. Douglass and Linda White.
    p. cm. -- (Basque classics series ; no. 1)
  Includes bibliographical references and index.
  ISBN 1-877802-52-2 (pbk.) -- ISBN 1-877802-53-0 (hardcover)
  1. Law--Spain--Vizcaya--Sources.  I. Monreal Zia, Gregorio. II. Douglass, William A. III. White, Linda, 1949- IV. Vizcaya (Spain). Fuero Viejo. English. V. Title. VI. Series.

  KKT9001.A17O426 2005
  349.46'63--dc22

                    2005008119

*Bixenti Zarraonandia eta Begoña Garetxanari,*
*Natxitxun, Bizkaiko itsaso zabalaren baztertxo horretan,*
*betirako atseden hartzen duten baserritar umil eta duinei.*
*Bihotz-bihotzetik esker onez.*

# Contents

# Acknowledgments

At the outset I wish to underscore that there was one especially relevant individual at the time of determining publication of this work, and who also contributed to its later development. I refer to William A. Douglass, who is named as a translator together with Linda White. Now and then his involvement went much beyond the already difficult task of searching for adequate expressions in modern English for a frequently confusing medieval juridical text and written in antiquated Spanish.

In the spring of 1986, while on sabbatical and living with my family in Reno, Bill and I realized several excursions together through the interior of Nevada. During one of those trips, on the road from Tonopah to Fallon, I commented on the status of a possible publication of the *Fuero Viejo de Bizkaia*, the Old Law of Bizkaia. Ten years earlier, I had expended considerable effort collecting manuscripts in order to critically reconstruct the composition of a customary law elaborated in the mid-XV$^{th}$ century by Bizkaians. I concluded the endeavor but, for various reasons, the publication of the final text has been delayed. We discussed the historical-juridical, institutional and anthropological merits of the Old Law, and Bill suggested that its publication would be well-suited for the Basque Book Series that he edited for the University of Nevada Press. Linda White would be responsible for the translation. To be certain, Linda assumed and completed the undertaking with competence and efficiency, however, once again the text languished due to my diverse professional responsibilities.

Two years ago, when the Center for Basque Studies committed to include the *Fuero Viejo* in its new Basque Classics Series, Bill generously offered to assist me with the project, possibly without calculating the full implications of his decision. In August of 2004, we reviewed the precepts of the Fuero, one by one, comparing the original Spanish to the English translation. His perspicacity, anthropological perspective, and knowledge of the traditional society of Vasconia contributed materially to our understanding of certain meanings of the original text. Over the last few months, during which Bill endured the painful loss of his spouse, he dedicated himself consummately to this publication, formulating valuable observations in regards to the structure and content of the Introductory Study and providing the Preface. Therefore, it is only fair to inform the reader of the extent of his collaboration in this work.

Ana Douglass assisted materially with her patient and professional editing.

I would like to extend my thanks to Marian Zarraonandía. In the autumn of 1975, while I was surrounded by the demands and urgencies of competitive examinations for a professorship, she assisted me and twice typed the entire manuscript while deciphering the problematic original calligraphy that had once impeded its reading

Finally, I am grateful to the Friends of Reno (*Amigos de Reno*), an association of academics from The Basque Country who have been visiting scholars at the University of Nevada-Reno's Center for Basque Studies. It was their efforts that secured the support for this publication from the Provincial Government of Bizkaia.

# Preface

The present work provides the Anglo reader with one of Europe's most important, yet little known, medieval legal codes—the *Fuero Viejo* or Old Law of Bizkaia.* Redacted in 1452, or in the waning years of the Late Middle Ages, its text provides intimate insight into a medieval world view at its moment of passing. Europe was still embroiled in (indeed obsessed with) the centuries-long crusade to rid the continent of

---

* Translator's Note: Bizkaia is the place name for both a Basque medieval Seigniory, a Spanish province and one of three components of Euskadi, or the present Basque Autonomous region within Spain. In the Middle Ages, it was rendered in English as Biscay, a seldom-used denomination at present. The confusion is compounded by the tendency of most historians writing in English about the area to employ the Spanish orthographic rendering of Vizcaya for the place name, which is then anglicized to Vizcayan for both the adjectival form and the nominal one for an inhabitant of the territory. The same can be said more or less for the entire spectrum of Basque place names. For example, the Gipuzkoan (Guipuzcoan) city of Donostia is more commonly rendered as San Sebastián, Gasteiz as Vitoria, Iruña as Pamplona and Gernika as Guernica.

In recent years, however, the Basque Language Academy (Euskaltzaindia) has developed its preferred orthography of Basque place names. It will be respected in the present work with the proviso that, when it differs from Spanish usage, for easier comprehension, the latter will be included in parenthesis upon its first occurrence in the text.

There are, however, certain exceptions. First, we will employ Navarra rather than the Basque Academy's Nafarroa, since, although part of the traditional Basque Country, Navarra constitutes its own autonomous region within contemporary Spain and accords official recognition to the former denomination. Second, we have conserved the original orthographic rendering of both surnames and place names in the text of the Old Law itself. Regarding them it should be noted that there was inconsistency or, more accurately, flexibility in the usage of the day. Thus, a name that would be standardized simply as Juan today, in addition to that rendering might assume the forms of Joan, Joannes, etcetera in the Late Middle Ages. It should further be noted that Romance or Old Castilian was the Seigniory of Bizkaia's administrative language, so in the Old Law, Basque place names, personal names and surnames were all being transposed from Basque or Euskara into a Romance format.

Finally, when relevant, we will be anglicizing the official Basque terms rather than their Spanish counterparts. Thus, the inhabitants of Bizkaia are treated as Bizkaians.

the infidel Moors. However, as yet it was unchallenged by the redefinition of humanity that would follow Columbus's first voyage a scant forty years later or the questioning of mankind's relations with the divine posed by Martin Luther's proclamations in the ensuing few decades. The Old Law, then, captures and codifies a system poised on the brink of tremendous geographical and intellectual expansion that would produce the Modern Age.

For the next half millennium, human history, if not exclusively Occidental, was certainly dominated by the West and the many contradictions inherent in its religious Reformation and Counter Reformation, the universalistic humanism of an Enlightenment and the particular nationalism culminating in configuration of the European states. It was a period punctuated by both the most abysmal wrongs and finest rights of humankind. The transatlantic imperialism of several new European powers contained the germs of both civilizing and Christianizing zeal and the unbridled human greed that justified genocide and human enslavement on a vast scale. Yet there was also the universalist humanism of an Enlightenment facilitating the scientific curiosity and creativity informing rational inquiry into solutions for such human miseries as disease, famine and poverty. In both the American and French Revolutions, human rights and individual liberty were both furthered; and by the late nineteenth and throughout the twentieth centuries, the issue of what constitutes social justice was being contested on a planetary scale by proponents of the socialist and capitalist models. Just exactly what constituted "progress" in each and all of these "modern" developments will likely be debated indefinitely, not only by the victors and vanquished but by future generations of historians.

Why is such a sweeping (and presumptuous) overview of history necessary for present purposes? After all, none of the European events and developments subsequent to 1452 were, of course, anticipated in the Old Law. Its most tangible value was to delineate quotidian life in one little corner of twilight medieval Europe, while also providing several glimpses into the precursive customary practices and consuetudinary law of an earlier age. Nevertheless, while a portrait of one manifestation of medieval reality, there is in the Old Law an even more intriguing prefiguration, when not outright exposition, of many features of what came to be regarded the key "western values." While, in 1452, Bizkaia was but a tiny Seigniory in the Kingdom of Castilla, or even before the birthing of modern Spain, in both spirit and substance many of the Old Law's precepts are stunningly "modern" or "contemporary."

The twin pillars of late medieval Bizkaian society were its primitive democracy and a secular judiciary. Regarding local governance, all

Bizkaian males were convened in periodic General Assembly both to legislate and, at times, to serve as the court of highest appeal in a major civil or criminal lawsuit. The convocations were announced by the sounding of horns from five mountaintops throughout the Land, as was the custom. While an assembly might be held elsewhere, Bizkaia's political epicenter was the town of Gernika, and more particularly its sacred oak. Beneath its canopy, in theory all Bizkaian males gathered to craft public policy, and an autochthonous judiciary tried those criminals whose offenses were sufficiently grave as to warrant incarceration, physical punishment and even death. Bizkaia's democracy was quite similar to that of certain Swiss cantons of the epoch and, like theirs, was primitive in the sense that, rather than representational, participation was direct and universal.

The Old Law was ever vigilant against external forces and influences, whether emanating from royal or ecclesiastical sources. As the condition for the allegiance of Bizkaians, upon assuming the throne of Castilla the new Monarch, in his or her capacity as Lord or Lady of the Seigniory, had to come to Bizkaia and, in several venues throughout the Land, swear to safeguard and respect its *fueros* (laws) and customs. The oath-taking route both terminated and culminated in Gernika. Under the Old Law, the monarchs were powerless to change Bizkaian law without the concurrence of the General Assembly.

Bizkaia lacked its own resident bishop and the power of both its local priests and external prelates was limited in the extreme. Most legal matters were deemed to be secular rather than ecclesiastical, hence were assigned by the Old Law to the civil rather than canonical court system. That secular jurisdiction was informed by autochthonous Bizkaian law rather than its wider Castilian counterpart. In most matters the *Fuero Viejo* accorded to all Bizkaians immunity from being tried by, and according to the precepts of, Castilian civil law; a Reformation, indeed, excepting for violations regarding dueling, no Bizkaian could be extradited and then judged outside the Seigniory.

Then there was the very legal status of Bizkaian citizenship. The Old Law makes certain clear social distinctions among the *hidalgos* or noblemen, the *labradores* or peasant tenants and *villanos* or commoner townspeople. However, there was clearly no feudal serfdom in the classic sense. Indeed, when, in 1526, the Old Law was reformed into the *Fuero Nuevo*, rather than further defining and reifying the social class distinctions, all Bizkaians were declared to be noble and of equal standing! This claim would eventually be extended to neighboring Gipuzkoa and Araba as well, and thereby became a "Basque," rather than exclusively "Bizkaian," privilege.

Probably the most modern (and extraordinary for the epoch) aspects of the Old Law were its treatments of both women and the rights of the individual. While women were not enfranchised, they nevertheless enjoyed full legal personage in almost every other regard. Far from being subjected to male authority, Bizkaian women owned property, which they were free to buy, sell and bequeath (albeit subject to certain restrictions that applied equally and identically to the property of men). Not only was the testimony of women admissible in court cases, in certain instances the Old Law actually required them to appear in the capacity of witnesses.

The rights of an accused were an overriding concern of the Old Law. There was the equivalent of the modern practice of posting bail. Either by providing a sufficient amount of one's own property or producing an "honest and propertied" *fiador* (guarantor) willing to ensure the party's court appearance and subsequent payment of any costs and fines ordered by the judge, a defendant was exempted from pre-trial incarceration. Indeed, the plaintiff as well was required to produce his or her own property and/or *fiador(es)* to meet possible court costs, retribution to an exonerated defendant and fines in the event that he or she lost the case.

But of particular interest, and an ancient echo of fundamental contemporary rights within Occidental law, were the defendant's immunity from double jeopardy and right of *habeas corpus*. It should be noted that the Old Law was explicit in this regard more than two centuries before England's vaunted and ostensibly watershed Habeas Corpus Act of 1679!

Given that neither the Bizkaians nor the Basques have ever attained statehood within a Europe parsed into states as its prime political players, it is scarcely surprising that Bizkaia's extraordinary politico-juridical system is little known, which is not to say that it went entirely unnoticed. In 1801, the German savant Wilhelm von Humboldt visited Bizkaia and declared it to be a truly unique "nation."[1] The eventual second American president, John Adams, visited Bizkaia in 1779. In 1787, he published in England a three-volume *Defense of Constitutions of Government of the United States of America*. Volume one was issued in its first American edition just prior to the Philadelphia Constitutional Convention and was read widely by the redactors of the Constitution of the United States of America.

Adams was defending his belief in a "federal democracy" in which the rule of "the one, the few and the many" would obtain. He argued for independent and balancing judiciary, executive and legislative branches of government. The legislative function would be divided between populist and privileged chambers. Both the chief executive and the legislators were to be elected through a popular vote. In short, Adams defended what was subsequently adopted as the American model of democratic government that persists to this day.

In mustering his arguments, Adams reviewed historical and contemporary examples of other democratic systems of government. While he voiced his criticisms of each, he found the most laudatory to be the "democratic republics," among which he included only certain Swiss cantons, San Marino and Bizkaia. Regarding the latter, Adams noted,

> "In a research like this, after those people in Europe who have had the skill, courage, and fortune, to preserve a voice in the government, Bizcay, in Spain, ought by no means to be omitted. While their neighbors have long since resigned all their pretensions into the hands of kings and priests, this extraordinary people have preserved their ancient language, genius, laws, government, and manners, without innovations, longer than any other nation of Europe."[2]

In 1810, or the advent of the century in which Bizkaia's laws and customs would be challenged and then overturned by the Napoleonic invasions and then Spanish central authority, William Wordsworth penned the following poem under the title "The Oak of Guernica."

> Oak of Guernica! Tree of holier power
> Than that which in Dordona did enshrine
> (So faith too fondly deemed) a voice divine
> Heard from the depths of its aerial bower—
> How canst thou flourish at this blighting hour?
> What hope, what joy can sunshine bring to thee,
> Or the soft breezes from the Atlantic sea,
> The dews of morn, or April's tender shower?
> Stroke merciful and welcome would that be
> Which should extend thy branches on the ground,
> If never more within their shady round
> Those lofty-minded Lawgivers shall meet,
> Peasant and lord, in their appointed seat,
> Guardians of Biscay's ancient liberty.[3]

Gernika's centrality as the most tangible symbol of not only Bizkaian but Basque liberty was enhanced even as the rights and privileges reflected in the Old Law and other iterations of Basque *fueros* were eroded in the aftermath of both nineteenth (the Carlist Wars) and twentieth (the Spanish Civil War) century battlefield defeats. In the 1850s, a disillusioned Gipuzkoan bard, José María Iparragirre, penned the song Gernikako Arbola (Tree of Gernika), which has become the *de facto* Basque national anthem. When sung today in the Basque centers of Boise, Buenos Aires or Sydney, Iparragirre's words never fail to bring tears to the eyes and pride to the voices of expatriate Basques. The first stanza proclaims,

| | |
|---|---|
| Guernicaco Arbola | The Tree of Gernika |
| Da bedeincatuba. | Is a blessed symbol. |
| Euscaldunen artean | Among the Basques |
| Guztiz maitatuba: | Dearly beloved: |
| Eman ta zabaltzazu | Holy tree, spread your |
| Munduban frutuba, | Fruit throughout the world, |
| Adoratzen zaitugu | While we render unto you |
| Arbola santuba.[4] | Our adoration. |

For the wider world Gernika has been immortalized as the quintes-sential *cri de coeur* against the horrors of war by Pablo Picasso's famed painting. The work freezes forever the terror felt by the thousands of defenseless civilians slaughtered when, on April 26, 1937, a market day in Gernika, the Luftwaffe launched what was arguably history's first aerial attack on a human settlement, killing 1,654 persons.

In conclusion, then, the Old Law both reflects and configures Biz-kaia as a unique society within both the Europe and Iberia of its day. Regarding the latter, Bizkaia was the only one of the several political entities constituting the Kingdom of Castilla, and subsequently Spain, to enjoy such privileged status. Indeed, it is fair to say that the Old Law is the foundational text of a people's identity, as well as the continuing claim by some Basques to political protagonism either within or with-out the Spain and France of the twenty-first century. The Basque case remains one of the thornier unresolved issues as Europe seeks to inte-grate and accommodate its stateless regions within that most ambitious of contemporary political projects—the European Union.

It is therefore most appropriate that the Center for Basque Studies of the University of Nevada, Reno, initiate its Basque Classics Series with publication and translation of this critical edition of the Old Law or *Fuero Viejo* of 1452. It is quite simply both the foundational and canonical text of Basque history.

William A. Douglass

# The Old Law and Its Contexts:

# An Introductory Study

# Part One

## I. A Geopolitical Overview

The presentation of an important medieval Bizkaian legal text to an Anglophone readership should perhaps be preceded by a short geographical and geopolitical overview of Vasconia and Bizkaia. Vasconia, which includes Bizkaia, is situated along the Atlantic coast of southwestern Europe where the Western Pyrenees reach down to the Bay of Biscay. Politically, the territory of Vasconia—or Euskalherria in Basque—is divided between France and Spain. A small portion—the French Basque Country or Iparralde—is continental, while the majority—the Spanish Basque Country or Hegoalde—is peninsular. While Vasconia is oriented toward the Atlantic, both geographically and historically, many of its rivers drain southeastward to the Mediterranean. Despite its modest overall size (20,000 square kilometers), the coastline, mountains and interior plains of Vasconia provide it with an array of climates and considerable human diversity.[5] Today there are slightly fewer than three million inhabitants in Euskalherria.

### 1. VASCONIA IN ANTIQUITY

The Basques are a pre-Indo-European people, one whose prehistorical affiliations are yet to be determined.[6] What is certain is that the Celts, the earliest of the Indo-European speakers to invade Western Europe, found a certain Pyrenean cultural complex already in place. The Greco-Romans Polybius, Strabo and Ptolemy, writing between the second centuries before and after Christ, were the first to reference the Basques and the closely-related Karistios and Bardulians (as well as the nearby peoples of Aquitania). By all indications, the inclusion of Vasconia within the Roman orbit was peaceful, and the acculturation of the southern or Mediterranean part of the country extensive. There was demographic growth, expansion of agriculture and animal husbandry, and development of mining and communications. It is likely that the former political structures were impacted and modified as well. Also mytho-religious beliefs and the autochthonous languages surely felt the impact of Latin, which indeed provided the latter with both concepts and loan words. Nevertheless, the Basque language survived in the majority of Vasconia's territory. Indeed, Basque proved to be the only pre-Indo-European and pre-Roman language in southern Europe to do so.[7]

For reasons that are unknown, during its final phase (the fourth and fifth centuries A.D.), the Basques changed their posture regarding the Empire. Indeed, they confronted directly Rome's successors and heirs, the Germanic tribes that created the respective Kingdoms of Galia (the Franks) and Hispania (the Visigoths). Frankish and Visigothic chronicles are replete with expressions such as *domuit vascones* ("dominated the Basques"), *vascones vastavit* ("devastated the Basques"), or *vasconum …infestantium…perculsi sunt* ("Infesting Basques were struck"), which seem to underscore the continual military actions of Frankish and Visigothic monarchs against the Basques, as well as the precariousness of the results. After the sixth century, Vasconia had secured its place within the historical atlases of political Europe.[8]

## 2. Bizkaia between Asturias and Navarra: The Creation of a Seigniorial Dynasty[9]

The arrival of the Mussulmans in the eighth century served as a political catalyst for the central Basques—those who would later become the Navarrese—to form a state, the Kingdom of Pamplona, known in later centuries as the Kingdom of Navarra. Allied with the Mussulmans recently installed in the Valley of the Ebro River, first they confronted the Merovingians and subsequently Charlemagne and the Carolingians. The new Kingdom of Pamplona promptly expanded to the west, and by the tenth century probably began its occupation of the western lands where Basque was spoken. Nevertheless, during the next three centuries it proved difficult to maintain the unity of the Monarchy's patrimony.[10] There was harsh competition with the powerful Kingdom of Castilla-León, which was expanding both its territory and influence while seeking a direct link with France through the western part of the Navarrese Kingdom. In effect, in 1200, Alfonso VIII of Castilla through conquest managed to absorb Araba, Gipuzkoa and the Duranguesado or Bizkaia (which had already fallen within the conqueror's orbit a quarter of a century earlier). The intrinsic viability of Navarra was diminished not only by the loss of territory but by virtue of the fact that the Kingdom was now landlocked.

The earliest mention of the term Bizkaia, referring to the present territory of that name, appears in the ninth century in an Asturian chronicle. A century later there is another reference to a Bizkaian count married to a Navarrese princess. Each prefigured one of the two poles—

Asturias-León-Castilla and Navarra—of political attraction for this western Basque land. By the eleventh century, the term and concept of Bizkaia are reasonably well documented. The territory of this original or core Bizkaia was situated between the Nerbioi (Nervión)/Ibaizabal Rivers and that of Deba. It constitutes a countship district of the Kingdom of Pamplona and is ruled by Eneko Lupiz, a Navarrese high functionary who governed Bizkaia for several decades. It is possible that he secured from the monarchs the right of hereditary succession, that is, the capacity to transmit to his successors the title and privileges of count. The attribution of this governance notwithstanding, there was a superior level of authority—what today we would call sovereignty—in the hands of the monarch. But the hereditability of the countship created a veritable dynasty of lords of the territory—the Haro family.[11]

The respective forces of attraction exerted upon Bizkaia by the Kingdoms of Castilla-León and Pamplona (or Navarra) are evident in the eleventh century. There is a period of alternation of both Kingdoms' sovereignty over Bizkaia. However, the very grave crisis of the Navarrese Monarchy in 1076 prompted Eneko Lupiz to accept the authority of the King of Castilla, a Kingdom in which Eneko's Bizkaian successors found an ample playing field on which to satisfy their nobiliary ambitions and expectations. If indeed it is certain that Bizkaia would quickly become reintegrated within the patrimony of the Kingdom of Navarra, at the end of the twelfth century the Bizkaian seigniorial dynasty—the House of Haro—becomes entangled definitively with the Castilian Court and drags along with it the countship.

3. The Seigniory under the Sway of the Castilian Monarchs and the Institutional Integration of the Countdom's Component Territories: The Bizkaian Core or Tierra Llana, the Duranguesado, the Encartaciones and the Villas

After the conquests of Alfonso VIII, and from 1200 A.D. throughout the late Middle Ages, Bizkaia, Araba, and Gipuzkoa (facilitated by the acquiescence of the Monarchy) fostered within the Castilian framework their expanding statutory political autonomy. In 1512, that which remained of the Kingdom of Navarra was itself conquered. Although it was incorporated into the Castilian Crown, its condition as a Kingdom was accorded ample respect. By the Modern Age, all of the traditional peninsular territories of Vasconia were dependents of the Castilian Crown, and thereby benefited from the Spanish Monarchy's quest for political hegemony in Europe, on the one hand, and the immense opportunities inherent in the colonization of the Americas, on the other.

Basques played a role in both undertakings in a manner out of proportion to their territorial and demographic importance.

Regarding the Seigniory of Bizkaia, after its definitive anchoring within the Castilian orbit, the house of Haro managed to round out the original countdom of core Bizkaia or the Tierra Llana by incorporating under its seigniorial authority two adjacent territories. Reference is to the Duranguesado,[12] situated to the southeast, and the Encartaciones,[13] located to the west on the left bank of the Nerbioi/Ibaizabal Rivers. In order to articulate the three territories, the lords utilized the institution of primogeniture that obligated the titleholder of the countship to maintain intact the elements constituting its patrimony and then to pass it on to his successor. This submission over several generations of the Tierra Llana, Duranguesado and the Encartaciones to the jurisdiction of a single lord and his officialdom created a kind of institutional unity among them. In this fashion the denomination of Bizkaia, which referred originally only to the Tierra Llana of the Seigniory, was gradually generalized to all three territories. Nevertheless, in the case of Bizkaia, as we shall see, a certain clear institutional distinction among the three territorial entities comprising the Seigniory is maintained throughout the Middle Ages (and into the Modern Age as well). The Old Law of 1452 reflects well this duality between the seigniorial unity of the whole, as reflected in some common institutions, on the one hand, and the politico-administrative singularity of each one of the territories, on the other.[14]

The political institutional complexity of the Countdom of Bizkaia was exacerbated notably by the creation of a complex of municipalities with special characteristics and collective political character—the so-called Villas. In the kingdoms of the Iberian Peninsula and Europe as a whole, during the eleventh century there was notable urbanization that produced population nuclei, each with their own statute according them a considerable degree of autonomy. In the case of Bizkaia, the process was delayed somewhat, but between 1229 and 1376, 21 *villas* were founded in core Bizkaia, the Duranguesado region and the Encartaciones. These included Orduña, Bermeo, Lanestosa, Plentzia (Plencia), Bilbo (Bilbao), Otxandio (Ochandiano), Portugalete, Lekeitio (Lequeitio), Ondarroa, Billaro (Villaro), Markina (Marquina), Elorrio, Gernika (Guernica), Gerrikaitz (Gerricaiz), Miravalles, Durango, Ermua, Mungia (Munguía), Larrabetzu (Larrabezúa), Errigoiti (Rigoitia). There was also the frontier town of Balmaseda (Valmaseda), founded in 1199, or before it was subsequently incorporated into the Seigniory.

The Villas, with their urban opportunities and certain foundational privileges, attracted the inhabitants of their hinterlands. The new set-

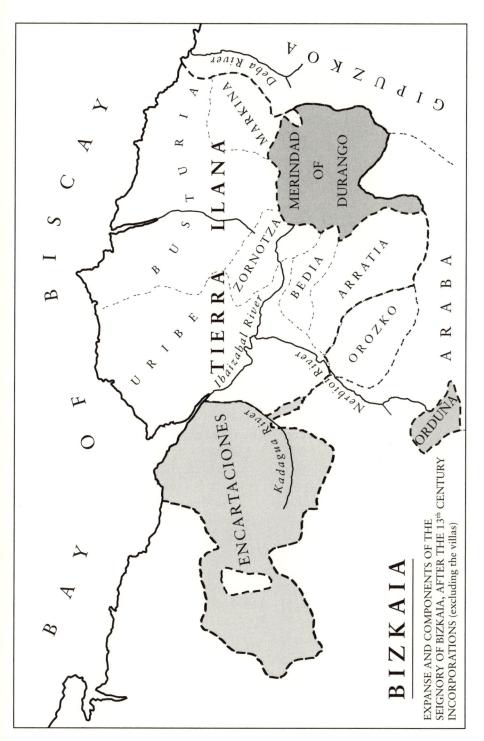

## BIZKAIA

EXPANSE AND COMPONENTS OF THE
SEIGNORY OF BIZKAIA, AFTER THE 13th CENTURY
INCORPORATIONS (excluding the villas)

tlers received as their collective patrimony seigniorial lands of the
founder, who might reserve certain rights for himself. In the *villa* there
emerged the institution of the *alcaldes* (in reality judges), as well as
other local officials. Over time the political autonomy of the *villa*
increased, culminating finally in the elimination of any dependency
upon the aristocratic officialdom operative within its surrounding
*merindad* or district. It should be noted, since it is reflected clearly in the
Fuero, that the Villas were subject to their own laws, which differed
from those of the rest of the territory. Broadstroke, the former was
based upon the founding charter and Fuero of the highly privileged city
of Logroño.[15] Reference is to a brief codex that was concerned with certain important aspects, both public and private, of the collective life of
a municipality. The normative gaps in that short document were bridged
with Bizkaian custom as lived in the surrounding countryside. Subsequently, however, and particularly after approval of the Ordinances of
Alcalá in 1348, all of the Villas (and notably the larger ones) were
increasingly subject to royal law. In effect, the Villas opted for Castilian
law regarding legal process and civil matters, at least in part. But regarding public law they continued to observe the custom of Bizkaia, that is
to say the Fuero of Bizkaia. And it is highly likely that in the smaller *villas*, those with a traditional way of life, Bizkaian custom continued to
apply in most aspects of both the private and public domains. In any
event, the appearance on the scene of this bloc, designated Villas, inaugurated a dual system of justice whose manifestations will be apparent
when we examine in detail the prescriptions of the Old Law.[16]

Nevertheless, in the Villas as well, the collective Bizkaian right of
primogeniture, with its unique seigniorial overtones, obtained. Additionally, the residents of the Villas were full participants in Bizkaia's
General Assemblies (*Juntas Generales*), the principal one being held
beneath the sacred oak tree of Gernika, where the body politic
addressed the problems and crafted the solutions within the Seigniory's
political life. Residents of the Villas enjoyed the same political rights as
all Bizkaians. They contributed taxes to the public purse. In short, the
Villas formed part of a larger political entity, even if they continued to
conserve their institutional personality as reflected in each of their local
charters.[17]

## II. Juridical Romanization, Castilian Royal Law and Bizkaian Law

The Old Law is the written exposition of the consuetudinary laws
of the Bizkaian community, compiled tardily if one's point of temporal
reference is that which happened in Castilla and in other peninsular
states, as well as in the rest of Europe.

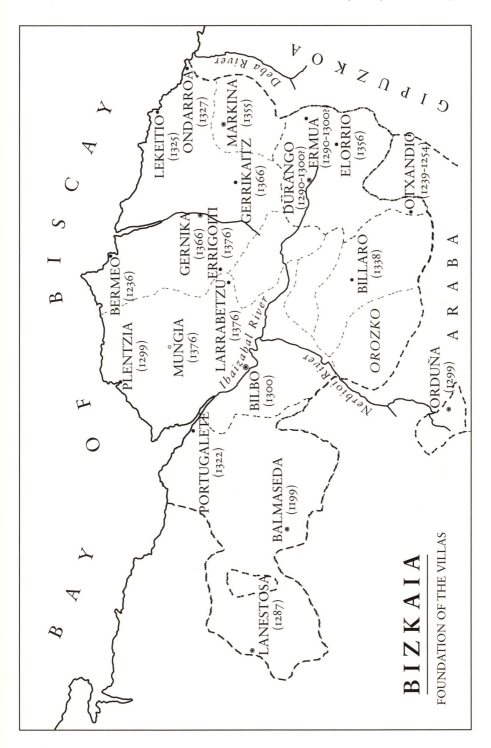

**BIZKAIA**

FOUNDATION OF THE VILLAS

In order to understand the meaning of Bizkaian custom, we must first consider, albeit summarily, the evolution of law in the Kingdom of Castilla-León—Bizkaia's wider political framework from the thirteenth century on—Spain and Europe. A critical factor in this part of the world has been its juridical Romanization, produced at two distinct and quite distant moments in time.

It is beyond our scope to develop a full treatment of Classic Roman law. I would simply note its manifestation during Roman domination—in Hispania and Galia from the third century B.C. to the fifth century A.D.—in various forms such as the founding of colonies of Roman and Latin citizens and the universal concessions of Latinity and citizenship. Roman law replaced totally or partially the laws of the indigenous peoples. The intensity of this juridical influence in western Europe varied according to the degree of cultural Romanization in a particular locale. The appearance of the so-called vulgar or adulterated Roman law in the Late Empire is a manifestation of the distance that obtained between official code and the reality of legal practice.

## 1. Medieval Custom

We noted earlier that the Basques rebelled against the Roman order in the final phase of the Empire, and that they regularly confronted the Frankish and Visigothic Monarchies. Consequently, effectively there was closure of most European locales in the Late Age of Antiquity to external juridical influences. Similarly, between the fifth century and the eleventh or twelfth, there is no external political hegemony established in or imposed upon Vasconia or Bizkaia. Here—as in the majority of the European territories of the epoch, and particularly between the eighth and twelfth centuries—it is the local society itself that creates its own law through various procedures: by generating authentic customs, by establishing pacts of different kinds or by receiving concessions of privileges. Roman law was forgotten. Justice came to be administered more informally as part of local practice invoked as "customary." That is to say, there was a certain *ad hoc* interpretation of the truth by a judge in search of solutions that were consonant with community opinion. Indeed, such decisions had to be acceptable to a community that participated fully in decisive judicial assemblies.[18]

Bizkaia participated in this more or less spontaneous creation of consuetudinary norms, as did other territories of the Cantabrian Cornice and the Pyrenees. This manner of generating law was also evident in the areas of Castilla repopulated by settlers from Vasconia and Cantabria.[19] The evolution of the juridical system of these territories was configured profoundly by this multisecular experience of social autonomy. That which transpired in the Late Middle Ages helps to explain the subsequent differences in their respective political organization.

## 2. THE RECEPTION OF ROMAN LAW IN THE LATE MIDDLE AGES

But there is a second historical phase of the penetration and influence of Roman law, as noteworthy as the earlier one and as extraordinarily decisive in the evolution of European law. Reference is to the outstanding, indeed almost exclusive, role played by the Justinian Code—particularly the Digest or Pandects—in both legal doctrine and the teaching of law in European universities from the twelfth to the nineteenth centuries. Throughout the Late Middle Ages and the Modern Age, there were teaching institutions and schools of thought devoted to the study, interpretation and construction of a legal system based upon Roman law, the canon law of the Catholic Church and Lombard feudal law. Initially, this was evident in the Italian universities and, subsequently, throughout those of the Holy Roman Empire, and including the universities of peripheral European countries. These were the schools of the glossaturs, the postglossaturs and the commentators (who employed the methods of the *mos italicus*) and of the French and Central European humanists (who worked with the *mos gallicus*).

The reception of civil law was not a solely academic phenomenon of enthusiastic erudites working with classic juridical texts that were considered to be the *ratio scripta* of jurisprudence. Rather, civil law penetrated progressively into Italian legal practice, as well as that of southern France, Spain, and later in the German Empire. The new legal system was spread in part by the movements of thousands of university students and their professors. They formed the new social group of the legalists and the lettered, and they influenced directly and decisively the elaboration of the curriculum and texts. The resistance by the lower classes and of the privileged estates did not prove an effective obstacle, faced as they were with the support that this nascent bourgeoisie gave to juridical Romanization.[20]

In fact, juridical Romanization was quite intense in southern France and in the states of the Spanish Levant (Catalunya, Valencia, and Mallorca). In the Kingdom of Castilla-León, the Monarchy wavered over authorizing the doctrines of the great Italian civil law experts and canonists as admissible in court. From 1427, in Castilla legal recourse was had only to the commentators who came after Bartolo da Sassoferrato and to the canonist Juan de Andrés.[21] Nevertheless, Romanism had entered the Castilian legal edifice through legislation.[22] Subsequently, we will consider in greater detail the evolution of juridical norms in the

Kingdom of Castilla, Bizkaia's broader legal setting in the Late Middle Ages.[23]

### 3. CASTILIAN ROYAL LAW, COMMON LAW AND THE DISAPPEARANCE OF LOCAL LAW

With its conquest of the Moors of Andalucia and Murcia in the second half of the thirteenth century, the Kingdom of Castilla-León became the most powerful realm on the Iberian Peninsula, as well as one of Europe's most important. Having fleshed out the Kingdom, the Castilian-Leonese Monarchs undertook reform of the complexity of juridical structures of their constituent territories with an eye toward greater uniformity. The effort addressed extraordinary juridical diversity. In addition to those territories (including Bizkaia) characterized by consuetudinary law, there were those in the realm governed by Frankish law. To the south of the Duero River, various systems of "frontier" laws and accommodations obtained. Finally, there was an extensive region in the southern meseta, parts of Andalucia and Murcia, governed by the *Fuero Juzgo*, a juridical code based upon the ancient Visigothic ordinances dating from the seventh century.

Fernando III (1201–1252) was the first monarch to conceive of a uniform legal code for the Kingdom, but it was his son, Alfonso X (The Wise) who would implement it. Alfonso X ruled between 1252 and 1284. For his juridical reform, he employed various law books that were both elaborated in his court and received from posterity. One of the latter was the *Fuero Juzgo* of his southern territories. He took the initiative in redacting three new books, the *Espéculo*, the *Fuero Real* and the *Siete Partidas*. The last two are of interest to this study.

The *Fuero Real* (Royal Fuero) was elaborated in 1255. It is a short code, based on the *Fuero Juzgo* and canon law. It addresses public, civil, penal and processual law. It became the municipal law of numerous population centers in the north of the realm, including the Basque territory of Araba beginning in 1331 A.D. The *Siete Partidas* became the most important work of Hispanic law and is universally renowned. It contains 2,500 laws arranged into seven parts. Among its juridical sources are the Italian glossators of Justinian Roman law and the commentaries of the Decretals of Gregory IX, as well as Lombard feudal law. According to tradition, the *Siete Partidas* were elaborated between 1256 and 1265, although their provisions did not enter into effect until nearly a century later. Consequently, the *Siete Partidas de Alfonso X el Sabio* came to be considered "the Spanish version of civil law." As Professor Lalinde has pointed out, this was more than a reception, that is, of the direct admission of the civil law texts into the epoch's legal system.

Rather, it was penetration equivalent to fundamental inspiration and to impregnation of the new law with precepts and guidelines.[24]

Alfonso X's attempt to produce a more unified juridical order for the Kingdom by elaborating or authorizing law books succeeded in the southern part of the realm through application of the *Fuero Juzgo*. Elsewhere, however, the King met opposition from the nobles and many municipalities who preferred to maintain traditional law. In a compromise with the King, implemented in the Cortes of Zamora of 1274, the Councils managed to conserve the ancient law, but the King retained direct jurisdiction in criminal suits of particular gravity, the so-called "Court cases."[25] Popular and aristocratic opposition was unable to impede a constant progression of a general law for the Kingdom. The *Fuero Real* and the *Partidas* eventually consecrated the Monarch's full competency to legislate and inspired political activism in the creation of norms (royal directives, permissions, provisions, ordinances, etc.). The Cortes achieved a colegislative competency as well, that they exercised through codes of law, prepared by the Royal Council (*Consejo Real*) and approved in Assembly by the Castilian estates, or by means of Codes of Petitions, elaborated through the initiative of any one of the estates represented in the Cortes and then approved by the Monarch. Of greatest interest to this study is the 1348 Ordinances of the Cortés of Alcalá, in that it established the order of preference and precedence of the sources of Castilian law.[26] After this date that code was applied in the Villas of Bizkaia in the guise of royal law.

A crisis of local and territorial law was one effect of the relative uniformity instituted by the legislative revolution of Alfonso X. The legal centralization contributed decisively to the decline of local law, through both the competition with royal law initiated in the thirteenth century and accentuated in the following one when the Ordinances of Alcalá required that, in order to remain in effect, a municipal *fuero* had to demonstrate not only its longstanding use but also that it did not contradict God's law, reason and royal law. No new *fueros* were granted nor existing ones confirmed. They began to be considered a relic of the past.[27]

In order to better understand what follows below concerning the specificities of Basque and Bizkaian law, it should be noted that the creation of a general law that displaced local codes is one of the fundamental parameters of the juridico-political modernity of the Castilian Kingdom. Obviously, there are other indicators as well, such as the growing independence from papal temporal authority as reflected in the *pase regio* (royal veto) and the beginning of control of the Church by means of the right of patronage, the delimitation of the Kingdom's frontiers and the official importance accorded the Castilian language. Already in the Late Middle Ages, and in a particularly early fashion in Castilla, there emerged a modernity based in monarchical absolutism once the limitations upon it by the former dualism or political corporatism of the estates was overcome. But, as we shall underscore, the crucial element in this process was the standardization of law and the corresponding enhancement of centralized institutions.[28]

## 4. The Subsistence of Bizkaian Law

Bizkaia and the other Basque territories integrated into Castilla in 1200 were exceptional in that their juridical evolution was inverse to that of the remaining territories of the Kingdom.[29] In the face of the aforementioned general legal standardization and disappearance of local law, Bizkaia conserved and developed its own legal system, with the relative exception of the Villas, which would receive royal law.

In order to explain the persistence of Bizkaian custom in the Tierra Llana, Duranguesado and the Encartaciones, we must take into account several factors. It should first be noted that two centuries passed from the time of the political integration of core Bizkaia into the Kingdom of Castilla-León about 1175 A.D. and the incorporation of the entire Seigniory into the Crown in 1379 A.D. During this period, the Lords of the House of Haro enjoyed ample political autonomy, and all the while the community's traditions of foral self-governance were becoming firmly established. By the time the Seigniory was finally incorporated into the Crown (1379), the Land possessed its own various and solid institutions: its peculiar justice system with its own judges (*alcaldes de Fuero*), officials such as the *prestameros* and *merinos*, internal jurisdictions— *anteiglesias* and *merindades*—with their own assemblies, recognized exemptions and liberties, the General Assemblies of Gernika and a rich and well elaborated body of consuetudinary law that was known as the "Fuero of Bizkaia." There existed a critical mass of features that had survived from earlier times. At the time Bizkaia was referred to as "a land apart," that is, not integrated into the Kingdom's common governmental structures. It was also said that Bizkaia "always wishes its *fueros* to be safeguarded and sworn to (be upheld)." In this fashion Bizkaia resisted homogenization with the royal order obtaining in the rest of the Kingdom and the centralization of power and authority that it implied.

When the grand bodies of Castilian law promulgated by the monarchs appeared on the horizon, followed by the plethora of norms legislated by the Cortes and ruler alike, Bizkaia's solid consuetudinary law proved to be sufficiently powerful to achieve a stalemate, a state of affairs defended well by Bizkaia's General Assembly backed by a well-structured Bizkaian community.

But the foregoing reality corresponded to but an important part of Bizkaia—the Tierra Llana or core Bizkaia, the Duranguesado and the Encartaciones. It did not concern the entirety of the Seigniory, since within it were the Villas with their royal charters and where Bizkaian custom was weakened in many legal domains by standardized royal law. Throughout the Land, the new municipal councils provided an influence and a demonstration effect of the normative aspirations and processes of the lords and, subsequently, the monarchs. The first manifestations of the normative capacity of the Lords of Bizkaia were evident in the Early Middle Ages in the capacity of concession of particular and general privileges that created, confirmed or amplified certain prerogatives. In the Late Middle Ages, such intervention was accentuated when rules of law were implemented that affected the municipalities specifically. In point of fact, within the bundle of powers constituting seigniorial authority—similar to those that made up the "regnum" or royal authority—there is that of the right to charter villages on the lands of the Lord; although in the case of Bizkaia, the founding of privileged settlements required the "consent of the Bizkaians" convened in General Assembly.

I indicated earlier that the Fuero of Logroño influenced the charters of the Villas and that it contained but a minimum of juridical rules designed to privilege the settlers. The many normative lacunae would be covered by recourse to the consuetudinary law of the surrounding territory, that is, by Bizkaian custom. The situation seems to have changed in the middle of the fourteenth century, in the aftermath of the Villa's new council's support of Castilian royal law. From then on the vacuum created by the paucity of detail in municipal charters was filled, at least officially, by the grand normative bodies of royal law. What is certain is that in the founding documents of the later Villas, or after Bizkaia's incorporation into the Crown, there is a tendency to cite the authority of the Ordinances of Alcalá of 1348. Bizkaian consuetudinary law remained an influence in the Villas, at least theoretically, but in the unfavorable position of custom versus law. The criteria for validating custom over law were quite imprecise, which supposed the weakening over time of the force of the former. Nevertheless, a part of the Bizkaian order would prevail in the Villas, singularly in the new law of the Hermandades (Confraternities), which concerned certain other common governing institutions, as well as in the authority of freedoms contained in procedural and personal matters that were in the process of constant expansion.

## III. Antecedents of the Old Law (*Fuero Viejo*)

1. THE EMERGENCE OF THE CONCEPT "FUERO OF BIZKAIA"

The complex of Bizkaian consuetudinary norms had crystallized in the Late Middle Ages into the concept of "Fuero of Bizkaia." Well before this juridical concept irrupted as such on the scene, there were two fourteenth century codes—the Codex of 1342 and the Ordinances of 1394. Both of these legal codes undoubtedly prefigured and formalized the foral concept as the Bizkaian legal order, sworn to be upheld by lords of Bizkaia and Castilian monarchs alike, and that were recognized to be clearly binding on all the parties.

The municipal *fuero* or charter of the Villa of Arzeniega in Araba, conceded by the Castilian King Alfonso X in 1272, has an article which gives to the residents, "the Fuero and exemptions that Bizkaia and the council of Vitoria have, that they shall have them well and fulfilled in every way as they are held in Bizkaia and Vitoria." One scholar was perplexed by the apparent incompatibility between the Fuero of Bizkaia, which is "seigniorial, archaic, consuetudinary and inspired in the book of *albedrío*," and that of Vitoria, which is a foundational *fuero* [charter] of a free *villa*."[30]

If a comparison is effected of the content of the first Bizkaian Codex or Fuero of 1342 and the more than forty precepts of the Fuero of the city of Vitoria, there are really no contradictions or incompatibilities. Rather, at their cores they are similar with the exception of the latter's more evident humanitarian concerns regarding punishment of crime. In both texts there are similar freedoms and exemptions, as well as certain approximations regarding the public patrimony, legal process and private law. It may be argued that we are contemplating similarities in two texts that are too removed from one another temporally, but it is a defect of those who would underscore their incompatibilities as well, which, in fact, do not bear up under close scrutiny. At the same time, it seems probable that all of the *villas* of Bizkaia experienced the same circumstances during their foundational phase, since their municipal charters were based upon the Fuero of Logroño and the custom of the Land. The latter would seem to have been so evident and ubiquitous throughout Bizkaia as to not warrant specific mention in the founding charters. Nevertheless, it did make sense to invoke influences from places situated outside of the ambit of the Seigniory, as was the case of Arzeniega and as occurred later in certain municipalities enclaved in valleys of northern Burgos.[31]

We are ignorant of the precise ways in which the norms of Bizkaian public and private law converged and crystallized into a more or less
homogeneous consuetudinary legal corpus. Ultimately, however, the
similarity in the customs of the constituent territories was sufficient for
them to become identified collectively as the Fuero of Bizkaia, which at
times was influential outside the Seigniory itself. There are certain documents, few in fact and proceeding from within Bizkaia, referring to the
application of the law by simply invoking the Fuero of Bizkaia. After
1353, different texts of the Collegiate Church of Zenarrutza, situated in
the heart of the Merindad of Busturia, expound that institution's stipulations with private parties regarding the concession of land in perpetu-
ity in exchange for an initial payment and the subsequent equal division
between the parties of the annual apple harvest and its cider. It is stipulated that the agreements are governed by the Fuero of Bizkaia. In effect,
they are dealings that would have been accommodated readily by Articles 148 and 151 of the Old Law of the following century (1452). There are
also examples of references in the fourteenth century to financial guarantees, property surveys, the regimen regarding mountain farmlands,
the required declarations of five judges, the stipulation that charitable
donations were not to exceed a fifth of a patrimony, and so forth—all
of which were surely reflective of the proper institutions of Bizkaian
consuetudinary law and consonant with articles included in the Old
Law of 1452.[32]

In any event, there is formal reference to the Fuero in both four-
teenth-century legal codices—that of Juan Núñez de Lara redacted in
1342 and that of Gonzalo Moro in 1394. They establish the principle that
the lords and monarchs alike of Bizkaia were required to come to the
Seigniory to swear to observe and safeguard its law.[33]

## 2. THE JUAN NÚÑEZ DE LARA TEXT (1342)

The redaction of Bizkaian consuetudinary law began in 1342, or
more than a century before the Old Law was written down. On the earlier occasion, local representatives and the Lords of Bizkaia, along with
their *alcaldes de Fuero*, gathered ritually beneath Gernika's oak tree that
was sacred to the Bizkaians. Don Juan Núñez de Lara, the consort of
Doña Maria de Haro, Lady of Bizkaia, requested information and a
statement from the assembled regarding three issues: that of the customary ways of imparting justice in the territory, that of the existing rights
in the commons (or mountainous lands), and, finally, clearer specification of the nature of the laws of Bizkaia. We do not know how the
replies were formulated, but they resulted in the drafting of a Codex
(*Cuaderno*). Its text was ratified the following year and again in 1376.[34]

The Codex consists of 37 articles, generally quite concise. We are presented with a brief document focused fundamentally upon penal and procedural matters. Accordingly, it was stated to be customary to summon delinquents to appear in person beneath the tree of Gernika (a procedure which will be spelled out more fully in the Old Law of the following century), allowing a certain period for them to comply, but declaring them to be outlaws should they fail to do so. Twelve crimes (including homicide, theft and the raping of women) merited the death penalty, and there were other punishments as well. The dwelling of anyone declared to be an outlaw was subject to demolition or of being burned to the ground. Officials were prohibited from entering without permission the house of a Bizkaian. Should they do so they were subject to heavy fines. Regarding process, there was a certain resistance to, or discomfort with, participation of ecclesiastical judges in the proceedings. And, finally, there is definition of certain economic freedoms that will be developed further in the next century: rights regarding the buying, selling, and felling of trees on the commons for firewood, house construction or as fuel for iron foundries. The Codex also addresses certain difficulties that had arisen concerning the founding of a *villa* or privileged town.

## 3. THE GONZALO MORO TEXT (1394)

Half a century later a new law was formulated, one that was neither entirely autochthonous to Bizkaia nor consonant with its consuetudinary law. Rather, it constitutes a repertory of measures designed to confront an exceptional state of unrest in the Seigniory. It will end up being the most important influence within Bizkaia's evolving penal code. It contains, if possible, even greater punitive overtones, and its geographic scope, in addition to the heartland of Bizkaia, encompassed (with certain adaptations) the Encartaciones and the territory of Gipuzkoa to the east. It seemingly appeared as a response of the community, supported by the King, to what has been called the "factional struggles" *(lucha de los bandos)*. Among the Basques, as elsewhere in Europe, the Late Middle Ages witnessed violent social confrontations. In the Basque case, initially, it was a conflict between the leaders of lineages (the great traditional lineages—not unlike Scottish clans—were primarily based in the rural districts) and subsequently a rural aristocracy with the inhabitants of the recently-founded urban nuclei or *villas*. The effect of the fighting was disastrous in every respect, and the wider community responded by creating defensive alliances and repressive Hermandades (Confraternities) supported by the Castilian Crown, which accorded them exceptional jurisdiction. The monarchs sent to the

Basque area officials with excellent technical skills to coordinate the structuring of the Hermandades. Gonzalo Moro, *corregidor* of the Seigniory of Bizkaia, would have been one of these magistrates. The *corregidor* was the officer who served as the King's paramount direct representative.

The Hermandades were organized in Bizkaia throughout the fourteenth century, but with uneven success. In 1394, Enrique II of Castilla responded to the petition of some Bizkaians to reform and relaunch their Hermandad by sending Gonzalo Moro to Bizkaia to do so. After overcoming fierce resistance from some proponents of the lineages, Gonzalo Moro convoked the General Assembly in Gernika. It appointed a redactive commission, comprised of representatives of the *merindades* and *villas* and, together with the *corregidor*, they elaborated a text that was then presented to a new General Assembly. The capitulary was read aloud, and the *corregidor* repeatedly asked the Bizkaians if there was anything in the text that was contrary to the law of the Land. This act of inviting the denunciation of discrepancies is known as the anti-law (*contrafuero*). In the month of October of 1394, the *Cuaderno de Hermandad* of Gonzalo Moro was approved and confirmed.[35] In the following months, a similar text (practically modeled on the Bizkaian one) is approved in the Encartaciones and, three years later, another in Gipuzkoa.

In establishing a new penal jurisdiction serviced by specified judges—the *alcaldes de Hermandad*—the Codex respected, insofar as possible, the traditional juridical powers of the *alcaldes de Fuero*. The latter continued to devolve their traditional function, albeit with certain interferences. Regarding the list of crimes and punishments, typically those concerning the struggle with the warring bands, there are many transgressions that are given the death penalty: such as homicide, bodily injuries, aggravated theft (repeat offenses increased one's punishment), extortion, the rape of women and adultery with a married woman. In other cases, punishment included mutilation of the ears or the right hand, the burning down of a delinquent's dwelling, banishment or prison, or a half or full year in shackles. In the case of robbery, return of the stolen property was required, as well as additional grave fines.

One should underscore the importance of penal procedure. In the first place, there was an original system for capturing delinquents surprised *in fraganti* or identified by the judicial authority. Reference is to the neighborhood "alarm," which is to say the obligation of all men to pursue a delinquent to the jurisdictional limits of their municipality, at which point the inhabitants of the bordering one took up the chase. The pursuit passed thusly from one municipality to another throughout the confines of Bizkaia.[36] The Codex regulates the procedures for filing a complaint or accusation as well. Reference is to the practice whereby the *alcaldes de Hermandad* went to the municipality within which a crime was alleged to have been committed and convoked the residents in order to secure their cooperation in the investigation. Finally, there is greater elaboration of the procedures for summoning an accused to appear beneath the tree of Gernika, how the defendant would be informed of the nature of the process, the possibility of incarceration and the requirement to provide guarantees of financial capability to satisfy the possible indemnities or fines in the event of conviction.

After its redaction, the Codex of Gonzalo Moro was applied in all of the instances covered by it. In the event of any unanticipated cases, there was then recourse to the earlier Codex of Juan Núñez de Lara. As a last resort, the *alcaldes de Hermandad* and *alcaldes de Fuero* together decided upon a punishment.

After 1394, then, within the Bizkaian legal framework, there coexisted two codices that were almost exclusively penal in nature. Practically all public and civil law remained consuetudinary and unredacted. It was the Old Law that would fill this void.

## IV. Fundamental Reasons for Elaborating the Old Law (1452)

The Proem to the Old Law lists the Bizkaians' motives in writing down their customary law. They had their consuetudinary norms that were applied according to *albedrío*, that is, through the judge's simple determination of what was just and appropriate regarding a contested situation, but only after taking public opinion into account. Nevertheless, there is the complaint concerning the wrongs that result from the lack of a written code—the Proem specifies the "damages and wrongs and errors" and laments the "many questions" that arise. It is necessary to know the law with exactitude "because the men knew what laws and usages and customs and exemptions and liberties they have, and were certain of them." They contrast the problems inherent in unwritten law with the advantages of a written code.

Lacking greater precision in the text, it is well to reflect upon other indicators as well as the context itself. We will focus upon three concerns that explain the Bizkaians' desire to redact the custom of the Land. First, there is the question of proving the existence and authority of consuetudinary law. Second, there is Bizkaian rejection of the procedures and possible legal solutions of canon law and of common law in general. Finally, there is the concern over the possible consequences of the reigning Juan II's failure to comply with the requirement to take the oath to safeguard the Fuero.

It is likely that, by the mid-fifteenth century, the Bizkaians were suffering from the problems inherent in proving points of the law largely with recourse to unwritten custom. The references of the Old Law are merely indicative, but fifty years later it was the most goading concern in the application of Bizkaian law. It is likely that this was the question at the heart of the invocation of the misfortunes caused by the lack of a written law code.

It is commonly accepted that written law need not verify its existence, but rather is known to everyone and particularly to the judges who apply it. There obtained in the Middle Ages as well the principle of *nemo ius ignorare censetur*, or "ignorance of the law is no excuse for violating it." However, applying consuetudinary law is more complicated, even in cases like that of Bizkaia where the judges are chosen from among persons in the social setting itself and therefore fully cognizant of local law. Nevertheless, there frequently arose difficulties regarding the very existence of certain norms and particularly their interpretation. In doubtful cases regarding the status of a custom, the judges sometimes had recourse to persons who knew about it. Reference is only to the uncertain ones, since many were uncontroverted and known to all. Regarding the former, the burden of proof fell to the parties to a lawsuit, and particularly the plaintiff. It became necessary to muster all legal recourses, from the invocation of precedents, to the examination of witnesses, etcetera. It was an expensive and risky undertaking, as well as a procedure that could also undermine the stability of the administration of justice. [37]

This challenge and difficulty in establishing the precise nature of the law itself was not unique to Bizkaia alone; rather, it was generic to all countries whose legal system was based upon a consuetudinary juridical culture. At times, to establish legal precedent, there was the consultation of a group of ten qualified persons—the proof of the crowd—who deliberated and then made a unanimous proclamation of the existence and the nature of the custom in question; at others, there was recourse to a particular authority or even to another jurisdiction. But, as we have said, habitually the results were at best mixed and were likely to create similar problems wherever these procedures were applied. For example, in the Ordinances of King Charles VII of France (1454), it is stated that the consequence of the application of custom in the different regions of the realm was that "frequently the lawsuits drag on and the parties suffer great expenses." [38] The same complaint would be heard often in Bizkaia. The fact that in the Seigniory all of the *alcaldes de Fuero* met together to resolve appeals was insufficient to dispel doubts—whether general or particular.

The written redaction itself provided proof of the authority of consuetudinary law, while at the same time the approval of the text was an occasion for the community to renew its consent and to reaffirm and consolidate the order. What is certain is that already in the thirteenth century, in other European venues, such evidentiary difficulties were a decisive reason for the writing down of consuetudinary law.

The second probable motive for the Bizkaians to redact their Old Law regards their resistance to the application in Bizkaia of canon law and the Kingdom's common law. Indeed, they were possibly conscious of attempts by some civil and ecclesiastical judges to weaken the custom of the Land itself by privileging civil rules taken from royal or canon law. The rejection of the sophisticated canonical procedures of ecclesiastical judges is apparent in Article 218, which states that in Bizkaia "in the legal cases the regimen of [canon and civil] law is not followed, nor are there proofs, nor in the judgments are the solemnities and subtleties of [canon and civil] law safeguarded" since the judges of the Church regard legal cases "according to the form of [canon and civil] law."

Finally, the Bizkaians faced the problem of the lack of the current Lord's oath to uphold the Seigniory's law. We will consider below the evidence that Juan II, King of Castilla (1406–1454), failed to take the oath to uphold the Fuero at any time during his several decades of rule. This must have been very disturbing to the Bizkaians. At the moment of demanding his oath, and/or of requiring it of all future monarchs, its nature and object were likely deliberated. What was the content of the oath that could be exacted from the Lord of Bizkaia upon acceding to power? To what was he agreeing? It should be remembered that over and above concern for respect of the extant legal code there was added another principle—that the law of the Land could not be modified excepting in the General Assembly of Gernika and with the consent of the Bizkaians. Thus, it was important to compile in written form their uncodified laws so that it was clear just what, during the sacred ceremony, the Lord was swearing to safeguard and uphold.

## V. Writing the Old Law

On June 2, 1452, the redactorial commission of the Fuero of Bizkaia that had been appointed by the preceding General Assembly of Idoibalzaga met in the church of Santa María la Antigua of Gernika.[39] It included the *corregidor* of all of Bizkaia, Pero González de Santo Domingo, and the five *alcaldes de Fuero*, four of whom were titular and one a *logarteniente* or assistant—reference is to two judges from the Merindad of Uribe (upon which were dependent those of Arratia and Bedia as well) and the three judges from Busturia. Present and forming a part of the commission were 22 personages whose surnames reflect their status as heads of important lineages. The assembled were assisted by two notaries—Fortún Íñiguez de Ibargüen, who would finally authorize and possibly redact the document, and Sancho Martínez de Goiri.

On initiating the session, the assembled remarked upon the wrongs that the Bizkaians had suffered by virtue of the absence of a written law. Conscious of the problem, "all the Bizkaians gathered together in their General Assembly of Idoibalzaga" had elected the commission and charged it with the duty and the authority to organize and compile in writing their unformulated law that was based on precedent. Once the text had been elaborated, they would present it to the King for confirmation. The assembled asked of the *corregidor* that he require an oath from each of them to fulfill their charge conscientiously. The *corregidor* agreed with the commissioners regarding their analysis of the problems and manifested his willingness to collaborate in the redaction. He applied the requested oath, following the traditional ritual (placement of one's right hand on the cross). The commissioners swore to comport themselves loyally and faithfully to the best of their understanding and in the service of God, the King, and the Bizkaian community. Then the *corregidor* warned them of the gravity of their sworn oath (*les echó la confusión de el dicho juramento*). That is, he enumerated the bad consequences of every kind that they would suffer should they fail to live up to their word. The *corregidor* then excused himself because he felt it better that he not participate directly in the redaction itself. He would later take part in the proceedings before the General Assembly, but only after the text was in hand.

The 30 members of the commission declared that the Lord of Bizkaia customarily swore to uphold the law of the Land and of its four different components—Bizkaia, Encartaciones, Duranguesado and Villas—upon assuming power. There is the assumption that the Lord knew about the obligation and its procedures, so the latter were not spelled out.

On July 21 of the same year, or 19 days after the commission began its work, the General Assembly convened at the customary site—beneath the tree of Gernika. It had been convoked in the usual ritual manner: the *prestamero* ordered his agent, the *sayón*, to sound the horns from the five mountaintops as ordained by tradition.

Present at the beginning of the Assembly were the *corregidor*, the five *alcaldes de Fuero*, the *prestamero's logarteniente*, the *merino* of the Merindad de Busturia, "and many other *escuderos* (esquires) and *fijos-dalgo* (noblemen) and *omes buenos* (good men) of the said Bizkaia." In several passages it is stated that all Bizkaians were in attendance, although it is evident that some were absent. The important point is that at this time the General Assembly was still universal in the sense that it was open to the public and not constituted solely by the representatives of individual *villas* and *merindades*. In this regard the public assembly was similar to those of some Swiss cantons.

Of the commissioners convened initially on July 2, 13 heads of lineages were present on July 21. The listing of their names on the latter occasion followed the same order as when enumerating the members of the commission, which perhaps reflects a hierarchy among Bizkaian lineages. The following are the names of those present at both gatherings and their order: Juan Sáenz de Mezeta, Juan García de Yarza, Juan de Sarria, Gonzalo Ybáñez de Marquina, Gonzalo de Aranzibia, Rui Martínez de Aranzibia, Ochoa López de Urkiza, Martín Ruiz de Alviz, Lope Gonçález de Aguero, Diego de Asua, Pero de Garay, Martín de Mendieta, Pero de Uriarte, and Sancho Martínez de Goiri, notary. Absent were Juan de San Juan de Avendaño, Ochoa Urtiz de Susunaga, Pero Sáenz de Salazar, Pero Urtiz de Aguirre, Martín Sáenz de Asua, Martín Ybáñez de Garunaga, Pero Ybánez de Alviz, Ochoa Guerras de Lexarrazun, and Sancho Urtiz de Arandoaga. On the other hand, on July 21 there were a few named individuals who were not in attendance on July 2: Juan Ruiz de Adoriaga, Juan Urtiz de Lecoya, Martín Ybáñez de Garaunaga, Martín Saénz de Mundaca, Pero Martínez d'Alviz, Juan Sáenz de Tornotegui [Torróntegui], and Sancho del Castillo. They were again assisted by the notary Fortún Íñiguez de Ibargüen.

On July 21, the members of the commission in attendance stated to the General Assembly the charge that they had been given by the earlier General Assembly of Idoibalzaga. They declared that they had completed their mission and that Fortún Íñiguez de Ibargüen—who was the authorized royal notary public of the King's court and in all his realms—had been responsible for the redacting of the draft. They asked the assembled to examine the text to confirm that which was valid and amend that which was not. The *corregidor* once again absented himself from the Assembly in order that his presence not inhibit the debates.

The assembled asked the notary to read out the text prepared by the commissioners. In a loud voice, he went through the document chapter by chapter so that his interlocutors could scrutinize, debate and approve them. Once completed, everyone present—including the judges "as private persons"—declared unanimously that it was their desire from then on to have the redacted text, and each of its provisions, as their law. They requested of the King and Lord of Bizkaia that he confirm the new legal code.

They then agreed to something that was surprising, given the civil law of the epoch. They ordered the judiciary of Bizkaia to apply the newly-approved law immediately, or before the Monarch's confirmation of it, in all civil and criminal matters. They held harmless the magistrates from personal liability in acting accordingly, and they pledged the property of all those present as financial guarantee to cover any damages or fines that might be forthcoming because of this posture. The use of any other legal code was expressly forbidden. The act finishes with the truly impressive statement, "concerning the above, all of the aforementioned *escuderos* and *fijosdalgo* and *omesbuenos* who were in the said General Assembly shouted, in one voice and of accord, 'it is right' (*vala*)."

When Enrique IV ascended the throne of Castilla in 1454, the Bizkaians sent their representative to the Castillan city of Segovia to ask that he come to the Seigniory to swear the oath, according to established custom. He alleged that he was unable to do so because of his involvement in the war against the Moors, but he took the oath to observe their laws on the spot, promising that just as soon as he was able he would travel to Bizkaia to renew it.

On March 10, 1457, the King was present in the church of Santa María la Antigua of Gernika. He was 32 years old. He was accompanied by three members of the Royal Council—the senior chancellor, the chief chamberlain and the senior *prestamero* of Bizkaia. It seems that the Bizkaians were not gathered in General Assembly; rather, they convoked a special meeting at which there were present four *alcaldes de Fuero*, four *alcaldes de Hermandad* and the notary Juan Pérez de Iturribalzaga. There were others as well, including the eminent heads of lineage, Joan Alfonso de Mújica and Martín Ruiz de Arteaga. The assembled reminded the King that, as was the custom of the community, upon arriving in Bizkaia to assume the lordship of the Seigniory, he should swear in various places to safeguard the laws. One of these venues was Gernika, the site of the present meeting. The King replied that such was the purpose of his visit. He then swore on the cross and the Holy Gospels to safeguard the laws of Bizkaia, as had his predecessors (often monarchs), to which were appended the usual attestations. There is no reference whatsoever, however, to any specific text, such as the Old Law of 1452 or the earlier codices that had been thereby safeguarded.

On August 26, 1463, there was a General Assembly in Gernika. Present were the *corregidor* Lope de Mendoza accompanied by three royal commissioners—a doctor and two licenciates. There appeared one *alcalde de Fuero* and eleven delegates from distinguished families elected by the Tierra Llana and twelve representatives of the Villas that were listed by precedence. Also present were six heads of lineage "and other *escuderos*." There were two notaries who seem to be Bizkaians. The assembled affirmed that they were empowered by the King and the community to examine and organize "the Codices and the law of Bizkaia" (*Los Quadernios e el Fuero de Vizcaya*), as well as to approve them. They affirmed that they had reviewed all the laws that the King had sworn to uphold. Consequently, it was ordered that in future all of the judicial authorities (of whatever kind) within the Seigniory follow the "said Codices and law and the law of the Tierra Llana" that the King had sworn to uphold and not deviate from them. Employing the authority confirmed upon them, they forwarded a letter of confirmation to the King and Lord of Bizkaia on the same day of August 26.

## VI. Transcriptions of Old Law Texts

The original text of the Old Law of 1452 has been lost, destroyed or mislaid. Consequently, we know its contents only from transcriptions made of it and then subsequent transcriptions of transcriptions. Since the copies were effected at different times spanning more than half a millennium, and for different purposes, they differ considerably. It is clear that compilation of a single critical edition of such a venerable text as this one first requires locating and examining all of the extant manuscript copies. Consequently, the editor faces a formidable heuristic challenge.

In preparation for this critical edition of the Old Law, during the 1970s I conducted a search in several archives. These included the Archive of the Chancellery of Valladolid (seat of the Tribunal of the Superior Justice of Bizkaia) and the archival resources of the Seigniory itself (the Provincial Archive and that of the General Assembly of Gernika). I also consulted archival collections in Madrid (at the National Historical Archive, the National Library, the Academy of History, the Royal Palace and the Naval Museum). Finally, the quest led to several family holdings as well (those of the Urquijo, Ibarra, Marco-Gardoqui, and Heredia-Spínola families, among others).

A considered examination of all the materials allowed construction of a certain genealogy among the manuscripts, as well as a classification of their type and content. From them were selected those which seemed best suited for formulating a single critical edition of the Old Law.

### 1. GENEALOGY OF THE TEXTS: *STEMMA FORIS VETERIS*

It was possible to authenticate the proliferation and sequence of the texts beginning with the original one that was redacted in 1452, since each states when (and at times why) it was produced.

In order to clarify what follows, I provide a summary diagram that outlines the *Stemma Foris Veteris*, or genealogical tree, of the different texts:

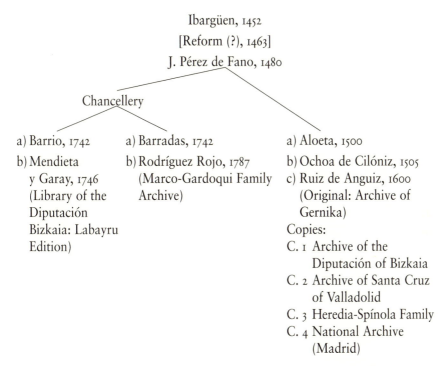

Ibargüen, 1452

[Reform (?), 1463]

J. Pérez de Fano, 1480

Chancellery

| a) Barrio, 1742 | a) Barradas, 1742 | a) Aloeta, 1500 |
|---|---|---|
| b) Mendieta y Garay, 1746 (Library of the Diputación Bizkaia: Labayru Edition) | b) Rodríguez Rojo, 1787 (Marco-Gardoqui Family Archive) | b) Ochoa de Cilóniz, 1505 |
| | | c) Ruiz de Anguiz, 1600 (Original: Archive of Gernika) |
| | | Copies: |
| | | C. 1 Archive of the Diputación of Bizkaia |
| | | C. 2 Archive of Santa Cruz of Valladolid |
| | | C. 3 Heredia-Spínola Family |
| | | C. 4 National Archive (Madrid) |

Thus far the original document approved in Gernika in 1452, and authorized by the notary Fortún Íñiguez de Ibargüen, has not been located. It is probable that the revision of 1463 included a few changes and possibly even serious modifications. In reality, the Old Law initiated its future course based upon the text that was approved in 1463, the *Quadernio de Vizcaya* (Codex of Bizkaia), that incorporated the two legal documents of the preceding century—that of Juan Núñez de Lara (1342) and the Ordinances of Gonzalo Moro (1394). Therefore, in the second half of the fifteenth century, there was the desire to consolidate within a single text the entire law of the Seigniory.

The lines of the three subsequent branches of the trunk of the authorized genealogical tree first pass through the edition compiled in Bilbo on August 2, 1480, by the notary Juan Pérez de Fano, at the request of a resident of Barakaldo. It is 70 pages long, with the text covering half of each sheet. Three Bilbo residents served as witnesses. The original has not survived, but the subsequent copies derive from it.

## 2. Toward the Joan Ruiz de Anguiz Manuscript (1600)

After the Fano copy, the chain that leads to the best manuscript has the following links:

On May 5, 1500, the notary Pero Ibáñez de Aloeta made a copy of the Fano text (or of the original?) at the request of the mayor of the Villa of Gernika. He did so in the presence of two witnesses. The text contains 118 half sheets of paper. It, too, no longer survives.

On May 14, 1505, Ochoa de Zilóniz, notary of the Merindad of Busturia, made a copy of the Pero Ibáñez text—which is expressly mentioned. The transcript was produced at the request of Diego de Anunzibay, and the notary was ordered by the *alcalde de Fuero* to produce it. Three residents of Gernika were present during the exercise. It encompassed 86 half sheets of paper. It, too, has been lost. It is clear, however, that this was the officially approved avenue for transmitting the Fuero, since the redacting commission of the New Law (*Fuero Nuevo*) of 1526 utilized the Ochoa de Zilóniz transcript as its point of departure, as did the Regiment of Bizkaia when reconciling the two codes. Such is acknowledged in the Proem of the New Law that we will examine subsequently.

On November 4, 1600, the notary Joan Ruiz de Anguiz certified that, upon entering the "*archivo de Biscaia*" (probably in the church of Santa María la Antigua of Gernika), he found there the law, which he corrected and reconciled. He did his work in said church. Present in the act, which was intended to underscore its seriousness, were the *síndico* (trustee) of the Seigniory and four other persons. Ruiz de Anguiz, originally from Murélaga and currently resident in Begoña, and a notary in the Tribunal of the *corregidor* and that of the Merindad of Busturia, was obviously well-qualified technically for the task. After he was finished, the Codex was returned to its place. The copy required 98 sheets of paper. Ruiz de Anguiz noted under the heading of authentication that the Codex that he had worked from was bound and sewn, and that annexed to it were the proposed reform laws of 1506 authorized by Juan de Arbolancha. Since this supposed reform was in the form of an annex to the main body of the text, he copied it separately on eight sheets, placing his mark upon them. The Ruiz de Anguiz copy of the Old Law is the most valuable, which explains why it is found in at least four different archives and libraries. A simple comparison with the other extant copies makes manifest its superiority—it therefore serves as the basis for this critical edition.

### 3. THE COPIES IN THE CHANCELLERY OF VALLADOLID PROCEEDING THE FANO TEXT

In effect, there are another two textual versions of the Old Law that derive from a copy of the Fano text (1480) in the Chancellery of Valladolid. That copy of Fano's work had been made in the seventeenth century and with regard to litigations pending before the Tribunal of the Superior Judge of Bizkaia, which was under the Chancellery. Unfortunately, this important Chancellery text disappeared at the beginning of the nineteenth century during conflicts between the government of the Spanish Monarchy and Bizkaian officials. But by then there were two series of copies descended from it, which were certainly deficient compared with that of Ruiz de Anguiz, yet indispensable for filling in its holes and correcting its defects.

#### a. The Mendieta and Garay Text (1746)

The Superior Judge of Bizkaia and of the Chancellery of Valladolid ordered in October of 1746 that an accurate copy of the Old Law deposited in its archive be effected. Four years later, Joseph Lucas de Mendieta and Joaquín de Garay, both secretaries of the Assembly of the Encartaciones, and utilizing said copy, made one of their own that was 237 pages long. It ended up in the Provincial Archive of Bizkaia. I have compared it with the Ruiz de Anguiz text in formulating this critical edition of the Old Law.

#### b. The Rodríguez Rojo Text (1787)

Once again the Superior Judge of the Chancellery, Josef Colón de Larreategui, dictated an act in December of 1776 that ordered expedition of a "certified copy of the general law called of precedent (*de albedrío*) that in this time is called Old Law." He said that the basic text derived from a legal case of the preceding century, and that it must have been the same text that was employed in 1742. The copy made to satisfy this mandate appeared eight years later. It was written by the notary Pío Rodríguez Rojo and is deposited in the archive of the Marco-Gardoqui family. It is the third text that I employ in formulating this critical edition, comparing it with the other that proceeded from the Chancellery (they generally agree, but there are a few discrepancies) and with that of Ruiz de Anguiz.

I indicated earlier the possibility that the body of the Codex—integrating the texts of Juan Núñez de Lara (1342), the Ordinances of Gonzalo Moro (1394) and the Old Law (1452)—was articulated in 1463, at which time it was both revised and all of its components approved.

Indeed, perhaps this revised text is the real point of departure for all of the subsequent copies. But there remains a conundrum. If Pérez de Fano made his copy in Bilbo in 1480, and Ibáñez de Aloeta did so in 1500 in Gernika, where did they get their text for copying?

It would seem natural that authorized copies would be made from a text on deposit in an official archive, and only at the request of an officer and in his presence. Otherwise, the danger of proliferation of fabrications is obvious. The proper controls are evident only in the case of the Ruiz de Anguiz copy. Fortunately, it is the one that has survived and, although it presents significant textual challenges, it has served well as the fundamental reference for this critical edition.

There remains another question with respect to the transmission and the disappearance of the texts. What happened to the Codex copied by Joan Ruiz de Anguiz (that of Ochoa de Zilóniz made in 1505 and which was still in the Provincial Archive of Bizkaia in 1600)? And what happened to the foundational text for the other series of copies that still existed in the Archive of the Chancellery in 1776? We simply do not know the dates of the disappearances, but they likely transpired as the result of the profound conflict between the Spanish Crown and Bizkaia (and the other Basque provinces as well) initiated at the end of the eighteenth century. It is enough to note how an aggressive Royal Order of 1805 obliged the Seigniory to open its archives to the scrutiny of the official Spanish historian Llorente. The Seigniory finessed this pretense of the King.[40] It should be noted that the text on deposit in the archive of the Chancellery of Valladolid was removed from there for official reasons that were never spelled out clearly.

## VII. Editions of the Old Law

At this moment of preparing a critical edition of the Old Law, it is well to recount the former ones and their characteristics. In the first place, I might comment on the tardiness of their publication. The appearance in 1526 of the New Law, which was reissued regularly throughout the Modern Age by the authorities, displaced and marginated the Old Law of 1452, thereby limiting its dissemination and even the awareness of it. As recently as 1864, in a debate regarding fiscal matters held in the Spanish Senate, the Bascophobe senator Sánchez Silva affirmed that he had never had the opportunity to examine the Old Law in order to compare it with the new one of 1526 because the Bizkaians had intentionally expunged the former from the Castilian and Seignorial archives. He was immediately informed of the abundance of copies of the Old Law. But there was still no attempt to actually publish one of them for the next 35 years.

### 1. THE LABAYRU EDITION (1899)

The credit for publishing the first edition of the Old Law goes to Estanislao Jaime de Labayru, who reproduced the text in his monumental *Historia General del Señorío de Bizcaya*.[41] Unfortunately, this otherwise superb Bizkaian historian utilized the Mendieta and Garay (1742) copy on deposit in the Provincial Library (*Biblioteca de la Diputación*). Although he knew of its existence (there was even a copy of it in the Provincial Archive of Bilbo), he ignored the Ruiz de Anguiz copy deposited in Gernika. That is to say, he took at face value only one copy, and that defective, of the Old Law. Throughout his published edition, Labayru drops articles, pronouns and prepositions, all of which tends to confuse the reader. There are serious textual omissions that change meanings and even obfuscate the text. There is also an abundance of transcription errors resulting from an incorrect reading. Such paleographic faults further undermine the reliability of the Labayru edition. Clearly, he was aware of the deficiencies of his text and tried to compensate for them with the unfortunate introduction of his own "clarifications."

### 2. THE ASTUY EDITION (1909)

The problems with the Labayru edition were immediately obvious with publication of his *Historia General*. It was known that there existed a different copy of the Old Law—one with a clearer and more intelligible text. It was on deposit in the Provincial Archive (*Archivo Provincial*) in Bilbo. It had belonged to the great Bizkaian patrician, Fidel de Sagarmínaga, who, along with his personal library, donated it to the Bizkaian provincial government or Diputación. It was the copy that Labayru either overlooked or ignored.

José Astuy began publishing the superior Ruiz de Anguiz text by installment in the daily newspaper *La Unión Vasconavarra* and the weekly *Euskalduna*. In 1909, he incorporated them into a book that he then produced in his own publishing house.[42] While informed by the best copy of all, unfortunately the Astuy edition includes all of the defects and errors that had been accumulating throughout the chain of transmission. To the problems of the Ruiz de Anguiz copy were added those of the subsequent copies based on it. The lector of the Astuy edition of the Old Law will appreciate the difficulty in reading it. Several of its precepts are simply incomprehensible.

3. The Edition of the Institute of Basque Studies (*Instituto de Estu-dios Vascos*) of the University of Deusto (1991)

In 1991, the Institute of Basque Studies of the University of Deusto published a volume that included the law of Bizkaia and of the other territorial components of the Seigniory. Consequently, it contains the laws of the Merindad of Durango, Ayala, the Encartaciones, and central or nuclear Bizkaia, as well as appendices of twentieth-century Bizkaian civil law. Despite the edition's pretense of being exhaustive, inexplicably two fundamental pieces of the Seigniory's general law are lacking—the 1342 Codex of Juan Núñez de Lara and the 1394 Ordinances of Gonzalo Moro. Both texts are ineluctable since, in a certain sense, they are the foundation of the Seigniory's law. Also missing is the Ordinance of Chinchilla, which is essential to an understanding of the fifteenth-century conflicts between the Seigniory and the Spanish Crown, as well as those in the eighteenth century.

The team charged with editing the 17 normative pieces of the 1991 edition[43] followed the advice and guidelines of the Aragonese civil law expert Jesús Delgado Echeverria. José Miguel Olea Euba authored the indices, although other members of the editorial team collaborated as well, and particularly Professor Itziar Monasterio.

The authors of this edition state that they have reproduced literally the text of the Old Law published in 1909 by Astuy.[44] Nothing needs to be added to my earlier criticism of it. On the other hand, the 1991 edition lacks any kind of introductory study. Nevertheless, the appended indices have a certain and indisputable value, whether referring to the *Voces del índice analítico, ordenado por temas* ("Words of the Analytical Index, Arranged by Themes"),[45] which illuminated the features of traditional law and facilitates formulating lines of inquiry regarding them, or to the corpus of more than 300 key terms in the documents. It is precisely for such strengths that the absence of the Juan Núñez de Lara and Gonzalo Moro texts is palpable. Had they been included, the indexical coverage of Bizkaian law would have been quite comprehensive. To this caveat may be added another, namely that the scope of the indices is greater than that of the present critical edition of the Old Law alone.

4. The Edition of the Old Law in the *Fuentes Documentales Medievales del País Vasco* Published by Eusko Ikaskuntza (1994)

In 1994 Eusko Ikaskuntza/Sociedad de Estudios Vascos (The Basque Studies Society) published as Volume 51 within its important collection of *Fuentes documentales medievales del País Vasco* (Medieval Documentary Sources of the Basque Country) a work entitled *Fuentes jurídi-*

*cas medievales del Señorío de Vizcaya* (Medieval Juridical Sources of the Seigniory of Bizkaia). A team with grant support from the Society reproduced the Joan Ruiz de Anguiz copy of 1600, preceded by introductory notes by José Luis de Orella commenting on the Labayru and Astuy editions.[46] This edition, in addition to the Old Law, includes the 1342 Juan Núñez de Lara manuscript and the Gonzalo Moro Ordinances of 1392. Which is to say, it reproduces the entire Codex of Bizkaia, although the editorial team does not elaborate on the point.

Of particular interest is the thematic index, as well as the onomastic and toponymic ones, that accompany the transcription of the texts.[47] There is, however, the problem that the entries (without discrimination) refer to three documents with different dates (1342, 1394 and 1452). Nevertheless, taken as a whole they do facilitate comparative study.

Without doubt, this edition is of greater interest than all the earlier ones, given that the editors transcribed directly the Ruiz de Anguiz copy. Nevertheless, it is not a critical edition in that it fails to effect comparison (and reconciliation) with all of the other extant authorized copies considered above. And, as was noted, the Ruiz de Anguiz copy suffers from numerous and essential omissions, a circumstance that could only be corrected by employing the copies in the Chancellery of Valladolid— that is, the Mendieta and Garay one of 1746 and that of Rodríguez Rojo (1787). Furthermore, the decision regarding the 1994 edition to retain the paleographic script added nothing to comprehension of the text while presenting the reader with an additional challenge. Indeed, the lector is left to sort out what should have been an editorial task. Reference is to working out a system of punctuation that clarifies the text.

## VIII. The Need for a Critical Edition of the Old Law

In preparing this critical edition of the Old Law, I have disqualified from consideration the copy of Mendieta and Garay (1746) used in both the Labayru edition and that of Rodríguez Rojo (1787) as a basic source text. I have done so because of their obfuscations. However, as indicated earlier, they have comparative value at times in the attempt to reconstruct, as far as possible, the original Old Law text. They also provide certain correctives to the serious defects in the Ruiz de Anguiz transcription, which otherwise is considered to be the most accurate. In effect, no one denies the superiority of the Ruiz de Anguiz text, which has been utilized for many editions—such as the ones by Astuy, the University of Deusto and the Society for Basque Studies. But it is precisely because of its strengths that the challenges that it also poses need to be considered. It is their reconciliation that justifies attempting a critical edition such as the present one. I will therefore examine the original Ruiz de Anguiz transcription directly, and thereby avoid the defects introduced to it subsequently in the process of producing the distinct editions based upon it, including the most recent one effected by the team of transcribers of the Society for Basque Studies.[48]

At the outset I might underscore the numerous minor transcription errors committed by Ruiz de Anguiz. Reference is to small mistakes that the reader can rectify easily by exercizing judgment and by being a bit critical, given that they do not in any way pose an insuperable obstacle to understanding the text. There are perhaps one hundred in all. The ones that concern us now are the most substantial, and they are of several types.

At times, instead of employing the appropriate term from what must have been the original text, another with a somewhat different meaning is substituted. The effect can be disorienting and confusing.[49] Comparison with other transcripts frequently clarifies the situation and facilitates recovery of the original, which is also verified by the context. At other moments, certain terms are omitted, which can modify the meaning of a phrase, even seriously in some cases. In effect, if the omission is limited to a word or two, it may have minor relevance,[50] but this is not true when whole series of words or more extensive sentences are lost. In such cases, which occur with a certain frequency in the Ruiz de Anguiz transcript,[51] the article in question may border upon the incomprehensible. Indeed, the disappearance of a conditional participle, that in itself might seem irrelevant, creates problems with meaning.[52]

The evident deficiencies in all of the copies and editions to date of the Old Law have made it difficult for historians in general, and legal historians in particular, to study comprehensively the juridical, economic, social and political reality reflected in this most interesting and important late medieval text. Researchers have limited their efforts to isolated consultation of particular points in the Old Law regarding certain issues regulated by the reformed law of 1526 (often called the *Fuero Nuevo*). Rather than studying the Old Law in its own terms, it tends to be regarded of interest only as antecedent to the New Law under consideration. Civil law historians, as specialists who have studied the Old Law more extensively, constituted the one exception.

At the same time, to date the position of the Old Law within the general framework of Spanish medieval law has not been determined sufficiently, nor has its importance been pondered properly. It is evident that the text constitutes the response of an embattled Bizkaian medieval tradition, threatened by Romanism as filtered through royal law, and applied amply in the Villas situated in the heart of the Seigniory. The legal solutions and procedures of *Ius Commune* simply contested openly the traditions and legal processes of the Land. On balance, the Old Law provides us with insight into an extraordinary universe, one that was partly in decline. It is practically our only evidence of an earlier tradition.

Finally, a reconciled and critically edited edition of the Old Law is germane to a proper understanding of the law of the Seigniory of Bizkaia during the Modern Age. A *prima facie* comparison of its contents with those of the New Law of 1526 reveals not only what they had in common but also the changes that had transpired in Bizkaia's juridical structures over the intervening 75 years. With this critical edition in hand, it is now possible to detail the evolution of the Bizkaian legal system during a particularly critical and transitional period of its development.

# Part Two

## IX. The Language of the Old Law

Like all of the preceding bodies of Spanish law, as well as the entire corpus of the area's extant medieval legal documentation, the Old Law is redacted in Old Castilian or Romance. However, it is clear that in Bizkaia at the time—at least in the Tierra Llana and the Duranguesado—Basque was the vernacular. One can assume that it was also spoken habitually in the majority of the Villas created in both regions during the Late Middle Ages. Nevertheless, it would not be until the following century that Basque was first written down. Consequently, throughout what is today Hegoalde, or the Spanish Basque area, in the fifteenth century Castilian was the language of all public and private documents, and was probably employed in at least certain administrative transactions and communications. At the same time, a part of the Basque population quickly acquired a degree of fluency in Romance, particularly urban and rural elites, persons engaged in commerce and seafaring, a part of the clergy and those charged with redacting and recording documents of any kind. Nor should we ignore the strong Basque presence in Castilian universities that was all out of proportion to the magnitude of the Basque population. This is well-documented for the Early Modern Age, or sixteenth century, and was quite possibly already evident in the fifteenth.

Several factors favored the use of written Castilian. Throughout Western Europe, after the thirteenth century, the Romance languages basked in the cultural prestige afforded by Latin. The Basque language is pre-Indo-European and fragmented into several dialects, each with a limited number of speakers. Indeed, the entire universe of Basque speakers was relatively tiny and simply incapable of providing critical mass for a literate tradition. Furthermore, in the fifteenth century it was divided politically among three Kingdoms (Castilla, Navarra, France). Within the Basque lands of the Castilian Monarchy, there was also a notable tripartite internal political distinction. Reference is to the Province of Gipuzkoa, the Hermandad of Araba and the Seigniory of Bizkaia.

The possible repercussions of the linguistic diglossia of the day—the use of a more or less official written language and the reality of a markedly different popular vernacular—had upon the redaction and approbation of the Old Law is unclear. Undoubtedly, it had a direct impact upon the work of the actual redactor, who seems to have been Fortún Íñiguez de Ibargüen. We have seen that he was a notary public authorized to act both at Court and throughout the Castilian Monarch's kingdoms and seigniories. He must have had a solid grounding in jurisprudence, enhanced by his practical experience with the law. It is not clear whether he held a degree in letters, although we might better assume so. Without formal training it would have been extremely difficult, if not impossible, for him to have shaped the Old Law out of such a complex normative labyrinth, and within a very short time frame. Nor can we assume that he had benefit of some earlier redaction that might have served as the foundation for the Old Law. By all indications his was an entirely new undertaking. At the same time, it seems likely that he knew at least some Basque, which would have been an obvious advantage in discussing details with the redacting commissioners. This supposition is based upon the surnames Iñiguez Ibargüen, which are both of obvious Basque derivation.

In relation to its language, there is a precept of considerable interest in the Old Law. Reference is to Article 110, which addresses the freedom of transmission of property, equating the right to give or bequest moveable property with that governing real estate. The precept is stated in negative terms, requiring that all of the items in the transmission be listed individually. It then underscores respect for what "the *Fuero Antiguo* of Bizkaia calls *urde urdaondo e açia etondo*." It then explains the scope of this Basque phrase, which encompasses pork products that happened to be present in the household in question, as well as therein any wheat, millet and barley harvested that year.

The precept poses several challenges. First, there is the explicit expression "Old Law of Bizkaia," which is the only instance of it in the entire text. Is reference to the consuetudinary law that is mentioned so frequently throughout the Old Law or to a possible earlier written version? Given that this phrase is singular within the text, it seems prudent to assume that it is yet another way of referring to custom (others include *usos, leyes, derechos, franquezas, fueros, costumbres*). Nevertheless, it is interesting that the substance of an institution is captured in a Basque language juridical aphorism. Indeed, it is the first, or one of the earliest, examples of a full expression or sentence in written Basque, and therefore possesses intrinsic historical linguistic interest. It also allows us to speculate that this was not a unique case and that prior to redac-

tion of the Old Law there might have existed other such Basque juridical aphorisms that synthesized institutions. It is known that among preliterate peoples such coined expressions are often employed to formu-
late rules.[53] In the Bizkaian case such was no longer necessary once the
Old Law had been redacted, which thereby codified custom into law.
The cited example might therefore be treated as an island known to us
in passing mention, the tip of a surrounding submerged continent of
similar aphorisms now lost. But this is obviously an hypothesis, since we
may be dealing with an isolated instance.

We cannot mine the Old Law for much additional evidence regarding the Basque language. There are a few isolated examples, such as
when the redactors use the expressions *"echar bidigaza"* and *"alzar
abeurrea."* From context it appears that reference is to objects placed as
signs or notices next to waterways on the commons by individuals
claiming the site for construction there of a dam and/or canal (*bidigaza*)
and a mill or iron foundry (*abeurrea*). The *bidigaza* was placed horizon-
tally (possibly in the watercourse), and the *abeurrea* was vertically
"raised." The *Diccionario vasco-español-francés* of Resurrección María
de Azkue (who knew the Bizkaian dialect and the folk customs of Bizkaia well) fails to mention *abeurrea*. Regarding *bidigaza* it refers to the
New Law of Bizkaia, in which the *bidigaza* custom for claiming private
use of public land continued in effect in the sixteenth century.[54]

Then there is the expression *"a locue"* or *"alocue"* that we will consider in greater detail below, and which refers to a gathering of the
*alcaldes de Fuero* to deliberate over an appeal of a decision handed
down by one of them. Is reference to the place where they met? Possibly, since in Bizkaian Basque the term *lekue* means "place."

## X. An Old Law of *Albedrío*

The Romance term *albedrío* (written *alvedrío* in the Old Law)
appears various times in the text and with semantic complications. As
stated earlier, a fundamental meaning of *albedrío* regards ascertaining
the truth and searching for the most equitable and publicly acceptable
resolution of a particular case. This presupposes that in a particular
instance there is no clearly established precedent within consuetudinary
custom (or law) that could be incontestably invoked and applied. Consequently, on occasion a judge had to come up with a new resolution.
But it could not be idiosyncratic and arbitrary, since it had to take into
account the community's collective sentiments and values, and quite
possibly be handed down in public assembly. In this sense *albedrío* is a
form of populist law.

This close connection between law and community is most evident in Bizkaia. There, until the end of the fourteenth century, or the time when the king's royal official, the *corregidor*, is implanted in Bizkaia, all lawsuits were ultimately decided before the General Assembly of Bizkaians, usually meeting beneath the Oak of Gernika. Even in 1452, or when the Old Law was redacted, the Bizkaian assembly remained the ultimate arbiter in the application of justice. We are obviously dealing with consuetudinary law in that the greater part of public, civil, penal and processual law remained unwritten. It was law applied by judges who were not formally trained legalists and within a judicial pyramid whose apex was the Bizkaian General Assembly.

The Old Law contains several references to its grounding in *albedrío*, all of which are basic to an understanding of how the Fuero and its precedents attempted to resolve Bizkaian society's legal issues and problems. Fundamental is the emphasis upon collective will regarding both the legitimacy and intrinsic worth of popular opinion. For example, Article 33 specifies that the decisions of arbitrators may not be appealed—neither to judges "nor *alvedrío* recourse to [judgment]" (i.e. to someone who might seek to reinterpret the case and thereby frustrate the collective will regarding it). Conversely, Article 61 refers to the *veedor's alvedrío* (i.e. discretion) in the matter of the number of guards that might be assigned to a prisoner's vigil. This measure would seem to be pragmatic recognition of the challenge posed by Bizkaia's warring bands in that the *veedor*, should he deem it necessary to prevent the escape of the defendant(s), might take extraordinary precautions.

Nevertheless, the foregoing are rather unique applications of the notion of *albedrío*. It is also possible to discern a frequent and mainstream employment of the concept throughout the Old Law. Indeed, the text closes with the statement "And each one of them [the Bizkaians] stated: that as the said *corregidor* knew well how the Bizkaians had their privileges and exemptions and liberties and other *fueros* that were of *alvedrío* and not in writing." The *corregidor* responded that effectively "it was true that the said Bizkaians had their own exemptions and liberties, as well as their usages and customs and Fuero of *alvedrío*, by which they judged and ruled themselves." And this concept of *albedrío* is repeated several times throughout the Proem—at times as the defining general characteristic of Bizkaian law and at others as one component of it. Thus, on occasion there is reference to their task of redacting "the exemptions …and the Fuero of *alvedrío*"; at other times particular components are listed and then qualified in conclusion as being "of *alvedrío*"—in this latter instance the meaning of the term appears synonymous with "precedent."

The most important declarations in the Old Law concerning the nature of the Bizkaian legal system are in Articles 205 and 218. The first prohibits the Bizkaians from appealing to the Lord outside of Bizkaia—without clarifying the procedures should he be present in it (which was a rare event)—regarding any civil or criminal suit initiated in the Tierra Llana (for those brought in the Duranguesado there were other recourses). Thus, they state that "their Fuero is of *alvedrío* and that any sentence or sentences handed down by such *veedor* or *alcalde* according to the *Fuero* of *alvedrío* and usage and custom of Bizkaia, could be commonly revoked by anyone outside the Seigniory of Bizkaia, because the Lord, or his officials, cannot be [well] informed about the said Fuero of the Land, being outside of the said Seigniory."

In the second precept, Article 218, after pronouncing against the interventions of ecclesiastical judges in lawsuits over the patronage of churches and other matters, their exclusion is justified accordingly: "In the said Countship, in the legal cases the regimen of [canon and civil] law is not followed, nor are there proofs, nor in the judgments are the solemnities and subtleties of [canon and civil] law safeguarded. And the said alcaldes and veedor judged these cases according to the unwritten Fuero of alvedrío and their usages and customs, without the appearance of a [civil law] trial. And the said archpriests, without maintaining this order, judge the lawsuits according to the form of [canon and civil] law, from which there arose much damage and many expenses for the inhabitants of said Countship."

Lalinde discerns in the insistence upon *albedrío* a "Castilianization" effect upon Bizkaia. *Albedrío* had been a key principle in the juridical life of Old Castile, and is indeed prominent in that Countship's founding and precedential myth, or in the *Libro de los Fueros de Castilla* or the *Fuero Viejo de Castilla*, regarding Castilla's relations with the Kingdom of León and inspired by the Visigothic *Liber Iudiciorum*. At a particular moment the Castilians abandoned this system and adopted the recycled Romano-canonical one, but that did not transpire in a more juridically conservative Bizkaia.[55] This interpretation seems valid, except regarding the origin of Bizkaian *albedrío*, given that it is not so clear that it was imported from the outside. Rather, it seems more likely that in the Late Middle Ages a similar system (*albedrío*) of formulating law was common over an ample zone, which included Castilla, Bizkaia and other territories as well. In any event, were one disposed to thinking in terms of the transposition of *albedrío*, it is more reasonable to speak of the likely exportation of it from Bizkaia to Castilla, given the history of the latter's repopulation by northerners during the Reconquest in the medieval struggle with the Moors.

We might also emphasize that the Bizkaian legal system, like those of other medieval Hispanic ordinances based upon consuetudinary law (Navarra, Aragón and, as stated earlier, Old Castile), shares much in common with English common law. The latter was elaborated from the twelfth century on through decisions emerging out of the populace's interaction with royal jurisdictions. We are, of course, dealing with cultures that were spatially distant from one another and subjected to differing conditions and influences.[56] Nevertheless, England and Bizkaia did have some actual contacts, and, despite their dissimilarities, there were certain parallels in their respective juridical development.

For instance, as in Bizkaia, English common law notoriously emerges out of territorial custom, from the "general immemorial custom of the Realm." Although we are unaware of the precise form of the sentences of the Bizkaian *alcaldes de Fuero*, they were likely dissimilar to the "writs" that were so basic to English common law. The writs were originally casuistic and subsequently based upon stereotyped formulas of a public nature that originated in the orders of the king. Nevertheless, the corresponding "actions" differed from those of the private realm of Roman civil law.

There is greater similarity with the Bizkaian case in the general judicial proceedings and the judgment of individual cases. Under English common law, the parties, or their representatives, can appeal before a tribunal a prior decision intended to resolve their litigation. In practice, the "cases" are determined according to a jurisprudential law code, which requires judges to operate within the parameters set by legal precedent and consonant with the principle of *stare decisis*. Accordingly, in neither England nor Bizkaia does the judge dictate law arbitrarily, but rather according to underlying rules. In the former it is the "substantial law," which is to say it takes fundamentally into account that which already exists. Both conscience and reason are brought to bear, but against the backdrop of an underlying social logic regarding the juridical principles operative within the society, its existing values and that which constitutes acceptable change within established parameters.

In both the English and Bizkaian systems, there is rejection of Roman law and the erudite jurisprudence elaborated in the medieval universities. In the English case, it is the evolution of the monarchy that impeded penetration of the continental civil law system (despite certain influences such as those underscored in the work of Bracton). In Bizkaia, which formed part of the Kingdom of Castilla, albeit with considerable and growing political autonomy under the Fuero, the pressure is greater to accede to royal law strongly inspired by Romano-canonical jurisprudence. And therefore it is the defense of the *albedrío* system, reflected in the redaction of "custom" in the Old Law, that becomes the prime mechanism for resisting efficaciously the penetration in the Seigniory of the institutions and rules of Romano-canonical civil law.

## XI. The Personal Scope of the Old Law: *Hidalgos* and *Labradores*

One of the key questions that arises out of a reading of the Old Law regards the identity of its social protagonists. Whose rights and obligations are outlined therein; who was subject to the Fuero's dispositions? There is constant reference to noblemen—whether in the common variants of *hidalgos*, *hijosdalgo* and *fijosdalgo*—or more infrequently *escuderos* (esquires) and *cavalleros* (gentlemen). There is occasional mention of the entirely different social category of the *labradores* (peasant tenants). I will therefore now attempt to profile these two social groups and determine, at least partially, their standing within Bizkaian society and its Fuero. In the final analysis, it is necessary to understand the personal scope within which the *Fuero Viejo* was applicable.

The characterization of the *hidalgos* corresponds to the emergence from the tenth century on of a specific social group, known as the *fijosdalgo* in Castilla and León and in their constitutent territories, and as *infanzones* in Navarra and Aragón. Both terms denote nobility, and at the same time membership is the lowest stratum of the noble estate. From the moment when it was diffused and established in Bizkaia, the Castilian term *hidalgo* prevailed in naming this social category, but also there is prevalent the equivalent Navarrese-Aragonese one in denominating as the Infanzonazgo the territory inhabited by *hidalgos*.[57] It should be remembered that in Castilian society there were distinct grades of nobility—"*hidalgos de solar conocido de 500 sueldos*,"[58] "*hidalgos de gotera*,"[59] who were poorer, as well as "*hidalgos de bragueta*."[60] The generalization of noble status to the inhabitants of Bizkaia gave them unique status as a collectivity within the Kingdom of Castilla.[61] *Hidalgos* and *infanzones* tended everywhere to enjoy a similar noble juridical regimen, particularly in the form of military privileges limiting their service to the king to certain days, as well as fiscal privileges that included exemption from taxes. They also had other advantages within penal and processual law, exemption from torture, etc. We will return to this subject when we consider the specifics of the Bizkaian statute.

The question of the juridical status of the *labradores* appearing on the tax rolls of medieval Bizkaia is far from clear. The matter requires further study, a most difficult undertaking given the scarcity of available documentation regarding the truly interesting questions. To wit, what

was the real social standing of this group, its size in relation to the mass
of landed *hidalgos* and its evolution?

We do have some reliable data. Certain aspects are clear: the
*labradores* on the tax rolls worked the Lord's lands and paid him a
*censo* or tax for the privilege. Their name *labradores censuarios* derives
from this payment obligation. The *censo*, or payment, of the individual
*labrador* was combined with that of the others to meet their collective
annual obligation to the Lord of Bizkaia of 100,000 *maravedís* in old
money or 200,000 *maravedís* in the newer so-called "white money."
While unspecified, it seems likely that each *labrador's* contribution varied and corresponded to the size and productivity of the individual tenancy. Since the global payment remained fixed, the individual's burden
could vary over time, increasing accordingly in periods of demographic
and/or economic crisis and contraction. Consequently, the *labradores*
had an intrinsic interest in the stability of their numbers, as is evident in
Article 208 of the Old Law. This tax apportionment was distributed
exclusively throughout the *merindades* of the Tierra Llana.

There is little evidence regarding the proportion of a household's
income that was taken by the *censo*, although there is one fourteenth-
century reference that estimates it to be one-fifth of the harvest.[62] In
Article 208 of the Old Law, it is called the *quarto*, or "quarter," which
seems a likely stipulation of magnitude. If these two fragments of information capture an increase over time in the Lord's demands, we may
have identified one other possible motive for redaction of the Old
Law—namely the desire to freeze the *censo* at one-quarter of the harvest, which, as we shall consider below, became one component of the
annual tax assessment paid to the Lord by the Villas.

We can also elicit certain aspects in the evolution of the residential
status of the *labradores*. In the foundational charters of a new *villa*, it is
commonly stated that the *labradores* who worked *censo*-encumbered
lands within its precincts were to be incorporated as residents into the
municipality. It seems that from then on said *labradores* paid their *censo*
to the *villa*, as successor to a former part of the Lord's patrimony, and
that the income from such *censos* was employed to meet a part of the
*villa's* annual obligation to the Lord. In 1376, the Lord gave the significant order to incorporate all of the *labradores* of the extensive
Merindades of Uribe, Busturia and Markina into the Villas of the same
names, with each *labrador* retaining the right to be incorporated into his
*villa* of choice.[63] And what transpired in the Tierra Llana's remaining
Merindades of Bedia, Arratia and Zornotza? Is it possible that they
lacked tax-encumbered peasant tenants? In any event, it appears that
the Lord's order was executed,[64] but we are unsure of the practical

effects of transferring the new status of resident (*vecino*) of a *villa* upon the former *labrador censuario*. It seems likely that the sum total of Bizkaia's *censos*, denominated in the Old Law as *el pedido*, or "the request" (but in actuality the Lord's assessment), was paid by that time by the Villas as a whole who also acted as the agencies for their collection. Such appears to be the best interpretation of Article 4 of the Old Law, redacted some 76 years after the *labradores* were incorporated into the Villas, which states "the Lords of Bizkaia have always had from the *labradores* in [and from?] the Villas of Bizkaia their tax assessment *pedido*." The concept is repeated in a most ambiguous manner at the end of the precept. It might be noted that this same ambiguous aura is retained in the New Law (*Fuero Nuevo*) redacted in 1526.

The *labradores censuarios* were residing in the Infanzonazgo (or Noble Land) of the *hidalgos*, that is, the Tierra Llana. If this were indeed the case, there would have been one effect: after adscription, from that moment onward all of the lands of the Tierra Llana would have been allodial. One might further speculate that the Lord's transfer in 1376 of the *labradores censuarios* of at least three *merindades* of the Tierra Llana to the Villas was an attempt to undermine the *hidalgos* (who were often the key protagonists in the wars of the bands). But, as is evident, we are formulating plausible hypotheses rather than recounting documented history.

An understanding of the Old Law, as well as the evolution of Bizkaian law in general, must be grounded in the process of the creation and diffusion of a growing awareness of Bizkaian identity as social standing. That is to say, there was the emergence of systematic leveling of juridical differences of all of the inhabitants, whether *hidalgos* or *labradores*, following a pattern of general ennoblement of all Bizkaians. Over time it manifested two distinct facets. On the one hand, there were the exemptions and liberties of the *hidalgos* who were proprietors of allodial holdings. On the other, as we have seen, there were the privileges conferred upon the inhabitants of the Villas, and then slowly extended to the *labradores censuarios* incorporated as residents into them (at least in the Tierra Llana). There was marked similarity in the content of the liberties of both, whether dealing with the exemptions and privileges of an *hidalgo* of the Tierra Llana or the resident of one of its Villas. In fact, it was this very confluence that would result at the beginning of the Modern Age in a general statute for all Bizkaians based on "Bizkaianness." That is, in the first half of the sixteenth century, and for various reasons, there is imposed throughout the Seigniory a common political identity of "Bizkaian," which implies that all residents of the Villas and the *hidalgos* of the Tierra Llana enjoyed identical political rights, as reflected in the New Law of 1526. Nevertheless, in the Old Law of 1452 we can already discern that process, along with certain ambiguities. The Old Law makes several declarations of rights that undoubtedly correspond to every inhabitant of the Seigniory, while at the same time specifying certain privileges enjoyed only by the residents of the Tierra Llana and others that pertain exclusively to *hidalgos*.

We might now examine summarily the legal standing of *labradores* (*censuarios*) in relation to the *hidalgos* as reflected in the three medieval bodies of Bizkaian law. We might first underscore that both before the incorporation in 1376 of the *labradores* into the Villas in Tierra Llana, as well as afterwards, the *labradores* shared certain political rights with the *hidalgos*.

In 1342, the *labradores* participate in the General Assembly that approves the Codex of Juan Núñez de Lara. It also confers upon them, along with the *hidalgos*, the only concrete right mentioned in the entire text—that of buying and selling as reflected in the exploitation of the town commons (before these were constituted into the privileged jurisdiction of the Villas). It is also certain that the Codex mentions only the rights of *hidalgos* regarding the division of communal forests with the Lord.[65] And there is differential penal treatment of a *peón* convicted of a robbery, although it is unclear whether the condition of *peón* is equivalent to that of *labrador* or that the difference regards the *peón's* lack of property with which to pay fines (which is the thrust of the precept). Regarding punishment of all other delicts, there is no social distinction made among the citizenry. The salient difference remains that between an unpropertied defendant and one with sufficient resources to respond to required guarantees and fines. I believe that to speak of a truly distinct social status between *hidalgos* and *labradores* there need to be additional and more significant reflections of difference.

Similarly, in the quintessentially penal code of Gonzalo Moro (1394), there is no discrimination whatsoever between *hidalgos* and *labradores*. This is particularly striking considering that the penal law of the epoch is one of the main contexts for manifesting status differences. It is genuinely surprising that, in a penal code *par excellence,* no distinction is made between *labradores* (and/or *peones*) and *hidalgos* regarding punishment for crimes. What is more, the Gonzalo Moro code rejects torture as a means of extracting truth in favor of other means. It rules out torture since Bizkaians were "commonly noblemen" (*comunmente hijosdalgos*). The text points, then, in two directions. The first underscores that the majority of the Bizkaian population enjoyed noble status, and, second, that it was therefore protected by the exemption of the nobility from such measures. In short, a noble privilege had been converted in practice to a general right.[66] At the same time, the *labradores* continued to share with the *hidalgos* the political right of attending the General Assembly.

Nevertheless, in the Old Law of 1452 certain differences between *hidalgos* and *labradores* are specified that should be contextualized. Article 208 discusses the distinctions, but seemingly more in the spirit of maintaining the Lord's income than regularizing the status of the farming collectivity, perhaps because there was little remaining to say or do regarding it given that (at least most of) the *labradores* were now residents of the Villas. The concern was that the abandonment of the tax-encumbered farms might prejudice collection of the Lord's assessment. From this article we see that the *hidalgos* had their own tributary farms, but ones that paid far less tax than did those of the Villas, hence the incentive for a *labrador* to move from the latter to the former. Here we may be dealing with the nobility's response to the (possible) attempt to undermine it in 1376 by transferring most of the *labradores censuarios* to the Villas.

In Article 209 the difference between *hidalgo* and *labrador* is underscored explicitly and somewhat emphatically. It prohibits them from entering together into treaties (or alliances), and from dueling one another, although we are uncertain as to the significance of the latter as noble privilege by 1452. Only *hidalgos* have the specified right, at their discretion, to fortify their dwellings. There is also explicit distinction between *hidalgos* and *villanos* (commoners or townspeople), the only use of the latter term in the entire Old Law text. We simply cannot say whether *villano* refers, as it seems, simply to "resident" of a *villa*, or whether it is a deprecative term of reference for non-*hidalgos*. The article notes that encarcerated *hidalgos* were charged 24 *maravedís* as the cost of their imprisonment while *villanos* paid half that amount. Nevertheless, on balance we might conclude that it is not the occasional mentions of such distinction that commands attention, but rather their paucity or near absence throughout the text.

## XII. The Territorial Scope of the Old Law: The Singular Problem of the Villas

I have defended the thesis that the Old Law barely discriminated between the *labradores* and *hidalgos* and, consequently, its norms were applicable to the entire population. However, to the population of what territory? It is necessary to consider the geographical scope within which the Old Law's institutional jurisdiction obtained. Earlier we identified four territorial blocs within the Seigniory—the Tierra Llana,

Encartaciones, Duranguesado and Villas. I will now examine the degree to which each is constitutive of the Old Law and reflected in it. It is clear that the basis of the Fuero is the corpus of law and custom obtaining in the Tierra Llana—nuclear or core Bizkaia—that is, the six Merindades of Busturia, Uribe, Arratia, Bedia, Zornotza and Markina, and undoubtedly that of Durango as well. At the same time there are many precepts that are applicable throughout the Seigniory, or in all four of its constitutive territorial blocs, each of which tends to be named in the particular article. We can safely assume in such cases that its precepts applied throughout the entire range of the referenced territories.

Regarding the territorial scope contemplated for the new text of 1452, there is a lengthy and ambiguous paragraph in the Proem to the Old Law regarding the protagonists of the redactive exercise, indirect references to the problems that motivated the creation of such a text and, above all, the geographic scope within which its precepts were applicable. To wit,

> And each one of them stated: that as the said *corregidor* knew well how the Bizkaians had their privileges and exemptions and liberties and other *fueros* that were of *alvedrío* and not in writing. And [he knew] as well the damages, harms and errors into which the said Bizkaians and those of the Encartaciones and the Durango region have befallen and befall everyday for not having, in written form as they could have been reasonably written down, and from which they would have been able to agree, as they could have, about said exemptions and liberties and *fueros* and customs.

And when the Proem refers to the Lord's oath, it repeats all of the geographical blocs within the Seigniory—as well it should. The oath was taken:

> in the aforementioned church of Gernika and in certain other places to safeguard all the privileges and exemptions and liberties and *fueros* and usages and customs in the Villas as well as in the Tierras Llanas of Bizkaia and in the Encartaciones and the Durango region...

The Lord's oath to safeguard the *fueros* is first sworn at a ceremony held in nuclear Bizkaia (Bilbo). While it is to be repeated elsewhere, after this initial oath-taking, the Old Law is valid throughout the Seigniory, that is, within each of its territorial units and for all of their institutions. The redactors are quite explicit and reiterative in Articles 1 and 2 regarding the territorial scope of the Old Law, as well as the freedoms that it safeguards. From an institutional standpoint, the Fuero undoubtedly encompassed the (probably minor) variation in the local *fueros* of the four individual territorial blocs within the Countship. Summarily, the Old Law outlines certain precepts that were the individual and collective rights and obligations of all Bizkaians. These include certain tax exemptions (Article 4), freedom of commerce justified by shared poverty (Articles 7 and 9), exemption from arbitrary demands of the Admiralty (Article 12), and access to certain personal liberties under processual law. Similarly, all Bizkaians are regulated identically in the purchase of land in Castilla and its registry (Article 10), the procedure for naming justice officials (Article 17), the rules for notary publics (Article 23 and 24) and certain prohibitions on association (Article 200).

While it is a relatively sparse complex of "public law," taken collectively the foregoing were a powerful set of core values at the subsequent moment of generating a Bizkaian common political identity.

With the exception of the few instances cited above, there are no other precepts in the Old Law that make specific mention of territoriality or of the direct articulation of the Tierra Llana with the Encartaciones and the Duranguesado, as well as with the Villas. We have already noted that, with the exception of certain aspects of the administration of justice, the Duranguesado shared the same substantive law with nuclear Bizkaia.

The question of the link between the Tierra Llana and the Villas, and the possible extension of the *Fuero Viejo* from the former to the latter, merits particular attention. The Villas enjoyed with the Tierra Llana the same system of freedoms declared in the Old Law, and the practice of holding together a single General Assembly, of singular institutional relevance, should be kept in mind. It is a feature that is implicit in the text, but without being elaborated explicitly. It is equally obvious that the Old Law did not encompass the entire body of Bizkaian public law, nor its private law either.

Regarding the Villas, there are provisions designed to deal with possible frictions with the Tierra Llana, and which reflect a certain rivalry or conflict of interests between their respective inhabitants. There is specific reference to respect for the market privileges of the Villas in Article 16, but at the same time underscoring the rights of Bizkaians to engage in commerce in their homes and in any *anteiglesia* as long as they adhered to the prices established therein by local authorities. Article 186 requires the residents of the Tierra Llana and the Encartaciones to support together an inhabitant of either who is detained by a judge from a *villa*. Particular jurisdictional issues arose when a resident of a *villa* litigated over heritable land that he or she claimed in Tierra Llana (Article 207).

Consequently, there are reflected in the Old Law the relational difficulties between the Villas and Tierra Llana that were endemic to them since the creation of privileged municipalities in the Middle Ages. Indeed, such frictions, at times quite grave, would continue until the first decades of the seventeenth century. But they did not prevent from the outset the Tierra Llana (core Bizkaia) and its institutions from being at the center of the Seigniory's public life. Bizkaia of the Merindades *de facto* constituted the magnetic pole and nucleus that energized the coalition of the four territorial blocs. It tended to provide the general features of Bizkaian law, although subsequently certain aspects of it might be qualified as particular to nuclear Bizkaia alone during periods of tension and rivalry. The Villas never demonstrated a desire to take the lead in the Seigniory; at most they managed to establish their own entity made up of the corpus of Villas. It should be noted that the Villas have no common Fuero; rather, the limited early Fuero of Logroño serves simply as the foundation upon which are erected the particular ordinances of each municipality. In their confrontation with the Tierra Llana, the Villas gained residents by incorporating the *labradores* into their respective territories, but at the same time they lost considerable ground when such important *villas* as Bilbo, Gernika, Portugalete, Bermeo and Markina were unable to maintain control over the ample territorial jurisdictions accorded them during their foundational moment.

At times names have creative force, and the inhabitants of the Tierra Llana retained from the outset the exclusive use of the names Bizkaia, Seigniory and Countship. This is reflected clearly in the Old Law, as well as available documentation of the previous two centuries. It was not solely a question of designating the Tierra Llana of Bizkaia—although such transpired at appropriate times—but rather referring to that area as simply Bizkaia. The other blocs do not have such pretense. They call themselves Villas *of* Bizkaia or Encartaciones *of* Bizkaia.

To complete our understanding of the territorial scope of the Villas themselves within which the Old Law was in effect, as well as the perception of their inhabitants regarding this important question, it should be underscored that the redactors in 1452 declared their intention to "write down and enumerate all the freedoms and exemptions and customs and usages and *alvedríos* and privileges that the said Villas and Tierra Llana had but not in writing." It seems that they wished to effectively redact a law that embraced the entire territory. It might be added that the *procuradores* of the Villas were present at the General Assembly of Gernika held eleven years later at which the Codex of Bizkaia, including the Old Law, was approved. And, in effect, the Fuero was applied generally regarding Bizkaian freedoms, in the matters of public law mentioned in specified precepts, and possibly in other areas of public life as well. But, on closer examination, we find that the precepts and other documentation of the epoch establish that in matters of civil law—family life, inheritance, property rights and others—the precepts of the Old Law applied solely in the Tierra Llana and Duranguesado. One should also note that, on the other hand, the law of the Encartaciones, despite following its own path regarding legal codification, was surprisingly similar to nuclear Bizkaia's concerning juridical structure.

It is really beyond the scope of the present work to track the relations among the several blocs after publication of the Old Law. But briefly it can be said that the institutional problems of Bizkaian unity continued for nearly two more centuries, or until there was an Agreement (*Concordia*), in 1630, that produced a satisfactory politico-administrative integration of the Villas into the Seigniory.[67] The historical climate had changed and an effective equalization of the *villas* and *anteiglesias* was implemented without distinguishing between "Seigniory or Villas, because all should be a republic without distinction."[68] The attendance of the Villas at the General Assemblies was maintained, and they acquired the faculties of both active and passive participation in the elections of officials of a Government of Bizkaia that from that time on represented fully the interests of the entire Seigniory. The precedence of the general magistrates over those of any of the blocs was affirmed. The blocs were to be taxed equally. The system of appeals was standardized: now an appealed lawsuit from a *villa* would end up in the tribunal of the *corregidor* and Bizkaia's deputies or Deputation (Chapter 3) that had replaced the former General Assembly.

Regarding the scope of application of the law, in 1628 there was an attempt to supercede the particular laws of the Villas with the Fuero of Bizkaia, which was to be applied "in and for everything." The Agreement of 1630 did not go quite so far, but it did establish that "if one of the said *villas* and city wished to abandon some law of those which it had and adopt others that are used in the Seigniory, and asking of the Seigniory in General Assembly that it pass the laws that they had thusly requested conforming them with those of the Fuero, let it be done"(Chapter 3). In fact various *villas* decided to adopt the Fuero of Bizkaia in civil matters over the following two centuries.[69] Such was the case of Elorrio with regards to inheritance (1712), certain *barrios* of Bermeo—Albondiga, San Pelaio and Zubiaur—more broadly (1737), and the extramural *barrios* of Otxandio (1818) and Billaro (1829).[70]

Finally, some comments are in order regarding the importance that noble status (*hidalguía*) would acquire in the institutional convergence of the period after approval of the Old Law. The Agreement established a unique procedure for establishing one's nobility in the Villas and the Tierra Llana (Chapter 9).[71] There was something very important at stake, that is, the interest of residents of the Villas in enjoying without contradiction the juridical status of Bizkaian and all of the political rights as such—including that of Bizkaian universal nobility. As a consequence, Bizkaian noble privilege became a strong integrative, even populist, force within the community in general. This was particularly so from the late fifteenth century on when such status became extremely useful for opening doors throughout the Spanish Monarchy—whether in Europe or Spain's ultramarine territories.

In sum, primordially the Old Law of Bizkaia is a Fuero of the noblemen of the Tierra Llana, but in large measure it became the law of all of Bizkaia and Bizkaians. At the same time, it represented an important step in the process of institutional convergence of all of the constituent blocs into a single Seigniory.

## XIII. The Seigniory of Bizkaia's Foundational Pact

The foundational myth of the Seigniory of Bizkaia as such was recounted by the Count of Barcelos in the first half of the fourteenth century.[72] According to the account of this Portuguese nobleman, the terms of the initial pact whereby the Seigniory was constituted are as follows: Froom, a brother of the King of England, accompanied by his daughter, came to Bizkaia and offered, if they would accept him as their Lord, to lead the Bizkaians in their struggle against the Asturian Count Don Moninho (Munio). Froom was victorious at the battle of Arrigorriaga, which was the foundational event of a dynasty of lords.

A century and a half after the Count of Barcelos' account, Lope García de Salazar, writer and warrior in an almost interminable internecine war between bands or lineages, repeats the story, but with some variation. In his version, the Bizkaians were resisting the King of León. However, he did not deign to do battle with them because they were not led by a king, the son of a king or anyone of royal blood. In short, they were unworthy opponents given the chivalric code of the day. Consequently, the Bizkaians selected as their leader Jaun Zuria, nephew of the King of Scotland.[73]

The scholar Andrés Mañaricua suggests that both sources were informed by an autochthonous oral tradition; if varied in their detail, they share a common core. The story is likely quite ancient.[74] But Lope García de Salazar adds a second element to his version of the foundational myth. He notes that in accepting Jaun Zuria as their Lord, the Bizkaians agreed to divide with him "the mountains and the pasturages (*selas* [*seles*]) and give him all of the dried and green wood that is not of fruit-bearing trees to take [as fuel] for the iron foundries and certain rights in the veins [of ore] that they worked, and they converted into commons for themselves [the nuts of] the oaks, beech and holm oaks for maintenance of their pigs. And they gave him some of the best lands in all of the districts on which to settle his *labradores* and so he had use of them, and [therefore should] not bother the *fijosdalgo*."[75]

Lope García de Salazar was alluding to the equally-divided owner-ship of the mountains and commons and the distributions of patronage over individual churches that is reflected in the bodies of Bizkaian legal codes, beginning with the Codex of Juan Núñez de Lara (1342). Articles 34 and 35 of it discuss the delimitation of ownership of pasturage (*seles*) between the noblemen and the Lord. The Old Law of 1452, approved in the General Assembly of Gernika, treats the same issues similarly. Its Article 11 states that in Bizkaia "all of the mountains, tracts and com-mons belong to the Lord of Bizkaia and to the *fijosdalgo* and towns equally (*a medias* or half and half)." The point is reiterated in the first sentence of Article 154. There is a similar arrangement regarding the right of patronage over churches or *monasterios* ("monasteries") owned by individuals, and which afforded them the ecclesiastical tithes. According to Article 216, half of the church patronages belonged to the Lord and the other half to the noblemen. The latters' share was justified on the grounds that they had won the land from the Moors and contin-ued to fight them, that is, they were defending the faith and needed resources to do so, including from the Church. But, by the middle of the fifteenth century, patronage or tenancy over individual churches was becoming anomalous within canon law. It had already provoked a lengthy conflict between the nobility and the Church, as well as formal reclamations by the Bishops of Calahorra and Burgos—such as that of 1390 in the Court of Guadalajara.[76] In the Old Law there is a petition to the King that he ask the Pope to legitimate the patronages, which was of course in the Monarch's interest as well, given that he was Lord of Bizkaia.

We are confronted by an issue that is both relevant and difficult to elucidate. The legend of the pact and the reality of the division of own-ership of the mountains and commons and church patronages both raise key questions regarding the antecedents and origin of the arrangement. Was there some sort of initial or founding pact between the community and Lord Eneko Lupiz when the jurisdictional Seigniory of Bizkaia was constituted in the eleventh century within the Kingdom of Pamplona, or was the agreement earlier or later? Or, indeed, are we dealing with an entirely different state of affairs?

The foundational pact has been the object of two types of interpretations. Some focus upon its political and institutional aspects and suppositions, while others view the pact as one expression of the socioeconomic evolution of the Bizkaian community. Perhaps there is room for a third syncretic interpretation.

If we raise the question of political pacting as it regards the reciprocal oaths between the Lord and the Bizkaian community, it is well to note the interest of the legal historian Lalinde Abadía in a legend that might be linked with the most important foundational myth of eastern Spain. Reference is to the Fuero of Sobrarbe that is so decisive in configuring the political imaginary of Navarra and Aragón.[77] For Lalinde, there was an autochthonous Bizkaian legendary substratum linked to relations between the Basques and England, to the Arthurian cycle and to the struggle for Bizkaian independence from the Kingdom of León, upon which the Lope García de Salazar interpretation, conditioned or inspired by the legend of the Fuero of Sorbrarbe, has been superposed. The connection had been posited as early as the sixteenth century by Coscojales.[78] He underscores certain features of the Bizkaian legend, which, as in the Kingdoms of Aragón and Navarra, have the function of strengthening or reinforcing political pacting within the community.

It is noteworthy that it was not Bizkaians alone who relate and interpret the legend, given that in addition to the account of the Portuguese Count of Barcelos, there is that of the "Chronicle" of the Castilian *corregidor* Cedeño (1545), albeit from the sixteenth century.[79] The legend narrates an anti-Leónese reaction, against whose authority a decisive battle was fought and won. And there is British leadership of the resistance, personified either by the brother of the King of England or the sister of the Scottish Monarch. Nordic characteristics are underscored throughout. The Lord is Jaun Zuria, the "White Lord," a physical feature that seemed evident in the seigniorial dynasty created in Bizkaia. Some of its lords are nicknamed "The Blond" or "The White."

Similarly, the Bizkaians, when referring to their norms and political organization, share with other people certain elements present in the legend of Jaun Zuria: the appearance of a foreigner as the first leader, one who was persecuted in his own land, one whose very foreignness facilitates his acceptance while at the same time imposing strict limitations upon his authority. There are other features in common such as victory over another people.[80]

There have been attempts to explain the origins of Bizkaia's foundational myth and the hypothetical pact between lord and community as simply a concern over the distribution of property rights. It is certain that, by the mid-fourteenth century, there was a legendary explication of such division that, as noted earlier, could have been extant for a long time. But for how long? If in fact it is true that oral tradition is the medium *par excellence* for information transmission in preliterate societies, or those with minimal written documentation, it seems overly optimistic to attribute to orality a capacity to recount accurately events transpiring 300 or 400 years earlier. How precise, then, is Bizkaian fifteenth-century oral tradition regarding the presumptive tenth-century existence of Momo, *comes bizchaiensis*, or under the aegis of Eneko Lupiz, the first ruler of Bizkaia—but not adequately documented until a century later? The legend surrounding him has intrinsic interest as one element in the formation of an autochthonous political identity, and as an expression of Bizkaian self-representation that is increasingly evident throughout the thirteenth, fourteenth and fifteenth centuries, but it is of scant reliability regarding the detail of Bizkaia's foundational reality. For this reason other possible explanations have been explored.

The medievalist García de Cortázar, recognized authority on the Seigniory's economic and social history, has underscored the legend in his analysis of the evolution of land tenure, squeezing as much as possible out of the scant information available for the Early Middle Ages. He postulates that there was an initial phase in which the economy of a small population turned upon extensive animal husbandry on land held collectively. Extended families were accorded usufruct, but not ownership, of mountain and valley pasturage. Several factors might have undermined free and exlusive tenancy. Among them was the Lord of Bizkaia's initiative in establishing privately-owned churches, with tithing authority within a particular jurisdiction, that thereby generated income for the seigniorial system. Both before and during the creation of *villas*—which were located strategically along trade routes and themselves constituted an important factor in the acculturation of Bizkaians into the Castilian world—the Lord was likely settling upon his estates the *labradores* or peasant tenants—possible successors of earlier serfs. There also emerged the *parientes mayores*, or senior lineage heads, who evolved into *fijosdalgo* (*hidalgos*), or noblemen, and who imitated the Lord by both exercizing patronage (and thereby receiving the tithes) of individual churches and settling rent-paying tenants (*labradores*) on their own lands. In short, both the Lord and the noblemen privatized the commons. In this regard, the period of foundation of the Villas (thirteenth and fourteenth centuries) was likely decisive. With them Bizkaia entered into a new phase regarding land tenure, reflected in the institutional articulation of the *anteiglesias* (parishes) or rural townships.[81]

Nevertheless, our documentation for the period is scant and such speculation has its limits. Without doubt, by this time there existed a strong seigniorial patrimony in Bizkaia, one that in part facilitated and accommodated the founding of the Villas, while at the same time raising occasional issues and problems regarding the inclusion of land "belonging" to *hidalgos* within the jurisdiction of the new privileged municipalities. We see this tension reflected in certain articles of the Old Law, which both state the Lord's ownership of Bizkaia's public lands, while restricting his ability to create (by conferring charters of privilege unilaterally) new *villas* without the consent of Bizkaia's General Assembly. And what was the origin of such seigniorial hegemony in Bizkaia? Why did the Lord have initial general tenancy over the lands of an unconquered (by him or his ancestors) area? After all, in the ninth century there is reference to Bizkaians' ownership of their territory, affirmed in the phrase *a suis reperitur semper esse possessas*. Conversely, it would seem that allodial lands (or free holds) were also quite common. Otherwise, the (uncontested by the Monarchy) contention in the Old Law, and subsequent codes and documents that all Bizkaians are commonly *hidalgos* or noblemen, makes no sense. Similarly, in the Fuero it is proclaimed and reiterated that one half of the mountain commons belongs to the *hidalgos*. One gets the impression that the redactors of the Old Law and their contemporaries regarded this dual symmetry in the ownership of the public patrimony to be something specifically and distinctively Bizkaian.

Finally, the thesis of the relatively late private appropriation of land in Bizkaia runs counter to the sanctity of the family patrimony that is quite evident throughout the Old Law. What is more, it is fair to say that the only land tenure regulated specifically by the Fuero is that of the nuclear family, but with the strong intrusion of the principle of the precedence of the property within an extended family that accords collateral kinsmen certain rights over its disposition. In the Middle Ages, it was customary to invoke the authority of "time immemorial" to legitimize contemporary custom and law, and such is clearly the case in the Old Law regarding family ownership of heritable land. There are but a few references to changes to it within recent memory. Nor was such family law the result of a few isolated novelties; rather, reference is to the generation of a complex and interconnected system of rules, which must have emerged only over a considerable period of time. Obviously, the private property system reflected in the Old Law was the one extant in the fifteenth century, but most of its features undoubtedly date from earlier ones.

In sum, we might propose a syncretic explanation that takes into account both an original system of communal shared property in Bizkaia as well as a subsequent pact between the community and the Lord. Widely extended in other parts of Vasconia, to this day there is a system of communal property held by the residents of various municipal jurisdictions. These are denominated *faceros* or *facerías* in Navarra and community of pasturage in Gipuzkoa. Under the *facerías*, the inhabitants of municipalities of valleys adjacent to the same extensive woods and mountain meadows share common ownership and, consequently, usufruct of such resources. The residents, rather than the municipalities in which they reside, are the titular owners of said rights in the *facero*. These *facería* arrangements have been in existence since at least the Late Middle Ages. We might suppose that in these zones of communal ownership the *facerías* are reflective of an original or antecedent system that was then maintained after the formal institutionalization of the municipal councils. It should be noted that the councils or municipalities, that is, the new administrative units, recognized the existence of both family property and that of the town commons as well that belonged to all residents within their jurisdiction. But there is clear persistence of the common ownership of the residents of dozens of municipalities of the *faceros* situated between adjacent valleys.

It would not be strange to imagine that a similar situation obtained in Bizkaia (although the evidence is less direct). But there, in the eleventh century, there was an institutional event of paramount importance. I refer to the concession by Navarra's monarch to a high governmental official or *comes*, the hereditary right to govern the Seigniory. It is quite possible that at this moment Eneko Lupiz, as a part of his countship, sought feudal authority over the woodlands, meadows and other resources that previously comprised the Bizkaian commons, putting the whole former system at risk with his pretensions. And in an attempt to preserve a part of their original rights, the community might have pacted with the Lord an equal division of said communal land, thereby satisfying in part (but only partly) his aspirations.[82]

## XIV. The Community

In the constitution of Bizkaia in the Middle Ages, there are two elements in play—the Lord and the community. On the one hand, as we have seen, there was the dynasty of the Haro family that acquired the right of heritable governance of the Seigniory in the eleventh century. In 1379, or three hundred years later, by virtue of such succession the pretender Don Juan (1358–1390) acceded to the Castilian throne. After this time the Bizkaian seigniorial and Castilian royal authority coincided in

the same person. Thenceforth, the powerful Castilian monarchs included amongst their titles that of Lord of Bizkaia.

We shall consider the figure of the Lord in greater detail below. For
now, the focus is upon the community as the second element configuring Bizkaia as a political entity. The Lord and the officials who exercise
power in his name—the senior *merino* and the *prestamero* (sheriffs in
the medieval sense of the term), and later the *corregidor*—have their
correlate in the Bizkaian community. Structured early on, there is a kind
of populist political counterweight to seigniorial power, one that will
play a crucial role, we might even say a surprising one (viewed compar-
atively throughout the Europe of the day) in public life. The dialectic
between the Lord and the community is key in the political evolution of
Bizkaia.

We might reiterate the points made earlier regarding the organization of a Bizkaian community conscious of its law. There is the probable pre-Roman origin of the population. It would remain free from
Mussulman occupation and therefore did not experience Christian
repopulation in the Early Middle Ages (as did much of the Iberian
Peninsula). In the *Chronicle* of Alfonso III (874 A.D.), there is a reference that asserts that there was no repopulating of Bizkaia during the
reign of Alfonso I (739–757) because these lands *a suis reperitur semper
esse posessas* ("were always possessed by their inhabitants").[83] What is
certain is that there is no clear evidence of the existence of an external
political authority operative in the territory during the Dark Ages (the
fifth to the ninth centuries). The local society was likely left in large
measure to fend for itself. It may have elaborated customs and usages
that, given their antiquity by the Late Middle Ages, might have seemed
constitutive of the community itself. Perhaps this fact influenced the
political process when officials of Navarra and then of Castilla gained
sway over Bizkaia, prompting necessary agreements or pacts with the
locals that configured diverse aspects of the public life of the Land. It is
that to which we referred earlier when we noted that Bizkaian foundational myths might have a certain basis in historical reality.[84] At the
beginning of the Late Middle Ages, and after the community's lengthy
incubation, there are *anteiglesias* and *merindades* with their assemblies,
and a representative body of the entirety of Bizkaian society—the General Assembly.

1. THE CONCEPT OF "BIZKAIA" AS SYNONYMOUS WITH THE BIZKAIAN
COMMUNITY

By 1452, the idea of an organized political community was clearly
evident throughout the Seigniory. This collective political subject is

known by the autochthonous name "Bizkaia," a term that possessed a communitarian meaning that transcended the purely territorial. As articulated throughout the Old Law, and within various other contexts, there are multiple references to this broader sense of community as polity. Thus, "all Bizkaia" (*toda Vizcaya*), that is to say all the community, will require of the *corregidor* (or the King's highest ranking representative) restraints on his right to hand out sentences outside of the established territorial limits (Article 196), as well as his support of those engaged in lawsuits initiated by residents of one of the Villas regarding property situated in Tierra Llana. Or there is anticipation of his forming a common front with the Seigniory (*juntar a Vizcaya*) in certain matters, as stated in Articles 206 and 207. He who kills someone "as an enemy of Bizkaia" is immune from punishment if he submits to ecclesiastical jurisdiction rather than the competency of ordinary secular justice (Article 214). "Bizkaia is obligated" to resist said ecclesiastical jurisdiction when it contravenes or "breaks" the Fuero, and Article 215 holds harmless anyone who acts in defense of the Fuero. In another context there is mention of a form of liability incurred by certain fraudulent parties who are thereby required to contribute to the "maintenance of Bizkaia," possibly by restituting the public expenditures that their imprudent behavior had cost the community.

The existence of the Bizkaian community as a political entity is reflected in certain primordial ways. Those which best express a communitarian spirit are reflected in the creation of the law, or the oath taken by the new Lord upon accession to office—which implies renewal of a constitutional pact. On the other hand, it is well to contextualize the rights inherent in the condition of being Bizkaian and a nobleman within the ambit of a politically defined society.

## 2. THE LEGISLATIVE FACULTY OF THE GENERAL ASSEMBLY

We might now consider the question of the community's participation in the creation of law. At an early time, although it cannot be determined with precision, the Bizkaians acquired important protagonism (and one that stands out in comparison with other European contexts) in the creation of law. We have already considered passages in the text that underscore the singular importance of the General Assembly in the elaboration of the Fuero, just as had been the case in the redaction of the two preceding legal codes, the Codex of Juan Núñez de Lara (1342) and the Ordinances of Gonzalo Moro (1394).

Direct intervention of the community in the creation of law was not exclusive to Bizkaia, given that it was known in other Spanish contexts. The assemblies of the Kingdoms of Navarra, Aragón and Catalunya had all achieved normative pacting competencies by the thirteenth and four-teenth centuries. Nevertheless, the radicality of popular protagonism in formulating legal concepts and praxis in the tiny Seigniory of Bizkaia is particularly noteworthy. There, either the General Assembly, or a com-mission appointed by it, is present in every phase of the legislative process.

In effect, it is in the General Assembly of Idoibalzaga that the Bizka-ians agreed to compile in writing their consuetudinary laws and cus-toms, and there that they named the redacting commission. In the delib-erations of the commission, the need for all Bizkaians to come together to debate and approve the resulting text is stated. They affirm regarding their laws that "the said Lord and King, as Lord of Bizkaia, could not take them away from them, nor add to them nor give them any new [ones] unless he should do so in Bizkaia, beneath the tree of Gernika, and in General Assembly and with the consent of the said Bizkaians" (Proem: paragraph 3). And when alluding to the Lord's oath taken in Gernika, it is stated "And afterwards he will come to Gernika beneath the tree where the Assembly is customarily held, [announced by] the blowing of the five horns. And there, with the consent of the Bizkaians, if some [laws] should be deleted and others amended, and with said agreement, he shall delete them and create new ones if need be."

When the General Assembly of Idoibalzaga empowered the com-mission to redact the Fuero, the *corregidor* excludes himself voluntarily from its deliberations and is also absent when the text is presented and discussed in full assembly. His behavior underscores the populist nature of the exercise. Neither the Lord nor his representative takes active part in the redaction; rather, it is their role to confirm the end result and then only after the Bizkaians had done so. It is also surprising that the Assem-bly then orders that the approved code enter into effect immediately, even before its royal confirmation, and holds harmless the local officials from any possible consequences for applying it. Such collective audaci-ty was largely unthinkable in the juridical climate of the epoch.

I earlier noted the requirement of the consent of the General Assem-bly in the creation of new *villas*. Article 11 notes "the Lord of Bizkaia could not order the creation of any *villa* in Bizkaia except in the Assem-bly of Gernika, [convened by the traditional] blowing of the five horns, and with all the Bizkaians giving their consent." There was an earlier practice in this regard, as reflected in the foundings of Plentzia (1299), Bilbo (1330), Billaro (1366), and Gernika and Gerrikaiz (1366). Their foun-dational charters declare that the new nuclei were constituted "at the pleasure of all the Bizkaians," "with the pleasure and with the will of all the Bizkaians."[85] The omission of expressed references to the agreement of the community in the charters of other *villas* does not necessarily mean that the Lords of Bizkaia bypassed the General Assembly in founding a *villa*. The Old Law was elaborated after the cycle of creating new privileged municipalities was over. There was simply no longer an opportunity for the Assembly to exercise this faculty.

3. The Rights of Bizkaians: Exemptions and Privileges

In speaking of freedoms in the plural, it is neither my intention to invoke the contemporary understanding of liberty nor to enter into the theological, philosophical and scientific debates concerning its nature in the abstract. More germane to an appreciation of the Old Law is the viewpoint of jurists regarding freedom within functioning political and social structures. Reference is to whether or not a particular polity is free to act without external constraints, whether it has declared its formal rights to such liberties and if mechanisms are in place to guarantee them.

The history of the concept of liberty predates considerably the attempts of Rousseau and Locke to elucidate the intellectual foundations of political freedoms, as well as before the late eighteenth-century declarations of rights by American and French revolutionaries.[86] It should be remembered that the latter were based upon certain English precedents, and even some from cities of Antiquity, and that in various places on the European continent during the Middle Ages there had been important expressions of tangible freedoms. In this latter regard, there were significant examples of medieval pactism in the eastern parts of the Iberian Peninsula—notably in Aragón, Catalunya and Valencia. The same was true of the Kingdom of Navarra. In the thirteenth and fourteenth centuries, certain liberties appear in foundational juridical texts as more or less explicit rights protected by certain guarantees of either a political or jurisdictional nature. Rather than an abstract and unsystematized statement, the texts tend to specify and then accumulate individual liberties that constitute a particular brand of freedom. There is usually a sequence in the elaboration of such political liberties: habitually they initiate with the individual estates—the nobility, the clergy, the merchants—and are subsequently generalized throughout society through their conversion into "national" freedoms.[87]

The Bizkaian case is of historical significance in this development of European popular liberties. There was an awareness of Bizkaian freedoms in the Early Modern Age, reflected in part in literature of the Castilian Golden Age, as for example in the chapter that Luján de Saavedra devotes to them in his famous novel.[88] The matter is also central within traditional Basque political thought, although at the beginning of the Modern Age its emphasis is more centered upon the claim of universal nobility for all Basques and rights inherent within such status.[89]

Nevertheless, there was longstanding awareness of the singularity of Bizkaian law and liberties. A Castilian chronicle regarding the reign of King Juan I (1379–1390) recounts how his Royal Council reminded the Monarch that, although it was true that Bizkaia followed faithfully the banner of the Monarchy of Castilla, it was "a separate land" and that the Bizkaians "always wanted their *fueros* sworn to and safeguarded and their own judges…and they do not consent to being judged by your judge or hear his judgments, unless there is a separate judge in your Court for it…and the Bizkaians are men of their own will who wish to be very free and treated very well."[90] This is not someone's personal opinion, but rather a pronouncement by the highest judicial and advisory organ of the Monarchy. Quite possibly it reflects the climate of opinion extant at the Royal Court after the recent incorporation of the Seigniory into the Crown in 1379.

The Old Law of 1452 contains several declarations regarding the freedoms and rights that correspond to the Bizkaians. We are not dealing with a table articulated systematically, as there would be in a modern constitution, but rather with unique and concrete freedoms stated in the style of the *Ancien Regime*, if applied in a general manner so that certain aspects constitute an antecedent of the modern concept of universal rights. We have seen earlier that in the Old Law the scope of individual rights is not always entirely clear, particularly given that on occasion the language refers to the freedoms and exemptions of the noblemen alone while on others there is no such qualification. Nevertheless, it must be remembered once again that six decades before the Old Law was redacted, or in 1394, in the Ordinances of Gonzalo Moro it is stated that all inhabitants of Bizkaia were noblemen (*hidalgos*).[91]

It is impossible to determine the origins of each and every freedom guaranteed by the Old Law. They probably date from different epochs and resulted from distinct actions and processes. At times they were likely the ratification and confirmation of existing circumstances of longstanding duration; at others they may have resulted from pacts or even onerous concessions by the Lord, with the community taking advantage of moments of crisis or weakness in his governance. Some may have been privileges conceded gracefully and gratuitously. But what really matters is the final outcome, however arrived at, which is the critical massing of freedoms over time that resulted in a privileged status for Bizkaians that was unprecedented within the comparative European law of the epoch.

Let us consider certain liberties:

a. Freedom from taxation is guaranteed by Article 4. It states that other than the *pedido* paid by the *labradores*, "the Bizkaians and those of the Encartaciones and from Durango never had another assessment nor tribute, nor sales tax (*alcavala*), nor monetary payments, nor services." The noblemen of these territories have always been free from "other tributes of whatever kind," as long as they remain in Bizkaia. At the same time, as we saw earlier, the collectivity of *labradores* who worked the King's lands paid 100,000 *maravedís* as *pedido*, but for reasons unspecified by the Fuero. It is unclear whether the payment was made as a tribute or as rent for use of private property. This confusion is common in similar European texts of the epoch.

b. Graduated exemption from military service is detailed in Article 6. The Bizkaians had to respond to the Lord's call to serve in the military ranks, and without salary, while campaigning as far as "the Malato Tree, which is in Lujando," a boundary marker of the Seigniory. If they went beyond the Seigniory's confines,[92] but without crossing the mountain passes leading into Castilla, they were to receive two months salary. For service beyond said passes, the salary was increased to three months.

c. Freedom of commerce is regulated in a contradictory manner, taking into account the alimentary needs of an Atlantic maritime population living in a land with scant agricultural potential.

From this there result restraints rather than freedoms. Article 7 prohibits removal from Bizkaia of foodstuffs that arrive by land or sea. Article 8 requires ships landing in Bizkaia to leave there one-half of their cargo. On the other hand, there is the positive measure preventing detention of French and Breton vessels and cargoes under letters of seizure or retaliation (royal authorizations for corsair activity). Breton and French vessels were allowed to offload freely the foodstuffs that they brought and then take on iron and any other merchandise (Article 9).

There is also the Bizkaians' freedom to buy and sell any kind of merchandise in their homes (there is specific mention of textiles and iron), a freedom that was not felt in principle to undermine the market privileges accorded to the Villas (Article 14). The right of Bizkaians to sell bread, wine, cider, meat and other foodstuffs is broader, since they can do so "in their houses and in any other districts" at a price fixed by the mayors of the *anteiglesia* where such sale is transacted. Without a doubt, this is a universal liberty because the declaration makes mention of both noblemen and peasants (Article 16).

Finally, there is another guarantee of individual initiative that accords to noblemen the right to construct on their properties a fortified house or an unfortified mansion (Article 162).

d. Various freedoms in the legal process are specified. The Fuero consecrates a right of capital importance in the epoch, namely that no judicial authority could cite a Bizkaian as plaintiff or defendant in either civil or criminal cases outside of Bizkaia, including in those so-called court cases of the Crown. We might note the crimes covered by the Courts of Zamora of 1274: "[causing a] certain death, raping a woman, breaking a treaty, violating safe conduct, burning down a dwelling, interdicting a road, treason, dueling and treachery." In effect, Bizkaians were exempted from being summoned and tried outside of Bizkaia for such crimes, with the exception of that of dueling (Article 13).

All of which should place maximum importance upon the Old Law's declaration that the authorities cannot detain or hypothecate the property of anyone without a judicial order, and that immediately upon a judge's order they had to release prisoners (Article 63). It is an early and surprising (for the times) example of Bizkaian *habeas corpus* that concerns judicial verification of the legality and the conditions of incarceration. In this regard, recall that the pioneering English "Habeas Corpus Act" dates from 1679! According to that law, which is a part of the "Glorious Revolution," an unconvicted accused defendant could request a *habeas corpus* ruling from the judge requiring the authorities holding him in custody to place him at the disposition of the tribunal in timely fashion in order that it certify the necessity and validity of the imprisonment in light of the pending charges.[93] In Aragón, there was a "manifestation law" (*manifestatio personarum*), enacted in 1398 and again in 1510, that allowed any accused to seek the protection of the highest judicial magistrate—i.e., the justice system—by entering prison under his direct control.[94]

Indeed, under the Old Law the authorities could neither accuse anyone nor initiate a criminal investigation without a judge's order, except in the case where someone was caught *in fraganti* with stolen property or in the act of fleeing the scene of a crime. Even then, once apprehended, the seigniorial officials had to place the accused immediately at the disposition of a judge and without imprisoning him themselves (Article 66). Nor could the authorities allege as justification of their own inappropriate actions that the person in question was of bad repute (excepting if the maligned individual were a vagabond). Authorities violating such structures were subject under the Fuero to the severe punishments reserved for judges and officials who act incorrectly (Article 67).

Finally, there was no double jeopardy for anyone absolved of a crime (Article 194).

e. The inviolability of the home is given singular treatment. Justice officials cannot enter the house of an *hidalgo* without his permission. They must remain at a distance of 8 *brazas* [95] (i.e., 14 or 15 meters) from it until allowed to approach, and then must enter the dwelling unarmed. The *hidalgo* is exempted from any punishment should he resist and even kill an official attempting to enter his house without permission. The only exception is if the *hidalgo* is harboring a known criminal or fugitive (Article 77).[96]

f. Among the specified civil liberties is that of guaranteeing with one's property the validity of one's contractual obligations. Any man or woman at least 25 years of age can underwrite his or her obligations with moveable goods or heritable land up to the full amount of their worth. And if such guarantee is proffered, the guarantor may not be incarcerated for an offense prior to trial (Article 192).

g. Freedom of movement from place to place and along the roadways, and without charge, is explicit (Article 198).

## XV. The Lord and His Oath

The oath of the Lord to respect the Bizkaian Fuero is central to the Old Law. Its first four precepts are devoted to this central feature of Bizkaian governance. Notably, an oath is a solemn promise to God to do (or abstain from doing) something. Taken while placing one's hand upon the cross and the Bible, or upon the host, which is the body of Christ, it is of a sacramental nature and fully binding. To break one's oath implies not only perjury but sacrilege, with all of the inherent temporal and spiritual consequences. The Infante Don Juan of Castilla affirmed that he would be endangering his soul were he to not comply with his oath to safeguard the Fuero of Bizkaia, given when he was received there as its Lord.[97]

Perhaps from the perspective of our desacralized world it is difficult to understand the extreme binding value placed upon such an oath, and its role in medieval public and private law. Monarchs employ the oath to ensure the community of respect for its law; subjects use it to display reverence for the monarch's authority. An oath might establish ties of fidelity and dependency between persons, or, in law, to guarantee the compromises relating to property or other obligations. In processual, civil and criminal law, it is central to both compromise and the determination of truth. As noted in the Old Law, there were specific churches, the so-called *iglesias juraderas*, for the oath-taking, whether public or private oaths.

Obviously, the oath to safeguard the *fueros* was important in the system of governance of the distinct Hispanic kingdoms, most notably that of Aragón.[98] Lacarra analyzed the practice of taking oaths for the Kingdom of Navarra.[99]

Regarding Bizkaia, there is evidence of the Lord's oath-taking two centuries before the redaction of the Old Law. One instance is legendary and is narrated by Lope García de Salazar. According to his account, the Lord of Bizkaia, Diego López III de Haro (1239–1254), reputed to be one of the most powerful Castilian magnates, failed to follow the custom of his ancestors and refused to take the oath. He was forced to relent by the threat of 10,000 Bizkaians to leave the Seigniory.[100]

There are four consistent testimonials from the fourteenth century regarding the celebration of the Bizkaian General Assemblies and their relation to oath-taking. The first refers to Diego López's presence in the General Assembly of 1308 held in Aretxabalaga. He requested to be exonerated from assuming the lordship and making "the corresponding solemn acceptance promise in favor of his niece María." According to the account,

> Since they arrived in Bizkaia, Don Diego has tried to assemble all of the good men of Bizkaia in that place where they are accustomed to hold the Assembly when they accept a Lord, which is Aretxabalaga.

There, the Bizkaians accepted his proposal and "received her as their Lady in the same manner that they used to [receive] the other Lords that were of Bizkaia."[101]

The second instance regards the document elaborated in 1356 by the Tierra Llana and the Villas guaranteeing a fidelity pact subscribed by Don Tello, Lord of Bizkaia, upon his marriage to Juana, the heiress of the Bizkaian lordship, and her brother King Pedro I. In the event of rupture of said pact, the guarantors agreed to accept the King as their Lord, stating,

> And if the said Doña Juana went along with Don Tello in disservice to the King, then we the said Bizkaians and [residents of the] Villas, received as Lord of Bizkaia, and we recognized the lordship of the said Lord King Don Pedro. Whether it angers or pleases the few or the many, coming said Lord Don Pedro to Aretxabalaga, which is in Bizkaia, sounding the five horns, and being in General Assembly, according to the custom of Bizkaia, and swearing the said Lord King Don Pedro that he will maintain and safeguard for

the Villas and for all the rest of the land of Bizkaia our *fueros*, and usages and customs and privileges, accordingly as have sworn those Lords that there have been in Bizkaia until now.[102]

In the foundational charter of Miraballes, drafted in 1374, it is noted that the future King Juan I (1358–1390) (who would not accede to the throne until 1379) had been Lord of Bizkaia since 1370, having come in person to Bizkaia while still the *Infante* or pretender to swear to respect and observe Bizkaian law.[103] Finally, when elaborating his Ordinances of 1394, Gonzalo Moro mentions several times the oath to safeguard the *fuero* of Bizkaia taken earlier by King Enrique III (1379–1406). While somewhat later than the Old Law, Mendieta's well-known painting of the monarch's oath-taking in the General Assembly of Gernika, when promising to safeguard the Fuero, is a graphic expression of the importance of said ceremony within the Bizkaian imaginary.[104] It might be noted that during the fourteenth century Aretxabalaga and not Gernika was the customary place for holding the General Assembly at which to receive the Monarch's oath. The centrality of the oath-taking within the Seigniory's legal system of the mid-fifteenth century is evident. The political community's underlying pact is actualized through the oath, which binds the Lord to maintain and safeguard the territory's law. For their part, the Bizkaian's pledge themselves to accept him as their Lord and to respect his prerogatives.

In the Proem to the Old Law, it is noted that the King of Castilla, Don Juan II (1406–1454), had yet to come to Bizkaia to take the oath to observe the *fueros*. He died two years after approbation of the Old Law, or apparently before making his appearance. As noted earlier, it seems that he had never carried out the prescribed ritual, which was anomalous given the fact that he had reigned for 48 years. Indeed, this situation may itself have prompted redaction of the Old Law, and particularly the final prescription that it be effective immediately and prior to its confirmation by the Monarch. But, in any event, there is statement that the King's forebears had always come to Gernika to take their oath before assuming the lordship of Bizkaia. The solemn royal promise was clearly felt to bind together the four blocs constituting the Seigniory. On the other hand, the royal oath is associated with the principle that Bizkaian law is created and modified through an interchange and agreement in the General Assembly of Gernika between the royal will and that of the Bizkaian community. By redacting the Old Law, the Bizkaians were outlining with clarity that which the Monarch would swear to safeguard and uphold.

The foregoing regards the Proem of the Old Law. Entering its corpus in the very first article, it is stipulated that anyone fourteen years of age or older, who by any means held title to the right of succession to the Bizkaian lordship, would have to appear in Bizkaia in person in order to take the oath. He or she could not delay for more than one year after acquiring the right of succession and/or attaining age fourteen. The oath was to be received by an ensemble of territorial blocs constituting the political entity of Bizkaia—the Tierra Llana, the Encartaciones, the Duranguesado and the Villas. The act of oath-taking was to be repeated in several places. After the swearing, the Lord (or Lady) was in possession of all his (or her) rights and authority. However, any delay in the oath-taking beyond the prescribed time frame meant that any seigniorial payments due (excepting income from the iron foundries) were in abeyance.

The Lord's route for oath-taking is specified as well. There is a first general swearing (the text insists that it is directed to all of Bizkaia and all of its social groups) held in Bilbo. Next comes the traditional place of Aretxabalaga and then the church of San Emeterio and Celedon in Goikolexea (close to the Villa of Larrabetzua). The Lord then continued on to Gernika where the General Assembly is convened. Again, according to the text, the Lord's presence beneath the Oak of Gernika was required were the law to be reformed, and only then with the concurrence of the Bizkaians. The itinerary finishes with a visit to the church of Santa Eufemia in Bermeo. There the Lord takes the oath while placing a hand upon a consecrated host held by a clergyman dressed in sacred regalia. In short, the circuit passes through the Merindades of Uribe and Busturia, or the heart of core Bizkaia.

## XVI. The Relationship between the Community and Its Lord: The *Pase Foral*

There is the clear conception in the Old Law of the polity as an entity consisting of two parties—the Lord and the community—each endowed with reciprocal rights and obligations. This prefigures an institution that emerges two centuries later and which will be denominated the *pase foral*. That is, the community would reserve for itself the competency of examining the Lord's dispositions (and those of his agents) to decide whether they were to be respected or not according to the preexisting law that the Lord had sworn to conserve. If affirmative, the corresponding royal resolution is authorized and applied. That is, it is given *pase* (passage), from which derives the institution of the *pase foral*. In the event that its dispositions contravene Bizkaian law, or what was called the *contrafuero*, it was opposed by the traditional formula of "to obey but not comply." This is an expression from medieval Castilian law that took root in the territories of Vasconia, and particularly Bizkaia, where it survived even after having fallen into disuse in its place of origin. The language of the Old Law states, "whatever decree that the Lord of Bizkaia hands down in opposition to the Fuero of Bizkaia shall be obeyed but not complied with" (Article 15). In other words, the authority of the King and Lord is acknowledged, but the particular measure is rejected on the grounds that it contravenes the community's law that the Lord had sworn solemnly to uphold.

There are two concrete applications of this concept specified in the Old Law. In order to defend the jurisdiction of the Tierra Llana regarding property situated therein against the claims by the Villas, Article 207 states that should someone appear with such summonses from the Lord "they shall be obeyed but not complied with." Furthermore, the principle is applied even more starkly with respect to papal dispositions, or those of some bishop, that are felt to contravene Bizkaian law regarding the patronages of privately-owned churches. Any ecclesiastical letter felt to be contrary to the Fuero "shall not be obeyed or complied with" (Article 217). In this case there is not the recognition of the obligation to obey that follows from the monarch's preeminence (even if he is to be subsequently defied).[105]

## XVII. The Administration of Justice

1. THE TERRITORY OF THE TIERRA LLANA AND ITS DEMARCATIONS: THE *ANTE-IGLESIA* AND *MERINDAD*

In order to comprehend the administration of justice within Bizkaia, we require at least a summary sketch of its administrative structure. In addition to the Villas, which comprised their own entity, there is the so-called Tierra Llana of core or original Bizkaia and the Duranguesado, within both of which the key territorial units were the *anteiglesia* and the *merindad*.

By the time that the Old Law was redacted in 1452, Bizkaia's territorial divisions of *merindades*, *anteiglesias* and *villas* were completely delineated and consolidated. The evolution of the administrative structure, initiated in the Late Middle Ages, was reaching its maturity. In some sense this had to do with the substitution of the attendance of all Bizkaians at the Assemblies by a representative model in which the *villas* and *anteiglesias* begin to send their delegates or assemblists empowered to speak for their appointing entity.

The rural townships (*municipios rurales*) or *anteiglesias* have their origin in the parishes that proliferated in Bizkaia after its Christianization and throughout the Late Middle Ages. The foundational charters of *villas* often refer to places that were first constituted as *anteiglesias*. The Codex of 1342 contains references to them as well. The Gonzalo Moro Ordinance of 1394 refers to the *fiel*, or mayor, of the *anteiglesia* who is responsible for the resources of the Hermandad and for organizing the first general convocation or "call" to all of the residents to assemble in order to pursue a criminal surprised *in fraganti* or fleeing a crime scene.

The church construction financed by the Lord or by wealthy families provided their patrons with an income from the tithes of the surrounding parishioners for whom the church was a focal point. It was there that they fulfilled their religious obligations and interred their dead in the adjacent cemetery or in family sepulchers or tombs within the churches themselves. Additionally, inside the temple—on festive days and during high mass—public announcements were made concerning the transmission of lands and other family property. Other judicial actions were solemnized and legitimated in similar manner. Meetings of local residents were held either within the church building or adjacent to its outer walls. The latter spaces were quickly covered and converted into the public fora that soon came to be called the *anteiglesia* or *eleizateak* ("church doors") in Basque. Later this denomination would be extended to all of the parish and, therefore, to the rural municipalities as a whole.

There are two governmental organs operative within the *anteiglesia*. On the one hand, there is the municipal assembly, which is known by various names. In Romance it is often called the "council" (*concejo*) or "open council" (*concejo abierto*), and even as the "stopped Cross" (*Cruz parada*). It refers to the moment in a religious procession when the priest, holding the local church's crucifix on high, stopped in order to permit the discussion of the *anteiglesias'* public affairs; in Basque, it was called the *batzar*. It was convoked by a ringing of the church bell. The assembly of residents deliberated their common concerns, including the organization of their collective life, administration and exploitation of their mountain commons, regulation of the pasturing of livestock, determination of the boundaries of private and public lands, road maintenance, etcetera. Additionally, the *anteiglesia* was the first line of defense regarding maintenance of public order and the suppression of crime. It was the *anteiglesia* that issued the first alarm or "call" (*apellido*) to pursue a delinquent. It was also involved in elections. One of its primary functions was the appointment of the *fieles*, who were given the authority to litigate in the name of the community and to represent it in the Assembly of the *merindad* or the General Assembly of Gernika. As

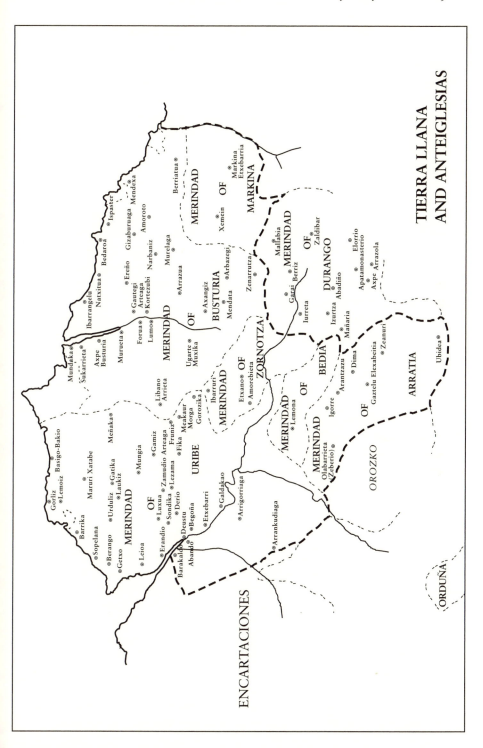

we have noted, the council also administered the public patrimony and could constitute the *anteiglesia* into a kind of military unit (particularly critical as counterweight to the epoch's warring bands). On the other hand, there is the figure of the *fiel regidor*, or mayor, elected by the residents according to customs that varied by locality (the drawing of lots, rotation, etc.). The scope of his office encompassed the provisioning of foodstuffs, inspection of roads, management of the public purse, the conduct of censuses, registration of property and the maintenance of public order. Shortly, we will consider his judicial function.

Regarding the origin of the other administrative division that we have mentioned, throughout the Middle Ages, in both the Kingdoms of Navarra and Old Castile, the realm was divided for administrative purposes into districts called *merindades*. This was true for Bizkaia as well, which at different points in its history formed a part of both Kingdoms. There is reference to one *merino* in the eleventh century, and by the fourteenth Bizkaia's *merindades* are completely delineated and consolidated. The first systematic enumeration appears often in Ordinances of 1394, in a listing of Bizkaia's *alcaldes de Hermandad*. It is evident that the *merindad* was regarded as an entity for the repression of criminal delinquency. In the Old Law of 1452, it is stated that "in the said Countship of Bizkaia there are seven *merindades*." To wit: "the Merindad of Busturia and Uribe and Arratia and Bedia and Zornotza and Markina and the said Merindad of Durango" (Article 57). Each *merindad* had its representative Assembly of the Merindad, in which the name of the *merino*'s assistant, or *logarteniente*, was announced publicly (Article 57). In fact, said Assemblies were apparently active during the foundational epoch of the Villas (thirteenth and fourteenth centuries). In 1451, or the year before redaction of the Old Law, there is reference to a meeting of the Assembly of the Merindad of Uribe.[106]

## 2. THE *MERINO, PRESTAMERO, CORREGIDOR* AND *ALCALDE DE FUERO*

The *merindad* was governed initially by the *merino*, or more precisely by a senior overarching one over the more minor *merinos* who acted in each of the districts. In the case of one *merindad*, Uribe, the Old Law stipulates that it had two *merinos*. Each *merino* could name an assistant or *logarteniente*. Then there was the *prestamero*, or sheriff, a figure of singular importance in the application of justice in Bizkaia of the thirteenth, fourteenth and fifteenth centuries.[107] The office was filled by persons pertaining to one of the Land's more prominent lineages. It was customary to name two *logartenientes* of the *prestamero*, one for the complex of six *merindades* specified in Article 57 of the Old Law and the other for the Merindad of Durango. In the fifteenth century, the office of *prestamero* is dominated by the Mendoza family, as mentioned in both the Proem and Epilogue of the Old Law. It is a period in which the honorific and financial rewards established for the office outweighed its political importance.

In any event, in this legal corpus the functions of the *prestamero* and *merino* are at times confused. Both are seen as implementing within the *merindad* the judicial orders and dispositions handed down by the General Assembly (or in the Modern Age by the Deputation or *Diputación*), the *corregidor* and the *alcaldes de Fuero*. But it is the *prestamero* who orders the sounding of the five horns to convene the General Assembly, a most important competency but one whose exact nature is unspecified in the Old Law. The *prestamero* is also in charge of the principal prison in Gernika, while the *merinos* are each responsible for the minor ones in the *merindades*. There is a complex of precepts in the Old Law specifying their fees.

The real authority of the *prestamero* and *merino* had undoubtedly been diminished by the arrival on the scene of the *corregidor*, or King's representative, after the Seigniory of Bizkaia's incorporation into Castilla in 1379, and particularly by Gonzalo Moro's lengthy and potent term of office.

A simple reading of the Old Law conveys the broad administrative and judicial faculties enjoyed by the *corregidor* in Bizkaia.[108] He was clearly the monarch's key political representative in the Countship, whether in the fifteenth century or the subsequent Modern Age. Nevertheless, at the end of the Middle Ages, the Bizkaians viewed the *corregidor*, who was always from outside the Seigniory, as a neutral figure in their internal politics, whereas the *prestamero*, of local origin, was likely to be a participant and even a partisan. The Old Law captures well this transitional moment in which the power of the *corregidor* is waxing and that of the *prestamero* is in decline.

The five *alcaldes de Fuero*, or judges, are of particular judicial importance and with competency beyond the limits of a single *merindad* (Articles 18, 19 and 28). There are two *alcaldes de Fuero* in the Merindad of Uribe, but with jurisdiction in those of Arratia and Bedia as well. The three *alcaldes de Fuero* based in the Merindad of Uribe exercised authority in those of Zornotza and Markina. The *alcaldes* were appointees of the Lord, selected from among the more prominent lineages (as is reflected in the listing of the participants in the redaction and approval of the Old Law). The fact that the appointments were in part honorific probably accounts, at least to a degree, for the conferral of juridical powers upon delegated *logartenientes* capable of advancing the legal process. The *alcaldes de Fuero* were to be residents of the *merindad* in which they were appointed, and "propertied and credible," that is, in possession of real property and sufficient solvency to warrant their financial capacity to meet the obligations of office, and particularly to pay the damages for any malfeasance.

We may now turn to the rules that governed the administration of justice insofar as they implicated the individual offices that we have just considered.

### 3. JUDICIAL INSTANCES AND RECOURSES

The administration of justice in Bizkaia seems at first blush to be extremely complex, but in fact this is not the case. The value of the object under litigation, the nature of an infraction and the scope of a judge's authority generated three distinct judicial circuits.

a. Viewed from below, there is within each *anteiglesia* and/or *merindad* a juridical structure that deals with minor matters. Verbal insults among residents and the failure to observe local ordinances are resolved by the *fiel* of the *anteiglesia* insofar as the amount of the possible fine or punishment did not exceed 110 *maravedís*. The accused could appeal the local decision to *fieles* of nearby *anteiglesias* for a maximum of three times. Should the accused press the right of appeal to the limit and then lose, there was the serious consequence of an 1100 *maravedís* indemnity to be paid to his own *anteiglesia*. Further appeal of the matter could be made to the *corregidor* only in the event that there was disagreement among the adjudicating *fieles* (Article 32).

b. Beyond the level of the municipality, there were certain *alcaldes de la Tierra* (judges of the Land), who dealt with disputes over movable property. The limit upon their capacity to fine or punish was a modest 48 *maravedís*.

Cases of greater consequence followed a different legal path. In civil suits *alcaldes de Fuero* were the judges of first instance. As noted earlier, their purview or jurisdiction was defined in terms of *merindades*. No Bizkaian could be required to appear before a magistrate in a civil matter unless first ordered to do so by an *alcalde de Fuero* (Articles 20 and 27). However, the *alcaldes de Fuero* could only intervene in a criminal matter when acting in consort with the *alcalde de Hermandad* (judge of the Hermandad). The latter office was created under the Ordinance of 1394 to deal exclusively with penal and criminal matters. Consequently, regarding criminal law, the *alcalde de Hermandad* was the magistrate of first instance, acting either alone or in consort with an *alcalde de Fuero*. In either case the accused could request to be tried by the *corregidor* instead, who in any event monitored criminal trials. Indeed, the Old

Law of 1452 confers upon the *corregidor* the jurisdiction of first instance in criminal cases (Articles 25 and 26).

The *alcaldes de Fuero* could act outside the confines of their jurisdictional *merindades* if accompanied by the *corregidor*, or if working together with the *alcaldes de Fuero* of other districts. The several transcriptions of the Old Law refer variously to the meeting as *a lecue, a locue* or *a loare*. In any event, the *alcaldes de Fuero* are required to heed the *corregidor's* request for assistance (Article 29 and 30).

The Old Law stipulates the time of day for court proceedings—from the "tercia" (9:00 a.m.) to midday, except in unusual cases. It appears that the cases were usually heard in the home of the *alcaldes* (Article 34), but, as noted, all of the *alcaldes de Fuero* might meet elsewhere (*a lecue*) to render a collegial decision regarding a particular suit. The name *a lecue* and its variations is a little enigmatic. The orthographic differences probably derive from the fact that the practice had fallen into disuse by 1600, or when the main copy of the Old Law was made. In this event, the transcribing notary would have been unfamiliar with the institution and its name (Article 197).

Finally, there is minute and strict specification of the fees and their source for *alcaldes* depending upon the nature of a case (Article 197). This schedule allows us to reconstruct the phases of the legal process and the corresponding actions of the judges. It is therefore possible to gain a clear overview of a judge's compensation and its sources.

The system is somewhat complicated regarding the process for appealing the decision of the *alcalde de Fuero*. Article 205 is key to our understanding, since it captures the transition from an earlier system under which the Bizkaian General Assembly was the court of last appeal to one in which the *corregidor* played that role.

The prime concern of the Fuero of 1452 is that appeals of judicial decisions not leave Bizkaia to be tried by the Lord or any of his officials. The prohibition corresponds to the Old Law's repeated declaration that the Fuero is of *alvedrío*, which is to say that it reflects the judge's freedom to investigate and then hand down a ruling conditioned by the extant consuetudinary law and custom of the Land. It states specifically that if the case is heard outside of Bizkaia there is considerable risk that the sentence will prove invalid, since neither the Lord nor his officials could possibly be conversant with the particularities of Bizkaian law and custom. There is, however, an exception. For whatever reason, lawsuits in the Duranguesado region may be appealed to the Lord. We do not know with certainty the appeal process within the Villas, although the logic of their origins in royal foundational charters would suggest that their appeals were heard by the *corregidor* as the highest royal official in the Seigniory.[109] Nor do we have a comprehensive overview of how the Villas might access the Lord as ultimate instance, although some of the foundational municipal charters do specify the geographical bounds within which their residents were subject to external judicial hearings. Notably, in a few cases there is mention of jurisdictions like Vitoria, Orduña, Medina and Laredo.[110]

The Old Law implicitly describes the path of the judicial appeals' process—one which seems to have been quite confrontational to a degree that seems extraordinary by modern standards. Thus, the sentence of an *alcalde de Fuero* could be appealed by the plaintiff or defendant successively to the second, third, fourth and then fifth *alcalde de Fuero*—who would then render the concluding decision of this phase of the judicial process—in short to the entire corpus of Bizkaia's *alcaldes de Fuero*, and this over a ruling in a minor matter! And if the outcome were still deemed unacceptable by the aggrieved party, the case could even be appealed to the *corregidor* himself. Only then was the verdict final. It does seem that it was possible (although the details are unclear) to combine all subsequent appeals into a single one. That is, rather than appearing successively before each of the *alcaldes de Fuero* it may have been possible to convene them *a locue,* and with or without the *corregidor*. The texts are inconclusive in this regard, but they suggest such a possibility. Thus, there are Articles 29 and particularly 197 (which mentions that "when the *alcaldes* gather *a locue,* which is a meeting of the *alcaldes* from each case, with or without the *veedor,* to decide cases of each *locue,*" and, it seems, to hand down definitive sentences regarding appeals and without further testimony). Similarly, Article 199 discusses the decision that contravenes the law and hence is now "appealed and comes before the *locue.*"

When the *corregidor* was not in Bizkaia, there was a special procedure that was probably reflective and a relic of an older legal system. In the event of the absence of the royal magistrate, after a sentence had been decided by the fifth *alcalde de Fuero* and the aggrieved still wished to appeal, said *alcalde de Fuero* requested the *prestamero* to convene the General Assembly, which would then hand down its decision.[111] In this case, if the aggrieved party still refused to accept the outcome, he could await the return of the *corregidor* to renew the appeal. It should be noted that there existed the legal possibility of involving the General Assembly to give a ruling even in the event that the *corregidor* was present in Bizkaia and available. However, there is explicit recognition that a judicial system could scarcely function in efficient and timely fashion if each decision required the direct intervention of the multitude. The Old Law notes that because of said procedures "there are great expenses in such councils," expenses that were probably insupportable for the parties to the suit should they have to pay them.

c. But, as we can appreciate, it seems that in Bizkaia by 1452 there was a growing tendency to have recourse to appeal decisions before the *corregidor* in the second or even the third instance.

Thus, it was the *corregidor*'s role to review appeal prompted by the sentences of the *alcaldes de Fuero* in civil matters (Articles 20 and 27). In criminal cases he might act as the judge of first instance or in consort with the *alcaldes de Hermandad*. This opened the door (Articles 25 and 26) to an evolution that would culminate, in the Modern Age, in according the *corregidor* exclusive competency in criminal matters

The *corregidor* was assisted by *logartenientes*, one for the six *merindades* of the Tierra Llana, another for the Duranguesado and a third for the Encartaciones (Article 21). Given that the *corregidor* and his assistants received salaries from the monarch, they were not entitled to any fees for their services in individual cases (Article 22).

4. THE RESTRAINTS ON JUDGES

Medieval Bizkaian law disposed of several means for controlling the actions of judges and officials. Reference is to "extraordinary recourses" available to the parties when the judicial proceedings were demonstrably flawed, not by human error but by culpable manipulation. At times this involves judges blatantly misapplying the law, ignoring established procedure or, finally, engaging in criminal actions.[112]

There is a fundamental mandate that the *alcaldes de Fuero* judge and sentence defendants in accord with the Codex of Bizkaia. Should this fail to happen, either party to a dispute can appeal to the *corregidor*, who, if he agrees with the aggrieved, is expected to punish the judge, but only after the latter has been given the opportunity to justify his contested sentence (Article 199). In the event that it is felt to be the *corregidor* who has contravened the Fuero, one could appeal his decision to the General Assembly, which would name its delegates to review the matter along with the *corregidor* (Article 206). In this fashion, the future role in the Modern Age of the Bizkaian deputies (*diputados*) is anticipated in the Old Law.

Finally, there is an exception to the precept that the lawsuits should not be tried outside Bizkaia. There is one extraordinary recourse to the Lord. Reference is to the circumstances in which the parties to a particular suit believe that the *corregidor* has acted irregularly or illegally in a particular civil or criminal case, one assumes regarding violation of either the substance or form of the Old Law. In this event, the Lord names a judge/commissary who pleads the case against the *corregidor*, whether the latter is present or defiantly absent. It is not clear whether this process required that testimony be received from the Bizkaians gathered together in General Assembly, or whether there was recourse to all of the *anteiglesias* of the Tierra Llana. There are faint suggestions in the Old Law in support of both procedures. In any event, if the *corregidor* is found to have acted contrary to the Old Law in rendering a judgment, he stood condemned. There was similar recourse against the fifth *alcalde* in the event that, standing in the stead of an absent *corregidor*, he had rendered an irregular definitive sentence (Article 205).

### 5. THE PROBLEM OF ECCLESIASTICAL JURISDICTION

Without doubt, by the fifteenth century Christianity was well established in Bizkaia. There are several manifestations of this. The political terrain is divided into the so-called *anteiglesias* or parishes. Canonical marriage was the most acceptable and prestigeful form of permanent sexual union. The sacred oath taken by the Lord in a designated church and invoking Christian symbols is the most important political ceremony. Christian oath-taking was employed widely to seal private transactions. Nevertheless, it is clear that the landowning sector of society, those with personal patronages in individual churches, had grave problems with the institutional Church. It seems that the two parties were contesting continuously the concept of private religious patrimony with the corresponding differences over jurisdiction regarding Church property (structures, lands, tithes).

The problem was as follows: in the Christian Occidental world of Late Antiquity, the rural churches were sometimes constructed and endowed by private parties. The benefactors sometimes regarded such a church and its corresponding income to be their private property, an interpretation that the Church opposed at first. Subsequently, there was greater permissiveness or flexibility, conditioned by the extent of the endowment, but without the Church conceding outright "ownership"— with the corresponding rights to all of the income—let alone exemption from any sort of ecclesiastical control. Part of the attempt at compromise was to permit the benefactor to appoint the particular temple's priest, a form of vigilance over the patrimony, as well as the right to receive support from the church's income should the benefactor subsequently become impoverished.[113]

But this was not the situation in Bizkaia, and the tension was ancient. The Codex of Juan Núñez de Lara of 1342 states that jurisdictional ecclesiastical authority within Bizkaia was exercised by the archpriests of the *anteiglesia* of Izurtza, in the Duranguesado (near the Villa of Durango) and of Arantzatzu in the Merindad of Arratia. In said text conflicts with Church tribunals are translucent; it ordains that, in suits regarding oaths of allegiance (by their nature acts of ownership and/or control over religious property), the summons were to be issued by the archpriests and not the bishop (Article 26). It also contains the final mandate that lawsuits regarding ecclesiastical authority be pursued and resolved by the archpriests, and never by the bishops or his vicars—as was the normal procedure under canon law. Under severe penalty, the Fuero orders that the summonses of the latter should never be respected (Article 27).

Before examining in detail the relationship between Bizkaians and ecclesiastical authority as reflected in the Old Law, it is well to clarify the scope of certain terms in the text. In the first place there are those of *monasterio* and *patronato*. Mañaricúa notes "*monasterio* is what our ancestors called that which today the historians of canon law call private church (*iglesia propia*), which later evolved into a patronage church (*iglesia de patronato*)."[114]

The Old Law states that in principle half of Bizkaian *monasterios*, that is "private churches," belonged to the *hidalgos* and the other half to the Lord. Titular Bizkaians with church patronages understood that their rights derived from the merits earned in the wars against the Moors. Given that, those conflicts continued (and their participation in them), as did the motives that justified an exceptional arrangement between Bizkaian noblemen and the Church. In any event, it was evident to the former that they needed to consolidate their rights over church patronage with written titles. They requested of the King that he obtain them from the Holy See. In the meantime, it was deemed necessary to carry on as before. Consequently, while the process of obtaining clear titles was in process, the Old Law ratifies the various defensive measures against ecclesiastical authority that were in place. The Fuero also underscores the gravity of the conflict with the Church.

First, it was necessary to deny the validity of any papal or episcopal letters of title to *iglesias propias*. Such letters were not to be obeyed or complied with (Article 217).

Second, Bizkaian territory and its inhabitants should remain exempt of ecclesiastical jurisdiction in all matters regarding the right of Church patronage (titles and other monetary income of the *hidalgos*, maintenance of the clergy, ownership of sepulchers and burial fees, and other property inherent in the right of patronage). It also stated that the intervention of ecclesiastical judges—archpriests and vicars—in such matters compromised the accepted and ordinary course of justice. It subjected the parties to suits complicated by complex canonical legal procedures, when the Bizkaian legal process was simple and of *albedrío*.

Consequently, the Old Law strictly forbids the intervention in the Seigniory of ecclesiastical authority, excepting in matters concerning it directly (heresy is mentioned, as are cases involving excommunication, theft or robbery of church property, incest by married persons and sexual relations among persons within four degrees of consanguinity, as well as other marital matters and ecclesiastical crimes). Regarding any other issues, persons who bring from outside Bizkaia documents of a bishop or ecclesiastical judge in order to intervene in a legal process were subject to the gravest punishment. They could be killed by anyone with impunity, given that the bearers of such documents were "enemies of Bizkaia" (Article 218).

At the same time, there was a strong aversion against supporting bishops, archpriests and vicars who merely wished to come to Bizkaia (presumably to intervene in its affairs). It is noted in the Old Law itself that such was prohibited in the *"Fuero Antiguo."* Consequently, any Bizkaian who facilitated such interventions was a "violator of the said *Fuero*" and would be relieved of all of his or her property. Any Bizkaian who killed such a facilitator of ecclesiastical intervention was immune from any punishment (Article 219).

There was also evident discomfort and care regarding the use by the clergy of the exceptional measure of letters of excommunication in trivial matters—such as thefts of vegetables, apples or livestock, as well as trespass in fields. According to the Old Law, recourse to such extreme measures was "a disservice to God and a usurpation of secular justice and a great danger to the souls." Consequently, the reading out of such letters of excommunication was punished and the matter remitted to the care of the *fiel* of the *anteiglesia* where the conflict transpired.

## 6. The Special Jurisdiction of the Iron Foundries

There existed in Bizkaia special treatment of iron foundries (Article 31). They had their own legal jurisdictions and judges that dealt with conflicts between the "iron men" *(ferreros)*—probably referring to the owners of foundries—and their workers, who are called *braceros* in the Old Law. The text of 1452 recognizes this singular authority, which in principle has the appearance of labor and/or social law (Article 31). It is quite likely that the *alcaldes* of the iron foundries ruled in accord with the provisions of their own special *fueros*.[115]

The smooth functioning of the foundries required a proper supply of charcoal and iron ore. Regarding the former, the rational exploitation of the forests demanded that they be managed well and renewed. The owners of the foundries had the right to obtain wood from the forests, first from the commons and then, if necessary, by purchase from the owners of private tracts. In the latter instance, the sellers had to sell at the price normally obtaining in the district, as estimated and confirmed by three good men. Furthermore, the foundry owners had the right of veto over timber sales to others, although in times of scarcity they were required to share the resource with the other foundries (Article 211).

The buying and selling of iron ore was only permitted at the foundries themselves. From this it followed that the scales were only located at the foundries and the points of fiscal control. That is, they were in the places where the weighing was part of satisfying the Lord's fiscal claims over iron production. The Old Law specifies the value ascribed to the *quintal* of refined iron (Articles 212 and 213).[116]

### 7. ROADWAYS AND RIGHTS OF WAY

Roads and rights of way were both specified in the Old Law. For better comprehension, we have consolidated several scattered precepts under Article 210 in the present critical edition. The dispositions regulated such matters as the width of roads and the rights of way that they engendered, as well as ensured that the network of roads linked the foundries with the seaports. The transportation of plowshares by public road, and the planting of trees and erection of fences along their borders, were all regulated.

## XVIII. Penal Law[117]

When preparing the penal precepts of the Old Law (1452), the redactors took into account the Seigniory's two previous ordinances—those of Juan Núñez de Lara (1342) and Gonzalo Moro (1394), both of which were almost entirely penal in nature. Consequently, a comprehensive understanding of the complete universe of late-medieval Bizkaian delicts and crimes (and their punishments) requires consideration of all three texts.[118]

In principle, the late-medieval Bizkaian penal code is a punitive system that configures the sense of community. It is always the public authority that prosecutes crimes, although the process must be triggered by a complaint. That is, a party initiates a case by invoking the so-called accusatory principle. The penal sanctions are of a similar public nature, and the redresses (*caloñas*) assume the guise of pecuniary punishments (both restitution to the damaged party and fines).

Nevertheless, behind this explicit public system as reflected in the three medieval corpuses of Bizkaian law, there was an implicit private one that in a sense both imposes itself upon and annuls the former. Through private agreements, which the Old Law refers to as the pardon (*perdón*), the parties to a dispute can reach agreement regarding the consequences of an alleged delict pending in the judicial process and thereby suspend completely the public proceedings. This radical right of an aggrieved party to pardon the accused perpetrator is completely foreign to the Romanist legal system and that of Castilian law in particular.[119] In any event, reference is to a hidden system, whose details are only glimpsed in the text, although their effects are quite evident. We do not know the specifics of how the parties came to their agreement, although we can imagine that it was probably an attempt at substitution for a former system of blood revenge. On the other hand, at the margins of its legal system, Bizkaia was clearly plagued by public disorder (*Blutrache*) of the worst kind, as reflected in the terrible struggles between warring bands.

In sum, we can discern in Bizkaian penal law three distinct classes, whose respective importance and incidence, nevertheless, we are unable to determine with certainty given the insufficiency of the information provided in the Old Law. In the first instance, there was an extralegal world of the private vendetta in which blood revenge applies. It was not only external but contrary to the law and, to the extent it might still obtain, was a survival of an ancient "code" that was no longer accommodated by the legal norms of the fourteenth and fifteenth centuries. The second order, also within the realm of private justice, was agreement amongst the parties to a dispute, possibly entailing the payment of compensation, and which resulted in the aggrieved's pardoning of the offender. The outcomes of this procedure were clearly recognized by the law, but were unregulated by it. This, too, was an extralegal arrangement, a sort of juridical arrangement negotiated directly by the parties themselves. And, finally, there was the system of public regulation of crimes and delinquency to which we now turn our attention.

In this regard, in general, fourteenth and fifteenth century Bizkaian penal law has many modern characteristics.[120] To be sure, there is certain severity of punishment that was introduced into the Kingdom of Castilla beginning with the reign of King Alfonso XI. But there is evidence of advanced subsequent evolution of the Bizkaian penal code, particularly in its introduction of subjectivity into the determination of what constituted crime and proper punishment. Reference is to a certain accommodation of the intentions of the accused to inflict damage, the protections against a too liberal interpretation of the code to include charges for crimes not clearly specified as such by it and a certain weighting of the punishments according to the gravity of the crimes to which they were applied. In some cases, punishment was lighter for a first offense and then increased for repeat ones. Furthermore, as we have seen when considering the status of *hidalgos* and *labradores,* the law was applied evenly and without consideration of the social status of either the plaintiff or defendant.

By 1452, Bizkaia had resolved, at least on the legal plane, the problem of the extreme and lacerating criminality that fed partially upon the internecine aggressions of the warring bands.[121] In effect, a century before the Old Law, the Codex of Juan Núñez de Lara had addressed the issue of homicide and the gravity of its diverse forms,[122] thefts,[123] attacks against persons and property[124] and abductions and the harboring of outlaws in private domiciles. In keeping with the spirit of the age, the corresponding punishments were quite severe. The Codex calls for the death penalty for a total of twelve specified crimes. There was also the possible punishment of burning to the ground a convicted criminal's house or destroying his possessions.

Half a century later, the Ordinances of Gonzalo Moro of 1394 would lengthen notably the list of crimes and punishments. Again, given the nature of the crimes in question, it seems evident that the wars of the bands provided the main motivation underlying formulation of the Ordinances. The novelties, when compared with the Codex, include penalties for wounding another, armed threats—particularly if they transpired during the General Assembly—extortions of money and property under threat of violence, dares, rape, the fabrication and transport of crossbows (felt to be a particularly deadly weapon) and providing assistance to fugitives (*acotados*) pursued by the authorities.

In the Ordinances, the death penalty is applied in at least fifteen circumstances. Possibly the sentences were carried out by drowning, or in the manner that the Old Law would refer to subsequently as execution by "natural death," which is to say by "ponding," a form of execution that seems to have been reserved for *hidalgos*. There were additional corporal punishments as well, such as cutting off a criminal's ears[125] or dismemberment of his hands. He might be demeaned publicly by being dragged through the streets with hands tied and a rope around his neck. He might be restrained by having a door closed upon one of his ears or by being put in stocks.[126] Finally, under the Codex he could be banished from the land for his crimes.

The redactors of the Old Law did not question the penal code that they inherited from the two texts of the previous century. To the contrary, they took them for granted and respected them scrupulously, not even bothering to reproduce all of their precepts in the Old Law. At most they made minor modifications or elaborations of a few of their precepts in the interest of expediency. They did, however, address certain new crimes that probably corresponded to developments in the wars of the bands—namely the introduction of firearms into the conflict and the resort to certain violations against property. Regarding the latter, the Old Law writes down the consuetudinary rules and practices designed to order and protect the agrarian regimen of the Bizkaian countryside. In effect, there are two groups of penal precepts of a differing nature and contextualized in different ambits. It is also possible that they were elaborated at separate historical moments.

The first group of new precepts is found in its own special section of the Old Law (Articles 38 through 48). They are related, although not exclusively, to the wars of the bands, which, in 1452, continued.[127] The escalation of the violence with the innovation of firearms exacerbated the threat to life and limb, dwelling and foundry, and even the year's harvest. The heightened social concern is clearly reflected in certain provisions of the Old Law. Article 38 applies the death penalty to anyone discharging any of the new firearms, which are listed individually (*trueno, lombarda, trabuquete* and *ingenio*). This maximum punishment is imposed as well on those who intentionally burned down another's dwelling or set fire to his fields, to him who uprooted or cut down five or more trees belonging to another, to him who vandalized a foundry, mill or their water power systems, to him who smashed or pierced an apple cider barrel and to those whose theft exceeded ten florins in value (Articles 39, 45, 48, 49 and 52).

In other cases, the punishment was meant to indemnify a damaged party, who received twice what he lost.[128] Additionally, there tended to be a heavy fine that would go to the Lord (in many cases it was five cows). The foregoing formula of indemnifications and fines were applied for arson on mountain tracts, stripping the bark of up to five trees or uprooting them, and plowing another's field (Articles 40, 45 and 210). Or the punishment might consist of an amount to be divided equally between the aggrieved and the Lord, as is the case with the 600 *maravedís* fine for the setting of a fire on the commons, or on one's own land that then spread to that of a neighbor, or the illegal placing or removing of boundary markers on another's property (Articles 41, 42 and 46). Curiously, insults are given little importance and come under the jurisdiction of the *fieles* of the *anteiglesias*.[129]

Further along in the document, there is a somewhat startling revisitation of criminal law beginning with Article 138, "Title of the Crimes and Punishments." In all, there are 22 clustered articles or precepts dealing with the ordering and protection of the agrarian regime (the freedom of movement, pasturing of livestock, planting of trees) and with the founding of iron foundries, the twin pillars of the medieval Bizkaian economy. Interestingly, the standard of most frequent punishment levied in such cases was a fine of 48 *maravedís*. Possibly this reflects an unmodified ancient and fixed tradition. The converse is also possible, namely, that it was a recent and planned elaboration.

Generally speaking, persons and their livestock could move about the roads and even across private lands (although in the latter case excluding carts and shod animals) without payment or fee of any kind (Articles 138 and 198). Consequently, land ownership is subjected to certain rights of way, but not to other actions defined as illicit. A trespasser who entered a field without the owner's permission, who used his animals for tasks without authorization or who pastured his livestock on another's field, particularly on valuable cultivated land, was liable for indemnities and fines (Articles 139, 140, 142 and 145). In the matters regarding damage done by livestock, the Old Law reckons punishments according to the kinds of animals and their adverse impacts. It discriminates between major and minor damages, whether the property in question was open or fenced and whether the offense transpired during the daylight or dark (this last measure seems to be a barometer of the herder's intentionality).

Another emphasis within the Old Law regards the importance of trees, and particularly apple trees (the source of cider, or the Seigniory's prime alcoholic beverage). Apple orchards appear to have been pretty ubiquitous throughout Bizkaia's cultivated landscape, whether planted next to dwellings or in orchards sited on one's own land, or that of another. In the event that one planted trees on another's land it seems that the harvest was divided between them equally, with the first party obligated to care for the orchard (Articles 148 through 151). Within a complex and somewhat confused set of regulations, one thing is clear: the Fuero emphasizes conservation of the apple tree, ensuring its cultivation and care throughout its life cycle. One has the impression that the well-being of the apple trees was of greater concern than the rights of the planter or the proprietor of the soil. The same does not hold for any other variety of tree. Anyone planting them on the land of another without permission risks losing all rights in the mature trees (Article 152).

Article 153 provides marvelous insight into a medieval world view that sought to regulate sunlight and shade. Reference is to the precept requiring the setback of one's trees from a property line so as not to cast shade upon any portion of a neighbor's holding. There is careful recognition of the size of the crown (and hence capacity to shade) of each variety of tree, the distance of the required setback varying accordingly. In any event, rather than serious penal law, we are here within the realm of mere norms governing agricultural practice, violations of which incur occasional sanctions of an administrative rather than penal nature.

At least as reflected in the precepts of the Old Law, Bizkaian "industry" (as opposed to agriculture) consisted of the milling of grain and the founding of iron. The Fuero states that there were numerous iron foundries in the Seigniory and elaborates several provisions regarding the construction and protection of them (and mills as well) (Article 157). Earlier we discussed the two terms in the Basque language—*bidigaza* and *abeurrea*—that refer to the markers used to lay claim, usually on the commons, to part of a waterway and building site of a foundry or mill. The former was critical since both were water-powered and required a dam and diversionary canal. In the event that one wished to claim part of the commons for such a project, he placed the appropriate markers and then announced his intentions publicly at the high mass of the church in the *anteiglesia* in question. In the event there were no objections or desire of the public to participate, the claimant had a year and a day within which to begin construction. Anyone who tampered with the markers in the interim was fined heavily (1100 *maravedís* for a first offense) and was subject to the death penalty for a second one (Articles 154 and 159).

It also happened that someone placed *bidigazas* and *abeurreas* on his own land that he held in common with partners and without their knowledge. In the event that they protested within the year and a day, the project was either paralyzed or the aggrieved had the right to participate in it by paying their prorated share of the costs (Article 155). The situation is graver should someone attempt to claim for construction of a foundry or mill another's private property (Article 159). All of these provisions are double-edged in that they both encourage the industrial development of the commons and the utilization of private holdings, while at the same time hedging the process with explicit and severe administrative and penal punishment of abuses.

The Old Law also recognizes that there is only so much water in a stream, and thus the proliferation of new foundries and mills on it could undermine the ability of the former ones to operate. Articles 157 and 158 state the minimum amount of water that must flow from upstream installations to downstream ones. Article 160 regards the water rights of abandoned foundries and mills.

## XIX. Legal Procedure

The cornerstone of Bizkaian trial law is the premise that the authorities only initiate a legal action at the behest of an aggrieved party. They are never to do so by virtue of their own authority, or by *pesquisa* (inquiry) as it was called in the language of the day. Articles 37 and 66 of the Old Law address this issue. It is the accusatory procedure that leaves to the parties themselves the fundamental initiative and protagonism in the course of justice. In Spain there exists a legal tradition that was already manifest in the seventh century in official Visigothic law as contained in the *Liber Iudiciorum*, and which was subsequently evident in the municipal *fueros*, in which there is the principle that "no one responds [before the justice system] without a complainant (*ninguno non responda sin quereloso*)."[130]

In reality, official justice, or that by inquiry, did apply in certain exceptional cases that are cited in the Old Law. They are explicated exhaustively, no doubt to avoid a broadening by analogy of the authorities' employment of judicial inquiry (something that was anathema to the Bizkaians). The broader legal authority of justice officials was limited to certain crimes that are of such singularly grave and public affront as to justify unilateral formal inquiries by the authorities. These included the harboring of fugitives, the investigation of persons with a clear public reputation of being robbers (rather than perpetrators of a single theft), rape, indecencies and the murder of a foreigner (given that otherwise there would be no one in Bizkaia to protest such a death) (Article 37).

These matters, while similar, did not coincide with the so-called Court cases (*casos de Corte*), which, given their grave nature, in other parts of the realm were reserved for direct royal juridical disposition. However, in the case of Bizkaia, it is quite possible that they were regarded to be Hermandad cases, as contemplated in the Ordinances of Gonzalo Moro (1394). Reference is to homicide, rape, the breaking of a treaty, violation of a safe conduct agreement, arson of a dwelling, treachery or perdition and threats.[131]

In short, for the most part a legal process could only be initiated by one aggrieved Bizkaian against another, and not by local or royal officials. Arguably, the emphasis was upon the avoidance of undue and potentially progressive external interference in Bizkaian affairs.

Throughout the Fuero there are several other safeguards as well for individuals implicated in a legal proceeding. There is avoidance of double jeopardy, in that a person who had been tried for a delict and absolved could not be retried for it, even if the aggrieved party alleged that there had been irregularities in the proceedings, including bribery of the judge (Article 194). Consequently, the principle of the legal protection of the individual's rights prevails over any other consideration. But the Old Law does contain one exception in the matter. Once a minor attains the age of majority, he or she can reopen a case regarding a decision rendered earlier that went against his or her best interests. In other instances as well, the Old Law is meticulous in safeguarding the interests of a (defenseless) minor who might have been ignored or abused by others or by application of a legal principle.

There is an additional provision within the penal code that regards a concern with equity. If an aggrieved party or his or her representative, pardons one of the accused of a crime, all of those implicated in it are thereby pardoned, except in the case where the individual is pardoned for a delict that differs from that (or those) of the other accused persons in the case (Article 195).

In the realm of civil law, it is prohibited to initiate an action over an obligation that had been met or satisfied. If it were proven that an ostensibly aggrieved party had wrongly accused someone for failing to perform, the plaintiff would have to pay the amount requested in the action for having acted in bad faith (Article 185).

## 1. Penal Procedure and Its Phases:[132] The Summons beneath the Tree of Gernika

Under the Old Law, procedure in a criminal case was as follows: it began with the complaint of an aggrieved party to a judge, which, if deemed to have sufficient merit, initiated either an investigative phase or a judicial instruction. If there is an accused person, he or she was ordered to appear beneath the Tree of Gernika. There, a hearing was conducted, which resulted in a finding of guilt or innocence, the latter being tantamount to absolution (*da por quito*) (Article 194). If, to the contrary, the accused was found guilty, then one of the aforementioned punishments was applied.

Of greatest interest, as well as somewhat surprising, was the so-called "summons beneath the Tree of Gernika" invoked frequently, but rather unsystematically, in the Old Law. Drawing upon the several references to it, the practice can be synthesized as follows: it seemed most frequent when the charges, if proven, resulted in the physical maiming or death of the accused. As noted earlier, the offended or affected aggrieved party initiated the process by complaining to the official empowered to deal with criminal cases—the *alcalde de Hermandad* or the *corregidor*, who then launched an investigation or simply issued an instruction once a preliminary hearing (without the defendant) was concluded. If the case was to be continued, then a law official, called the *sayón*, was issued an executive order to cite and summon the accused to appear in person within 30 days at a hearing beneath the Tree of Gernika (Articles 50, 52 and 60). In the interim, the defendant could not be apprehended, although there was the enigmatic exception that the accused could be so imprisoned in cases that did not carry the possible punishment of physical maiming or death (Article 52). This seems counterintuitive. What it does suggest is that the summons beneath the Tree was applicable in at least some civil matters as well; however, the Old Law is largely silent regarding the details.

In the event that the accused answered the summons in a criminal case, he or she was provided with all of the testimony taken to date. In the event of a civil suit, the defendant received a copy of the judge's preliminary instruction and the testimony, either without the names of the witnesses or a list of the accusing witnesses but without their individual depositions (Article 50). In short, there was a clear attempt to protect the anonymity of accusing witnesses or to at least obfuscate how and the extent to which each contributed to the accusations.

Once the accused or accused persons arrived in Gernika, he, she or they were placed in the preventive custody of the *prestamero*. There is reference in the Old Law to "yielding to the chain (*acudir a la cadena*)." We know little else regarding the circumstances of such detention, excepting that its duration and harshness varied according to the gravity of the possible punishment in the case (Article 61). The judge mandated the length and place of the detention—it could even be town or house arrest (Article 64). The detainee was responsible for the expenses of his or her incarceration, so there is some detail in the Old Law regarding its circumstances. The judge was the only one who could order the release of a prisoner. Should the defendant(s) escape, the *prestamero* was held responsible and could even receive the punishment that would have corresponded to the accused in the event of conviction for the crime in question (Article 68).

Those who failed to answer the citation or summons to appear beneath the Tree of Gernika were declared outlaws (*rebeldes*), and their movable property was seized by the *prestamero* who then kept it (Article 59). Such fugitives were designated *acotados* or persons outside the law, and there were serious consequences for harboring them (Article 52).

## 2. Concerning Dares and Duels

As in Castilla, in Bizkaia of the Late Middle Ages there were legal procedures for the nobility regarding dares and duels. They were a residual manifestation of the trials by ordeal of the Early Middle Ages. It is necessary to consider them, even if but summarily.

It is well known that medieval thought did not distinguish between the natural and supernatural orders, given that God the Creator is present in all of His works and acts equally in the realms of both nature and of history. The deity is the ultimate authority in justice and law. Consequently, there is the need to implicate Him in the search for juridical solutions, imploring His intervention through magical juridical rites designed to ascertain the truth. The trial by ordeal (that of placing an accused's hand in boiling water, the battle of the candles, etc.) assumes God's familiarity with occult matters and His willingness to reveal the truth in juridical disputes through certain rituals specified in the law. The same thinking underpins tolerance of duels, whose outcome could be interpreted as God's will. It was based on the premise that, if two disputants engaged in fair and equal combat, God would grant victory to the morally correct one.[133]

Beginning in the Late Middle Ages, the Church's opposition to them first reduced and then abolished trials by ordeal or irrational means for determining guilt. There is no reflection of them in the Old Law; however, we might note that in Bizkaia (as elsewhere) there was considerable resistance to the abolishment of the duel.

The Old Law mentions a special procedure in matters of threats, dares and duels (Articles 13 and 209). The references are minimal and regard only the *ex post facto* situation; consequently, one must refer to Castilian law to understand the legal mind set. The dare is equivalent to challenging another's belief or truth—it constitutes announcement of the beginning of true enmity between the parties. It also signals the initiation or consequences of a juridical dispute or contest. He who issues the challenge must accept the other's *fiadores'* guarantee that he will respond to the charge. Should the challenger fail to accept such representations, it is he who assumes the mantle of enmity. Indeed, in this case the accused can even kill his challenger with impunity. Such a challenge does not necessarily lead immediately to a court case in itself because it can be the result of reaction to an existing judicial dispute.

The duel has much in common with the dare, excepting that it is limited to *hidalgos*. It can accompany another demand. Consequently, the *Partidas* declare that any *hidalgo* accused of killing, wounding, dishonoring, detaining or causing any other *hidalgo* to take flight, without first issuing a challenge to him, are all grounds for a formal duel. But it can also be issued independently of such actions and stand alone. The duel is formalized when the challenger heaps upon the accused certain defamations, such as calling him evil, traitorous or perfidious. In the *Fuero Real*,[134] these are the standard accusations for a duel.[135] Both the *Fuero Real* of the mid-fourteenth century and the Ordinances of Alcalá of 1348 ordain that a duel can only be held at the Royal Court.[136] From this there follows the provision in the Old Law whereby dueling is the only exception to the principle that Bizkaians cannot be tried outside of the Seigniory (Article 13). Once permission for the duel is conceded by the King, the implicated *hidalgos* engage in a joust, the mounted combat underscoring their social status as *caballero* (horsemen=gentlemen). According to the *Partidas* (VII, 4), such sanctioned dueling is but one manifestation of the more widespread practice of "the men of the towns and the villages" in which the combat "tends to be on foot." The outcome of the duel was felt to determine the validity of the accusation. If the challenger died on the field of combat, the accused was liberated of the charge; if it was the accused who died, in a manner of speaking he was also liberated from the obligation of confessing to his wrongdoing. If both were unhorsed, yet survived, then both were dishonored and neither was satisfied nor vindicated in the matter.[137]

3. CIVIL PROCEDURE

The phases of the Bizkaian legal procedure in civil cases, and the formalities that are observed in each one of them as reflected in the Old Law, differ considerably from modern legal practices. We shall now examine briefly the different stages of civil law procedure, focusing our attention upon its imitation, the appearance of the parties before the judge, the means of examination and determination of proof and the sentence.

i. The Demand, Guarantors and Seizures of Property

The manner of initiating a civil suit varied according to whether it regarded movable property or real estate. Both parties to such a lawsuit are normally required to provide personal guarantees and those of "landed" and "credible" *fiadores* or guarantors who ensure that the proceedings unfold in timely fashion and then underwrite any assessed damages in the event that their party to the dispute cannot or will not perform. Indeed, each party's *fiadores* play a pivotal role in the proceedings. It is they who assemble to cast the lots that will determine before which *alcalde de Fuero* the case will be tried, and even determine the date for the hearing (Article 167).

In the event that a defendant occupying a disputed property fails to provide a sufficient personal guarantee and/or a *fiador* or *fiadores* within a graduated time frame, the plaintiff can demand the defendant's eviction and the plaintiff's immediate possession of the litigated real estate (Article 168).

There is also rich symbolism in the Old Law when it addresses the matter of property offered as security by defendants. In the event that movable property is seized to cover the expenses and damages of the suit, then the defendant has a tight time frame within which to impede physical removal of the property by providing *fiadores*. If the defendant fails to meet the deadlines specified in the Old Law, then the plaintiff can sell the seized property until the amount owing is realized. Indeed, the law allows the aggrieved to return for subsequent seizures and sales until the full obligation is met (Article 168).[138]

## ii. Appearance before the Judge

Within the agreed time frame, the parties to a suit appear before the selected *alcalde de Fuero*. If he deems it necessary in order to ensure timely procedural progress in the case, and payment of any damages determined by it, he may order that some or all of the *fiadores* increase their exposure. He may even require one of the parties to provide different (more qualified) *fiadores*. In this event, the original ones are released from their commitments (Article 164 and 166).

At the same time, once having appeared, the defendant could request prolongation of the process in order to prepare a response to the accusations. He (or she) might be given nine days in which to do so, but with the proviso that the defense correspond directly and solely to the principle charges.

Failure to appear triggers instantly the imposition of a punishment by the judge (Articles 164, 165, 166, 172 and 174).

## iii. The Oral Nature of the Hearing

With the appearance of both parties on the appointed day, the hearing commences. It is a key characteristic of Bizkaian legal procedure that oral testimony is paramount. This stands in marked contrast to the Romano-canonical law adopted increasingly by the monarchs of Castilla-León, which relies in part on written depositions. In Bizkaia the parties appear before the *alcalde de Fuero* on the appointed day and present their arguments orally. At the hearing, the entire process (including the allegations, the posing and opposing of exceptions, counter charges and the verdict) is conducted orally. The *alcalde de Fuero* is required to tear up publicly any prepared written statement presented by the plaintiff(s) or the defendant(s) or their representatives (Article 170).

## iv. Concerning Proof

A public document establishing prior title or claim to a contested property, prepared by a notary and attested to by three credible witnesses, had full legal force as proof. This modern means of establishing proof obviated all others. But there were more traditional acceptable proofs within Bizkaian law, largely regarding the role of strong and credible *fiadores*. By providing them it was possible to establish a prior (undocumented) sale, bequest or mortgaging of a house or other real estate. If one wished to claim the entire property, it was necessary to provide six *fiadores*; if the claim were for only a part of it, the testimony of three *fiadores* sufficed (Articles 186 and 187).

The mode of constituting financial underwriting when there were insufficient *fiadores* for one of the parties in the *anteiglesia* in question is particularly original. In a land dispute everyone concerned with the case went to the property and, "after having measured the boundaries around it," two *fiadores* were chosen there to take an oath regarding their findings, the *alcalde de Fuero* setting the date for this at the local church designated by the tradition for oath-taking. There follows an elaborate casuistry regarding procedure when it is impossible to find sufficient *fiadores* locally or some are deceased. The oath given is itself viewed as a form of proof, as will be seen shortly.

## v. The Sentence and Appeals

The *alcalde de Fuero* is always required to render a judgment on the spot, and not after subsequent deliberation. He cannot drag out the process. Nevertheless, the *corregidor* has the authority to prolong sentencing in both civil and criminal cases, but after such intervention, the verdict is final (Articles 170 and 196).

We have considered the various judicial instances of appeal earlier. Here, suffice it to say that in appealing a case from one judge to another, neither the plaintiff nor the defendant was permitted to introduce new evidence or demands. However, upon reaching the appeal level of last resort, i.e. one before a tribunal composed of the *corregidor* and/or all of the *alcaldes de Fuero* meeting *a locue*, new arguments were admitted (Article 175).

## vi. Legal Representation (*Personerías, Voceros, Señores de Pleito*)

The procedures contain certain prohibitions against legal proxies. Consequently, it is punishable to give one's power of attorney to the resident of a *villa*, if in said *villa* there exists an identical prohibition of conferring such authority upon an inhabitant of the Tierra Llana. Similarly, it is prohibited to confer power of attorney upon clergymen, except in cases which, because of their *ratione personae* nature, approximate or come under ecclesiastical jurisdiction (those suits against other clergymen, those regarding minor orphans, widows or *miserabiles personae*). It should be kept in mind that all of the aforementioned groups are understood within the ecclesiastical jurisdiction to be *ratione personae*. Nor is it necessary to formalize power of attorney when conferring one's defense upon one of his or her *fiadores*, since such *fiador* is regarded to be already involved in every respect in the case (Articles 190, 191 and 192).

4. Processual Guarantees: The Oath, Guarantors and Judicial
Embargoes

In the transcourse of justice there are several processual measures
to ensure that the parties to the dispute are able to respond to their possible liabilities. These include oath-taking and, in a different vein, financial warranties and judicial embargoes.

The oath is a declaration by one of the parties concerning the verac-
ity of an event or an intent under the threat of divine punishment in the
next life for lying and possible castigation in this world should the false-
hood be discovered—the delict of perjury. Processually, the oath-taking
is employed in the Old Law for the investigation of truth, although it
can also be used to avert bad faith by one of the parties.

We can appreciate how the Bizkaian legal order rests upon the personal guarantee to an extreme. In general, the purpose is to provide
guarantees of restitution for any damage caused by the unfortunate acts
of one of the parties to a dispute, whether in the legal process or in
negotiations outside its framework. Any obligation of whatever nature
is therefore to be backed up with *fiadores* under various denominations.
They are distinguished by their nature as persons who are "trustworthy
and propertied," "landed," etcetera. Their function in a particular case
is also frequently specified—whether they be guaranteeing the redress of
wrongdoings, the integrity of auctions, the honesty of transactions, the
authenticity of truncal consanguineal inheritance claims or simply the
intention to comply with the law. On occasion the guarantors multiply,
given that the original designees might be required to produce others to
ensure full capacity of his or her party to comply with any eventuality.

Under the Old Law then, we have diverse circumstances in which
some persons meet the contractual obligations of others. There are
*fiadores* for ostensible wrongdoings, who use their guarantee that an
accused will face trial to prevent preliminary detention or who prevent
someone from being tried simply for being of bad repute. In the case of
public sales of property, the buyer provides *fiadores* to guarantee that he
or she will pay the amount of the winning bid. Parties to a litigation are
required to provide both *fiadores* to guarantee that they will abide by
the outcome and to pay any restitution and damages that result there-
from. *Labradores* who were detained for abandoning a landholding
subject to taxation to inhabit one of a tax-exempt *hidalgo* were required
as a condition for their release to provide *fiadores* guaranteeing that
they would return to the tax-censured farm within six months (Articles
67, 69, 73, 75, 76 and 208). Other *fiadores* attest to the legitimacy of suc-

cession regarding the inheritance of truncal property. In sum, it is their role to ensure that the law is followed and fulfilled.

The judicial embargo (and the extrajudicial as well)—called the *prenda* or pledge in the Old Law—complements the personal guarantee and that of the *fiadores*. Through it the authorities deprived an accused of the free disposition of his or her property to prevent the elusion of the responsibility demanded by law. One assumes that this measure was taken in cases where the accused was unwilling to post a personal guarantee, appear before the court or was openly rebellious. However, in criminal matters, in Bizkaia the accused was simply detained. We might also note that at the initiation of a lawsuit, the *fiadores* could be required to post *prendas vivas* (living pledges), meaning livestock as a condition for continuing with the legal process (Article 167).

## XX. The Nature of Property

Those writing treatises between the twelfth and eighteenth centuries regarding property rights as one facet of civil law followed the dogmatic lead of the *Institutiones* established by Justinian in the sixth century. As is well known, such systematization was assumed by the legal scholars of the philosophical school of Natural Law and, with more or less minor modifications, in contemporary legal codes.

The Old Law does not concern itself in this regard with everything that is likely to be found in a modern legal code, nor even with the entire range of property law found in some medieval redactions of consuetudinary law. Rather, the Fuero limits itself to certain property matters that its redactors deemed essential and/or that were provoking major problems within the judicial system.

### 1. A TYPOLOGY OF OWNERSHIP

Within the precepts of the Old Law, on occasion the estates or landed property of the *hidalgos* are distinguished from those of the taxed or "censured" households (*casas censuarias*), or, which is really the same, the free or allodial landholding is differentiated from the tenure of the *labrador*. This was a common distinction throughout the Europe of the Late Middle Ages.

In Bizkaia the entirely untaxed or allodial landholding of the nobility is found primarily in the Tierra Llana. Its freedom from encumbrances both defined and was defined by its proprietor's noble status. The *labrador's* tenure might be held within the estate of an *hidalgo* or, more commonly and widely in Bizkaia, constituted a "right of occupancy" of a tenure of the Lord's patrimony. Thus, the Lords of Bizkaia held farmland and conceded use of it to peasant tenants for an indefinite period, while nonetheless retaining real and immediate control over agricultural exploitation. The Lord's ultimate ownership of the peasant tenant's holding therefore constituted an authentic royal right.

Within the text there is always a differentiation between truncal or inherited property and that acquired by one's own efforts. However, the truly ubiquitous distinction is a binary one between so-called movable and immovable property or real estate. In medieval Europe the classification of property as either movable or immovable follows the tradition established in Roman law. Immovable property regards things that cannot be transported and which generally produced a rent or income. At present it is common to refer to such property as *bienes raíces* (real estate) or *heredades* (country estates). It is more difficult to define movable property, that is to say, that which can be moved from one place to another and which can be treated independently of the site where it happens to rest. The Old Law, as will be seen, takes the existence of the two classes of private property for granted and then limits itself to enumerating some examples when regulating inheritance practices. The protection afforded by law to movable property is weak. If lost, there are few recourses for its recovery. On the other hand, it is the preferred object of legal seizure as guarantee of compliance of its owner with his or her obligations before the law.[139]

Regarding property ownership, the Old Law distinguishes three habitual kinds. First, there is purely individual ownership over which the proprietor exercised absolute title and latitude of disposition. This primarily regards movable property. Second, there is immovable property or real estate (dwellings, land, mills, foundries). Medieval European law generally distinguishes between two classes: 1) the "proper" or patrimonial holdings that in Spanish are termed *troncales* (truncal), *de abolengo* (ancestral), etcetera, and 2) "earned" or acquired ownership in land and/or structures acquired in one's lifetime. One's truncal immovable property comes through inheritance from paternal or maternal ancestors, that is, it is received within the family. It is the object of considerable restriction whether regarding disposition *inter vivos* or transmission *mortis causa* (with or without a last will and testament).

Perhaps it is inappropriate to speak of "family property," given that not only its usufruct but final disposition (at least initially) was up to the individual owner. Nevertheless, according to degrees of consanguinity, the relatives of a proprietor held a preferential right to reacquire inherited immovable property. Indeed, they could reverse its sale to a third party by offering to pay the same accorded amount within a year and a day.[140] In the event of the owner's death, his or her close consanguineal relatives had a right of succession, which limited the freedom of the testator to name a nonrelative as heir or heiress. The owner had to make the selection of one or more successors from amongst the closest relatives.

In sum, it should be noted that the major part of the Old Law is devoted to family ownership, which was also the case in other Basque and Pyrenean consuetudinary law codes. If the owner of movable property was free to dispose of it by sale or bequest, the same was far from true regarding immovable property. The truncal variety of immovable property was clearly fettered by the legal claims of extended kin. However, even if in theory one could dispose freely of property earned or acquired honorably within one's lifetime, in certain subtle ways it was included within the truncal property regimen and was not alienated easily from familial control. The property distinctions were both subtle and interconnected.

Finally, there is the issue of the commons, i.e. ownership of the mountain lands, which was held equally by the *hidalgos* and the Lord of Bizkaia and the access to them. It seems quite likely that communal ownership of mountain pasturage in a pastoral society was the original form of proprietorship. By the fifteenth century, such ownership continued to be important, but the Old Law limits treatment of it to a declaration of its existence, while dedicating but a few precepts to the protection of public lands and access[141] to ferns (used as bedding for stabled livestock) and a wood supply. As with the tenures of the *labradores*, there is a distinction to be made between ownership and usufruct. Regarding the latter, the inhabitants of a settlement had access to the woodlands and mountain pastures surrounding their tenant holdings. It was a right held by the community as a whole rather than its individual members. Probably the remaining practices on the commons, notably the pasturing of livestock, were regulated by such generally accepted consuetudinary practices that their inclusion in the text of the Old Law was not deemed necessary by the redactors.

## 2. The Lack of Prescriptive Time Limits upon Property Rights

There is a final solemn declaration in the Old Law to the effect that in Bizkaia there is no prescribed time limit on either the acquisition of property rights and obligations or their extinction (assuming the existence of a clear title and the belief and trust that it was obtained legitimately). Claims to inheritance, other ownership rights and demands regarding fulfillment of contractual obligations were therefore made habitually without reference to time frame. This could easily give rise to difficulties regarding burden of proof, since original parties to the matter might be deceased and/or the documentation regarding it unavailable (Article 178).

Lacking formal temporal limits, the disputes could be further exacerbated by the inevitable evolution over time of a *de facto* arrangement into a legal right. As in other places, the passage of time itself influenced the strength of a claim to a legal right. The Old Law guarantees possession of houses and estates that had been acquired peacefully and whose ownership was uncontested for a year and a day. Regarding such property, *hidalgos* of the Tierra Llana shared the attenuated year-and-a-day prescription with the inhabitants of the Villas who were influenced by the Fuero of Logroño. Indeed, it was a legal formula very characteristic of the broad geographical area influenced by Frankish law. In order to acquire the holding, the claimant presented the *alcalde de Fuero* with a *fiador* and two witnesses who swore that he or she was the rightful proprietor. The judge was limited to simple recognition of the ownership claim, without ruling upon its validity, perhaps due to the Romanist influence of the Ordinances of Alcalá (1348). It required that the claimant produce other proofs—the so-called "just title" and, possibly, an act of "good faith." In this event, the earlier Bizkaian practice of conferring ownership simply through the testimony of a *fiador* and two witnesses was frustrated.[142]

The Old Law recognizes ownership over contested property only after two or more years of possession of it, and then with the oath of the *fiador* and two witnesses. However, the legal process in such cases is lengthy, particularly when the witnesses are from outside the *anteiglesia* in which the property is situated (Article 177). The continuous uncontested possession of truncal property for ten years extinguished all possible disputes. In this event, the oath of a *fiador* alone confirmed the possessor's claim. In the event that someone disputed ownership after the ten years, the possessor was not even required to respond (Article 178).

### 3. The Sale of Immovable Property and Other Forms of Transmission

The Old Law is concerned with two questions regarding the voluntary or forced transmission of ownership of immovable property. On the one hand, it requires strict observance of the formal public announcement of a sale. On the other, it accords close relatives a preferential right of acquisition. Reference is to the first right of refusal that accords preferential treatment of a relative over a willing buyer and the right of retraction that allowed recuperation of a property by a relative after sale to a third party. The two concerns are present whenever there is the pending transmission of ownership or possession of truncal property: whether through voluntary sale or that ordered by a judge to satisfy the owner's obligations, as well as any of civil origin (such as those deriving from satisfaction of the punishment after conviction for a crime). They were also applicable in the event that a truncal property was hypothecated temporarily to guarantee a loan. They were even observed regarding public announcement of an *inter vivos* contract whereby parents transferred ownership of a family patrimony to one of their offspring.

Thus, publicizing the transmission of truncal property was a key institution of the legal order. Given the familial nature of immovable property in Bizkaia, it was necessary to respect the expectations of one's relatives regarding truncal rights of ownership. The best guarantee of doing so was to publicize one's intent to sell or to transmit such property. Reference is to the "announcement" (*llamamiento*) of the sale or contract. This type of public notice had to be made on three successive Sundays in the church within the jurisdiction where the property was located (Article 84). It was to be "done publicly before all the people on Sunday at the time of the high mass, with a ringing of the bell, before the whole town" (Article 92). Such public announcement, or something similar, is common to medieval law throughout the Hispanic world. It had the dual purpose of lending transparent certainty to the transmission of property while respecting the rights and expectations of relatives regarding the familial or truncal property.

After the announcement there were three possibilities:

a) If the relatives appeared with a *fiador* guaranteeing that they would match the highest bid, then they were awarded the property. One's offspring, grandchildren or other consanguineal relatives held a preferential right of purchase, but they lost it if they failed to appear at the announcements (Articles 84 and 89).

b) If the relatives in question fail to appear at the announcements (or exercise their right at that time), the seller is free to proceed with the sale with its own specified payment schedule (Article 84).

The relatives could also exercise a retroactive right of acquisition in the event that the seller had failed to meet the announcement's requirement. The closest consanguineal relative had the first right of refusal, and it had to be exercised within a year and a day. In such an event, the price of purchase was set by three "good men." The manner of appointing them is outlined clearly, as is their procedure in determining value and the ways in which the purchase was to be paid (in three equal time specific payments) (Article 84). Navarrese-Aragonese law observes this same time frame of a year and a day in such matters, another clear reflection of the shared institutional connections within a broader "Basque" legal system.[143]

c) The sale of property at public auction to cover debts had its own procedures. In such event, distinction is made between movable and immovable property. The latter was sold to meet obligations only in the event that the proceeds from the sale of one's movable property were insufficient to do so. Furthermore, the owner of the property in question could interrupt its forced sale by providing *fiadores* willing to guarantee that the outstanding obligations would be met. After the announcement on the third Sunday, the movable property in question was auctioned off. Any implicated immovable property was held for a year and a day before becoming subject to public sale (and only then in the event that its owner had failed to satisfy otherwise the outstanding obligation). We might note that in this case the principle of truncality was clearly affirmed (Articles 79, 80, 81 and 83).

The sale of truncal immovable property to meet one's obligations after conviction for a delict was held on the Sunday of the third announcement (i.e. without waiting for a year and a day). The delinquent owner's closest relatives were given preference. If no one bid on the property, the *anteiglesia* where it was located could acquire it for two-thirds of its appraised value (Article 90).

## XXI. The Family, Matrimony and Matrimonial Rights in Property

### 1. THE NUCLEAR AND EXTENDED FAMILY

The family system described in the Fuero falls somewhere between the extended and nuclear family models. On the one hand, as we have noted, extended kinsmen are clearly empowered with respect to a nuclear family's property. While there is no clear delineation of a lineage principle in any of the Old Law's precepts, it was operative to at least the fourth degree of consanguinity. In fact, the lineage was the critical component in the wars or struggles of the bands. The concept of the vendetta or personal vengeance was quite apparent. That is to say, the rule was that any offense against an extended family member obliged the others to assist and redress the affront. But this reality, which is described so graphically in Lope García de Salazar's *Bienandanzas y fortunas*, is not reflected in law, excepting the matter of truces. It should also be noted that the formal composition of such lineages is not specified, although their scope seems to have been fairly extensive. It is also possible, even probable, that kinsmen played a part in the swearing of oaths regarding one's innocence and, in particular, providing the required financial guarantees.

Nevertheless, such considerations do not place the Bizkaian family in the ranks of extended family social systems, as configured by the Roman *gens*, the German *sippe* or the Serbian *zadruga*.[144] Regarding Bizkaia then, reference is not to an extended family system with clear legal parameters spelled out in specific norms. Rather, as reflected in the body of the law, in Bizkaia there existed a developed system of official public justice, distanced from and paralleled by another rooted in the concept of family solidarity. Furthermore, the scope of the Bizkaian extended family apparently did not go beyond the limits within which the aforementioned truncal rights over heritable property could be exercised. Perhaps it is valid to say that in the Old Law we are witnessing the evolution towards a more restricted definition of family, excepting in the realm of patrimonial immovable property rights.

## 2. The Establishment of Canonical Marriage

At the end of the Late Middle Ages, canonical marriage—the blessed union—was fully established in Bizkaia. Within the norms of the Old Law, there is scant evidence of any other form of sanctioned permanent sexual union, although this does not mean that in real life there were not other arrangements such as concubinage. Indeed, Article 203 speaks to limitations upon the rights of priests to transfer heritable property to their (illegitimate) offspring. Nevertheless, in the Seigniory, as in the rest of Spain and Europe, by the fifteenth century, the Church exercised a legislative and jurisdictional monopoly over marriage,[145] leaving to lay tribunals only the matter of its economic arrangements. This explains why the Old Law is silent regarding the validation of marriage—the subject of debate by canonists. At the same time, there was no consideration of an issue that seems to have been a veritable plague in certain other European jurisdictions. Reference is to clandestine marriages and the attendant problems of the rights of offspring of such religiously unsanctioned unions. In sum, the total acceptance of canon law regarding marriage obviated the need for the Old Law to specify any norms concerning the minimal age for contracting marriage, impediments to it, annulments, etcetera.

## 3. Community Property and Dowering

We shall now consider in summary fashion the economic regimen of marriage, which was within the purview of secular legislation and, consequently, an important matter regulated by the Old Law. In the case of Bizkaia, there coexisted two property regimens supporting a married couple: on the one hand, a general system regarding community property, which came to be known by the equivocal term of *gananciales* (gains), and, on the other, as a subsidiary system, a dowering regimen that in some measure underpinned the spouses' retention of separate property rights. In Spain there is a scant, yet excellent, corpus of scholarship regarding the subject.[146] The Bizkaian system has recently been the object of serious study.[147]

### i. The General Principle of Absolute Community Property

The concept of community property implied that all or a part of the patrimonies of both spouses be converted at marriage into their common property, and that upon the death of one of them, there is a division between the heirs and the surviving spouse. Its origin has been attributed to a primitive German system,[148] Christian influences,[149] or, as Font Rius has suggested, results from a concurrence of both.[150] In northern Spain it might just pertain to a traditional autochthonous family structure. It is a system found in various parts of medieval Europe, particularly in Germany and in central and northern France. Hinojosa believes that it was the general practice throughout northern Iberia during the first centuries of the Reconquest, although it became evident from the twelfth century on in written customaries. In any event, by the Late Middle Ages, it is found more selectively, particularly in Bizkaia and certain Pyrenean territories.

In reality, there were different modalities regarding community property in Spain and Europe.[151] There existed, as in the Bizkaian case, the full or absolute communal concept that encompassed all of the spouses' property, whether movable or immovable, inherited or acquired, and which required the consent of both consorts before alienation. In the event of the death of one of the spouses, the patrimony was divided equally between the survivor and the deceased's heirs. In certain Cantabrian localities, the territory adjacent to Bizkaia, this practice was known as the Fuero of Vicedo, Viceo or Eviceo.[152] A similar system is found in the Fuero of Baylío, applicable in certain localities of Extremadura.[153] Nor should we forget that in southern Portugal there existed a system of communal property called the *Cartas de meatade*. At the same time, there were communal property practices that were less encompassing.[154] Then, too, there is the German *Gütereinheit* and the *Mainplévi* of certain Belgian localities that privileged the husband regarding the administration and disposition of ostensibly community property. There are other examples in which the communal concept regarded only the real estate and movable property acquired during the marriage.

In the Old Law of 1452, the community property regimen is absolute. The text is explicit in this regard. Article 96 states that the communal concept applies to movable property, its ownership as well as usufruct, and without reference to the size or amount that each brought to the union. Article 117 repeats that all movable property, and immovable property as well, are communal and shared equally. Communality of spousal property is even more explicit in Article 100, which stipulates that the surviving spouse received one-half of the union's movable property to dispose of freely as she or he wished.

The majority of scholars who have considered these precepts of the Old Law speak of a regimen of unconditional and universal community property, one that obtains and continues even if the couple remains childless.[155] Nevertheless, there are those who argue that, in the absence of offspring, upon the death of one of the spouses the movable property, and any that is immovable but acquired during the marriage, becomes the survivor's personal patrimony.[156] In any event, it is clear that in the Bizkaian system, once there were offspring, all of the procedures regarding community property were in effect.

## ii. Dowering and Marriage Gifts As a Subsidiary Matrimonial Property Regimen

At the point of considering dowering, the second of the matrimonial property regimens in Bizkaia, it is first necessary to take into account the existence in Iberia and Europe of two distinct dowry systems. On the one hand, there is the Roman regimen that obtained in the Late Middle Ages in certain regions of Spain, southern France and Italy. In those areas, the Roman dowering system had been maintained at least partially and was included into civil law in the eleventh through the thirteenth centuries—in the case of Castilla-León by means of the *Partidas*. Habitually, in this system there was separation of the property of the parties to a marriage, but with an obligation of the wife's father, mother or other relatives to dower her as a contribution toward allaying the couple's future household expenses. The groom received and administered the dowry, although he was not free to dispose of it. In the event that a marriage was dissolved, the dowry was restored to the wife or her heirs.

But there was also another dowering concept, the Visigothic, denominated by the polysemic term of "marriage gifts" (*arras*), evident in the *fueros* of the Late Middle Ages. The marriage gifts are given by the groom to the bride out of certain of his own property. Since future ownership is reserved for the children of their union, in practice what is being transferred is usufruct during the recipient's lifetime rather than outright ownership. The principle also applies to property acquired by the couple during their married life (which is held equally by them). Medieval law imposed limits upon the amount of property that could be included in a dowry.[157] The purpose of the marriage gift is distinct from the dowry; its twofold intent was to celebrate the marriage while providing certain security to a widowed wife after her husband's death.

The Bizkaian dowering regimen deviated considerably from both the Roman and Visigothic concepts. In fact, when the Old Law addresses dowries and wedding gifts, it outlines a different system. There are three distinctions. In Bizkaia, a dowry is dual in that it is constituted by property from both the husband and wife; it regards only immovable property, and there are no limits upon the amounts in question, given that all inherited real estate could be included (Articles 96, 97 and 100). Consequently, it is possible to state that in Bizkaia the general principle of absolute community property ownership considered earlier coexisted and overlapped with the dowering regimen. Taken together these factors configure a Bizkaian dowering system that is quite distinct from the Roman or Visigothic ones discussed above. The practical effect of this Bizkaian dual dowering system conflates, while also underscoring, their separate property ownership, if such was the will of the parties contracting marriage. Consequently, for legalists it is difficult to describe the system in simple or dogmatic terms.[158]

Constitution of the wedding gift had to meet several requirements and formalities. The will to provide one had to be expressed before witnesses or a notary, and the truncal property had to be specified. *Fiadores* guaranteeing the representation of the promised object had to be provided, and there was a *traditio* or symbolic handing over of it. From a formal point of view, of singular interest were the marriage gifts involving two, three or more houses, iron foundries or mills, particularly when situated in different *anteiglesias*. Regarding consummation of the "tradition" or handing over of the specified properties, it was sufficient that the beneficiary take possession of one of them—for example, a house or manor. In this event, those intervening in the constitution of the dowry went to the house or manor in question, and the beneficiary received there a roof tile, tree branch and a fistful of soil as signs of possession—including other properties listed in the agreement. The *fiadores* took part in this act as well (Article 99).

Regarding the actual management of properties within this dual (separation of ownership) dowering regimen, the Old Law is silent. It is to be assumed that it followed the same procedures that obtained for community property.

In general, the principle that dowered property will end up with the children of the marital union obtains, whether because the parents transmit it through joint action or through the individual will and testament of each of the spouses. Children from other marriages of either of them are excluded. Consequently, the wife transmits to their children proprietorship or usufruct of dowered properties received from the husband and vice versa (Article 103, 104 and 121).

4. Consent of the Wife in the Sale of Her Property and the Regimen of Marital Debts and Obligations

Within historical comparative European law, the status of women, married or not, is extremely variable. There are legal systems that accord women more or less equal rights to men; others, on the contrary, incapacitate women permanently, subordinating them to male authority—whether that of her father, husband or other relative. There are also intermediary cases.

The SenatusConsultumVeleianum, in the year 46 A.D., incapacitated women as possible guarantors for a third party. Castilian law adopted this Roman legal position. Half a century after approval of Bizkaia's Old Law, in the Kingdom of Castilla, it was legislated that a married woman could not enter into contracts without the permission and ratification of her husband, unless a judge should rule otherwise formally (beginning with Law 55 in the *Laws of Toro*).[159]

Bizkaian norms, to the contrary, establish nearly complete equality and symmetry of spouses in this regard, and particularly regarding patrimonies. The complementarity is not as absolute regarding witnessing of wills and testaments. Such instruments are attested before a notary solely by men. However, there are the two cases in which wills and testaments are attested to without the presence of a notary; one requires three male and two female witnesses, and the other two men and one woman. In these instances then, we might underscore that a feminine presence is prescribed (Article 128).

A prime rule of the Old Law is the requirement of a woman's consent in the sale of her property. If she fails to agree, any sale that implicates that half of the couple's patrimony pertaining to her is null and void, which is not consonant with the community property principle (Article 122).

The distinction is maintained in other ways as well. Regarding the mutual obligations of the husband and wife, the Old Law distinguishes between civil ones and those regarding the commission of a crime. To wit, the wife is not required to forfeit her property over civil obligations contracted by her husband. Nor is she liable for payment of retribution should her spouse engage in criminal activity—whether murders, robberies or other illegal acts. The same holds true for the husband and his property with respect to his wife's behavior. Nevertheless, there is one distinction between the sexes regarding one spouse's liability over a criminal act committed by the other. Even if the wife is aware of her husband's intentions to commit a crime, she is not thereby implicated unless she takes an active part in its commission—in which case she is equally culpable. However, if a knowing husband fails to impede a crime about to be committed by his wife, then he stands equally guilty. In such case he receives the identical punishment as his spouse (Article 118).

Even if she is aware of them, a wife is not responsible for the civil debts and financial guarantees contracted by her husband, unless, and with the agreement of her spouse, she knowingly assumes the obligation. The burden of proof that the obligation is mutual is upon the creditors. This is consonant with the restraint upon a husband who sells his property to pay his debts from including that which corresponds to the wife. Nevertheless, he does enjoy a lifetime usufruct of her property. Once he dies she is free to dispose of her property as she sees fit and without reference necessarily to their offspring (Article 119 and 120).

## 5. GUARDIANSHIP AND WARDSHIP

The Old Law abstains from addressing the general regulation of the status of children, given that, as occurs throughout the Occident until the Protestant Reformation, in Bizkaian society the matter is governed by canon law, the same as marriage. In the fifteenth century, regarding filiation, the Church mandated exclusively. In this matter, civil law simply accommodated the various distinctions established under canon law. It should be recalled that only the offspring of sanctioned unions enjoyed full rights, whereas those born out of wedlock were deemed illegitimate. The two categories of offspring were not treated equally under the Old Law. Among the "natural" or illegitimate ones, further distinctions were made concerning legal status. Those whose parents were free to contract marriage at the moment of conception or birth were legally distinct from the issue of prohibited or reproved unions (e.g. children of adulterous liaisons or of priests or nuns—that is, "children of damaging and punishable sexual intercourse" as stated in the legal texts of the day). Illegitimate offspring were incapacitated in certain political ways and in matters of succession.[160] Thus, in the Old Law, they are not taken into account in the transmission of the property after death of an intestate person.

The Old Law provides few precepts regarding the parent-child relationship. However, like other medieval consuetudinary redactions,[161] it is concerned with the guardianship of orphaned minors. Their protection and tutelage is consigned to a third party who is responsible for an orphan's education and the administration of the minor's property. This institution derives from Roman law, which defines testamentary tutelage, as well as that which is established subsidiarily by a magistrate. Such guardianship terminated at puberty, that is, at 12 years of age for girls and 14 for boys. Guardianship for *sui iuris* persons under 25 years of age was established from the third century A.D. on. Within comparative European medieval law, there was tendency over time for public intervention in guardianship to increase, usually by a magistrate naming of a guardian from amongst the orphan's relatives, or ordering the creation of an inventory of all of the minor's movable and immovable property. There could also be the requirement of rendering an annual accounting of the administration of the property in question.[162] In Castilla, the *Partidas* of Alfonso X, dating from the second half of the thirteenth century, introduced the Roman system.[163]

Under Bizkaian law, the guardianship (*tutela*) of children or heirs 14 years of age and younger might be stipulated in a last will and testament. The designated guardian—and it was not permissible for one spouse to designate the other for this purpose—had to appear before the judge within 30 days of being named to provide respectable and financially secure *fiadores* who would guarantee that the guardianship be carried out properly. The guardianship was constituted officially once the judge had received the designated guardian's oath and accepted the proposed *fiadores*. But what happened if the designee failed to comply or refused to accept the responsibility? In this event the obligation passed to the minor's two closest adult relatives, one from the father's side and the other from the mother's, who were then obligated to take the oath and provide the guarantees. If neither parent named a guardian nor the closest relatives were willing to serve, then the judge might force the latter to do so under threat of penalty. Within 30 days of being named guardian, one had to effect and make public an inventory of the minor's property (Articles 131 and 134).

There existed in Bizkaia the practice of wardship (*curatela*), i.e. the institution of protecting minors between the ages of 14 and 24 years of age. In this case, the ward had the right to elect his or her guardian and reject a close relative even if he or she aspired to this role. At the same time, if the minor failed to exercise this prerogative, and the guardian was named in the testament or, lacking that, close relatives were serving as guardians, the judge (as with the guardianship of minors younger than 14) could oblige the person named in the testament or the relatives to assume the obligation under threat of punishment (Articles 133 and 134).

Consonant with the ward's freedom to elect his or her guardian, the Old Law recognized the minor's right to terminate the arrangement upon attaining 18 years of age, or once he or she is deemed self-suffi-cient. In this event, the 18-year-old petitioned the *alcalde de Fuero*, who would determine the person's capacity to care for himself or herself and manage the property in question. If the petition was granted, the judge asked for an accounting of the property from the guardian—the profits and income from the minor's patrimony (Article 136).

## XXII. Inheritance[164]

To understand Bizkaian succession requires situating its practices within the broad continuum of such systems manifested in the compar-ative law of the epoch. The Old Law contained a considerable number of rules regarding succession, that is to say, concerning the transmission of the patrimony from a deceased individual to a living person or per-sons, whether by means of a testament, or, lacking such an instrument declaring will and intention, by means of supplementary legal norms. Bizkaia had a custom of *inter vivos* succession, the universal donation or transfer of the family patrimony activated either by an agreement signed with the designated heir(ess) at his or her marriage or some time thereafter. Strictly speaking, this was not testamentary succession but rather a contractual arrangement whereby the parents ceded the prop-erty to that son or daughter who was assuming responsibility for the family household, usually upon his or her marriage. We can begin with this practice.

### 1. *Inter Vivos* Succession: The General Donation

In medieval Bizkaia it appears likely that the general donation or transfer of truncal family property *inter vivos* was the most frequent avenue for the transmission of the patrimony from parents to children. The donors or widowed donor transmitted ownership of the house and its appurtenances to a legitimate descendant with the condition of receiving food and shelter (*mantenimiento*) for their lifetime and of being attended to properly upon death (*enterramiento*). In reality, and taking into account that testamentary succession was unknown in the Occident during the ninth, tenth and eleventh centuries, recourse to suc-cession pacts was a somewhat common practice in those countries with consuetudinary law. Nevertheless, in other parts of Europe—as well as in medieval Spain[165]—on occasion there were *post obitum* effects at play, whereby the transmission of the property was delayed until the moment of the donor's death.[166] At other times the donors in an *inter vivos* pact reserved to themselves a lifetime usufruct of the property. In the Bizkaian case, however, the all-encompassing transmission took place fully and immediately, subject only to the aforementioned conditions (*mantenimiento* and *enterramiento*).[167] There was a similar institution in Navarra.[168]

We might ask if the donor or donors could validly hand over to the heir(ess) all of the truncal immovable property making up the household and its movable goods as well. Indeed, truncal immovable property could be transmitted in its entirety in this fashion, but the same was not necessarily true of movable property. Rather, if such was the intention, the latter had to be listed in the document item by item. There was, however, one exception. The Old Law speaks of a juridical phrase that captured a consuetudinary norm—*urde urdaondo e açia etondo*. As we noted earlier, it is the oldest known aphorism in the Basque language, and it is accompanied in the text by a detailed explanation of its significance and scope. Article 110 explains that by invoking this phrase it was understood that the donation included pork products, the breeding pigs, stored grain, the year's millet and barley harvest, a chest, a cauldron, tablecloths, spades, hoes, axes and any bed and bedding found in the dwelling.

There are two features of the general donation that should be taken into account. The first regards the event in which the recipient dies before the donor and without having left legitimate offspring of his or her own. In this case, usufruct of the property reverts to the donor until such time as he or she designates a different recipient or recipients, and there is a new transmission of the patrimony. The second provision regards the circumstance in which the recipient physically harms his or her father or mother. Under this eventuality, the recipient forfeits the patrimony, unless during the year after the episode it can be shown that the donor and recipient had talked out their differences or that they had eaten or drunk together at the same table (Articles 113 and 116).

At the same time, should the donated or transmitted patrimony include a family sepulture—either within the church itself or in an adjacent cemetery—it is to be treated as any other truncal property. However, should the recipient's disinherited siblings or other relatives lack a sepulture of their own, they retained a right of burial in the familial one. The only unique privilege accorded to the lawful recipient was the right of burial at the head of the plot (Article 115).

## 2. Testamentary Succession: Freedom and Constraint in the Disposition of Property

The mechanism for succession that manifests most directly the intent of the *de cuius* is the testament, which is the unilateral declaration by word and document of the future course of the ownership of part or all of a patrimony after the testator's death.[169] Shortly, we will consider the formal characteristics of the Bizkaian testament. For now we would underscore the fact that within comparative European law the testator's freedom of disposition was not unlimited, given that the law tended to require "reserve" of a part of the patrimony for close relatives (both descendant and ascendant) called legitimate or reserved heirs. It was a means of protecting the family. It is precisely in these limitations placed upon the donor's freedom to exercise *de cuius* will, or, seen differently, in the reserve requirement, that the diversity of succession systems is most manifest.

Within the European comparative legal framework, there exist two models regarding that portion of a patrimony excluded from transmission solely according to the testator's will. In countries of Romanist legal traditions, those of written law, the legitimate heirs have a right to a portion of that which would have corresponded to them had the *de cuius* testator not made a will. And, in the event that the testator had attempted to deprive them of this portion, they could seek annulment of the document by virtue of *querela inofficiosi testamenti*. The intent is to avoid the abuses of disinheritance.[170]

By way of contrast, the countries with consuetudinary legal systems utilize the concept of the reserve, a different institution that consists in the rights of all of the family members who could claim participation in the succession—the lineage—to a significant portion of the patrimony, as much as two-thirds or more of the truncal property in question. As a consequence, the testator disposed of only a small portion of his or her patrimonial property, to which would be added acquired movable property. But if the testator failed to respect the reserve rule, those affected thereby were not in a position to actually annul the testament; rather, they could only litigate regarding the excess amount disposed of by exercise of the testator's will that should have been part of the reserve.[171]

In the Pyrenean ordinances of Aragón, Navarra (*Fuero General* II, 4) and Bizkaia, the freedom to make a testament is all inclusive but restricted to the circle of possible legitimate heirs. There is therefore operative a blend of the concept of a universal reserve with that of the right of the testator to elect one or more heirs or heiresses from the pool of legitimate claimants.

3. Testamentary Succession under the Old Law

As do other medieval ordinances, the Old Law distinguishes between the succession to the truncal immovable patrimony and movable property, applying different rules to each. As noted earlier, in Bizkaia the testator enjoyed absolute freedom in naming the successor(s) to movable property. In the case of truncal immovable property, however, the possible recipients had to be selected from among one's legitimate descendants or close relatives.

i. Absolute Testamentary Freedom Regarding Movable Property

In effect, the proprietor of movable property could do as he or she wished (*fazer lo que quisiere*), as is stated in Articles 114 and 126. In other words, the donor had all-encompassing freedom of election regarding the disposal of such property, whether during his or her lifetime or at the moment of death. According to Article 111, he or she,

> may give and bequest all that property or part of it to any person or persons that he or she may wish, whether they be strangers or relatives, or do what he or she wishes with it or even keep it not bequesting it even if there are legitimate children or other heirs, descendants, forebears, or distant [relatives].

For the Old Law, movable property includes cows, pigs, livestock in general, linen and wool clothing, gold, silver and "any other movable property" (Article 111). To this should be added the enumerated appurtenances of the household deemed to be inherent to it under the customary *urde urdaondo e açia etondo* concept.

ii. Freedom of Election amongst the Legitimate Heirs Regarding Immovable Property

Freedom of election is more restricted regarding immovable property because the testator had to select as heir(ess) one or more persons amongst the legitimate descendants. Albeit within each degree of kinship, the testator retained a full capacity to select and decide whether,

> any man or woman who had legitimate children by a legitimate marriage may give, in life as well as at the moment of death, all his or her movable property and immovable real estate to one of his or her sons or daughters, by giving and leaving some quantity of land, small or large, to the other sons or daughters, even though they are of legitimate marriage. (Article 105)

In the event that there were no legitimate descendants, the immovable goods had to be transmitted to the propinquitous relatives, but reserving to the testator the faculty of freely electing the recipient(s) from amongst them. Thus, Article 126 specifies,

> that a man or woman who had no inheriting offspring could not leave any immovable property that they had as an inheritance to anyone else except to closest relatives from the line from which the inheritance originated.
>
> ...he or she could not bequest nor give away the said immovable property, except to his or her heirs. It may be given to whichever of the close relatives that he or she desires, as long as the other close relatives are provided with some part of the real estate, as much or as little as [the donor] wishes.

The immovable property then, necessarily had to end up with "descendants or propinquitous relatives." What is more, no other donations or transmissions could be effected as long as such potential claimants were living, which underscores the extreme extent to which the principle of truncality was operative (Article 114).

The Old Law did allow the testator who lacked legitimate descendants to freely transmit up to a fifth of his or her immovable property outside of the circle of close relatives. The practice regarded donations "for the soul," that is, donations to the Church to provide for the expenses of caring for one's soul (suffrages, pious charities, etcetera). This appears in the Old Law as a novelty. Prior to its implementation, and without exception, truncal immovable property had to go to the "closest relatives from the line from which the inheritance originated." Nevertheless, this new provision was conditioned. A fifth of the immovable property entered into consideration only in the event that the *de cuius* testator lacked sufficient movable property to ensure his or her post-mortem spiritual needs (Articles 114 and 126). This freedom of disposition of a quota *pro anima* is present in Castilian law, but after challenges was eventually replaced by a legacy of *ad pias causas* donations.[172]

The Old Law established the following ordering of the claimants from among the legitimate descendants: offspring, grandchildren, and "natural" children of either a single mother or "the man's woman." The children of unsanctioned unions received only a token inheritance, "something of recognition." They were excluded entirely from succession to the immovable property, unless they were legitimized by royal order (Article 105). Such was not the case, however, regarding movable property—over which the donor exercised complete freedom of election (Article 105).

The Old Law does not rank close relatives according to their strength or priority of claims. However, one imagines that the same calculations of consanguineal kinship that obtained in the Occident since the fourth century A.D. applied in Bizkaia as well. The Fuero does mention calculation of lineal ascendant relatives (parents, grandparents, greatgrandparents), on the one hand, and collateral (*de traviesa*) ones, on the other. Accordingly, there are 1. parent, sibling, sibling's offspring, i.e., nephew or niece, 2. grandparent, grandparent's sibling, first cousin, second cousin, and 3. greatgrandparent, greatgrandparent's sibling, uncle or aunt once removed, second cousins.[173] It may be presumed that the calculation began with the "closest relatives from the line from which the inheritance originated," with the election transpiring first from among those candidates qualifying within the closest degree of relatedness to the donor.[174]

And what of the remaining offspring, nephews and nieces, etcetera, that is, those who were excluded by the donor? We have noted that they were to be given "an amount of land, little or great," which reflected that the testator, by mentioning them in this fashion, far from according preference, was in fact disinheriting them.[175] It is a practice that Bizkaian law shares with its Navarrese and Aragonese counterparts. In those lands as well, the disinherited received a symbolic amount: five *sueldos* in the movable property and five in the immovable in the case of Aragón, and five *sueldos* of weak carlins and corresponding parcel of communal land in Navarra.[176] The latter provision was meant to ensure that the disinheriting did not at the same time deprive the excluded person of his or her status of *vecino* in the community.

Finally, we should note that, in calculating the testator's estate in Bizkaia, the immovable property acquired during his or her lifetime was conjoined for succession consideration with the truncal or lineal patrimony that he or she had received (Article 112).

## iii. The Forms of Bizkaian Testaments

The Old Law devotes several precepts to testamentary forms or modalities. It might be noted that while the testament was the preferred form of succession in Rome, it practically disappeared in the aftermath of the Germanic invasions. For at least three centuries, it was an unknown institution in the Occident. It does not reappear clearly until the twelfth century, at first in urban settings and later, more slowly, in the countryside. Its diffusion was related to the Crusades, the omnipresence of canon law and the growing reception of (Roman-influenced) civil law. The Church had particular interest in supporting testamentary succession, given that it facilitated the provisions of post-mortem donations and endowments to ecclesiastical institutions. At the same time, the diffusion of the testament reflects in itself a social change, that of the rise of individualism regarding the nuclear family and property.

Throughout the Occident, by the fifteenth century, the written document was the customary form of making a will and testament. It was usually a public act before a notary, magistrate or even a priest, and normally in the presence of two witnesses. The holographic testament, redacted, dated and signed by the testator alone, was not well regarded in the Middle Ages. Similarly, in this period the *nuncupativo* or oral testament was rarely evident.[177] In Bizkaia successory reality was, as we have seen, usually effected by *inter vivos* donation of the patrimony by the parents to one (or more) of their offspring. However, the Old Law's extensive detailing of the written testament suggests that its use was not uncommon.

The Old Law encompasses distinct testamentary modes. They may be classified by the testators, persons who effect a coexecuted will (*testamento mancomunado*) or by proxy (*testamento por poder*), and by the manners of authorization or authentication (testating before a notary as opposed to the quotidian practice of doing so in the presence of three witnesses).

The two testamentary modes in Bizkaian law as defined by the persons exercizing their will were found in other lands as well, but, given their importance, persistence and perfection in the Seigniory, they ultimately came to characterize Bizkaian succession practices. In the first place, there was the coexecuted testament of the husband and wife effected at any time during their lifetime whether in sickness or in health (the *testamento mancomunado*). Such a testament was irrevocable for at least a year and a day, even though one or the other of the testators should die in the interim. If they should both survive for longer, they could revoke the agreement and recapture the right to freely make out a new will and testament in favor of a different beneficiary (Article 125). This coexecuted common testament of the two spouses is also found in Navarrese and Aragonese law.

The *testamento por poder* was designed for the situation in which someone does not wish to make a will while alive. It was possible for him or her to give his or her proxy to another—usually a husband to a wife or vice versa, but also to another person altogether. The designated individual subsequently decided upon the recipient(s) and saw to the distribution of both the movable and immovable property in question (Article 127). Conceptualized in principle as a vote of confidence, the practice was widely prevalent throughout the Iberian Peninsula in the

Middle Ages. The *Fuero Real* of the thirteenth century denominated this "testament by commissary" (Article III, 5 and 6). The institution, with the scope delineated in the Old Law, survived in Bizkaia even after it had disappeared in other places.[178]

Viewed in terms of the modes of authentication or authorization, Bizkaian law recognized three testamentary forms. Reference is to the nature of the public act whereby a testator declares intent with respect to the post-mortem distribution of his or her property, while ensuring that it could be verified if later contested by the disinherited.

First, there is the testament effected before the notary. The so-called "notarial testament" is mentioned only indirectly in the Old Law, although it was underscored therein as the most perfect form of declaring one's ultimate intent. It had to be witnessed by three males (Article 128). Since it is cited in passing and only at the end of the article, possibly this was still fairly exceptional at the time of the redaction of the Old Law.

Second, there was the ordinary testament, which was related to the notarial one in many respects but effected without his presence. In the settled districts, it was customary to have five witnesses—three men and two women—assuring the authenticity of such a will (Article 128).

Finally, there is the uniquely Bizkaian testamentary form that later came to be called *hil-buruko* ("of the deceased head") in Basque. The Fuero notes that, given the mountainous terrain and sparse settlement of the Bizkaian countryside, it was often difficult to find a notary and five witnesses, particularly when the testator faced unexpected and imminent death. It was therefore possible for him or her to make out a testament in the presence of three witnesses—two good men and a woman. Subsequently, they might be required by a judge to take an oath in church to the effect that they were present when the testator expressed his or her last wishes (Article 128).

## 4. LEGITIMATE SUCCESSION

The possible lack of foresight by the *de cuius* testator regarding the ultimate destiny of the patrimony required that there be legislative or consuetudinary norms to cover various eventualities. In the Iberian Peninsula, as in the rest of Europe, there were different systems of legitimate succession according to epoch and geography. Specifically, in Spain of the Early Middle Ages, there were three distinct modes for effecting succession after a person died intestate: the Roman, the Visigothic and, finally, a system that became manifest during the Reconquest. We should keep these in mind when trying to specify the nature of Bizkaian succession practices as reflected in the Old Law.

As noted earlier, legitimate succession is the result of the tendency of the Old Law to recognize the successor's rights of family members, which placed limits upon the capacity of the owner of a patrimony to alienate it from the family circle. In this regard, there is an interaction between the testamentary norms and the ordering of legitimate claim for heirship. The restrictions that this places upon the disposition of property are necessarily reflected in law. Thus, Roman law required that a quarter of the patrimony be reserved for family members with a right of succession, a quota that Visigothic law raised to four-fifths. On the other hand, over time greater restrictions were placed upon the *de cuius* right of the testator regarding the candidates for legitimate succession.

But for our purposes, it is more relevant to consider the more proximate system of the Late Middle Ages (that of the epoch of the Reconquest), which differed from both the Roman and Visigothic ones. Across a broad expanse of northern Iberia, the household is the basic social unit, although, as we have seen, the formation of an independent nuclear family did not mean that it was disentailed from blood kinsmen known collectively as one's *parentela, raíz y herencia*. From this standpoint, given that the husband and wife were in equal legal standing, with respect to matters of succession, so were their respective *parentelas*. Consequently, just as within testated succession, the bulk of the patrimony ends up obligatorily in the hands of the relative or relatives elected by the *de cuius*; in the event of the intestate estate, the patrimony passes, according to the law, to the closest relatives of the deceased.[179]

The order for legitimate or legally ordained inheriting in Bizkaia was as follows: legitimate offspring (with exclusion of children of single mothers, the issue of adulterous unions, etcetera), grandchildren and then the closest relatives from the family line of the patrimony in question. In this latter eventuality, which normally transpired only when the deceased failed to effect an *inter vivos* transfer and then died intestate, the close collateral relatives of the deceased spouse received the part of the couple's immovable property that originated in their lineage (Article 106). At play is an evident principle of truncality (*ius recadentiae*) whereby the patrimony reverts to its place of origin, or "trunk," in such fashion that the ascendants who are not related to said patrimony are excluded from succession. Consequently, there is strict application of the *paterna paternis, materna maternis* rule, as if there were two quite separate and autonomous succession complexes within the household, and, within each, an ordering or ranking of claims.

The fate of property acquired from a non-kin stranger is not clear. The Old Law is silent regarding its disposition in the process of an intestate succession that benefits the propinquitous relatives of the deceased.[180]

We might conclude that Bizkaian intestate succession is closely related to testamentary inheritance, given that they share several norms in common. They both rely on the same order of succession calculated on degree of relatedness to the deceased (with the exception that, in the event of intestate succession, illegitimate offspring are excluded). But both coincide in their legal measures to prevent the immovable patrimony from leaving the family circle. Stated differently, they share a certain coerciveness in this regard. If anything, the principle is more evident in the event of intestate succession than inheritance by virtue of a testament. In the latter case, the testator does have certain flexibility in disposing of a part of the patrimony—movable property and (up to) the one-fifth that could be earmarked for one's soul—whereas in the intestate transfer, all of the property forms a heritable mass to be transmitted within the circle of relatives as defined by the law.

# Part Three

## XXIII. From the Old Law to the New Law (*Fuero Nuevo*)

### 1. THE FIRST REFORM OF THE OLD LAW IN 1506: THE PROBLEM OF AUTHENTICATING CUSTOM

Publication and implementation of the *Fuero Viejo* did not resolve entirely the issue of their authority and force, both matters of primary concern to its redactors in 1452. The writing down of custom should have eliminated doubts regarding the existence of the norms, but it was not to be. On the one hand, not all of the body of custom was included in the Old Law, while, on the other, the written norms had to be verified by custom itself. The one point that the interested parties and the jurists could agree upon was that Bizkaian law was consuetudinary in nature.

Bizkaia is emblematic of the problems spawned in ascertaining proof within any consuetudinary legal system, as well as the difficulties of accommodating changes of it. This was quite apparent in the crisis of 1506. On February 11 of said year, the General Assembly met in Gernika. Present was the *corregidor*, Cristóbal Vázquez de Acuña, as well as distinguished persons from the Seigniory and the *procuradores* "of the councils and *anteiglesias*." The *corregidor* said that he had been in office for a year during which he had observed in his hearings much confusion and debate regarding what constituted proof in the application of some articles of the Old Law. He had prepared a text outlining the conflictive points. He read it to the Assembly, and its delegates were in agreement with him. Rather than act immediately, they followed the customary procedure, which was to empower amply two lettered men—Ugarte and Victoria—and the *corregidor* to study the matter. The normative solutions adopted by this delegated commission were to be valid, each of the assembled guaranteeing compliance with their person and property.

The commissioners met in Bilbo on February 28. Accordingly,

> *They spoke at length about certain matters, and especially about the said laws of the Fuero of Bizkaia and about the said ancient*

*usages and customs of said Countship, [that] from time immemorial until now [have been] observed and safeguarded.*

*And using the authority given to them by said General Assembly, they said that they had been made aware of the great damage and expense that the residents and inhabitants of the said Countship incurred on account of the great difference and variety that there has been and is in the understanding of some laws of the Fuero of Bizkaia and other cases, in which there has been and is a need of a declaration because there have not been nor are there laws that speak about such matters. And if there are some, they allege that [they exist] from mouth to mouth (*rebocadas*) [i.e. as oral custom], and others [are] limited and interpreted as pleases each person. And others, for going against usage and custom, [are] abrogated and derogated.*

*Accordingly, it happens and has happened that the judges and* corregidores *of such Countship, with [contrary] information given them by the lettered, prosecutors and notaries and other persons regarding the same matter, ruled and determined on one occasion in one way and on another in another. Which has caused and causes the great variety and difference that there has been in the understanding of said laws and the proofs regarding their usage and custom that are agreed and have been agreed upon.*

Subsequently, the commissioners get at the heart of the matter:

*Experience has shown that proofs that have been given and are given against the laws of the Fuero are very prejudicial and damaging to the said Countship, because being as there are public and secret opinions and partialities, and given that some are adversaries of others, even though for one party there is the written law, the adversarial party, in order to prevail and forgetting the commonweal of his Land and in derogation of the privileges of the said Countship from which he on other occasions was possibly helped and benefited, places the judges in great confusion and conflict, offering to provide information and to present witnesses, and otherwise proving many times the opposite of the truth.*

*And if this is allowed to happen, very quickly and in a brief time the* fueros *and privileges of the said Countship would be lost and destroyed by false proofs and corrupt witnesses.*

It was necessary to arrange the pertinent declarations into articles, or *capítulos*, in order to "appeal to Your Highnesses that you order them confirmed and approved." Then they were to be incorporated into the text of the Fuero. The eleven adopted declarations or laws were written down by the notary Juan de Arbolancha in the presence of witnesses.

The Reform, as it was called, tended to reinforce the authority of the Fuero, freeing the Old Law from the former of effects proof by custom, while clarifying explicitly those articles that had led to the greatest controversies.

In the first place, the commissioners ordered a literal application of the Fuero, ruling out the allegation of one of the parties to a suit that such and such a norm lacked authority (Article 1). Furthermore, the Reform formalized the practice of requiring delinquents to appear beneath the Tree of Gernika, extending it to all crimes for which the accused were liable for corporal punishment. It also exempted those accused of lesser crimes from preventive imprisonment if they posted financial assurances to guarantee their appearance before the court (Article 2). Just as in the subsequent redaction of the Old Law, the principle that the administration of public justice in a matter primarily concerns the parties to it is maintained. The right of the accuser to suspend the proceedings by pardoning the accused is clearly respected (Articles 2 and 3). Such right of suspension could, however, compromise the execution of justice itself. Therefore, in grave matters (homicides realized with arrow or treachery during periods of formal truce), the Reform authorized the judge to continue the legal process. In all other cases, if the parties came to an accord at any point in the proceedings, the judge was required to drop the matter (Article 5).

The Reform retained the law whereby the *prestamero* or *merino* could kill an accused defendant who had failed to respond to a summons without first hearing his side of the story. But this measure was limited to grave homicidal matters. In the other cases, the delinquent, whether fugitive or in custody, had the right to a trial (Article 6). The general absence of torture in Bizkaia meant that it was oftentimes necessary to base judgments upon circumstantial evidence. However, such proof alone could not result in a death sentence, mutilation or any other corporal punishment, neither to the forfeiture of property nor to banishment from Bizkaia for a period longer than three years (Article 7). Along the same humanitarian lines, it was prohibited to give out a death sentence for a robbery entailing less than ten florins. This was apparently anticipated in the Ordinance of Gonzalo Moro (1394), but not observed. Now it is declared that in order to apply the death sentence for robbery it had to be "very enormous and great in quality and quantity" (Article 8). It is quite probable that the generalization of noble status among Bizkaians influenced this increasingly evident restricting of recourse to the death penalty (Article 8).[181]

There is confirmation of the authority of the Fuero in excluding the testimony of witnesses in matters regarding loans of money. As long as it was given in the church designated for oath-taking, the oath of either the plaintiff or defendant was deemed sufficient. In cases regarding borrowings (*dares e tomares*) of movable or semimovable property, the rules of evidence in the common law of the Kingdom prevailed (Article 9). The customs formulating a definitive sentence based upon prior evidence, and a summary order before detaining the accused or summoning him or her beneath the Tree of Gernika, were affirmed. The senior judge (*juez mayor*) of Bizkaia and the Chancellery, alleging that practice was contrary to both common and royal law, opposed it while favoring the requirement of credible testimony of witnesses or of the presentation of new evidence at a plenary trial. Harsh measures were adopted against lawyers who contravened Bizkaian custom and witnesses who altered their plenary trial testimony given during the investigative phase (Article 10). Finally, the Bizkaian norm that prevented disclosure of the name of the accused in a complaint was reaffirmed clearly. Rather, the brief was limited to specifying the events, and their time and circumstances, etcetera (Article 11).

It is not clear that the Reform received royal confirmation, and there is no evidence of its application. However, it seems to have been enforced, given that nearly a century later it was considered to be a part of the Bizkaian code. In effect, on November 14, 1600, Joan Ruíz de Anguiz presented a draft of this reformation of the Fuero in the Church of Santa Maria la Antigua of Gernika. The *síndico* of the Seigniory and other notables were present at the opening ceremony, presentation of the Reform and close of the act. It was agreed that the Reform would be included as an annex to the Codex of Bizkaia (which, as noted, already contained the Codex of Juan Nuñez de Lara of 1342, the Ordinances of Gonzalo Moro of 1394 and the Old Law of 1452).[182]

## 2. TRANSFORMATION OF THE OLD LAW INTO THE NEW LAW (1526)

The underlying problems with the Old Law remained unresolved, even by the Reform. Consequently, 20 years later the Fuero was again under consideration by the General Assembly of Gernika in its session of April 5, 1526.

It is possible to ascertain the birth of the New Law through an act of proceedings that precedes the text. Present in the Assembly were the Licentiate Pedro Girón de Loyasa, the *corregidor* and possible representatives of the two major warring factions, the Oñacinos and Gamboinos—Juan Alonso de Mujica, Lord of Aramaiona, and Juan de Arteaga y Gamboa, Lord of Arteaga. They were accompanied by family members of the senior lineage leaders (*parientes mayors*). The *procuradores* of the *anteiglesias* of the Tierra Llana were present as well. Their summons to the Assembly and presentation of their credentials followed established custom—the so-called ancient matriculation (*matrícula antigua*) that would continue to be observed until abolition of the foral regimen in 1877. Importantly, there is no mention of representatives of the Villas. Two notaries were provided to witness the acts—Iñigo Urtiz de Ibargüen possibly a descendant of the notary Fortún Iñiguez de Ibargüen who was one of the authenticators of the Old Law of 1452, and Martín de Basaraz.

The assembled continued to be preoccupied with the authority of law. The central question was the force of the earlier Reform and probably that of the Old Law of 1452. They declared that it was necessary to eliminate obsolete norms and still extant customs not redacted in writing. The assembled observed that the actual Fuero:

> ...*was written and organized anciently in a time when there was no serenity and justice, nor as much influence of the lettered, nor [as much] experience with case law in the said Seigniory as at present (Praise be to God). For which reason there were written in the said Fuero many things of which there is no longer need, and others that in the same manner, and with the course of time and experience, are now superfluous and are not discussed. And others that at present are necessary for peace and order of the land and the good administration of Justice, were not written into the said Fuero, and they are employed and practiced through usage and custom.*
>
> *And at times regarding these there are lawsuits, and the parties to them suffer much fatigue and expense in proving that which is of use and of custom and is safeguarded. And the same happens regarding proving how the other laws that are written in the said Fuero are employed and practiced. And regarding [them] many expenses, and fatigues and lawsuits, and differences [of opinion] multiply, and often the judges are in doubt when deciding the case.*
>
> *And to obviate the said expenses, lawsuits, differences, and [unclear] proofs, that are thusly multiplied among the parties, and [to guarantee] that the said laws of the Fuero of Bizkaia be clearly and better understood and clarified, removing from them that which is superfluous and useless and unnecessary, and adding and writing in the said Fuero all that remains to be written and that by*

*usage and custom is practiced. And so as to write and reform the said Fuero, and its laws in every necessary regard, so that concerning the way the said Fueros were written, there be no necessity for the parties to prove anything with respect to whether the laws of the said Fuero are used and safeguarded or not, and thereby the parties be relieved of the burden [of providing] such proofs and expenses, and so that the law that are in the said reformed Fuero be safeguarded and according to them the lawsuits of thus said Seigniory be decided and judged, they agreed:*

*That they should appoint lettered persons of science and [good] conscience, and experienced regarding said Fuero, usages and customs and freedoms of Bizkaia, and empower them to examine the said Fuero, which is written, and its laws, and the privileges that this said Seigniory has.*

To realize the task, they gave ample authority to thirteen persons considered to be knowledgeable about the Fuero, individuals of "science" and good "conscience." The commission was made up of the *corregidor*, three bachelors and one licentiate, an *alcalde de Fuero*, and seven other persons. In their reforming of the Fuero, they were admonished to act with the greatest respect for the public interest and with maximum integrity. They were to add and delete certain provisions, while limiting the scope of others. They were to organize the body of laws systematically. They were given 20 days in which to complete their task. Once completed, they were to meet with the Regiment (*Regimiento*) of Bizkaia (as delegated organ of the General Assembly) to revise the text, redact it in final form and provide the document with a seal of approval. Then it was to be forwarded to the King for royal confirmation. In that event the reformed Fuero would determine the administration of justice in all legal matters within the Seigniory, as well as outside of it in suits among Bizkaians (*fuera de ella entre vizcaínos*), in cases heard before the Royal Tribunals (*Reales Audiencias*) of Granada and Valladolid, before the Senior Judge (*Juez Mayor*) of Valladolid and before all of the tribunals of "these kingdoms" (under the Crown of Castilla) without need of additional proof. They also empowered the Regiment to designate the *procuradores* who would take the final text to the royal court.

On August 10, 1526, the commission met in the house of Martín Sáez de la Naja on the outskirts of Bilbo. The *corregidor* exacted the obligatory oath from each of the assembled to fulfill his task honestly. He advised them that they were not to leave Bilbo for 20 days, from the present moment onward. They proposed meeting twice daily, from six to ten in the morning and from one to five in the afternoon. They were given the text of a Fuero of Bizkaia signed by Ochoa de Cilóniz "in order that the aforementioned delegates examine its laws and reform them." Thenceforth, that version of the Fuero would be denominated the "Old" (*Viejo*) one.

The commissioners worked at an accelerated pace that might be considered excessive. The 20th of August, or but ten days after beginning their work, they declared that "they had reviewed the Old Law to the best of their awareness, and reformed it, removing that which was superfluous, and including and writing other things that they had as Fuero and custom that were not in the first writings [i.e. the original text]." The notaries read out loud the new stipulations "because it was necessary that there be written in a new book that which they had taken from the said Old Law and that which they had newly written down of their *fueros* and customs, and all in good order and style."

The bachelor Martín Pérez de Burgoa, a lawyer of the Seigniory, and Iñigo Urtiz de Ibargüen, the *síndico*, were charged by the commission with redacting the final text. After swearing to effect the reforms, taking into account "the said old and new *fueros*," they were to go to the church of Santa María la Antigua of Gernika, there to organize the text into titles and chapters, and in good stylistic resolution, but without adding or deleting anything that had not just been approved by the commission. It seems to have been a purely technical procedure, since once the text was redacted it had to be passed again by the commission for final approval. Both notaries declared that they were in possession of the text of the Old Law and the reformed ones, and they were disposed to carry out their assignment.

Nevertheless, it seems that they did not complete their work within the agreed time frame, since the next day (August 21), the commission met with the government of Bizkaia—the Regiment—in the de la Naja house. Given the transportation system of the epoch, a round trip in the same day between Bilbo and Gernika would have been impossible, without even factoring in the time required to redact changes to the text of the Fuero. The two notaries produced the book that Iñigo Urtiz de Ibargüen had personally redacted, and which incorporated the resolutions of the reformers, as well as a copy of the Old Law. They then proceeded to compare the two texts, law by law, underscoring the changes in the new redaction with respect to the former one. The Regiment and the commission declared that the New Law "was good" and in accord with that which was the Fuero of Bizkaia. It only remained to fine tune the final draft, then have the two notaries authenticate it before giving Bizkaia's final seal of approval to the *Fuero Nuevo*. The Regiment then deliberated regarding the appointment of the *procuradores* who would transmit the text to the King's court for royal confirmation.

It would be the same Iñigo Urtiz de Ibargüen and Pedro de Baraya who, in the Seigniory's name, presented the text of the *Fuero Nuevo* of Bizkaia to Emperor Charles V in Valladolid on April 8, 1527. It might be noted that the haste surrounding the elaboration of the text was absent with respect to its presentation for royal approval. In any event, two months later, or on June 7, the *Fuero Nuevo* was confirmed. Permission to publish it was granted by the Monarch and, on July 3, the General Assembly of Bizkaia so ordered. In 1528, the printer Juan de Junta delivered the galley proofs (set in Gothic lettering) to the press in Burgos. The printed text included the oaths of confirmation of Bizkaia's Fuero taken by the Catholic Monarchs Fernando and Isabella, Queen Juana and Emperor Carlos V.

The subsequent vitality of the Bizkaian Fuero, both in the Modern and the Contemporary Ages, is reflected in the fact that there were seven editions of it published from the sixteenth to the nineteenth centuries. This suggests considerable circulation of the document, particularly given the limited territorial and demographic importance of Bizkaia. One obvious demand for the Bizkaian Ordinance was the need for Bizkaian authorities to supply copies of the New Law to tribunals throughout the Spanish Monarchy to inform their deliberations in cases involving Bizkaians tried outside the Seigniory. Although we are uncertain of the extent to which Bizkaians actually enjoyed such protection of "personal law," it is clear that the government of Bizkaia took great care in making the Fuero available to such tribunals.

Each successive edition of the *Fuero Nuevo* published during the foral period,[183] incorporated the oaths of confirmation taken by Castilian monarchs since publication of the last one. After the print run of the first edition was exhausted, it became necessary to reprint the document. A second edition of 5,000 copies was published in the city of Medina del Campo in 1575.[184] Unfortunately, it contains many omissions and typographical errors. The third edition (3,500 copies), called the Huidobro text, was realized in 1643 in Bilbo. It is possibly the most painstaking, and it is rather readily available to bibliophiles.[185] The fourth edition, which likely had a reduced print run, was effected by the printer Zafra in 1704. It includes an inventory or table of laws prepared by the Licentiate Echávarri.[186] Egusquiza published the fifth edition in 1762.[187] Curiously, this text incorporates the confirmations of Fernando VI, Carlos III, and even Carlos IV, the last of which would have indeed been unlikely since he did not accede to the throne until 1788! It seems obvious that we are dealing with pages intercolated into the text after its initial publication. Sometime between 1780 and 1788, Egusquiza's widow turned a sixth edition of the *Fuero Nuevo* over to the printer.[188]

In the period of foral crisis, or the late nineteenth century, there were additional editions, some of which had more or less official authorization. Such was the case with that of 1865, published by Juan E. Delmas,[189] official printer of the Seigniory. Then there was the estimable popular edition of Fermín Herrán (1897), which included an inventory of the titles (articles) and laws.[190] There were two other editions in the same century: that of Juan Soler in 1898[191] and another published in Mexico almost thirty years earlier (1869).[192]

In the last century there have been several more editions of the *Fuero Nuevo*. These include those of Darío de Areitio,[193] Adrián Celaya,[194] and the one prepared by the Section of Foral Civil Law of the Institute of Basque Studies of the University of Deusto, based on the Delmas text.[195]

## 3. COMPARING THE OLD LAW (1452) WITH THE NEW LAW (1526)

As we have just seen, the redactors of the New Law of 1526 relied heavily upon the text of 1452 elaborated in Gernika. Most of the latter's normative content was approved as written. While this is not the place to effect an exhaustive comparison of the two texts, we might consider this continuity both in terms of content and form. I would note that the Old Law was oriented towards the Modern Age rather than simply serving as a compilation of a medieval legal system. Similarly, the 1526 redaction was a further projection towards the present. Nevertheless, it sought to preserve that which was substantial in the medieval Bizkaian Ordinance.

We will first consider the most evident correlations in the two texts. Then we will analyze certain evident novelties as a means of finally mentioning developments that modified profoundly the foundations of the Old Law of 1452.

The normative changes are most imperceptible in the realm of public law, excepting certain aspects of the redaction itself that generally respect the Old Law's formulation. All of the Old Law's important public law precepts are retained in the New Law; indeed, there is even care in preserving their order of appearance in the text. In effect, regarding the Lord's oath-taking, exemptions from military service and taxes, freedom of commerce, processual legal guarantees, the creation of new *villas*, the *pase foral* and the appointment and duties of justice officials, there is a clear attempt to retain both the same substance and form of the Old Law in the new code.[196] These were the matters that Bizkaians most esteemed as essential to their political system.

Similarly, regarding penal law the two codes are similar, but with some modification. The New Law organizes the two sections on penal law in the Old Law into a single one. It also softens some of the penalties, inspired no doubt by the humanitarian trend at the beginning of the Modern Age.[197] At the same time, some of the industrial and agrarian precepts of 1452 are decriminalized and become strictly civil matters, although retaining much of the flavor of the original.[198]

In matters of property law, there is likewise great similarity between the two codes.[199] Regarding guardianship and the custody of minors, the New Law follows the Old.[200] The succession to property *inter vivos*[201] is retained and, with but small changes, so are the testamentary and intestate transmissions of property.[202] The rules for formulating a will and testament remain the same.[203]

A sense of continuity is reflected in other areas as well. For example, there is similar treatment in the two codes regarding roadways,[204] the production of the iron foundries,[205] the bounds of ecclesiastical jurisdiction,[206] regulation of the hunting of wild boars[207] and the obligation of the nobility to protect an inhabitant of the Tierra Llana who was prosecuted by a judge from a *villa*.[208]

But there are certain novelties as well, ones that confirm or complete tendencies already apparent in 1452. In 1526, the declaration that the Bizkaians were the titular beneficiaries of the freedoms protected under the law is clearer (compare Articles 76, 162 and 182 of the Old Law with 24.2 and 16.3–4 of the New Law). The 1452 text is more ambiguous in this regard. Regarding certain concrete liberties, the open and ample terror of the Old Law is maintained. At the same time, the specific prohibition against torturing Bizkaians, since all were considered noblemen, is explicit in the New Law (1.12 and 9.9). There is consecration of "Bizkaianess" in the matters regarding freedoms, that is to say, a conferral of said status upon all inhabitants of the Seignory, although the New Law does retain the restrictions that prevent *labradores* from leaving their tenancies.[209] The New Law further stipulates that the privileges inherent in the status of Bizkaian should apply to its inhabitants even when outside of the Seigniory (1.16). This was a quite useful privilege in the Modern Age, given the massive emigration of Bizkaians to the Kingdoms of Castilla and León, as well as the American colonies.

Imbued with their values and preoccupied with sixteenth-century nobiliary concerns, Bizkaians managed to introduce into the New Law of 1526 precepts that were lacking in the Old Law. I refer to the prohibition against according Bizkaian residency to Jews, Moors, and non-nobles (1.13–15). The requirement of accrediting one's "purity of blood" as a condition for Bizkaian status would characterize, until the twentieth century, the world view of the Bizkaians, as well as the native inhabitants of all the Basque territories.

There are other, perhaps less important, innovations that are reflective of the first reforms promoted by the Catholic Monarchs. In large measure they reflect reception of general norms of the Castilian Kingdom. Thus, there is regulation of gambling, punishments for keeping public concubines, restrictions of celebrations regarding first masses and weddings, the mourning practices of bereaved family members, etcetera.[210]

There were important innovations in the administration of justice that underscore both an institutional evolution within the Seigniory and the growing complexity of the Spanish Monarchy. The jurisdictional authority of the General Assembly was delegated to the general deputies of the Seigniory. And the direct right of appeal to the highest instance of the Lord-King is displaced by the Monarchy's most elevated organs of justice, reserving nevertheless to Bizkaians special treatment. Reference is to the appearance, within the Chancellery of Valladolid, of a Bizkaian forum in which appeals from the Seigniory were heard.[211] This was quite exceptional within the Castilian Monarchy, since no other territorial unit comprising it enjoyed similar treatment.

In listing the changes introduced by the New Law, particular attention must be given to civil and criminal procedures. This was no doubt the area in which the Old Law posed the greatest challenge of interpretation, and where application of consuetudinary law could generate maximum confusion. The Old Law formulated certain procedural precepts with extreme concision. On the other hand, it failed to address broad areas, a vacuum that was to be bridged by recourse to "custom." It is possible that better delineation of these omissions was one of the important motivations behind the reform of 1526. Nevertheless, we only mention this in passing since a full comparison of the two texts in this regard would be so lengthy and convoluted as to be unnecessary for present purposes.

Bizkaian law in the Modern Age, as developed in the New Law of 1526 and its subsequent interpretation and elaboration since the nineteenth century within the final phase of Spanish civil law codification by both Bizkaia's Senior Judge and Spain's Supreme Tribunal, has been the subject of many studies. In the 1880s the Spanish legislators agreed to accept the legitimacy of certain Bizkaian civil norms that were then appended to the Spanish Civil Code of 1889. This tolerant stance necessitated the elaboration of memorials and studies regarding the fundamental institutions of foral law. There was an attempt to order it and facilitate its application in the courts. This effort was continued over several decades and was not interrupted until the Spanish Civil War that began in 1936 (although some of the earlier studies were actually not published until after the conflict).[212] The study of Bizkaian foral law was interdicted for a quarter of a century. Then, in 1965, the legal historian Adrián Celaya inaugurated a new phase by publishing his renovative monograph, which has been followed by many additional works. Since then, he is considered as the master source regarding traditional Bizkaian law.[213]

There have been at least two attempts to situate the Seigniory's public and private law within the wider context of Basque law in general, employing a controlled comparison of the different institutions throughout Vasconia's several component territories. The work realized by Marichalar and Manrique[214] was regarded in its time to be particularly innovative and meritorious. The work of Jesús de Galíndez, conducted in exile and without easy access to the necessary bibliographic resources, should be acknowledged as well since it contains valuable interpretations and intuitions.[215]

In fine, it has been the purpose of this introduction to contextualize a most extraordinary medieval law code—the Old Law or *Fuero Viejo* of Bizkaia. It is now time that it speak for itself.

# Notes

1. Unamuno 1925: 294.

2. Adams 1851: 310.

3. Wordsworth 1892: 439.

4. Mendibil 1999: 266.

5. For an exhaustive classic study of the physical and cultural geography of Vasconia *cf.* Carreras Candi (1911–1925). Caro Baroja (1980) provides a general overview of Basque history and culture.

6. Altuna 1998; Caro Baroja 1942; Sánchez Albornoz 1929. For treatment of the Basque-Iberianism hypothesis *cf.* Caro Baroja (1942, 1943).

7. For broad discussion of the origin, evolution and circumstances of the Basque language *cf.* Tovar (1959).

8. Sayas Abengoechea 1999.

9. For a critical evaluation of the historiography, and particularly its juridical and institutional dimensions, regarding the last decades of the Middle Ages in Vasconia *cf.* Díez de Salazar Fernández (1988) and García de Cortázar (1977).

10. Lacarra 1972a.

11. Echegaray y Corta 1952; Gárate 1951; Mañaricúa Nuere 1984; Monreal Zia 1973; *Obispados*... 1964; Ortega Galindo de Salcedo 1953; Serrano 1941.

12. Caro Baroja 1981: 243–293; Monreal Zia 1974: 37–39; 266–292.

13. Etxebarría Mirones 1994. Regarding the legal system of this extensive Bizkaian region *cf.* De la Cuadra Salcedo (1916).

14. Monreal Zia 1974: 13–50; 238–292.

15. Gibert 1973; Martínez Díez 1975.

16. Basas Fernández 1972.

17. Monreal Zia 1974: 62–84; 213–236.

18. García-Gallo 1982c.

19. *Fueros locales*... 1982; González Alonso 1996; Martínez Díez 1979.

20. Concerning the evolution of European law and the impact of Roman law upon it *cf.* Cannata (1996); Gilissen (1979); Wesenberg and Wesener (1985; Wieaker (1995).

21. Pérez de la Canal 1956.

22. Regarding the reception of Roman law in Spain *cf.* Font Rius (1967); Petit (1982).

23. Regarding the general evolution of law in Spain *cf.* García-Gallo (1982c); Lalinde Abadía (1966, 1978a).

24. Craddock 1981; Font Rius 1967; García-Gallo 1951–1952, 1984, 1986b; Pérez Martín 1984.

25. Iglesia Ferreirós 1971b.

26. Coronas González 1995, 1996; Pérez Martín and Scholz 1978.

27. The most reliable and complete guide to local law in the Iberian Peninsula is the work of Barrero García and Alonso Martín (1989). Prior to its publication the canonical treatment was the classic study by Muñoz García (1847).

28. Torres Sanz 1990. The article echoes the broad debate in recent decades regarding the political nature of the Crown of Castilla/León in which authors such as García de Cortázar, Valdeón, Naeff, Tomás y Valiente and González Alonso have taken part *cf.* references in footnote 11 on page 170 of Torres Sanz (1990). For elucidation of the concept of the modern state *cf.* Maravall (1986); Naeff (1943); Strayer (1981).

29. More or less the same can be said for the Basque territories within France and other of its Pyrenean ones as well *cf.* Ourliac (1953).

30. Martínez Díez 1974.

31. The question of the extraterritorial authority of the Fuero of Bizkaia has been examined in several works. In particular *cf.* Areitio y Mendiolea (1928); Plaza Salazar (1899).

32. Enríquez Fernández and Sarriegui 1986. In particular *cf.* the documents of 1353 (pp. 8–9), 1379 (pp. 10–14), 1398 (pp. 43–49), 1407 (pp. 74–76), 1411 (pp. 85–87), 1415 (p. 99), 1416 (p. 27), etcetera.

33. It is believed that first the Codex of Juan de Lara (1342) and then that of Gonzalo Moro (1394) formalized the concept of the "Fuero de Bizkaia" and that both codices were the object of the successive oaths. The first was ratified by the Lord in 1343 and later in 1375. When elaborating his Codex, the Corregidor Gonzalo Moro stated that he had the authority to approve and confirm the legislative efforts of the Bizkaian General Assembly and that the King was not opposed to the oath that he had to take to safeguard the *Fuero*. With the confirmation of Moro's Codex, its norms entered into full force, and reinforcing them was the Lord's oath that was only taken once (at the moment of his accession to the lordship of the Seigniory). Consequently, the confirmation and the oath–taking to uphold it were distinct actions. The former predates the latter. Once approved, it was anticipated that the newly confirmed text would be both the basis of, and encompassed within, the scope of the new oath.

34. It was published by Labayru y Goicoechea (1968), including a seventh volume and an epilogue to volume II (pp. 403–408). There are also the works of Hidalgo de Cisneros, Lagarcha Rubio, Lorente Ruigómez and Martínez Lahidalga (1986). The latter reproduces the Codex of Juan Núñez de Lara (pp. 38–52).

35. It was published by Labayru y Goicoechea (1968 II: 497–509), utilizing a copy that was employed in a sixteenth-century lawsuit between the Villas and City (of Bilbo) and the Tierra Llana. It was also published by Galíndez Suárez (1934). Its most recent publication was by Hidalgo de Cisneros, *et. al.* (1986: 52–77), utilizing the manuscript of Ruiz de Anguiz (1600) archived in Gernika. A critical edition of the Ordinances of Gonzalo Moro of Bizkaia and those of the Encartaciones is currently under preparation.

The Bizkaian Hermandades have been analyzed by Orella Unzué (1986). The study of this institution with better data and improved historiography continues and represents a considerable advance over the pioneering research of Balparda (1932).

36. The *apellido* has been studied by García de Valdeavellano (1947).

37. Regarding this problem *cf.* Pissard (1910) and Poudret (1987).

38. Article 125 in the *Ordonnance de Montils-les-Tours* of 1454 reproduced in Gilissen (1979: 270–271).

39. The place where the General Assembly habitually gathered in the fifteenth century was a stone's throw from the walls of the Villa of Gernika and the site itself pertained to the bordering Anteiglesia of Luno. It was, therefore, in the Tierra Llana and under its jurisdiction. It was land belonging to the Seigniory. The setting encompassed several elements: first there was the oak tree, which was replaced by a sapling as it aged and died. Then there was a raised stand, with seating, that in the Modern Age was occupied by the *corregidor* and the two general *diputados* (deputies). We might presume that in the sessions of 1452 the persons mentioned in the Proem and Epilogue of the Old Law were seated there. The elevated stand was separated by steps from the third element, a plaza laid out with seating constructed from lime, sand and gravel. It was for the assembled. It was there that they met until the beginning of the seventeenth century. It was the only legitimate place for holding the main General Assembly. Finally, there was the church for oath taking, situated 15 paces from the tree. At first it served only for receiving the oaths of the lords and kings, for celebrating the elections of the Seigniory's officeholders and served as the archive of Bizkaia. Later the use of the church, called Santa María la Antigua, changed and the structure had to be rehabilitated. The building that first served as the oath taking church was prepared for the task by the Corregidor Gonzalo Moro in the early half of the fifteenth century, probably a few years before the redaction of the Old Law. Other important modifications to the structure were effected in the seventeenth century, between the years 1642 and 1653. It was necessary to modify the church to receive the delegates to the Assembly, who began to hold their regular sessions there after that time. The plaza beneath the tree came to be utilized only during the constitutive reunion at which the authority of the delegates was recognized. It seems that the sacristy was used as an archive. The *Fuero Nuevo* prescribed in Law 18, Title 1 that the Archive of Bizkaia was to be installed in said church "In which the privileges, documents and seals were to be kept." *Cf.* Echegaray (1922) and Monreal Zia (1974: 359–374).

40. Mañaricúa Nuere 1971: 292–294.

41. Labayru y Goicoechea 1968 III: 145–214.

42. Astuy 1909.

43. The work *Bizkaiko Foru Legeria = Legislación foral de Bizkaia* (1991) contains the following texts: *Fuero Antiguo de la Merindad de Durango* (14th century); *Fuero de Ayala* (1373), and modification of it in 1469; *Escritura de iguala y avenencia* (1487); *Fuero de Avellaneda* (1394); *Fuero de las Encartaciones y el Fuero de Albedrío* (1503). Also, and following the denominations adopted by the editors, the *Fuero Viejo de Vizcaya* (1452); *Reforma del Fuero Viejo* (1506); *Fuero Nuevo* (1526); *Escritos de Unión y Concordia* (1630), the charters of incorporation of Billaro, Otxandiano, Elorrio and some Barrios of Bermeo; *Apendices* (1900 and 1928); *Compilación de*

*Derecho Civil de Vizcaya y Álava* (1959); and the partial modification of the *Derecho Civil Foral* (1988).

44. *Bizkaiko Foru Legeria = Legislación foral de Vizcaya* 1991: XIV.

45. To appreciate the value of this table, suffice it to say that there are dozens of concepts under the rubric of civil law (sources, territorial scope, rights of the individual, rights of family members and lineage, inheritance and bequests, etcetera). The same is true of penal law, processual law and public law. The entry "Varios," which is the analytic index *per se*, contains selections with as many as 350 words *cf.* *Bizkaiko Foru Legeria = Legislación foral de Vizcaya* (1991: 479–548).

46. Hidalgo de Cisneros et al. 1986 VI: 77–204.

47. For a thematic index *cf.* Hidalgo de Cisneros et al. (1986 VI: 205–210) and for an onomastic and toponymic one pp. 211–216.

48. The transcribers were prone to certain omissions, such as the exclusion of the following sentence in the Proem of the Old Law: *para ello tomó e resçibió juramento a los sobre dichos e cada uno de ellos.*

49. For example, and following the order of the precepts: *vecinos* when it should be *bocineros* [Article 2]. The transcribers were prone to certain omissions, such as the exclusion of the following sentence in the Proem of the Old Law: *buenos* for *vecinos* [3]; *apelado* for *capitulado* [27]; *fuere* for *Fuero* [29]; *como* for *mismo* [34]; *en siando* for *fiando* [35]; *sa* for *se* [61]; *lo* for *so* [64]; *qualquier* for *quandoquier* [68]; *cumplimiento* for *pedimento* [71]; *cárcel* for *casal* [73]; *ajuramiento* for *aforamiento* [75]; *en ronque* for *en renque* [79]; *fame* for *firme* [81]; *veedor* for *vendedor* [86]; *edad* for *heredad* [91]; *domingo* for *dinero* [94]; *vino* for *vivo* [121]; *es* for *se* [128]; *años* for *daños* [131]; *si* for *así* [137]; *o no* for *solo* [138]; *e* for *que* [141 y 172]; *villas* for *viñas* [145]; *ninguna en tiendas* for *ninguna, entiéndase* [145]; *los* for *e*; *exigos* for *exidos* [168]; *ordenarían* for *ordenaban* [154]; *e si* for *así* [159]; *caso* for *e si* [167]; *que* for *quién* [206]; *sin* for *si* [212]; *contas* for *cartas* [217]; *si* for *se* [220]; *frutos* for *furtos* [221].

50. Thus, for example, in Article. 19, the numeral *dos*; *en Vizcaya* in Article 37; Article 44 *e presunciones*; Article 55 *biña*; Article 59 *pode*; Article 64 *que* ; Article 73 *su, en zepo*; Articles 78 and 89 *alguno*; Article 103 *estos*; Article 120 *ni*; Article 140 *non*; Article 164 *que, diere*; Article 170 *defensiones*; Article 172 *que*; Article 205 *ni*; Article 206 *se*.

51. These are the notorious cases of the loss of linkage of words and phrases. Examples include: *de los tales pleitos los alcaldes de la merindad de Busturia* [Article 20]; *no pueda vender ni enagenar los tales vienes de que primero fiziere donación* [113]; *que lo pueda dar a qualquier o qualesquier de sus hijos que quisiere, así como podría dar de los otros sus bienes raíces. Pero si los otros sus herederos* [115]; *que ella fizo* [118]; *los agüelos que los tales llamamientos* [137]; *e puede ser que sean parçioneros en el suelo de la ferrería o molino* [156] *o el fiador del uno o del otro dieren qué prendas tienen, e que le prenda si no quiere echas suertes ni aplazar a la parte ante el alcalde de el Fuero* [167]; *que no lleve más delante de aquella casa sus prendas hasta que traixa tal fiador...; mostrando primero ante el alcalde con los fiadores que así los apartó. E después que puesto el demandador (e quando el demandador)...; o fiador de le cumplir de Derecho sobre la tal demanda. E seiendo así requerido en la forma sobredicha, si no le quisiera dar buenamente las prendas...* [168]; *de ningún vecino de la Tierra Llana, non tome procuración alguna* [190]; *ni de*

*sus almas. E porque muchas bezes los escuderos fijosdalgo e omes buenos de dicho Condado...* [219].

52. For example, this occurs in Articles 58 and 59.

53. Gilissen 1979: 38–39.

54. Title 24, Law 4 of the aforementioned *Fuero* states "...the estates and usufructs of Bizkaia belong to its *hixosdalgo*; and some throw *bidigazas* in the rivers and creeks that pass through those estates, and place at the same time *abeurreas* (which are a sign of that house) to put in that location of those signs the dam of an iron foundry, or mill or wheel or that structure for an iron foundry or mill or wheel. And they do so surreptitiously and for the purpose of appropriating for themselves said property [by] keeping there for a year and a day the said *bidigaza* that was thrown into the water..."

55. Lalinde Abadía 1986.

56. Baker 2000; Caenegem 1963; 1988. Schwarz-Lieberman von Walhendorf 1977.

57. Michelena 1968.

58. This is a nobleman who, under the ancient *fueros* of Castilla, had the right to receive 500 *sueldos* (a monetary unit) as satisfaction for any injury inflicted upon him.

59. A nobleman whose nobility was recognized only within the community where he was domiciled and whose privileges were lost should he change residence.

60. Nobility conferred upon a man for having fathered seven consecutive legitimate sons.

61. Cf. Andrés de Poza's "Ad Pragmáticas de Toro et Tordesillas," a previously unpublished manuscript on Basque nobility that was subsequently included in the *Gran Enciclopedia Vasca* (1981 XIV: 497–679).

62. Founding charter of Elorrio in Iturriza y Zabala (1967 II: 256–257).

63. Iturriza y Zabala 1967 I: 1228–1229.

64. It might be noted that the *labradores* of Arbazegi and Bolibar chose to become *vecinos* of Gerrikaitz. Cf. Iturriza y Zabala (1967 I: 267–268).

65. Articles 18, 28, 29 and 34 of the Codex of Juan Núñez de Lara published in Hidalgo de Cisneros, et al. (1986: 43, 47, 48).

66. Regarding torture cf. Tomás y Valiente (1997b).

67. Regarding the conflicts that arose between some of the Villas and the Seigniory's central institutions from 1514 on, including with the Encartaciones and Duranguesado, cf. Monreal Zia (1974: 97–140, 225–266, 285–292).

68. Chapter 5 of the Concordia [The entire work was published in Labayru and Goicoechea 1968 V: 674–676].

69. Monreal Zia 1974: 136–138.

70. The petitions of the various collectivities, their progress in the General Assembly and its resolutions are compiled in *Bizkaiko Foru Legeria = Legislación foral de Bizkaia* (1991: 397–407).

71. Labayru y Goicoechea 1968 V: 575. Regarding this subject cf. Monreal Zia (1974: 137) as well.

72. Mañaricúa Nuere 1971: 148–158. For a more literary perspective of the legend *cf.* Bilbao (1982) and Juaristi (1980).

73. The Count of Barcelos wrote the *Livro dos Lihnagens* between 1323 and 1344 (reproduced in Herculano [1856: 230–390] of which pages 258–261 treat Bizkaia). Regarding Lope García de Salazar *cf.* García de Salazar (1967 IV: 7–9) and Guerra (1914: 6).

74. Mañaricúa Nuere 1971: 151–152.

75. García de Salazar 1967 IV: 8–9.

76. The episcopal protests and the *hijosdalgos* replies to them are to be found in the *Crónica del rey don Juan I, primero de Castilla* (1953: Chapter IX). The subject was also addressed by Mañaricúa Nuere (1950: 144, fn. 33).

77. Concerning the political influence of the legend of Sobrarbe in the constituting of the Aragonese Monarchy *cf.* the bibliographic references in Lalinde Abadía (1969, 1975b, 1980, 1985) and Giesey's (1968) classic work *If Not, Not. The Oath of the Aragonese and the Legendary Laws of Sobrarbe.*

78. This is echoed by Iturriza y Zabala (1967 II: 113, fn. 247) when he refers to the pacts and conditions imposed upon Jaun Zuria.

79. Published in Labayru y Goicoechea (1968 I: 382).

80. Lalinde Abadía 1986: 144–145.

81. García de Cortazar 1978; 1984; 1988.

82. Regarding the themes of the commons, *facerías* and community property *cf.* Cillán Apalategui (1959); Galan Lorda and Zubiri Jaurrieta (2002 I: 417–424, 459–469); Nieto Alejandro (1964: 307, 380–381); Soria Sesé (2002).

83. Ubieto Arteta 1961: 38.

84. Monreal Zia 1974; García de Cortázar, Arizaga Bolumburu, Ríos Rodríguez and Del Val Valdivielso 1985.

85. Iturriza y Zabala 1967 II: 212, 230, 251–252, 259–260, 263.

86. Regarding the problem of political freedom from a legal standpoint *cf.* Morange (2000); Rivero and Moutouh (2003).

87. García-Gallo 1980; Lalinde Abadía 1980.

88. Luján de Saavedra, Mateo. *La segunda parte de la vida de Guzmán de Alfarache.* Capítulos VIII-XI, Valbuena Prat 1946: 635–653.

89. Monreal Zia 1985a. For a contrary view *cf.* Otazu Llana 1986.

90. *Crónica del rey Don Juan primero de Castilla...* 1953 I: 127.

91. Balparda 1999.

92. To understand the social and economic background of the economic freedoms of the Old Law *cf.* Echegaray y Corta (1923); García de Cortazar (1966); Suárez Fernández (1959).

93. Baker 2000; Duker 1980.

94. Lalinde Abadía 1975b.

95. In the Old Testament the *braza* is equivalent to four "forearms" ( = 1.80 meters); in the Ancient World it was 1.776 meters. From the fifteenth-century on, the Castilian marine *braza* was six feet ( = 1.68 meters). Consequently, we might presume

that the eight *brazas* mentioned in the Old Law approximated a distance of 14–15 meters.

96. Regarding this particular freedom in comparative Hispanic perspective *cf.* Pascual López (2001).

97. *Colección documental...* 1986: 20–21.

98. Jesús Lalinde Abadía is the fundamental scholar of Hispanic pactism, the political system whereby the monarchs take an oath to respect the juridical order of the realm's communities. The following are this illustrious legal historian's principal works regarding the matter: (1966 particularly pages 358–362); (1970); (1972); (1974: 62–63), (1975a); (1975b) particularly paragraphs 199, 236, 248 and 254); (1979); (1980). Regarding the Castilian pactist tradition and projection of it into the New World *cf.* García-Gallo (1980).

99. Lacarra 1972b.

100. Labayru y Goicoechea does not find any merit in the Lope García de Salazar fifteenth-century narrative, referring as it does to a presumed Bizkaian revolt two centuries after the fact. Labayru y Goicoechea notes, "Such an assertion is not supported by any historical document" (1968 II: 220).

101. *Crónica del rey Don Juan, primero de Castilla* 1953: 127.

102. Labayru y Goicoechea 1968 II: 374–376; García-Gallo has treated this episode as well (1986a: 92–93).

103. *Colección documental...* 1986: 21.

104. Liñán y Eguizábal 1897.

105. Regarding the *pase foral* in the neighboring Basque territory of Gipuzkoa *cf.* Gómez Rivero (1979).

106. Monreal Zia 1974: 144–167.

107. The term *prestamero*, derived from *préstamo* (or "loan"), underscores that the period of service is finite. *Cf.* García-Gallo (1986: 97).

108. For treatment of this official in subsequent centuries *cf.* Ortega Galindo de Salcedo (1965).

109. In their foundational period—between 1299 and 1376—the inhabitants of all of the Villas situated in core Bizkaia made their legal appeals before the judges of Bermeo; later the residents of certain Villas—Elorrio and Gerrikaitz—had their appeals heard by the judge of Tabira and those of Miravalles appealed in Bilbo. In all cases, the forum of last appeal was before the Lord of Bizkaia. The last three Villas to be founded—Mungia, Larrabetzu and Herrigoiti—appealed directly to the Lord. *Cf.* Monreal Zia (1974: 75–76).

110. Accordingly, there are the foundational charters of Bermeo and Lekeitio. *Cf.* Iturriza y Zabala (1967 II: 201, 208, 247).

111. Are we dealing with an autochthonous tradition or with German influence? Given the difficulties with accepting the latter conclusion, it is plausible to think that in Hispanic justice of the Late Middle Ages there is particular emphasis upon popular assembly. In the municipal *fueros*, we find the community of free men implicated in the administration of justice and the pursuit of persons declared to be public enemies. *Cf.* Riaza and García-Gallo (1934: 766). Lalinde Abadía invokes the assem-

bly of free men (*mallum*), presided over by the king, count or their substitute, who administers justice comprised particularly of persons of great prestige for their honesty (*prohombres, probi homines*) (1978a: 893). There has been discerned in the original popular assembly (*mallum*) a passive context within which to impart justice, given that the impulse and direction of the matter corresponded to the parties to it. In which case we are dealing with a process realized through *coram populo*.

112. Lalinde Abadía 1978a: 924.

113. Bidagor 1933; García-Gallo 1950: 69, 107; Rodríguez Gil 2000; Torres López 1928.

114. Mañaricúa Nuere 1950: 483.

115. Basterra 1894; Enriquez Fernández *et al.* 1994.

116. The *quintal mocho* of Bizkaia weighed 71,452 kilograms and was unique to the territory. *Cf.* García-Gallo (1997: 275).

117. For Castilian penal law in the Early Middle Ages and its wider Spanish counterpart *cf.*; Díaz Palos (1954); Du Boys (1872); Gacto Fernández (1990); Gómez Jiménez de Cisneros (1948); Gutiérrez Fernández (1866); Hespanha (1987); López Amo Marín (1956); Mendoza Garrido (1999); Montanos Ferrín and Sánchez-Arcilla (1990); Sánchez (1926); Tomás y Valiente (1982). Regarding the treatment of particular delicts *cf.* Collantes de Terán de la Hera (1996); González Alonso (1971); Masferrer Domingo (2001); Morales Payán (1997).

118. There are several differing treatments of Bizkaian penal law. *Cf.* Beristáin, Larrea and Mieza (1980); Pérez-Agote 1972; Galíndez Suárez 1934.

119. For the treatment of this question during the Modern Age *cf.* Tomás Valiente (1997a). He discerns considerable continuity in the institution: under the appearance of gratuitousness, the pardon is applied to many delicts, but "the legal and judicially recognized efficacy of such pardons was incomplete, given that they did not normally imply termination of the process nor did they absolve the accused of criminal liability." (pp. 2, 912).

120. For a general description of the penal system of medieval Hispanic kingdoms *cf.* López-Amo Marín (1956) and Machado Bandeira de Mello (1961).

121. Pérez-Agote 1972.

122. For a comparative perspective *cf.* Roldán Verdejo (1978); Sánchez Arcilla (1986).

123. García de Valdeavellano 1949; Rodríguez Mourullo 1962; Sainz Guerra 1998.

124. Gibert 1957–1958; Orlandis Rovira 1944.

125. Arco 1957; García Marín 1980; Puyol Montero 1997; Ruiz Funes 1934. In a recent doctoral thesis presented at the University of Navarra (Pamplona), Segura Urra analyzes punishment in Navarrese medieval law and concludes that being hurled over a cliff or drowning were the means of execution of a convicted nobleman or *infanzón*, whereas all others were garroted, particularly for theft or robbery. We are ignorant of other possible corporal punishments. The analysis, of course, regards a different political context than Bizkaia; nevertheless, there are demonstrable juridical connections in various domains between Bizkaian and Navarrese Law.

126. Lasala Navarro 1951.

127. Arocena 1969; Banús 1975; Caro Baroja 1957; Echegaray 1895.

128. Alonso Romero 1985.

129. Castilian literature of subsequent centuries depicts Bizkaians as cholerics. It seems that the insult was widespread. *Cf.* Martín Rodríguez (1973). For the relation between insult and honor *cf.* Fernández Espinar (2001); Sánchez (1917); Serra Ruiz (1969).

130. Riaza and García-Gallo 1934: 761, 767. For treatment of the accusatory process *cf.* López Ortiz (1942–1943). Regarding initiation of a legal process by public officials *cf.* Cerdá Ruiz-Funes (1962); Procter (1966).

131. Lalinde Abadía 1978a: 615–616.

132. Regarding the course of penal procedure in Castilla *cf.* Bermejo Castrillo (1997). For treatment of penal procedure in the *Ancien Regime cf.* Gutiérrez Fernández (1804–1806).

133. Tomás y Valiente 1988.

*134. Fuero Real...* 1979 IV: 22, 24.

135. Several municipal and territorial *fueros* regulate dueling. *Cf. El Ordenamiento...* 1983: Article XXIX; *Fuero Real...* 1979 V: 21; *Fuero Viejo...* 1: 5; *Las Siete Partidas...* VII: 3; Ureña y Smenjaud 2003 V: 21.

*136. El Ordenamiento...* 1983 32: 4; *Fuero Real...* 1979 IV: 21.

137. The dare and the duel have been analyzed extensively by legal historians. *Cf.* Beneyto (1948); Cabral de Moncada (1925); García González (1962); Iglesia Ferreirós (1969, 1971a); Otero Varela (1955, 1959); Pérez Prendes (1999); Riaza Román and García-Gallo (1934); Torres López (1933).

138. There is no judicial intervention in the matter; rather the plaintiff acts *ex propia auctoritate*. As argued by Riaza y García-Gallo, the seizure referred to herein has a different meaning—that of taking control of someone's asset to ensure or guarantee that the judicial intention will be met (1934: 768). Regarding the nature of the extrajudicial seizure *cf.* Hinojosa Naveros (1955a) and Orlandis Rovira (1942–1943) who both agree with Riaza and García-Gallo regarding its significance.

139. Regarding the classification of property and forms of its ownerwhip in the Middle Ages *cf.* García de Valdeavellano (1949, 1977b); García-Gallo (1959); Lalinde Abadía (1962).

140. Regarding the right of retraction *cf.* Lacruz Berdejo (1959–1960); Sáinz de Varanda (1947–1948).

141. Regarding communal property in Spain, in addition to the sources listed in endnote 82 *cf.* Altamira (1981); Beneyto (1932). For the situation in bordering Gipuzkoa *cf.* Cillán Apalategui (1959).

142. Cabral de Moncada 1926–1928; García de Valdeavellano 1977b; Mier Vélez 1968; Ramos Loscertales 1951.

143. Celaya Ibarra 1973; 1986; Lacruz Berdejo 1959–1960; Sáinz de Varanda 1947–1948.

144. Gaudemet 1963.

145. Aznar Gil 1989; Carle 1980; Fonsar Belloch 1995; Gaudemet 1987; Iglesia Ferreirós 1988; Montanos Ferrín 1980; Olmos Herguedas 2001; Stone 1990.

146. Collantes de Terán de la Hera 1997; Font Ruis 1954; Martínez Marina 1845; Merêa 1913, 1943.

147. Martín Osante 1996.

148. Lemaire 1928.

149. Roberti 1919.

150. Font Rius 1954.

151. García de Valdeavellano 1956; Martínez Gijón 1957–1958; Pérez-Bustamante 1983.

152. Mouton Ocampo 1915; Porras Arboledas 1998. Seemingly, it was applied as well in an extensive part of the Encartaciones under the name of *Fuero de Vecino* cf. Martín Osante (1996: 127–128).

153. Boza Vargas 1898: 301–303; Cerro y Sánchez Herrera 1974; Madrid del Cacho 1963; Martínez Pereda 1925; Minguijón 1960; Terrón Albarrán and Muro Castillo 1977.

154. García de Valdeavellano 1977c.

155. Balparda 1903: 47; Celaya Ibarra 1986: 161; García Royo 1952 II: 130–131; Uriarte Lebario 1912: 14.

156. Jado y Ventades 1923: 531.

157. Regarding the general historical features of dowering under Spanish law (denominations, ownership, assurances, disposition, bases for exclusion) cf. Bermejo Castrillo (2001); Cárdenas (1884); Lalinde Abadía (1989: 716–717); López-Cordón (1994); López Nevot (1998); Merêa (1952).

158. Celaya Ibarra 1986: 162.

159. Gámez Montalvo 1998: García-Gallo 1966, 1982b; Hinojosa Naveros 1955b; Luiz-Gálvez 1990; Ourliac 1966.

160. Gacto Fernández 1969, 1971.

161. Mêrea 1947; Otero Varela 1956.

162. Gilissen 1979: 560–561.

163. Brenan Sesma 1996; Martínez Gijón 1971; Merchán Álvarez 1976.

164. García de Valdeavellano 1977a; Lalinde Abadía 1961.

165. Font Rius 1954; Marín Padilla 1992; Rubio Sacristán 1932.

166. Zink 1993.

167. Monasterio Aspiri 1994.

168. Aizpún Tuero 1945; Lafourcade 1992.

169. García-Gallo 1982a.

170. Fabre 1930; Pascual Quintana 1955.

171. Flemish custom was similar to its Bizkaian counterpart in this regard, given that the reserve was a universal requirement (excepting certain provisions for pious purposes). *Cf.* Planche (1925).

172. Lalinde Abadía 1978a: 834–835; Riaza Román and García-Gallo 1934: 718, 720. For monographic treatment of the topic cf. Maldonado (1944). Of interest as well is the work of García de Valdeavellano (1977d).

173. García-Gallo 1997: 267. With this graphic it is possible to effect a comparison of the distributions of the Roman and canonical computations of propinquity. *Cf.* Gilissen (1979: 592–595) for an overview of both Roman and contemporary computations, as well as the Germanic one. *Cf.* also Champeux (1933).

174. For the computation of the succession of ascendants *cf.* Letinier (2001).

175. Esjaverría 1914.

176. Pascual y Quintana 1955.

177. García-Gallo 1977.

178. Lalinde Abadía 1978a: 819–820.

179. Mouton y Ocampo 1915.

180. Chalbaud y Errazquin 1898. In a monograph on the subject of forced succession in Bizkaia, Gorka H. Galicia Aizpurua has elaborated a detailed reconstruction of this succession modality as reflected in the Old Law. Certain hypotheses, such as that of the assimilation into the property regimen of immovable property acquired from strangers, are not underpinned with explicit precepts, but this analyst argues persuasively, and with a conceptual framework derived from positivist civilists, a theory regarding the attribution of the property to cross relatives (2002: 29–105).

181. Regarding the death sentence *cf.* Ruiz Funes (1934).

182. The document of transfer consisted of eight folios, as may be appreciated from the Ruiz de Anguiz transcription of the Codex.

183. Regarding the editions of Bizkaia's *Fuero Nuevo* during the period in question (the more than three centuries after the New Law was published in 1528 until its abrogation in the late nineteenth century) *cf.* Areitio y Mendiolea (1977); Herrán (1977).

184. *El Fuero...* 1575.

185. *El Fuero...* 1643.

186. *Fueros...* 1704.

187. *El Fuero...* 1762.

188. *Fueros...* 178?.

189. *Fueros...* 1865.

190. *Fueros...* 1897.

191. *Fueros...* 1899.

192. *Los Fueros de Vizcaya* 1869.

193. *El Fuero...* 1950.

194. *El Fuero Nuevo...* 1976.

195. *Fuero Nuevo...* 1991.

196. There follow the correspondences between the texts. The first number of each equation regards the precept of the Old Law and the second is composed of the title and law of the New Law: 1 = 1.1; 2 = 1.3; 3 = 1.2; 4 = 1.4; 5 and 6 = 1.5; 7 = 33.1; 8 = 33.2; 9 = 33.3; 10 = 1.6–7; 11 = 1.8; 12 = 1.9; 13 = 1.19 y 7.1; 14 = 1.10; 15 = 1.11; 16 = 33.4; 17 = 2.1; 18 y 19 = 2.3; 21 = 2.2; 23 = 2.10; 23 y 24 = 6.1 to 6; 25 = 8.25–26.

197. 38 = 34.9; 39 = 34.10; 40 = 34.11; 41 = 34.12; 42 = 34.13; 43 = 34.14; 44 = 34.21; 45 = 34.15; 46 = 34.17; 47 = 34.18; 48 = 34.19; 49 = 34.20; 138 y 139 = 34.8; 140 y 141 = 34.6; 142 = 34.7; 144 = 34.5; 145 = 34.2–3; 146 = 34.4; 147 = 35.11.

198. It may be appreciated by comparing the two codes: 148 = 25.1; 149 = 25.2; 150 = 25.4; 151 = 25.3; 152 = 25.4; 153 = 25.5; 154 = 24.4; 155 and 156 = 24.5 y 24.6; 157 = 24.7; 158 = 24.8; 159 = 24.9; 160 = 24.10; 162 = 24.2.

199. 79 = 17.1; 84 = 17.6; 84 y 85 = 17.6; 87 = 17.4; 88 = 17.4; 90 = 17.5; 90 = 17.5; 91 = 18.1–2; 92 = 17.1–5; 93 = 17.3; 94 = 19.1; 95 = 19.3.

200. 131, 132, 133 = 22.1; 135 = 22.2; 136 = 22.3.

201. 110 = 20.13; 111 = 20.14; 112 = 20.16; 113 = 20.17; 114 = 20.18; 115 = 20.19; 116 = 34.22.

202. 105 = 20.11 (21.6); 106 = 21.8; 107 y 108 = 21.12; 126 = 21.10; 127 = 21.3.

203. 125 = 21.1; 127 = 21.3; 128 = 21.4.

204. 210 = 27.2; 211 = 27.3.

205. 213 = 28.1; 214 = 28.2; 215 = 28.3.

206. 216 = 32.1; 217 = 32.2; 218 = 32.3; 221 = 32.3.

207. 222 = 31 (a single law).

208. 223 = 30 (a single law).

209. 36.1–2.

210. 35.1–7.

211. 11.11–19–23, 27.6, 29.3–4–9–10.

212. Angulo Laguna 1983; Areitio y Mendiolea 1985; Echegaray y Corta 1950; Esjaverría 1914; Fairén Guillén 1946; García Royo 1952; Isábal 1915a, 1915b; Jado y Ventades 1923; Lecanda y Mendieta 1888, 1889; Solano y Polanco 1918; Vicario de la Peña 1901.

213. Celaya Ibarra 1965, 1966, 1970, 1972, 1975a, 1975b, 1975c, 1976, 1984, 1986, 1991, 1993, 1996.

214. Marichalar and Manrique 1868.

215. Galíndez Suarez 1947.

# Old Law of Bizkaia of 1452[*]

## Critical Edition

---

[*] Translator's note: In the following perambulatory material to the text of the Old Law itself, the headings in brackets [ ] were added as guides to the reader and do not appear in the original.

# I.
# Proem

GENERAL ASSEMBLY OF GERNIKA OF 1463:
    Approval by the General Assembly of the Codex and Fuero of 1452—I-A
    Remembrance of the Oath Given by Enrique IV in 1457—I-B
    Confirmation of the Oath by the Royal Commissioners—I-C
    Text of the Fuero of Bizkaia Approved in 1453—II-A

## I-A—Approval by the General Assembly of the Codex and of the Old Law of Bizkaia of 1452

Beneath the Tree of Gernika, where it is customary to hold the General Assembly, on the 26th day of the month of August, year of the birth of Our Savior Jesus Christ one thousand and four hundreds and sixty and three years.

This said day, being at said place and gathered in General Assembly, convened and charged for that which will follow below, the *corregidor*, the *deputados* of our Lord the King, and *alcaldes de Hermandad*, and *procuradores* and *deputados*—and *mannes* and *escuderos*, *fijosdalgo*, (and) *omesbuenos* (goodmen) of the Villas and Tierra Llana of said Countship.

Especially being in said Assembly the honorable gentleman Lope de Mendoça, senior captain of artillery and war supplies of the King our Lord, and his *corregidor* and *veedor* in the said Bizkaia and Encartaciones, and the doctor Fernán Gonçález de Toledo, and the licenciates Pero Alfonso de Valdevieso and Juan Garçía de Santo Domingo, delegates provided by the King our Lord in the Countship of Bizkaia, with the said Encartaciones, and Pero Martínez de Alviz, *alcalde de Fuero* of Bizkaia and *alcalde de Hermandad* and of the Villas and Tierra Llana of said Bizkaia and Encartaciones.

And additionally, being present in said Assembly Juan de Avendanno, and Ochoa Vrtiz de Guecho, and Rui Martínez de Albiz, and Juan Martínez de Hendedurua, and Martín Vrtiz de Hea, and Pero Ruiz de Saldívar, and Martín de Uriarte, and Lope Sánchez de Arana, and Ochoa López de Vrquiça, and Pero Martínez de Albiz, resident of Varroeta, and Joan Ynniguez de Mendieta, delegates elected and provided by the Tierra Llana of said Countship.

And additionally, being present in said Assembly Lope de Mendoça, senior *prestamero* standing in for the honorable gentleman Juan Hurtado de Mendoça, senior *prestamero* of said Bizkaia and Encartaciones. And additionally, there being in said Assembly, Martín Yuannez de Marecheaga, *procurador* of the *villa* of Vilbao, and Juan Pérez de Çearra, *procurador* of the *villa* of Tavira of Durango, and Juan Fernández de Arbieto, *procurador* for the city of Ordunna, and Martín Yuannez de Anguelua, *procurador* of the *villa* of Lequeitio, and Martín Sanz de Martiarto, *procurador* of the *villa* of Castro de Vrdiales, and Sancho de Çubialde, *procurador* of the *villa* of Hondarroa, and Lope de Meave, for the Villaviçiosa of Marquina, and Lope de Vrquiça, *procurador* for the ferrous *villa* of Hermua, and Juan Pérez de Yrnolaga, *procurador* of the *villa* of Plasençia, and Furtún Saenz de Salazar, for the *villa* of Portugalete, and Martín Yuanez de Berrioçaual, for the *villa* of Helorrio, and Martín de Mendiola, for the *villa* of Herriguita.

And therefore, being in said Assembly, Gonçalo Yuannez de Arançibia, and Martín Ruiz de Meceta, and Fernando de Varroeta, and Fernando de Verna, and Rodrigo Yvánnez de Jaurigui, and Rodrigo de Çornoça, and other *escuderos* of the said Countship. And in our presence, Lope Sáenz de Arana and Juan Yvánez de Unçueta, notaries of the said Lord King, and at the aforementioned witnesses, the said Lord's *corregidor* and delegates of the said Lord King and of said *Hermandad*, stated that by virtue of the power that each of them had from said Lord King and from said Countship and Hermandad and Tierra Llana of Bizkaia, and in the best form and manner of which they were capable and which law required of them, they approve and approved as correct the Codices (*Quadernios*) of Bizkaia and the Fuero of Bizkaia and the Hermandad that they have now reviewed anew and organized and capitulated. That, at the same time, they have now once again capitulated and organized all of the valid laws, exemptions, and liberties that they were ordered to safeguard by said Lord King and which said Lord King has sworn [to uphold].

That they order and ordered that those *juezes* and *justicias* of said Countship, as well as the *alcaldes de Hermandad* and *prestameros* and *merinos* and any other justices and judges, as well as any other persons of said Courtship and Hermandad, and to each and everyone of them, that from now on they safeguard and comply with and protect and meet the provisions of the said Codices and Fuero and Capitulary, and of each of its provisions at every moment of worldly time, and that they do not abuse nor go beyond nor go along with nor consent to abuses or the going beyond to the detriment of that which is contained in the chapters of the said Codices and Fuero and Capitulary, under the discretion of the said Lord King, and under those penalties contained in the said chapters and in each one of them.

The tenor of that said Fuero, that they have thusly reviewed, organized and agreed to anew, and the chapters of which are as follows:

## I-B Remembrance of the Oath to Safeguard the Old Law (*Fuero Viejo*) of Bizkaia Given by Henry IV in the General Assembly of Gernika on March 10, 1457

Lope de Mendoça, *corregidor* of Bizkaia and of the Encartaciones, the doctor Fernando Gonçalez de Toledo, and the licenciates Pedro Alfonso de Valdevieso and Juan García de Santo Domingo, delegates assigned by the King our Lord in the said Countship of Bizkaia with the said Encartaciones, we examined the laws of the Tierra Llana of Bizkaia that by said Lord King were sworn to and ordered to be safeguarded by the *cavalleros* and the noble *escuderos* of the Tierra Llana of said Countship of Bizkaia, accordingly as is contained at greater length in said oath that said Lord King took in the matter, the tenor of which is that which follows:

> *In Santa María la Antigua, close to the town of Gernika that is in Bizkaia, ten days of the month of March year of the birth of our Savior Jesus Christ of one thousand and four hundreds and fifty and seven years [March 10, 1457]. There being present the very noble and powerful King Don Henríque, King of Castile and of León, our Lord, who might God let live and rule for lengthy and good times. In my presence, that of his secretary and public notary, and of the witnesses enumerated below, there appeared before the said Lord King Furtún Sáenz de Villela, Martín Ynniguez de Çuasti, and Ynigo Sáenz de Yuarguen, and Pero Martínez de Alviz,* alcaldes de Fuero *of the Tierra Llana of Bizkaia, and Martín Sánchez de Villela, and Fernán Pérez de Verna, and Juan Pérez de Yvarguren, and García de Anchian,* alcaldes de Hermandad *of it, and Juan Pérez de Yturribalçaga, notaries of said Lord King,* procuradores *of the* cavalleros, escuderos *and* fijosdalgo, *and* labradores, *and other persons of the said Tierra Llana and Countship of Bizkaia, and Joan Alfonso de Muxica, and Martín Ruiz de Arteaga, as residents and distinguished persons of them.*

> *Thusly, and in the name of the said* cavalleros *and* escuderos *and* fijosdalgo *and* labradores *and other persons of the Land and Countship of Bizkaia, they stated to the said Lord King that, regarding what is of the Fuero, and usage and custom, whenever a new Lord comes to Bizkaia to receive overlordship of it, said Lord*

*must take an oath in certain customary places of the said Land of Bizkaia to safeguard all of its laws and privileges and good usages and good customs and exemptions and liberties and favors and lands that it has and has had from former Lords.*

*His Lordship knows that, and once he had assumed overlordship of his realms, the* procuradores *of said Bizkaia went to the city of Segovia to request that he come to take said oath. And because His Lordship was presently going off to war against the Moors, and because he was occupied with his other duties, he took the oath there [in Segovia]. And at the same time [he promised] as soon as possible to come in person to the said Land of Bizkaia to take said oath.*

*And that later His Highness had come there, and that the said church of Santa María la Antigua of the said town of Gernika was one of the places in which His Highness would have to take said oath, that they supplicated, requested and asked him to take according to said custom.*

*The said Lord King stated that he had come there to take said oath, and that it pleased him to do so. And then he stated that he swears and swore to God and to Holy Mary and on the words of the Holy Gospels, wherever they may be found, and upon the sign of the Cross that he touched physically with his right hand, and which was taken from the main altar of said church, and which has a crucifix on it, to all of said* cavalleros, escuderos, fijosdalgo *and* labradores *and other persons of whatever status and condition there be of the Seigniory of Bizkaia, to safeguard their* fueros *and privileges and good usages and good customs and exemptions and freedoms and grants and lands and offices. And according to the best and most compliant ways that they were safeguarded by the Lord King Don Juan, of glorious memory, his father, and of the other Lord Kings that there were or have been in Bizkaia.*

*Said oath having been taken, the said* alcaldes de Hermandad *and* alcaldes de Fuero *and* procuradores *of the said land, and the aforementioned distinguished persons of it, together in its said name, asked of me, the said secretary or notary noted below, that I give them a [written] copy of testimony [of oath] or two or more, so that they might be made public.*

*Witnesses who were present: Miguel Lucas, senior chancellor of said Lord King, and Pero Sarmiento, his chief chamberlain, and Juan Furtado de Mendoça, senior* prestamero *of Bizkaia, all of his Council, the* marechal *Pero de Ayala and Juan Fernández Galíndez,* cavalleros *of the said Lord King, and others.*

*And I, Alvar Gómez from Ciudad Real, secretary of our Lord the King and his Chamber [personal] notary and his notary public in his Court and in all his kingdoms and seigniories, was present in one of the said swearings when the very exalted and powerful prince, the King and our Lord, the King Don Henrrique took the aforementioned oath and solemnity. And by his order and at the request of the said* alcaldes *and* procuradores *and aforenamed persons, I wrote thus public instrument. In witness whereof I herein affix my seal—Alvar Gómez.*

## I-C Letter Confirming the Royal Oath of the Fuero by the Royal Commissioners in the General Assembly of August 26, 1463

And insofar as for their part they have requested of us that we gracefully safeguard the following: with this letter we ordain that their said *fueros* be safeguarded, thusly and as best they were safeguarded until now, and accordingly as the said Lord King ordered that they be safeguarded. Consequently, we order that they be given this letter signed with our names, and sealed with the seal of the notary and the notary public listed below. Done in the town of Gernika, on the twenty and six days of the month of August, year of the birth or our Savior Jesus Christ, of one thousand and four hundreds and sixty three years.

# II

## II-A Text of the Fuero of Bizkaia Approved in the General Assembly of June 2, 1452 [and possibly revised in 1463]

In the name of God the Father and God the Son and of the Holy Ghost, who are three persons and one true God.

On the second of June in the year of our Lord Jesus Christ of one thousand and four hundreds and fifty and two years, in the church of Santa María la Antigua in Gernika, being present in said location the honorable and prudent Pero Gonçález de Santo Domingo, *corregidor* and *veedor* for our Lord the King in the land of the Countship and Seigniory of Bizkaia and in the Encartaciones, in my presence, Fortún Ynniguez de Ybarguen, public notary of said King in his court and in all his kingdoms and seigniories. And, along with other witnesses to be mentioned below, there appeared Fortún Sanz de Villela and Ynnigo Martínez de Çuasti, and Ynnigo Sanz de Varguen, and Pero Martínez d'Alviz, *alcaldes de Fuero* of Bizkaia for the aforementioned King; and Ochoa Sanz de Gorostiaga, *logarteniente* representing the *alcalde* from

Bizkaia, Diego López de Anuncibay, *alcaldes de* [said] *Fuero* for the said Lord King, and Juan Sáenz de Meçeta, and Juan Garçía de Yarça, and Juan de Sarria, and Juan de San Juan de Avendanno, and Ochoa Urtiz de Susunaga, and Pero Sáenz de Salazar, and Pero Urtiz de Aguirre, and Martín Sáenz de Asua, and Gonçalo Yvannez de Marquina, and Gonçalo de Arançibia, and Rui Martínez de Arançibia, and Ochoa López de Urquiça, and Martín Ruiz de Alviz, and Martín Yvánnez de Garunaga, and Pero Yvánez de Alviz, and Lope Gonçález de Aguero, and Diego de Asua, and Pedro de Garay, and Martín de Mendieta, and Pero de Uriarte, and Sancho Martínez de Goyri, a notary, and Ochoa Guerras de Lexarrçacun and Sancho Urtiz de Arandoaga.

And each one of them stated: that as the said *corregidor* knew well how the Bizkaians had their privileges and exemptions and liberties and other *fueros* that were of *albedrío* and not in writing. And (he knew) as well the damages, harms and errors into which the said Bizkaians and those of the Encartaciones and Durango region have befallen and befall everyday for not having, in written form as they could have been reasonably written down, and from which they would have been able to agree, as they could have, about said exemptions and liberties and *fueros* and customs. And to write down and arrange said exemptions and liberties and usages and customs and *fuero* and *albedrío*, all of the said Bizkaians, being assembled in the General Assembly in Ydoyualçaga, that elected and empowered them, in that as one and with the said doctor and *corregidor*, they would organize, proclaim and write down said exemptions and liberties and usages and customs and *fueros*, and *albedrío* that said Bizkaians had, in the most correct manner that they reasonably can in order that they may be preserved. Because being thusly written down and proclaimed, his royal highness the King and Prince, Lord of Bizkaia, can confirm them as his Fuero and then exemptions and liberties and usages and customs would be safeguarded.

Therefore they asked and entreated the aforementioned doctor and *corregidor* to please receive from them and from each one of them a proper, and that he desire to arrange and write down the aforementioned in cooperation with them.

And then the doctor and *corregidor* said that it was true that the Bizkaians had their own exemptions and liberties, as well as their usages and customs and *fuero* of *albedrío* by which they judged and ruled themselves. And because they were not written down, much harm was done and many questions were raised. Consequently, it pleased him to count himself as one of them in arranging and writing down the said exemptions and liberties and usages and *fuero* and *alvedrío* and in all that was in God's service and of the said Lord King, and the common-weal of the land.

And to that [end] he accepted and received an oath from the afore-mentioned and from each one of them, making them place their right hands physically on the cross while swearing their oath. Each one of them swore to God and Holy Mary and on the sign of the cross that they touched physically with their right hands, and on the words of the Holy Gospels, wherever they might be, that they and each of them would declare, organize and write down well and faithfully, and with-out deceit or artifice or ardor [without partisanship], the said exemp-tions and freedoms and usages and customs and *fueros* and *alvedrío* that the Bizkaians have and had and that they would do so to the best of their God-given ability in such a manner that it might serve God and the said Lord King, and the commonweal of the said Land and the Bizkaians who dwell there.

And all of the aforementioned and each and every one of them said that they swear and swore to do so.

And later the said doctor and *corregidor* swore them in by saying that by so doing [fulfilling their pledge] all-powerful God might help them in this world of the flesh and in the other world of the souls. And if they were to do otherwise, God would treat them harshly and dearly in this world of the flesh and fortune, and in the other of souls as [He does] with those who take the holy name of God in vain. Each and every one of the aforementioned responded to the swearing in by saying: amen.

The oath having been thereby sworn, then the said doctor and *cor-regidor* stated that since he was busy with certain matters in the service of the said Lord King, he consequently ordered and ordained that all the aforementioned agree on and declare and organize and write down the said exemptions and freedoms and usages and customs and *fueros* of *alvedrío* that the Bizkaians have always had and have, and by which they maintain and have maintained themselves and judge and judged themselves in the most just manner that they could and to the best of their God-given ability. And once the laws were written down and organized, he would see them and all other Bizkaians together. And they should beg the most exalted Lord and Prince and King that it please him to confirm such exemptions and liberties and *fuero* and their good usages and customs by virtue of which they would be able to live and maintain [themselves] because men would know and be sure of what *fueros* and usages and customs and exemptions and freedoms they had.

And reaching an agreement, the aforementioned, without the said doctor, said the very exalted King and Lord Don Juan, as Lord of Bizkaia, had to come to swear before them according to the practice and the custom of his predecessors, the past Lords of Bizkaia.

He had to take the oath in the aforementioned church of Gernika and in certain other places to safeguard all the privileges and exemptions and liberties and *fueros* and usages and customs in the Villas as well as in the Tierras Llanas of Bizkaia and in the Encartaciones and the Durango region because said Villas and Tierra Llanas have *fueros* and customs apart from the written privileges of said Villas.

And the said Lord and King, as Lord of Bizkaia, could not take them away from them nor add to them nor give them any new [ones] unless he should do so in Bizkaia, beneath the Tree of Gernika in General Assembly and with the consent of the said Bizkaians. To avoid falling into the errors and wrongs and injuries into which they have befallen before, it was well to write down and enumerate all the freedoms and exemptions and customs and usages and *alvedríos* and privileges that the said Villas and Tierra Llana had but not in writing, at which time the said King and Lord should come to swear to safeguard them and to confirm them and give them as *fuero*.

They said that the exemptions and freedoms and usages and customs of the said Bizkaians, and that they had all presently agreed on, and which had always been safeguarded for them by the said Lords that there have been in Bizkaia, were the following.

### 1.   How and in What Manner the Lord of Bizkaia Must Be Sworn.

First they said that the Bizkaians have as law and usage and custom that whenever a new Lord succeeds in the Seigniory of Bizkaia, whether he succeeds in the said Seigniory of Bizkaia and the Encartaciones and Durango by the death of another Lord who went before him or by any other title.

That if such Lord who newly succeeds in the said Seigniory of Bizkaia is fourteen years old, he must come in person to Bizkaia and there he must take the oaths and promises and confirm for them [the Bizkaians] their privileges and usages and customs and exemptions and freedoms and laws and lands and grants which they have from him.

And if he is older than said fourteen years, and on behalf of Bizkaians, those from the Villas, as well as from the Tierra Llana, the said Lord of Bizkaia, who newly succeeds in said Seigniory, is required to come to Bizkaia to these places where he should take an oath to confirm their freedoms and exemptions and laws and usages and customs, within one year of the day when the requirement should be met [i.e. the day he accedes to the throne].

If he does not come, then the Bizkaians, those of the Villas, as well as those of the Tierra Llana of Bizkaia, the Encartaciones and Durango need not respond to the petition of the said Lord King, Lord of Bizkaia, nor to his treasurer or tax collector, nor should they receive or obey his letters until such time that he comes to swear and confirm the said exemptions and privileges and freedoms and laws and customs and lands and grants.

And from that day on which he comes to take said oath, all Bizkaians, accordingly those of the Villas as those of the Tierras Llanas of Bizkaia and of the Encartaciones and those of Durango, shall accept him with all the petitions and rights that the said Lord of Bizkaia has in Bizkaia, and they shall obey his letters and comply with his orders as they would their own Lord. But if the aforementioned demands are passed over [i.e. the King fails to appear to take the oath] after the said year from the day [of succession] required by Bizkaians had passed, then he has no right to assess [them], excepting only the fees for the iron foundries which the Lord might have in Bizkaia, whether he comes to swear or not.

2. **That Even If the Lord Does Not Come to Swear, the Officials Shall Occupy Their Offices.**

They also said that since the *veedores*, *prestameros*, *alcaldes*, *merinos*, *sayones* and *bozineros* were in the habit of occupying their offices, they would do so, whether the Lord came to swear or not, except in such cases where the said Lord of Bizkaia, after coming to swear, should find a reason to deprive them of office.

3. **What, Where and How the King and Lord of Bizkaia Must Swear.**

Furthermore they said that when the King and Lord of Bizkaia comes to Bizkaia to take the oath at the gates of the city of Bilbo, he must [place his hands] in the hands of some of the inhabitants of Bilbo and promise as King and Lord to keep and safeguard for the Villas and Tierras Llanas of Bizkaia and Durango and of the Encartaciones and all those residents therein, all the privileges and exemptions and rights and laws and usages and customs and lands and grants that they have received from him, according to what they had received in previous times and what was reserved for them. And afterward he must come to Aretxabalaga and the Bizkaians there must receive him and kiss his hand as Lord.

And afterward he must go to the church of San Meteri y Çeledon, and there he must swear on the consecrated body of God, held by the priest dressed in his priestly vestments that he will truly safeguard and maintain and have safeguarded and maintained all the exemptions and liberties and laws and usages and customs that all Bizkaians, as well as those of the Encartaciones and Durango, that *cavalleros* and *escuderos*, *fijosdalgo* and *labradores* had and have traditionally and until now, in the lands and grants that they received from the King's father, as Lord of Bizkaia, and which they received from him and from the other Lords in the manner and form that they had them and made use of them.

And afterward he will come to Gernika beneath the tree where the Assembly is customarily held, [announced by] the blowing of the five horns. And there, with the consent of the Bizkaians, if some [laws] should be deleted and others amended, and with said agreement, he shall delete them and create new ones if need be and shall confirm all the liberties and exemptions and laws and usages and customs that said Bizkaians have, and the lands and grants that the said Bizkaians had and have from the King and from past Lords, and in the manner that said lands and grants were used until now.

And upon going to Bermio, he must go to Santa Eufemia and before the altar of Santa Eufemia, place his hand on the consecrated body of God, while the priest in his vestments holds it in his hands, and swear that he will well and truly safeguard the liberties and exemptions and privileges and usages and customs of the Bizkaians, those from the Villas as well as from the Tierras Llanas of Bizkaia, and the Encartaciones and from Durango have possessed until now and in the manner in which they have had them.

### 4. How Much Is the Tax of Bizkaia and Who Must Pay It.

They also said that the Lords of Bizkaia had always had from the *labradores* their certain tax assessment (*pedido*) [and?] in the Villas of Bizkaia. And depending on the privileges granted to those Villas, they had always received said taxes in the amount of sixteen pieces of old money for each quintal of iron processed in the foundries of Bizkaia, and of the Encartaciones and of Durango [in payment] of the firewood from the mountains. And from their monasteries. And half of the reserved green timber in the accustomed mountains. And their mountain pastures (*seles*). And the *prebostades* of the Villas. Income derived from rights of patronage over an endowed church.[*]

And the Bizkaians and those of the Encartaciones and from Durango never had another assessment nor tribute, nor sales tax (*alcavala*),

---

[*] Reference is not to monasteries of religious orders; the word refers in this case to a particular church over which a benefactor, in this case the King, held claims.

nor monetary payments, nor services. Before all the noble Bizkaians and the Bizkaian *fijosdalgo* and of the Encartaciones and of Durango were always exempt and free and relieved of all assessments and services and monetary payments and sales taxes and whatever other tributes of whatever kind, being thus in Bizkaia and in the Encartaciones as in Durango, as in the Villas, excepting the taxed assessment (*pedido*) that said *labradores* have to pay in each one year [and] the same in the Villas, to the Lord of Bizkaia, for the privileges that were given to them by the Lords of Bizkaia.

5. **Concerning the Same Service.**

Furthermore they said, concerning service, that the Bizkaians must render [it] to the Lord of Bizkaia, according to how their ancestors served the Lords who were in Bizkaia before, on land as well as on the sea.

6. **Concerning Salary [for Military Service].**

Furthermore they said that the *cavalleros* and *escuderos* and *fijosdalgo* from the Villas as well as the Tierra Llana from the said Countship of Bizkaia were always used to and accustomed to going wherever and whenever the Lord of Bizkaia wanted them to, without any salary, for whatever reason he would call them into service, serving as far as the Malato Tree which is in Lujando. And if the Lord in his lordship should order them to go beyond said Malato Tree, then the Lord owes [them] two months' salary if they have to go as far as the mountain passes, and three months' salary if they must go beyond the passes. And being thus paid at the accustomed place, the *cavalleros* and *escuderos* and *hidalgos* of the Countship are accustomed and have been to accompany the Lord in his service wherever he might send them.

And if the said Lord did not give them the said salary at the Malato Oak, from then on they were not prepared nor accustomed to go beyond that point. And the *cavalleros* and *escuderos* and *fijosdalgo* were used to and accustomed accordingly, and such was always safeguarded for them by the Lords of Bizkaia.

7. **That Foodstuffs that Come into Bizkaia Shall Not Leave without Permission.**

Furthermore the said Bizkaians stated and agreed that they had as law and usage and custom and exemption and freedom that once bread and meat and barley and salt and any other foodstuffs entered Bizkaia whether by sea or by land, and had been unloaded in the land of Bizkaia, no one should dare to take them out of Bizkaia by sea or land, except with permission of the *Hermandad* of the place where such foodstuffs were located, under penalty of losing the bread and salt and barley and legumes and whatever other foodstuffs there might be, in the following manner: half for whoever seized it and the other half for the Lord.

But the King, as the Lord of Bizkaia, could take wheat and bread and legumes for his border fortifications, if needed, as well as for his provisioning of merchant vessels and warships. And [seagoing vessels and warships] could take baked bread and wheat and flour and meat and foodstuffs for a specific voyage, but not to sell. And if it were proven that it was sold, the ship or ships on which the foodstuffs were [carried] would be forfeited, half [to go] to the denunciator and the other half to the Lord.

## 8. That Half of the Sustenance That Comes by Sea to the Coast Shall Remain in Bizkaia.

Furthermore they said that they had as a *fuero* and custom that any foreign ship that should come with foodstuffs to the coast of Bizkaia should unload half of such food and sell it in the prescribed manner, and the other half may be taken wherever desired, except to the enemies of the King, and thus of the Lord of Bizkaia. And if one should carry food to the King's enemies and it be proven against him, then anyone may take the foodstuffs and the ship from him without penalty.

## 9. That Ships Carrying Foodstuffs Shall Not Be Seized for Reasons of [Letters of] Reprisal, or Privateer's Commission, If They Belong to Friends of the King.

Furthermore they said that in the Land of Bizkaia and of the Encartaciones and of Durango is very mountainous, and wheat is neither sown nor harvested, nor do they have other foodstuffs with which to support themselves, except for the wheat and barley and meat and salt and broad beans and other legumes which customarily come to them by sea.

And through reprisals and privateers' commissions which are carried out against the Bretons as well as against the French, who are friends of the King our Lord; and since the ships and foodstuffs that are brought by the said French and Bretons are seized by those who have such privateers' commissions and [letters of] reprisal against them, [neither] the Bretons nor the French dare to come to the Bizkaian coast and that of the Encartaciones with any foodstuffs on their ships. For that reason this coast—the Villas as well as the Tierras Llanas of Bizkaia and the Encartaciones and of Durango—is in great need and suffers a shortage.

For that reason they very humbly implore the said Lord King that he do them the favor [of commanding] that after the Bretons and French, and any others who are friends of the said Lord King, arrive in the coastal ports of Bizkaia or of the Encartaciones or their natural harbors with foodstuffs, their goods shall not be seized nor shall such foodstuffs be taken nor shall their ships nor any other item of theirs [be taken] because of any letter of reprisal or any privateers' commission that anyone holds against the Bretons, the French and other friends of the said Lord King, [but] rather that [the King] shall order them to come and load and unload their foodstuffs freely and unmolested and sell them.

And that [the Bizkaians] may sell iron and any other merchandise that [the shippers] would like to take away, as long as it is not foodstuffs nor other forbidden items, and the shipper may take those items anywhere he likes as long as they are not [intended] for the enemies of the said Lord King, as Lord of Bizkaia.

And let it be [the King's] will that the following prohibition be implemented in the courts of the Villas, as well as those of the Tierras Llanas of Bizkaia and of the Encartaciones: that neither their cargoes nor those [ships] which bring foodstuffs shall be subject to seizure [to satisfy an unfulfilled pledge] and shall be allowed to go freely and quit the ports and natural harbors, as is hereby stated.[*]

10. **The Lands and Grants of the Bizkaians Should Not Be Transferred [as such] to Castillian Registries, Nor Should the Registrars Allow Them to Be So Registered.**

Furthermore all the Bizkaians, those of the Villas as those of the Tierra Llana of Bizkaia, [and] of Durango and of the Encartaciones stated that many Bizkaians and persons from Durango and others who are not from Bizkaia, neither of Durango nor of the Encartaciones, buy lands that some Castillian subjects of our Lord the King had in Castilla for large amounts of *maravedís*. And once the lands were purchased, the [purchasers] went to the registrars in the Castillian places where they had bought the properties. They registered and transferred them in the registrars' books [as Bizkaian] so that the said lands of said Bizkaians and non-Bizkaians would be included in the tax assessment of Bizkaia,

---

[*] Letters of reprisal and privateers' commissions were presented to privately-owned armed vessels by heads of state, allowing those vessels to make raids on the ships of unfriendly nations. Evidently, these letters and commissions were not always rescinded after formerly unfriendly nations became allies or friends.

and the *maravedís* of the rents of the production of the iron foundries that the Lord of Bizkaia should have annually. For that reason, the Bizkaians who from time immemorial held lands and grants in Bizkaia, are harmed and damaged by the transfer of such purchased lands. Because the *maravedís* that there should be from such lands and grants do not come here to Bizkaia.

For that reason they ask as a favor of said Lord King, as Lord of Bizkaia, that he command the registrars, that from now on, whenever person or persons, whether Bizkaians or from elsewhere, buy land from someone who lives or resides outside of Bizkaia and of the Encartaciones and of Durango, that they order and prohibit that the registrars effect such transfer of said land gained and purchased from a vassal who lives in Castile by said Bizkaians or person from the Encartaciones or Durango, or others from elsewhere, to the tax assessment and rents of Bizkaia and of the Encartaciones and of Durango.

And if some have purchased and obtained [lands] up until now from someone who does not reside in Bizkaia, Bizkaians and the *veedor* and the *alcaldes* will be paid first from the lands and grants and salaries and incomes that they have from said Lord King and Lord of Bizkaia, before paying the purchase of such lands that were bought and obtained from those who do not live in Bizkaia, nor in the Encartaciones, nor in Durango that were transferred to the registries and assessments and rents of Bizkaia, etc.

**11.  That No Villa Shall Be Created by the Lord of Bizkaia, Unless He Is Present in the Assembly of Gernika.**

Furthermore the Bizkaians had as law and usage and custom that the Lord of Bizkaia could not order the creation of any *villa* in Bizkaia, except in the Assembly of Gernika, [convened by the traditional] blowing of the five horns, and with all the Bizkaians giving their consent. Since all of the mountains, tracts and commons belong to the Lord of Bizkaia and to the *fijosdalgo* and towns equally (*a medias*), he cannot create any *villa* nor order one created, nor make it a terminus, in any [land] belonging to the said *fijosdalgo* and towns, etc.

**12.  That There Shall Be No Admiral in Bizkaia, Nor Shall the Bizkaians Be Subject to Any Admiral.**

Furthermore the said Bizkaians, those from the Villas as those of the Tierra Llana de Bizkaia and Durango and of the Encartaciones, stated that they have been exempt and free by usage and custom, for as long as can be remembered, from having any admiral or admiral's official [in Bizkaia], from answering his call, from obeying his commands either at sea or on land, and from paying any tribute or tax there might be for anything that they take with their ships at sea or on land, since the said Villas and Tierras Llanas have always belonged to and still belong to the King, as the Lord of Bizkaia, and not to anyone else. [The Bizkaians] have always obeyed and will obey the letters and orders of that Lord, as if he were their Lord, which do not go against their *fueros* and usages and customs and privileges. The Lord of Bizkaia, as Lord of Bizkaia, never had an admiral in the Seigniory of Bizkaia, nor does he have one today.

### 13. That the Bizkaians Cannot Be Summoned Outside of Bizkaia, Even by Their Lord, but Rather Only Before Their Own *Veedor* and *Alcaldes*.

Furthermore the said Bizkaians and inhabitants of Durango and the Encartaciones and the Tierras Llanas stated that they are exempt from answering in any venue any summons that might be directed at them by the Lord of Bizkaia or his officials, for any suit that someone might file against them, or that they might have against another, because of wrongdoing that they have committed or done, or over an inheritance, or because of a contract that they might make in the Tierras Llanas. Rather whoever wanted to file a suit regarding such contracts and wrongdoings and inheritance that were agreed to or committed or held in the said Tierra Llanas must do so before their *veedor* and their *alcaldes* and not before anyone else outside of the jurisdiction of Bizkaia and the Encartaciones and of Durango, unless the *veedor* and *alcaldes* and *prestamero* and the *merino* of the said Tierras Llanas should fail in their duties [in which case] they may be summoned by order of the Lord King to wherever the Lord of Bizkaia might be, even if he be outside of the Seigniory of Bizkaia.

Otherwise no one from the said Tierras Llanas is obliged to comply with such a summons, even if he is summoned in one of the cases that is reserved by law for the court of our Lord the King, unless he was summoned for dueling. Whoever should be summoned for that reason must appear before the Lord of Bizkaia wherever he might be in the entire Kingdom of Castile, and there the problem must be resolved wherever the said Lord is to be found. And that they ask of him the said Lord King the favor that he might wish to preserve for all Bizkaians their exemptions and freedoms and usages and customs.

### 14. That the Bizkaians Are Free to Buy and Sell in Their Homes, Preserving Their Customs and Privileges to the Villas.

Furthermore all *fijosdalgo* are free and exempt to buy and sell in their homes, and to receive textiles and iron and other merchandise, whatever it might be, the privileges, usages and customs which they have enjoyed until now being preserved for the Villas, unless some persons received privileges from the Lord of Bizkaia which are contradictory, in which case those privileges are safeguarded.

## 15.  Decree from the Lord.

Furthermore whatever decree that the Lord of Bizkaia hands down in opposition to the Fuero of Bizkaia shall be obeyed but not complied with.

## 16.  Freedom to Sell in Their Houses.

Furthermore they said that the *fijosdalgo* and *labradores* of the Tierras Llanas of the Countship of Bizkaia shall be exempt and free to sell bread and wine and cider and meat and other foodstuffs in their houses and in any other districts, at the price [fixed by] the *fieles* of that *anteiglesia*.

## 17.  Concerning Justice Officials.

Furthermore they said that all of the justices of Bizkaia and of the Encartaciones, the *veedor*, as well as the *prestamero* and the *alcaldes* and *merinos* and *sayones* and *vocineros*, are appointed by the said Lord of Bizkaia.

The *veedor* and *prestamero* and *alcaldes* and *merinos* must be appointed by the said Lord of Bizkaia and not by anyone else.

And the *sayones* and *vocineros* shall be appointed by the *merinos*, each one in his *merindad* or [and] in the usual places.

And if it should happen that in places where there used to be said *vocineros* and *sayones* there are vacancies, then those *bosineros* and *sayones* must be replaced. And if it is agreed to replace them, the *alcaldes de Fuero* should appoint them, and if the *alcaldes*, each in his own *merindad*, cannot agree on the appointments, then they should meet with the *alcaldes* of other *merindades* and if those *alcaldes* cannot agree, then the *veedor* shall appoint them.

And the Lord shall assign to those *sayones* and *vocineros* the accustomed *fogueras** accordingly as was the usage and custom in times past and until now.

---

* The *fogueras* (hearths) were the family units or households used by the *sayónes* and *vocineros* for calculating and collecting taxes.

18. **The Lord Shall Appoint Five** *Alcaldes,* **and the** *Veedor* **Will Be Wherever the Lord Wishes.**

Furthermore they said that they had as *fuero* and usage and custom in Bizkaia that there should be five *alcaldes* [*de Fuero*] and that these should be appointed by the Lord. It should be noted [that there are] three in the *merindad* of Busturia and two in the *merindad* of Uribe.

And each of these should be a landowner and credible, and in his *merindad* and each should be a resident of the *merindad* where he is *alcalde.*

Furthermore the Lord shall appoint a *veedor* and a *prestamero* wherever his Lordship wishes.

19. **Concerning Those Same** *Alcaldes de Fuero.*

Furthermore let it be known [that] the five *alcaldes de Fuero* of Bizkaia have their separate jurisdictions, which are as follows: the two *alcaldes* of the Merindad of Uribe shall be in charge of the lawsuits of that *merindad* and the three *alcaldes* of the Merindad of Busturia [shall be in charge of those] in Busturia.

But at times one or more of the *alcaldes* of the Merindad of Uribe take charge of suits which pertain to the Merindad of Busturia and, having no jurisdiction, they give orders for the confiscation and auctioning off [of property]; and even though those *alcaldes* reside in the Merindad of Uribe they have their *logartenientes* in the Merindad of Busturia. And the *alcaldes* of Busturia behave in this same way.

Which they said was against the *fueros* and customs of the Land of Bizkaia, and against the best interests of its residents, since neither the *alcaldes* of one *merindad* nor the other can legally hear a case from the other *merindad* since it is out of their jurisdiction, except for [cases of] appeal in which the *alcaldes* of the Merindad of Uribe can take charge of cases which were first prosecuted and concluded before the *alcaldes* of the Merindad of Busturia; and in this same way the two *alcaldes* of the Merindad of Uribe shall hear cases in that Merindad and the *alcaldes* of the Merindad of Busturia shall not, unless it were by appeal, [the case] being first prosecuted and concluded before the said *alcaldes* of the Merindad of Uribe in the manner set forth above, since that was always the *fuero* and custom there.

And whatever might be done or ordered by the said *alcaldes* in another manner is not valid.

## 20. Concerning the [Court of] First Instance.

Furthermore let it be known that according to anciently preserved custom in Bizkaia, the *corregidor* and the *veedor*, whoever they might be, may not take charge of any civil suits, except in criminal cases and [those] of injury, without those civil cases first being prosecuted and concluded before the *alcaldes de Fuero* of Bizkaia, and afterward in order of appeal to the *corregidor* and *veedor* as [a] higher judge.

But here lately they have been taking charge of any and all civil suits, delivering summons to anyone regarding inheritances as well as debts and disputes, and drawing up petitions and executing documents, and forfeiting people's property. All of which the *corregidor* and *veedor* were doing against the customs and to the detriment of the said *alcaldes* and residents of the Tierra Llana.

And consequently they said that, according to said *fuero* and custom, any *corregidor* and *veedor* that there might be in Bizkaia should not and could not take charge of any civil suits of any nature, except in the course of an appeal, [the case] being first prosecuted and concluded before the *alcaldes*, and afterward [brought before] the *corregidor* as a superior judge in the course of an appeal. Nor can he hand down any decision to divide any inheritance, nor execute any documents, nor issue any summons against any person for any civil cause, unless the one so summoned should be a vagrant who has no worldly goods to offer as security, [but he may issue a summons in] criminal and personal injury cases ordering that someone go to give testimony in investigations or in some case that came before him.

And if someone were summoned by his order, except for the above-mentioned reasons, and the person summoned appoints a *fiador* as a guarantee that he will comply with the law before his *alcaldes*, he will not be required to go in fulfillment of that summons, and the one who summoned [him] shall pay a fine of six hundred *maravedís* to the summoned person. And if by not complying with the summons [a person] were to be accused of contempt (*reveldía*), he shall not be required for contempt to forfeit his guarantee, nor shall he be considered in contempt. And if the *prestamero* or the *merino* or the *sayón* or anyone else were to seize the guarantee because of that contempt, he could prevent them doing so without any penalty; and if he could not prevent them [from taking his surety] by himself and he were to call [for assistance] upon the residents of the *anteiglesia* where such happened, they should defend him and protect him under penalty of one thousand and one hundred *maravedís* to go to the party that was thus summoned and [whose guarantee was] seized.

## 21. Where, How and How Many *Logartenientes* Can Be Appointed.

Furthermore [they said] that the *corregidor* cannot appoint more than one *logarteniente* to carry out his duties in the Merindades of Busturia and Uribe and Arratia and Bedia and Zornotza and Markina, and one other *logarteniente* in the Merindad of Durango.

And the Durango *logarteniente* may not carry out his duties nor officiate over any legal arguments outside of the said Merindad of Durango. But the *logarteniente* for the other said *merindades*, whoever it may be, may carry out [the duties of office] and officiate over any criminal and civil legal arguments in the said Merindad of Durango, as well as in the other aforementioned *merindades*. But if the *veedor* would like to appoint someone to undertake investigation of some special suit, he may do so and appoint whomever he wishes, even though he has the aforenamed *logartenientes*.

## 22. The *Corregidor* Shall Not Receive Anything from Anybody.

Furthermore since the King our Lord of Bizkaia has, as he has always had in Bizkaia, a *corregidor* and *veedor,* and pays them a salary as it pleases His Lordship, any *corregidor* and *veedor* of Bizkaia is expected to carry out his duties without being paid any salary by the Bizkaian people.

And for that reason neither the *corregidor* nor the *veedor* nor any *logarteniente* or commissioner of theirs shall receive any salary or anything for carrying out said office, nor [for] undertaking and making investigations or any inquiry, be it specialized or general, and he shall carry out his duties without receiving any remuneration whatsoever [from anyone other than the King], under pain of falling into the situation in which by law befall the judges who receive a bribe.

## 23. Concerning Notaries.

Furthermore the *corregidor* shall receive any notary of good reputation from the Countship of Bizkaia, as well as the Villas and the Tierra Llana, in whatever civil or criminal suit that the plaintiff might bring, and before whomever he wishes, to handle his suit and undertake his investigation, since such has been the custom in times past until now.

## 24. That Notaries Who Come from Outside [Bizkaia] Shall Leave Behind Their Records.

Furthermore any notary from outside the said Countship who works with the *corregidor* and *veedor* shall leave all the records that passed through his hands in the keeping of some notary of good repute who is a resident of the Countship, and he shall not take them away or carry them out of the Countship. And in order to do and safeguard and comply, he shall appoint well propertied *fiadores* who are residents of the said Countship, and the notary shall take an oath in Santa María of Gernika swearing to do this. And until the notary complies with the aforementioned, he shall not have use of the said office, nor will the said *corregidor* receive him in any other manner.

**25. That the *Alcalde de Fuero* Shall Not Preside over Criminal Cases, or How and When [Exceptions Shall Be Made].**

Furthermore the *alcaldes de Fuero* shall not accept any criminal action, nor carry out any investigation, except in conjunction with the *alcalde de Hermandad*. And with the *alcalde de Hermandad* they may accept the case and make inquiries and proceed with the case, but not without the *alcalde de Hermandad*. But if the plaintiff [who] files a suit with both the *alcalde de Hermandad* and with the *alcalde de Fuero* wishes to go before the *veedor* with the inquiry that the *alcaldes* undertook, he may do so, and the *corregidor* may preside over and proceed with the case with the *alcaldes* or without them, even if the suit be filed and the inquiry undertaken by the said *alcaldes*, according to the law of the Codex of Bizkaia and in the manner required by it.

**26. One Who Is Summoned to Appear beneath the Tree [of Gernika] May Present Oneself before the *Corregidor*, Even Though Summoned by Another Judge or an Inferior *Alcalde*.**

Furthermore if the *alcalde de Hermandad* alone, or in conjunction with the *alcalde de Fuero,* both together, has accepted a suit and undertaken an inquiry and summons someone [to appear] beneath the tree of Gernika on a certain date, and the person summoned should prefer to present himself or herself before the *corregidor* [instead], he or she may do so. And the *corregidor* may preside over the case from that moment on even though the summons was issued by the *alcaldes*.

**27. Concerning [Who Shall] Preside over [Civil] Suits.**

Furthermore [they said] that the *alcaldes de Fuero* shall preside over all civil suits, and not the *corregidor* nor the *veedor*, except in the course of an appeal according to [what] is capitulated above.

**28. That the *Alcaldes de la Tierra* Shall Not Preside over [Cases Concerning] a Higher Quantity than Forty-Eight *Maravedís* in Old Money.**

Furthermore let it be known that the Merindades of Arratia and Bedia are under the jurisdiction of the *alcaldes* of the Merindad of

Uribe. And in Arratia and other *anteiglesias* and *merindades* they have *alcaldes de la Tierra* who have jurisdiction over and preside over suits brought before them concerning movable property, up to the amount of forty eight *maravedís* of old money. But sometimes, in some cases, the *alcaldes de la Tierra* preside over suits of even greater value than the forty eight *maravedís* at the request and consent of the parties [involved].

Therefore they said that they had as *fuero* and usage and custom that no *alcalde de la Tierra* from such *merindades* and lands could preside over suits of greater value than the said forty-eight *maravedís* of old money, even if it were at the request and consent of the parties [involved], unless it were at the request of the parties and on the authority of one of the *alcaldes de Fuero* [in which case they] could preside and pass sentence.

Any local *alcalde de Fuero* or *alcaldes de la Tierra* who go against this [rule] shall suffer the penalty of one who carries out the duties of office under foreign jurisdiction. And whatever sentence or sentences are handed down by any or all of them shall be worthless, even if it were given at the request and consent of both parties.

And the plaintiff who files such a suit shall have to pay the defendant the penalty of forty-eight *maravedís* in old money. And if the defendant does not wish to demand this fine, then the *alcalde de Fuero* may demand the fine from [the plaintiff] for himself within nine days, but not after nine days have passed.

But since in some such places they have the usage and custom of appearing before the *alcaldes de la Tierra* first, and not before the *alcaldes de Fuero*, whether [the case] is about real estate or movable property, regardless of how much money is involved, the said *alcaldes de la Tierra* shall draw lots in the presence of the *alcaldes de Fuero*. And in such a case the above-mentioned penalties shall not be in effect for appearing before the *alcalde de la Tierra*, but rather they shall follow [those customs] according to how they were followed and safeguarded up until now.

Furthermore it shall be [done] in this same manner in the Merindad of Busturia as well as in the Merindad of Uribe. And these *alcaldes de la Tierra* shall not receive any fees, except for six *maravedís* for each judgment they hand down.

## 29. Concerning the *Alcaldes de Fuero*.

Furthermore whenever the *alcaldes de Fuero* wish to work with and be with the *corregidor* and *veedor* in some location, [they may do so] even if it means that one or more of the *alcaldes* of the Merindad of Uribe has to go to the Merindad of Busturia, or one of [the *alcaldes*] of the Merindad of Busturia to the Merindad of Uribe, or in suits judged

by the *alcaldes* assembled a *locue*<sup>*</sup> and without the *corregidor*. [In this
latter case] the *alcaldes* of one *merindad* may preside over and pass
judgment in the others' *merindad* together, without any penalty. Because
this has always been the usage and custom in Bizkaia.

### 30. Concerning Those Same *Alcaldes de Fuero*.

Furthermore they said, that according to *fuero* and usage and custom of Bizkaia the *alcaldes de Fuero* were required to go wherever the
*corregidor* and the *veedor* should call them within the said Bizkaia to
consult with them and to judge any complaint or civil or criminal suit
[at any time].

### 31. Concerning the *Alcaldes de las Ferrerías* (Judges of the Iron Foundries).

Furthermore they said that there were *alcaldes de ferrería* in Bizkaia, and they were to preside over and judge the suits that occurred
between the owners of the foundries and the workers. And those
*alcaldes* were to preside over those cases [only] and carry out [their
duties] according to usage and custom, and nothing more.

### 32. Concerning the Presiding over Cases by the *Fieles* (Mayors).

Furthermore they said that they had as *fuero* and usage and custom
that the *fieles* of the *anteiglesias* of the Land of Bizkaia may sit in judgment and hand down penalties and punishments in cases regarding
insults and violations of their *anteiglesias*' ordinances. And these *fieles*
shall carry out [their duties] and shall preside over [cases involving] a
quantity of up to 110 *maravedís*.

And concerning the sentence that such *fieles* shall give in each of
their *anteiglesias*, there shall be no appeal [neither] before the *alcalde de
Fuero* nor before the *veedor*, unless [the appeal is to go] before the *fieles*
of another *anteiglesia*.

And if the *fieles* of the second *anteiglesia* find that those of the first
handed down a valid judgment, then he who appealed shall pay double
the penalty. And once the *fieles* of the second *anteiglesia* confirm the
penalty and sentence, if an appeal [is made] to a third *anteiglesia* and
the *fieles* of the third *anteiglesia* confirm the first two sentences, then he
who appealed [the case] shall pay 1,100 *maravedís* to the *anteiglesia*
where that [violation] occurred.

---

<sup>*</sup> A meeting of all of the *alcaldes de Fuero* in order to review the appeal of a deci-
sion handed down by one of them.

And if the *fieles* of the second *anteiglesia* or the third overturn the first sentence, then the [first] *fieles* shall pay the amount to the person against whom the sentence was passed.

And if the *fieles* of the three *anteiglesias* should be discordant and should not agree, then in such a case the party who feels injured may appeal to the *veedor*, [and] the sentence handed down by the *veedor* shall be valid.

### 33. Concerning Arbitration.

Furthermore they said that they had as *fuero* and usage and custom that if some persons had a question, complaint or debate among themselves in the Tierras Llanas of Bizkaia about any civil matter, and if in order to rid themselves of such complaints and questions and debates they wish to put [it] in the hands of arbitrators, they may do so according to their wishes with the authority of one of the *alcaldes de Fuero*, and in no other manner.

And any sentence or sentences handed down by such arbitrators shall be binding, as if it were the sentence of the *alcalde de Fuero*; but, before they hand down a decision, those arbitrators shall make the parties [involved] each provide two *fiadores* to [guarantee that they will] be present, comply with, and pay whatever might be ordered and determined. And there shall be no room for appeal nor *alvedrío* recourse to [judgment] of a good man, nor for any other appeal.

### 34. Concerning the Time for Hearing Cases.

Furthermore the *alcaldes de Fuero* shall hold their hearings in the houses where they reside, once a day from the hour of tierce* until noon and not afterwards, unless there is a case or cases left over to which they are assigned by the *prestamero* or the *merino*, or other cases that may require it. And in those cases which last the whole day, the parties shall be given a time at which they may appear before such an *alcalde*, and he shall hear them as if they had appeared before noon.

And if the *alcalde* was not going to be at home, he should leave another in his place to hear the complaints and deliberate. But there shall be no suit until he returns to his house, unless both parties find him wherever he is in his jurisdiction. And both parties shall be required to go and keep their appointment at the house of the *alcalde* before whom [the case] is pending.

---

* Tierce = the canonical hour of 9 a.m. Thus, the *alcaldes* held audiences daily for three hours until noon.

And if the *alcalde* does not act accordingly, he shall pay the costs of that day to the parties [involved] and he shall be constrained by the *veedor* to pay them.

### 35. Concerning Suits over Income and Allowances.

Furthermore they said that they had as *fuero* and of custom in the Tierra Llana of Bizkaia that the suits that arise over income in trust, as it is with other properties in Bizkaia, and the suits that arise over living allowances, shall be judged by the *alcaldes de Fuero* of Bizkaia, and according to its *fuero*.

### 36. Concerning the Summons.

Furthermore they said that they had as *fuero* and of usage and of custom that any investigation concerning civil or criminal wrongdoings that might be committed in Bizkaia for which some person or persons should be summoned, must be made public under the tree of Gernika where the Assembly is held.

And those involved and implicated by the investigation must be summoned [to appear] under the said tree according to *fuero* and usage and custom, and outlawed there if they fail to appear within the allowed time.

And if some of those who were outlawed for the wrongdoing they had committed should wish to save themselves and face the charges before the plaintiffs, they must do so if they can, under the tree of Gernika where the Assembly is held. And there they must be heard and judged, and there they must be acquitted or condemned, and not in any other place, unless the accuser and the accused both agree that the hearings may be held in another place, and not under the tree of Gernika.

But the outlawed cannot be exonerated, even if both parties consent, except under the said tree. And the *prestamero* may hold the accused prisoners where it is understood that they may be kept more safely, as long as he brings them to the hearings at the said location of Gernika.

And if the accused or accuser should say that they are afraid or [that they] fear coming to the said location of Gernika and to there face the charges of their enemies, [let them] tell the *veedor* and *prestamero* and *alcaldes* of whom they are afraid, and the aforementioned *veedor* and *prestamero* shall provide security for such an accused or accuser, and for their lawyers and witnesses and servants, from those whom such an accused or accuser shall demand it. And those against whom such security is demanded by the accused or accuser or by each of them, for themselves and all the aforementioned persons, shall give [protection] in the form and manner that shall be ordered by the said *veedor* and *prestamero* and *alcaldes* and by each of them, for themselves and all the aforementioned from those whom the said accused and accuser said that they had distrust and fear.

### 37. Concerning the Investigations.

Furthermore they said that they had as a usage and custom, exemption and freedom all of that contained in the chapters written below.

First they said that they had as *fuero* and usage and custom, exemption and freedom that no general investigation, nor any other investigation, may be carried out by the Lord of Bizkaia in Bizkaia, nor by his officials, without [a] plaintiff unless regarding condemnations of outlaws, or extortioners, or regarding a man wrongly defamed as larcener, thief or extortioner, or about *rechaterias*, or about slander.

And where such cases are concerned, as well as in similar ones, the *veedor* or the *alcalde de Hermandad* may better learn the truth. And furthermore, [this shall include cases] concerning the death of a stranger who has no relative to contest [his death], and [in cases] concerning the rape of a woman.

### 38. No Piece of Artillery, Lombard [Ancient Cannon], Catapult or Firearm Shall Be Discharged, etcetera.

Furthermore they said that no one shall use any artillery, firearm or catapult against anyone else, not against friend nor against enemy, nor during truce or without a truce, in the entire Seigniory of Bizkaia and of the Encartaciones and Durango.

And anyone who fires a piece of artillery, lombard, firearm, catapult or any of these against a friend or against an enemy, during a truce or outside of a truce, shall die the death of a perfidious person. And the Lord or head of lineage who orders him to fire, shall suffer the same penalty.

### 39. They Shall Not Set Fire to Houses, Nor to Grain Fields.

Furthermore no one shall dare to knowingly set fire to burn [a] grain or wheat field or houses, [neither] during a truce nor outside of a truce, under penalty of that person or persons being put to natural death.*

---

* Possibly refers to death by drowning in which there is no bodily wounding or mutilation.

## 40. They Shall Not Set Fire to the Mountains.

Furthermore [they said] that any person or persons, women as well as men, who set fire to any mountain which results in the burning of any trees or mountain pasturage (*seles*),[*] of another person or persons, shall pay double the damage and forty-eight *maravedís* of old money as a fine, and [give] five cows to the Lord.

And if the one who sets the fire is younger than fourteen years old, and if he or she has no money with which to pay, and if it is proven that he or she did it under orders from his or her father or mother or his or her master, then that father or mother or master shall pay the aforementioned fine.

And if it cannot be proven [that the minor took orders from another], then he or she shall not be received into his or her house again under pain of said penalty, and that boy or girl shall have his or her ears cut off. And if the perpetrator is older than fourteen, he or she shall receive the same punishment and spend six months in the stocks.

## 41. Concerning Whoever Sets Fire to the Commons.

Furthermore whoever knowingly sets fire to the mountain [forest] which is known to be on communal land, even if [the fire] does no other harm, just for daring to do so shall have [to pay] a penalty of six hundred *maravedís*, half to the accuser and the other half to the Lord. And any member of the population can denounce and accuse [him or her]. And if the one who sets the fire is under fourteen years of age, and does not have [the money with which] to pay, he or she shall spend four months in the stocks.

## 42. Concerning One Who Sets Fire to His Own Property.

Furthermore whoever sets fire either to his or her [own] property, fern lands, or gorse thicket, may do so in such a manner that the fire does not spread to the neighboring property or to any communal land. But if someone sets fire to his or her property and the fire spreads to a [neighboring] property or to communal land, he or she shall pay the

---

[*] The *sel* was established by felling trees and brush in the forest and then burning the clearing to fertilize and stimulate the growth of pasturage. The livestockmen sought to reburn the *sel* periodically, which could easily expand into extensive wildfires. In fact, even today, or long after the production of charcoal for iron foundries is no longer practiced, Basque villages retain strong ordinances against setting fire to the commons in order to stimulate mountain pasturage, but at the expense of saplings and mature trees on the commons.

aforementioned penalties. Since, because of the setting of those fires and the burning of the forests, the iron foundries do not have a supply of charcoal. Consequently a great disservice is done to the Lord and [he suffers a] loss of his income and [there is] damage to the lands.

### 43. Concerning Those Who Remove the Bark from Trees.

Furthermore whoever peels or removes the bark from another person's trees, for up to five trees shall pay double the damages, and an additional forty *maravedís* in old money for each tree to the owner of the trees and [shall give] five cows to the Lord.

And if the trees were on communal lands the aforementioned penalties shall be [divided] half for the accuser and the other half for the Lord.

And if he or she peels and removes the bark from more than five trees, the one who removes the bark shall suffer the same penalty as the feller of trees (See Article 45 below).

### 44. Concerning the Proof of Such Fires and Damages.

Furthermore the mountain ranges where such fires are set, and [where they] harm such trees, are on unpopulated mountains and in places where there could not be any eyewitnesses by whom wrongdoing may be proven.

Therefore they say that, although there be no other eyewitnesses, it may be attested by the forest wardens, and if it cannot be [attested] by the forest wardens, it may be so by the public opinion of the land and by the belief that there exist vehement presumptions [of guilt]. And such proof and presumptions may be accepted as established proof against such an agent or agents, even though there are no eyewitnesses.

### 45. Concerning One Who Knowingly Uproots Trees, or Cuts Them Down.

Furthermore anyone who knowingly cuts down or uproots more than five fruit-bearing apple trees or more than five fruit-bearing walnut trees, or even five grapevines, shall be put to death and dies naturally. And moreover, if he or she has [the money] for payment, let him or her pay the damages to the owner of the apple trees, vines or walnut trees.

And whoever shall cut down fewer than five apple trees, grapevines or walnut trees, whether they are bearing fruit or not, let him or her pay double the damages to the owner and five cows to the Lord, and pay additionally as punishment forty-eight *maravedís* in old money for each tree. And this fine shall be for the owner of the injured property.

And concerning all other trees, such as fruit cherries and sour cherries and medlars and oaks and ash and chestnuts and willows, let [the offender] pay double the damages to the owner for up to five [trees] in addition to the forty-eight *maravedís* and the five cows to the Lord; and for more than five [trees] let him or her pay double the damages and five cows to the Lord, etcetera.

### 46. Concerning Boundary Stones.

Furthermore if any person places or removes boundary stones on another person's property without the order of a judge, let him or her pay 600 *maravedís* as a fine for each boundary stone for the first offense, and for the second offense double the said fine to the owner of the property, and for the third offense he or she shall be put to death, once an investigation is carried out and the truth is known.

### 47. Concerning He Who Trespasses upon Another's Property without Legal Authority.

Furthermore they said that they had as *fuero*, usage, and custom that anyone who trespasses upon another person's property, in any manner whatsoever, and by force and against the will of the possessor, without the possessor first being heard, as he or she should be, thoroughly [and his or her rights having thereby been] superceded by *Fuero* and by law, that he or she who trespasses thusly on another's property loses any right that he or she [might have had] in it, and if he or she had no right, that he or she should pay as much [as the value of the property] as a fine.

### 48. Concerning He Who Damages Foundries or Mills, or Any Part of Them.

Furthermore whoever shall knowingly break the wheel, forge, mill, locks of the water reservoir or [its] walls shall be put to death.

### 49. Concerning He Who Knowingly Spills the Cider out of Barrels, etcetera.

Furthermore whoever knowingly upsets or tips over cider [barrels], or cuts a hole in the barrel in such a way that all or the major part of the cider is spilled, shall be put to death for it, etcetera.

### 50. Concerning Those Summoned beneath the Tree and Who Present Themselves.

Furthermore they said that they had as *fuero* and of usage and of custom that whenever the *veedor* or *alcalde de Hermandad*, before whom a [legal] complaint has been made concerning any wrongdoings, robberies or larcenies, calls [people to appear] beneath the tree of Gernika, and conducts an investigation and inquiry. Afterward those who are summoned and present themselves before that judge may ask for a transcript of the investigation in order to claim their right[s].

And it was *fuero* and custom in Bizkaia to order the transcript of such investigations be given over in their entirety in the case of criminal actions. And if the case were not criminal, a transcript is given of the words and depositions that the witnesses spoke and testified to, without their names on it, or the names [are given] without the declarations and depositions.

And consequently they found the custom to be reasonable and good. But if the amount [of money] involved in the complaint is less than ten florins, demanded of the one or those who by that investigation are found to be guilty, then the accused need not appear beneath the tree, but rather let them be given a time to appear so that they may speak to the charges. And if the accused appears or asks for a transcript, in such a case let him or her be given the transcript of the investigation without the names of the witnesses or [let him or her be given] the names without their testimony and depositions, moving what was at the beginning to another part, and that in the other part to [still] another part. So that he or she who receives the transcript of the names shall not know which is the first or second or third witness. And the transcript of the testimony and depositions [of the witnesses] shall be given in this way, and not in any other manner.

51. **Concerning Thefts and Their Fines.**

Furthermore, according to the law of the Codex of Bizkaia, anyone who steals or robs ten florins or more deserves the death penalty, and for fewer than ten florins must pay double the amount that he or she stole to the injured party, and a fine of a seventh of the amount [stolen], two-thirds [of it] to the *Hermandad* and onethird to the Lord.

And at times it happens that although someone has been robbed of more than ten florins, for which the wrongdoer should die, the plaintiffs drop the criminal [charges] and press civil charges. And in such a case the *prestamero* shall demand from the accused a fine of a seventh of the amount stolen, claiming that it is a civil case.

Therefore they said that they had as *fuero* that if the plaintiff presses charges civilly, then criminal charges shall not be pressed against the accused even if the amount it is said [that he or she took] were greater than ten florins, worth 50 *maravedís* each.* And if the accused is condemned, he or she shall have to pay double that which he or she stole to the owner of the stolen property and the costs [of the legal proceedings], and a seventh of the 500 *maravedís*, but nothing more.

## 52. That Who Are Summoned Cannot Be Taken Prisoner Until Thirty Days Have Elapsed, etcetera.

Furthermore they said that they had as *fuero* and usage and custom that whenever an investigation was made by either the *veedor* or the *alcaldes de Hermandad,* or one of them, into any complaint that was filed concerning the death of a man or other criminal cases, if through the investigation it appears that some person or persons committed the crime, the judge cannot arrest the wrongdoers unless they are first summoned according to the Fuero of Bizkaia, and the thirty days allowed by the summons have elapsed, and they are [declared] outlaws.

But if the investigation were made into a theft, and it is discovered by the judge that some persons should be prosecuted, the judge may order them imprisoned at his will before or after they are summoned. And this may be done in cases where the wrongdoers and those accused by the investigation will not suffer the death penalty. And if they might receive the death penalty, they cannot be taken prisoner until they have first been summoned, as stated above.

## 53. That Summoned Who Present Themselves for Some Crime Cannot Be Accused of Any Other, Until They Are Free of the One for Which They Were Summoned.

Furthermore they said that they had as a *fuero* and custom in Bizkaia that when some person or persons are summoned beneath the tree of Gernika in any criminal case, and present themselves before the judge, until the day they are acquitted or condemned, neither anybody nor somebodies may accuse them in any other criminal case whatsoever, nor may any investigation be carried out against them concerning any other case. And those who have been summoned may not be required to respond to more than one accusation or complaint until the case [for which they were summoned] is concluded, and they are at liberty, excepting when they have not yet appeared [on the first charge]. And this shall hold true as long as the lawsuit or accusation is not malicious, imagined or contrived. And if contrived and imagined and malicious,

---

* Florins varied in value because of the changes in the metals used in their minting.

then the accused shall go free by means of *fiadores* who shall pay for his release from prison, and he shall not be personally imprisoned.

### 54. Concerning Truces.

Furthermore because truces tend to be lengthy, [and the] Bizkaian *fijosdalgo*, being very warlike, often dare to commit many evil deeds and murders.

They said that they had as *fuero* that the Lord of Bizkaia could impose one truce, and no more. And this of ninety days among his vassals since it was his will.

And after ninety days, if by chance the *veedor* or *prestamero* or the *alcaldes de Fuero* should advise the *fijosdalgo* of Bizkaia who are fighting and wish to challenge each other and those [who] wish to reinstate the truce [that those who wish to may] grant a truce to each other and [those who] do not wish to give or grant a truce shall not enter any *villa* in the Seigniory of Bizkaia, nor [shall they enter] any of its iron foundries, nor the houses of its *labradores*, nor that of any one of them may they enter any house that belongs to a *labrador* of the said Lord King, nor their *villa*, nor the roads.

And if by chance they should act contrary to this, or any part of this, let [that person] spend forty days in the stocks, and moreover let him or her pay double all the damages that he or she had demanded, for having asked, even though they did not accede to the demand that was made, etcetera.

### 55. That the *Prestamero* and *Merino* Shall Not Go Beyond That Which the Fuero Allows and Demands of Them.

Furthermore they said that whereas the *prestamero* as well as the *merinos* of the said Bizkaia would [sometimes] put themselves in a position to act and proceed beyond what they should do and what they were ordered to do by the laws of the Codex of Bizkaia, they shall not do so.

Consequently, no *prestamero* or any *merino* shall go beyond nor act beyond that which is contained in the said laws of the Codex under the penalties contained therein, etcetera.

### 56. How Many *Logartenientes* the *Prestamero* Can Appoint and Where They Must Be From.

Furthermore they said that much damage was done because there are many in Bizkaia who call themselves *prestameros*. And so that the people may be sure of knowing [who is] the *prestamero*, and [so] that they shall know of whom to ask if some injury is done to them.

They said that they had as *fuero* and usage and custom that the senior *prestamero* in Bizkaia may not appoint more than one *logarteniente* who shall carry out [the duties] of said office in the Merindades of Busturia, Uribe, Arratia, Bedia, Zornotza and Markina. And another *logarteniente* in the Merindad of Durango. Since in ancient times that was the custom, and thus it should be maintained, according to the law of Royal legislation.

Such *logarteniente* shall be propertied and credible and [shall be] from outside the Countship of Bizkaia. And he shall be received as a *prestamero* in the General Assembly of Bizkaia under the tree of Gernika, and providing good *fiadores* [who are] credible and solvent, who are from the Countship of Bizkaia, in order to pay for and satisfy whatever may be judged against him [the *prestamero*] by the *corregidor* and *alcaldes de Fuero* of Bizkaia. And to provide his guarantee before any person of said Countship who shall bring a suit against him [the *prestamero*] for violating the *fuero*.

And in this same manner, he shall be received in the Assembly of Gerediaga. The *logarteniente* who is appointed in the Merindad of Durango may not carry out [the duties] of said office in the other *merindades*, but only in that of Durango.

And the *logarteniente* of the other *merindades* may carry out [the duties of his office] throughout the Countship, in the Merindad of Durango as well as outside of it. And the *prestamero* may appoint another who may travel in his name with the *logarteniente* of the *prestamero* in order to safeguard, demand, receive and look after the fees that belong to the office of the senior *prestamero*, but not to carry out any seizure of property. Furthermore the senior *prestamero* may carry out the duties of his office in person anywhere he happens to be in the Countship, even though he has his said *logarteniente*.

### 57. Concerning the *Merindades* and Their *Logartenientes*.

Furthermore there are seven *merindades* in the said Countship of Bizkaia. To wit: the Merindad of Busturia and Uribe and Arratia and Bedia and Zornotza and Markina and the said Merindad of Durango. And in each one of the said *merindades* there is a *merino*, except in the Merindad of Uribe which has the services of two *merinos*, even though it is one *merindad*.

These *merinos* each secretly appoint *logartenientes* in their *merindad*. And one day appointing one, and another day appointing another, in such a manner that the people do not know whom to heed and with whom to deal, from which [there] arises disservice to the Lord King, and injury to the Land.

And for that reason they said that they had as *fuero* and custom that any *merino* from the *merindades* may appoint one *logarteniente* and no more, each in his own *merindad*. And this *logarteniente* shall be a credible and solvent man, and shall be appointed publicly in the Assembly of that *merindad*, providing credible and propertied *fiadores*, in accord with what is contained in the aforementioned chapter.

But the senior *merino* who thus appoints his *logarteniente* may not carry out [the duties] of the office nor act as *merino* while he has that *logarteniente*, until he [the *logarteniente*] is presented publicly, and according to how he was received. Nor may the senior *merino* or any-one on his behalf, perform any duty excepting the one that was thus approved in the Assembly. And if each one of the senior *merinos* wish-es to carry out [the duties of his office] himself, he may do so if he has not appointed any *logarteniente* or if he wishes not to. In such a man-ner that only one person functions as *merino* in each *merindad*.

## 58. Concerning the Merindad of Uribe and the *Logartenientes* That There Must Be in It.

Furthermore the said *merinos* of Uribe until now have been accus-tomed to having and carrying out [the duties] of said office, one in one year and the other in another, and in other divisions of time. And [dur-ing] the time of the year that one carried out the duties of office, the other did not. And recently both were carrying out [the duties of office] at the same time, as if they [each] had the whole *merindad* entirely. And so that the office of *merino* may function in Uribe according to how it has and was accustomed to until now, and [so that it may function] according to what [has been described] in each of the aforementioned *merindades*.

They said that from now on, if the *merinos* who are [in office] now, as well as those who might be in the future in the Merindad of Uribe, can both agree between themselves on one *logarteniente*, then they may appoint [one] in the manner described above. And if they do not agree to appoint one *logarteniente* for both, then each may appoint a *logarte-niente* who shall serve as *merino* in his place. [And those *logartenientes*] shall be equal and shall carry out [the duties] of the said office during alternate years in such a way that no more than one *merino* shall carry out [the duties] of office in the *merindad* [at any time].

And if both *merinos* should not agree, or not want to come to an agreement and do the aforementioned, then both *merinos* shall go before the *veedor*, and they shall continue to carry out [their duties] according to his decision.

And until they are in agreement by means of the aforementioned manners, neither one nor the other shall dare to carry out [the duties] of said office. And if they do so, he who so acts shall incur the penalties that are established against those who carry out [the duties] of office without authorization. And moreover anyone from the *merindad* may oppose them and prevent them from making any seizure or attachment [of property], without [suffering] any penalty. And if they should not be able to stop them, and they take something, then [the *merino*] shall incur the penalty for violating [property] and [the victim] may file a suit against that [*merino*] who did such a thing before the *veedor* or before the *alcaldes de Fuero*, or before any of them and wherever the claimant would like, etcetera.

## 59. Concerning the Movable Property and Fees from Those Summoned beneath the Tree.

Furthermore in the summonses that were issued under the tree of Gernika for any wrongdoings, crimes and evil deeds, those who were summoned and did not appear were in contempt. For such rebellion, the movable property of such summoned persons is awarded to the *prestamero* of Bizkaia.

Because of that, they said that they had as *fuero* and usage and custom that the *prestamero* of Bizkaia shall not have or receive any fee, payment or salary [from the Bizkaians] for any summons that he makes under the tree of Gernika for such cases. And if the *merino* of the Merindad of Busturia should issue a summons because the *prestamero* is not available, in the case that such summons are issued by the *merino* in the Merindad of Busturia, the movable property of summoned persons in default shall go to the *prestamero*.

And if they [the summoned] were rebellious, the *merino* shall receive twenty-four *maravedís* for each summons, whether many people were summoned or just a few, whether many or just one. And he shall not dare to receive a larger quantity for any summons he might issue, [under pain of] penalties established in the law, and [he shall have to] pay double the amount of any excess that he should receive.

## 60. Concerning the Summonses of the *Sayón* and His Fees.

Furthermore they said that they had as *fuero* and custom that any summonses beneath the said tree may only be issued by order of the *veedor* and the *alcaldes* and the *prestamero* or the *merino*. And for such sessions the *sayones* shall receive a salary of six *maravedís* for each man who was summoned, up to three persons, and no more, even though [the number of] persons summoned was much greater. But recently the *sayones* had been receiving six *maravedís* in salary for every person who is summoned, even if many [people] are thus summoned.

Consequently they said it was necessary to maintain the custom in the following manner: that the *sayón* who must issue said summonses shall have as his salary for each summons six *maravedís* [for] up to three persons who are thus summoned. But he shall not receive more even though many people are summoned, under [pain of] the penalty incurred by whoever takes more than [is customary] in such a case, that is, paying double the amount that he received, etcetera.

## 61. Concerning the Custody of Prisoners.

Furthermore they said that the *prestamero* and the guards of the prisoners are very costly for those who are thus summoned under the tree of Gernika and who present themselves [there], [because judges] appoint many jailers to them and make the prisoners maintain the guards in a most unreasonable manner, [and] for that reason some of those who are summoned do not dare turn themselves in because they cannot afford such large fees, even though they wanted to appear [and submit] to the chain because they were summoned. For which reason many were and would become outlaws unjustly, from which results great disservice to the King and harm to the Land.

Therefore they said that they had as *fuero* and usage and custom that whenever any person or persons were summoned beneath the tree of Gernika in a criminal case for which they must suffer a corporal punishment if the case be proved against them, the person or persons summoned who presented themselves to the chain, and were handed over to the *prestamero*, shall be put in good prisons, and in that place that was possible and according to what the judge ordered. And he shall appoint loyal men as jailers in the following manner: if one, two or three present themselves, then one jailer shall guard them; if four, five or six [present themselves], then he shall appoint two jailers for them; and if more than six present themselves, he shall not appoint more jailers or guards for the rest. And the prisoners shall give the two guards an allowance according to how those prisoners passed [their time] and were cared for while they were in that prison.

And if the *prestamero* should like to appoint more jailers and guards, he may appoint them by paying for them himself, without any more fees from the prisoners. But if the *veedor* feels for some just reason that more guards should be given to some prisoner or prisoners, and that said [prisoners] should pay those [guards], it shall be within his right as *veedor* to so order.

And in no other way shall the *prestamero* or his jailers and guards dare to receive a greater sum, or any allowance, under penalty of losing their office.

## 62. Concerning the Prisons of Those Summoned.

Furthermore inasmuch as those summonses and cases for which people are summoned are of many and varied types. It is not reasonable that he who does not deserve corporal punishment should have as much prison [time], or as great a penalty as he who shall receive corporal punishment, such as death or the loss of a limb.

Consequently they said that they established that when a person or persons were summoned and presented themselves in the manner described above, each one should be imprisoned according to the quality of the case, the penalty he might receive if he were condemned, who he is, and who accused [him]. This shall be overseen by the *veedor*, the aforementioned costs still not increasing, but [rather] decreasing.

And the *prestamero* and the *merinos* shall be required to comply with the judge's orders, whether in detaining or liberating, and those prisoners paying those costs [of their] confinements that they should, under penalty of that which the judge might impose on them.

## 63. The Taking and Releasing of Prisoners Shall Be with a Judge's Order.

Furthermore they said that they had as *fuero* and usage and custom that neither the *prestamero* nor any *merino* could take any person prisoner without a judge's order, nor could he hold a prisoner in his power after the judge who ordered him detained had ordered him released. And the *prestamero* and the *merinos* shall be required to comply with the judge's orders, in taking [prisoners] as well as in releasing [them], under pain of penalties that might be imposed by the judge, [and] the prisoners shall pay appropriate costs and jailer's fees.

## 64. Concerning the Guards of Those Already Sentenced or Detained in a House or *Villa*.

Furthermore because some people are summoned beneath the tree of Gernika for a case in which the *veedor*, after they have appeared before him, orders that they be imprisoned for a certain limited time, or orders them not to leave a house or *villa* or some limited area. That in any and such cases it is not reasonable that such people have guards.

Therefore they said that they established in such a case or similar ones that the person or persons who were thus condemned should not pay any fee or allowance whatever to jailers or guards. And if [the officials] should want to guard them, they should pay [the guards] themselves; and [the guards] shall not receive any bribe or allowance except for their usual jailer's fees in the following manner: twelve *maravedís* from a commoner (*villano*), and twenty-four *maravedís* from an *hidalgo*, under the aforementioned penalties.

## 65. Concerning the Escape of a Prisoner.

Furthermore some prisoners in the custody of the *prestamero* or *merino*, because of being poorly guarded or because of not being assigned good jailers and good prisons, have fled by breaking out of jail or by other means, so that the accusers or plaintiffs cannot see justice done.

And so that the *prestameros* or *merinos* or guards of the prisoners shall be more diligent in guarding them, and [so that] the plaintiffs shall have justice and not lose their right, they said that they ordered that the *prestamero* or *merino* who held that prisoner or those prisoners in their custody should be required to guard them well or provide guards for guarding [them], so that those prisoners shall not escape through negligence, poor vigilance or poor prisons.

And if they should not [guard the prisoners well], and such a prisoner or such prisoners should escape, then the *prestamero* or *merino* who was holding them shall be required to pay the plaintiff double what the prisoner would have had to pay [him]. And if such prisoner were in custody and involved in a case where he might be required to pay something, and if he was imprisoned in a criminal case, then let [the *prestamero* or *merino*] have the same punishment as the accused would have had were he in custody.

And the *prestamero* or *merino* cannot be excused from said punishment by saying that the [accused] escaped through negligence of the guards. And if the *prestamero* or *merino* pays to the plaintiff that which the fugitive should have paid, he shall have the right to pursue the fugitive to recover the payment, etcetera.

## 66. When the *Prestamero* or *Merino* May Accuse [Someone] and Carry Out an Investigation without an Order from the Judge and Detain Prisoners.

Furthermore they said that they had as *fuero* and usage and custom that no *prestamero* or *merino* could accuse anybody, or carry out any investigation, or proceed in any manner, without the order of a competent judge, unless someone were apprehended red-handed (*con cuero y*

*con carne)*\* with some stolen object, or fleeing in from some wrongdoing that he had done.

And if he should apprehend someone red-handed with the stolen
object and fleeing in such a case, he may take him prisoner and then
bring him before the judge, but he shall not take him prisoner in any
other manner, nor release him or any others thus apprehended without
the order of a competent judge once they have been taken, [nor shall he
free] any other prisoners that he has in his custody, except by order of
a competent judge under the aforementioned penalties pertaining to
those who free prisoners, etcetera.

### 67. Concerning More of the Same.

Furthermore they said that they had as *fuero* and usage and custom
that no *prestamero* or *merino* shall dare to take any person prisoner by
[simply] saying that he is a criminal, guaranteeing [payment of possible
damages], or require him to provide *fiadores*, without the order of a
competent judge, unless the one who is said to be a criminal should be
a vagabond and of bad reputation. And if he should arrest anyone else,
let him pay for the injuries done to the one who was apprehended, and
pay penalties according to what is contained in the law of the Codex of
Bizkaia, etcetera.

### 68. Against the *Prestamero* Who Releases Prisoners with the Guarantees of *Fiadores*, etcetera.

Furthermore it happens many times [that] some prisoner or prisoners were in the custody of the *prestamero* for some criminal case [and]
the *prestamero*, sometimes by order of the *veedor* and sometimes without his order, hands over and releases those prisoners [upon the presentation of] *fiadores* and receives from those *fiadores* an obligation to produce that prisoner or those prisoners into his custody, or to pay very
large sums [if they fail to do so].

Consequently they said that they ordered that whenever the
*prestamero* should receive *fiadores* obligated to bring prisoners into custody or pay some great sum, their obligation shall not be worth [more],
nor shall those *fiadores* be obliged [to pay] more than 600 *maravedís* in
old money, even though this law and other laws may have been rejected. Inasmuch as in times past, except for recently, they had this as *fuero*
and usage and custom in Bizkaia.

---

\* A medieval expression that has disappeared. The literal translation is "with hide
and flesh"—reference possibly being to nakedness, i.e. flagrantly and without cover.

### 69. The *Prestamero* Shall Receive One-Tenth.

Furthermore they said that they had as *Fuero* and of usage and of custom that if the *prestamero* or *merino* has to publicly sell or auction off any property belonging to anyone by order of the judge, he shall have as his fee one-tenth of the sum received from that public sale or auction. And from this one-tenth, the *prestamero* or *merino* shall pay the *sayón* one-tenth of his one-tenth of the proceeds. And he shall receive no more salary for any public sale and auction that he performs, except for the *per diem* of 24 *maravedís* for the auction day on which the *prestamero* or *merino* carries out the auction. And if the senior *merino* should not carry out the auction by himself, or if it were done by his *logarteniente*, he shall receive 12 *maravedís*, and no more.

### 70. The Fees of the *Sayón* for Church Summonses.

Furthermore they said that [they had] as *fuero* and usage and custom in Bizkaia that the *sayón* shall receive six *maravedís* for each summons he must issue in the church from that property which is publicly sold, and those *maravedís* shall be paid by the one at whose request the summonses are issued. And no *sayón* shall dare to go beyond what is described herein, and they shall be required to do this and comply with this, etcetera.

### 71. How Much, When and How the *Prestamero* Must Receive His One-Tenth and His Fees, etcetera.

Furthermore sometimes the *prestamero* or the *merinos* do not wish to carry out judicial seizures without first being paid their entire one-tenth of the [proceeds of the] judicial seizure, and the office of that *prestamero* or *merino* expires because of death or some other reason. And afterwards those who requested the judicial seizures must again pay fees to another *prestamero* or *merino* for seizing or auctioning off the property which was seized, and for carrying out the obligation or sentence. Accordingly, there are many damages and costs to men.

Consequently they declared and said on this subject that they had in Bizkaia as *fuero* and usage and custom that any *prestamero* or *merino* shall be required to judicially seize whatever property he must, by receiving half the fee [normally received] in money or in movable property from the [person] who requested the seizure, and after the property's sale at auction the other half [of the fee shall go] to the *prestamero* or *merino* who performs the auction. But if the judicial seizure or auction should be performed as a result of some crime, the *prestamero* or *merino* who carries it out shall be required to do so without receiving his said fees until the person who requested the auction has received what is due him. And afterward [the *prestamero*] shall receive [his fee] from [the proceeds] from the seizure and public sale of the property of the defendant, etcetera.

### 72. Concerning When There Are Many Obligations and Creditors.

Furthermore it sometimes happens that the *prestamero* or *merino*, by virtue of an obligation or sentence for whatever amount it may be, judicially seizes the property of a person or persons who are indebted to many [people]. And afterwards, at the appointed hour of the summonses or auction of that property, there appear creditors who hold debts against the person whose property is being auctioned, and his property. And the *prestamero* or *merino* who does the judicial seizure demands one-tenth of [the amount of] all those debts that appear afterward which was an unlawful and unreasonable state of affairs.

Consequently they said that they ordered that any *prestamero* or *merino* who carried out the judicial seizure or auction should have one-tenth of the [amount of the] first debt for which that judicial seizure or auction was held, and [should not have] any fee or tenth of the other debts which might appear afterward, since that was *fuero* and usage and custom in the matter, etcetera.

### 73. Concerning the *Fiadores* of Reparation or Auction.

Furthermore the *prestamero* or *merino* who carries out the judicial seizure or auction shall receive from the buyer at auction *fiadores*, honest and well-to-do men according to the Fuero of Bizkaia, at the time of the auction to assure that the buyer will pay for the property. And the same goes for the *fiadores* of real estate when the judge so orders. When the *fiadores* of the judicial seizure or of real estate are taken prisoner [to satisfy a default], according to the Fuero of Bizkaia, [they shall be held] until they comply and do what they became *fiadores* to do, but not in chains. He [the *prestamero* or *merino*] may give them a house for a prison or [limit them to] a *villa* and its terminus, imposing upon them a penalty of seven hundred *maravedís* if they leave that location or place without permission and without the order of a competent judge. And those *fiadores* who [leave without permission must] pay the penalty to the *prestamero* or the *merino* who holds them in the stocks [upon their capture]. But they [the *fiadores*] shall not have [to pay] any allowance or any fee for guards. Since they said that that was the *fuero* and custom in Bizkaia.

74. **The Fees of the *Prestamero* or the *Merino* for a Seizure [of Property].**

Furthermore the *prestamero* or the *merino* who might have to carry out a seizure shall not receive more than a dozen *maravedís* in salary. And if that seizure was one that must be carried out by the *sayón*, the *sayón* shall receive six *maravedís*.

75. **Concerning the *Fiadores* Who Must Be Supplied in the Executions [of Property Attachments].**

Furthermore they said that they had as *fuero* and usage and custom that when some *prestamero* or *merino* carries out a seizure and execution [of attachment] of someone's property by order of the *alcalde*, if at the time of the seizure, the owner of that property appoints a *fiador* to assure that he will comply with his obligation, saying that he wants to show that he has paid or been forgiven his debts, or [giving] some other reason for which that seizure and execution should not take place. And if he so states and alleges during the appraisals [of the property], then the *prestamero* or *merino* who was to carry out that seizure and execution may not auction off that property until [the matter] is decided by the *alcaldes* with a definitive ruling. But while [the case is] pending, the *prestamero* or *merino* shall go ahead with the appraisals until the moment of the auction, and this shall obtain for movable property as well as real estate. And if the person whose goods were seized was not in the Land [of Bizkaia] during the appraisals, but should come and oppose the seizure and appraisal before the property is auctioned off, then he shall be heard according to his legal right, and not after the property [has been] auctioned off, etcetera.

76. **Concerning Those Same *Fiadores* and Executions.**

Furthermore they said that they had as *fuero* and usage and custom that if by chance the person or persons whose property was sold publicly or seized should appoint *fiadores* in the aforementioned manner in the above law, appear before the *alcalde* and oppose such seizure and announcements and appraisals for any cause or reason, he shall not be given a transcript nor shall he be heard until he posts propertied guarantees as security with one or two *fiadores*, accordingly as the *alcalde* might order.

And if he posts real estate as security, that seizure shall be undone, and he shall be heard according to his legal right. And if he were unable to post security and should want to hand himself over to the custody of the *prestamero* or *merino* in charge of the seizure, once he is in custody he shall be heard as if he had posted security. And if he were to post security and be defeated in the case, the *fiadores* of real estate, being in the custody of the *prestamero* or *merino*, shall make payment according to the Fuero of Bizkaia, as the *alcalde* orders. And if he should not post security and he should be defeated while in the custody of the executor [*prestamero* or *merino*], the property which was judicially seized shall be auctioned off according to the Fuero of Bizkaia. And if they [the properties] have [already] been auctioned off, [then] they shall turn them over to the buyer; and if the auctioned property does not cover the entire payment [of debt], he shall be a prisoner until the payment is made or until he provides good propertied *fiadores*.

77. **That *Prestamero* Shall Not Enter the House of an *Hidalgo* [for the Purpose of] Attaching [Property].**

Furthermore they said that they had as fuero and usage and custom that when any *prestamero* or *merino* was to carry out a judicial seizure [of property] by order of the judge in the house of some *hidalgo*, [and] that *prestamero* or *merino* is ordered by the *hidalgo* not to come to his house or enter it, [then] neither the *prestamero* nor the *merino* shall dare go closer to the house than eight *brazas** nor carry out any seizure, but the *sayón* may do so under orders of [the *prestamero* or *merino*].

And the *sayón* may enter the house and carry out the seizure [of property], without carrying any weapon, except for a rod one cubit** in length in his hand.

And if the *prestamero* or *merino* or their men were [to come] closer than eight *brazadas* and reach the house against the order of the *hidalgo*, or if the *sayón* should enter there with weapons, the *hidalgo* may defend [his property] and resist him without [incurring] any penalty, and if in doing so there should occur any injury, death or other problem, the *hidalgo* shall not be accused nor shall he be blamed at all for what happened.

But if the *prestamero* or *merino*, understanding that some outlaw or wrongdoer is inside, should [wish to] enter that house for [the purpose of] taking into custody and detaining the fugitive or wrongdoer, he may enter that house and remove him, even though the owner of [the

---

* *braza, brazada*: two names for a unit of measurement equal to 5.46 feet or 1.6718 meters. Hence, eight *brazas* would be 43.68 feet.

** Cubit: linear unit of measurement equivalent to the length of the forearm, from 17 to 21 inches

house] demands that he not enter. And the *hidalgo* shall not dare to deny him [entry] under penalties established by law.

### 78. That Justice Officials Shall Not Be Resisted and When They May Be.

Furthermore [if] the *prestamero* or *merino* were to carry out a judicial seizure and attachment, or seizure of property by order of an *alcalde*, or arrest someone by taking him prisoner, or be in the process of confiscating [the property] of other outlaws or wrongdoers, [and] some person or persons prevent him from doing any or all of the aforementioned things, then that obstructor [of justice] shall be investigated and summoned to Gernika.

And if it were the case that a criminal or other wrongdoer that [the *prestamero*] caught red-handed were taken [by the obstructors] against the will of the *prestamero* or *merino*, then that person or persons, being convicted by investigation beyond a doubt, shall incur the death penalty. And if the capture that he made was of one of those prisoners who shall be required to pay [money] for the things [he did], then [the obstructor of justice] shall be made to pay [a fine amounting to the payment of] one-seventh of the sum involved. However, where the *prestamero* or *merino* has not captured an outlaw or public thief, a man who is not condemned in any way by the judges or whose property has not been judged [as attachable], then by promising before the *alcaldes de Fuero* [to provide] the *prestamero* or *merino* [with] *fiadores* [to guarantee that he will] face the charges, he may be released and the matter dropped, [and] there shall be no fine, but rather the *prestamero* or *merino* shall be required to pay damages to the person to whom the injustice was done.

But if the [person] who was taken from the *prestamero* was arrested for criminal reasons, then the *prestamero* shall be required to release [the obstructors of justice] only after they provide *fiadores* [who will guarantee to deliver the accused when his case is heard] before the *alcaldes de Fuero*, etcetera.

### 79. Concerning Sales.

Furthermore they said that they had as *fuero* and usage and custom that when some property that has been seized must be sold, it shall be sold and auctioned off in this way.

If judicial seizure were made of movable property and real estate of a debtor, [sale of] those properties shall be announced publicly, three consecutive Sundays, and before the townspeople, in the *anteiglesia* where the properties were [located], at the hour of the high mass. And on the third Sunday the movable property shall be auctioned off to the highest bidder. And immovable properties, being thus announced, shall be held for one year and a day. And after one year and a day have passed, [their sale] shall be announced on three more Sundays in the aforementioned manner, and on the third Sunday they shall be auctioned off to the highest bidder. But if some close relative who has a right to buy them should wish to have those properties, let them be auctioned off to that relative at the price set by three good men, even though there be another buyer who would give more for them, etcetera.

### 80. Concerning the Announcements of Sales of Movable Property and Truncal Real Estate.

Furthermore they said that they had as *fuero* and usage and custom that the executor who had to auction off those properties in the aforementioned manner shall sell the movable property by making the sales announcement [and] naming each individual item, and [shall not announce] the movable properties in combination with the real estate. Whatever is done in any other manner shall not be valid.

### 81. That If the Movable Property Is Enough [to Pay the Debt], Then the Truncal Real Estate Shall Not Be Sold, etcetera.

Furthermore those executors, [seeing that the sale of the] movable property amounts to the entire payment of the debt, sometimes sell and auction off the truncal real estate which they said made no sense.

Consequently they said that they had as *fuero* and of custom that if the [sale of] movable property amounted to the entire payment of the debt, the real estate shall not be sold.

But if, during the appraisal at the time of the auction, the debtor or any other persons provide a *fiador* to guarantee their legal obligation, the executor shall assign all those thus opposed [to the auction] a time on the third day so that they may appear before the *alcalde* by whose order the seizure was made. And the auctioned property shall remain in that state until the auction is affirmed, and there is another order from the *alcalde*. And [if the value of] the personal property and real estate are enough for the payment of the debts, the debtor shall not be taken prisoner, etcetera.

### 82. Concerning When and How a *Fiador* for the Auction Can and Should Be Provided.

Furthermore it sometimes occurs that at the time when property is auctioned off, some [people] who have a right to that property, who should receive some quantity of money [in damages], cannot provide any *fiadores*. And later they appear before the *alcalde* on the third day, and the men are in doubt as to whether or not those who did not provide *fiadores* at the time of the auction should be heard concerning their demand.

And to decide this question they said that they had as *fuero* and custom and they ordered by law that, if at the time of the auction of property, or while the people were in church hearing mass on that day, nobody provided a *fiador*, then that auction shall be valid. And even if the person who wants to file a suit should appear before the *alcalde* on the third day, he shall not be heard.

But if at the time of the auction, the owner of the property or any other person provides a *fiador*, the executor appoints a time for that person to appear before the *alcalde*. And on the third day others who did not provide any *fiadores* should appear at the assigned time before the *alcalde*, their case shall [also] be heard, even though they did not provide *fiadores* at the time of the auction, just as if they had provided [them]. But if [a person] does not provide a *fiador* at the auction or does not appear before the *alcalde* at the time assigned by the executor, his demand shall not be heard.

## 83. That the Buyer of the Auctioned Property Shall Make Payment to Whomever the *Alcalde* Orders, etcetera.

Furthermore it often happens that when some people's property is sold [to pay off] debts in the aforementioned manner, the buyers of [the property] either pay the *prestamero* or *merino* who carries out the attachment [of property], or sometimes [they pay] the creditors without an order from the *alcalde*, over which many suits are filed, because the executors do not pay what they receive to the creditors, and because the creditors do not give receipts to whom they should.

Therefore, they said that they ordered and mandated that whenever anyone bought property that was being auctioned off [to pay] a debt, the buyer shall make the payment to whomever [he is] so ordered by the *alcalde* who ordered the property sold, and not to any other person. And if they give it to someone to whom they should not, they shall pay it again to whomever they should.

## 84. How Real Estate Should Be Sold.

Furthermore they said that they had as *fuero* and of custom that, if someone should wish to sell some real estate, let him first announce how he wishes to sell it in the *anteiglesia* where the property is located on three consecutive Sundays.

And if he should sell without first making those announcements, and afterward some close relative [who is] closer to the family line from which the property originated than is the debtor, should provide a *fiador* within a year and a day, [guaranteeing] the price set by three good men, it shall be necessary to give that close relative the property at the price set by three good men.

And if within a year and a day, having knowledge of that sale, no one provides a *fiador* or asks for the property, but after the year and a day have passed, someone appears, he may not ask for nor have that property.

And if he had no knowledge [of the sale] and he swears that he did not know about it within the year and the day, that close relative may then ask for and have that property by right of purchase for the said price [any time within] up to three years from the day the sale was made. And the [original] buyer cannot avoid [this] by saying that he was not asked [for the property] within a year and a day, since it is not reasonable that one who had no knowledge [of the sale] should lose his right [to the property]. But the price of the property shall be had by the [original] buyer regardless of whether it be more or less than the amount he bought it for, and this price shall be set by three men who shall be chosen as follows: each of the parties involved shall choose one man, and the third shall be chosen as intermediary by the *alcalde de Fuero*. He who buys the property [for] that price shall make three payments spaced over the year.

And if the seller of the property should announce [the sale] in church on three Sundays as aforementioned, and some of the close relatives appear and provide a *fiador* in order to buy and make the payment at the said price according to what the *alcalde* orders, then that sale shall be made to him as described and not to any other.

And if at those announcements some close relative does not come forward, from that time onward the owner of that property may sell it to whomever he wishes, and no close relative may make any demand of any kind of that buyer. But if the property were sold for a price less than 120 *maravedís* in old money, the buyer shall make the whole payment as soon as he buys it and shall not make three payments spread out over the year.

## 85. Determining the Closest Relative for Purchasing Real Estate.

Furthermore they said that they had as *fuero* and of custom that the close relatives' right of purchasing real estate shall belong to the nearest relative who comes from the family line from which that property originates, and not [to] any other.

And if there were many close relatives who have the relatives' right to purchase [the property], each one shall have his part as it pertains to him. And if the nearest relatives should not buy [it] or wish to buy [it], then any other relative or close relation of that [family] line, not more than four times removed, may ask for and have the right to purchase that property, and not any other relative who is not of that line, no matter how closely related they might be, etcetera.

86. **That Those Who Provide *Fiadores* [to Guarantee] a Purchase or a Sale during the Announcements Shall Be Required to Carry through with the Sale and Purchase, etcetera.**

Furthermore they said that they had as *fuero* and of custom that when a person makes the three announcements in church in order to sell his property in the aforementioned manner, any of those relatives who wish to buy [it] may provide two *fiadores* [to guarantee that they will] pay the price ordered by the *alcalde*, and the seller [shall do] the same [to guarantee] to sell it. And after [the *fiadores* have been] thusly designated by both the buyer and the seller.

And after the buyer and seller have both provided said *fiadores*, the one to the other, the seller may not avoid [the sale] by saying he does not wish to sell, nor [may the] buyer [avoid purchasing] by saying he does not wish or is not able to buy. In either case the one shall make the other fulfill [his obligation] through the *fiadores* that were assigned, and shall make [him] pay the costs as they were assessed by the *alcalde* under the oath that the one who wanted to comply [with his obligation] would do so, etcetera.

87. **The Relative Who Comes Forward during the Announcements to Buy the Real Estate Must Buy All of It or None of It, etcetera.**

Furthermore some people make announcements in the church to sell all their real estate or some of it. And one or more of their relatives provide *fiadores* [to guarantee that they will] buy and pay for part of that real estate, saying that they will buy what pleases them. But if that relative were to have the choice of buying the part of the property that he wants and not buying the part that he doesn't want, it would be a great blow to the owner of the property who wishes to sell.

Consequently they said that they had as *fuero* and of custom that if the relative of the seller should wish to buy all the property that is being sold, then he shall have it as described above. And if he should not want all of it, then he may not buy or have any part of it, unless the seller should consent to that. And the owner of the property may sell it to whomever he wishes, even though the relative or relatives say that they want part of it, and after the owner of the property sells it, whether to relatives or strangers, then the purchase is valid for that buyer, and neither the relatives nor anyone else may take it from [the buyer] if the owner does not consent to it.

## 88. Concerning the Appraising Good Men and How They Should Be Chosen.

Furthermore they said that they had as *fuero* and of custom that when the buyer and the seller went before the *alcalde de Fuero*, the one in order to sell and the other to buy the property thus announced for sale at the price [set by] three good men, the *alcalde* shall order the parties [buyer and seller] to each choose a good man, and they both [shall choose] a third between them in order to appraise the property.

And the appraisers thus chosen, the parties shall go where the property is located at the time ordered by the *alcalde* and under the penalties [imposed by him if they do not comply], each one shall escort his own appraiser and both [shall escort] the appraiser chosen in common, and whatever price is set on that property by the three appraisers, the two together with the third, shall be valid.

And the buyer shall pay that price to the seller in money and in three equal payments, in the following manner: one-third when the price is set, another third six months after [the first payment] and another third in another six months.

And when the seller receives payment of the first third [of the selling price], he shall provide two *fiadores* to the buyer in order to insure [delivery of] the property. And when the seller receives the second third of the payment for that property, he shall provide the buyer with strong *fiadores* according to what was ordered by the *alcalde*. And when the seller provides the said strong *fiadores*, the buyer shall provide two propertied *fiadores* to [guarantee that he will] make the third payment, and he shall make the payment in six months' time, as aforementioned. And if he does not make the complete payment at the said time, the *fiadores* shall be required to make the payment as well as any expenses, their property being held as security. And the *fiadores* shall look to the buyer who appointed them to recover their losses. And no [other] *fiador* may assume the obligations of the *fiadores*.

## 89. When the Children, Grandchildren and Descendants of the Seller May Buy the Property.

Furthermore they said that they had as *fuero* and of custom that when someone sold some estate or property, whether it was announced in church or not, once it was sold, no child, grandchild or descendant of the seller may have or buy the property at the price set by three good men, unless they appeared at the church announcements. But [if] during those announcements, the child, grandchild or other descendant should provide *fiadores* [to guarantee the] purchase and payment in the aforementioned manner, then he may have [the property] before any other relative. But if the sale were made by the father or the grandfather without making the said announcements, no child or grandchild may sue the buyer.

### 90. Concerning the Sale of Property for Crimes, etcetera.

Furthermore they said they had as *fuero* and of custom that whenever it was necessary to sell real estate because of some criminal wrongdoing that the owner of the property committed and was convicted for, [the property] shall be sold and auctioned off to the highest bidder on the third Sunday without waiting one year and a day [of the sale having been] announced in the church.

But if some close relatives should want to buy [the property], they shall have it before any others, the property being appraised in the aforementioned manner, and removing [from the price] one-third of what the property was appraised for. And the buyer's payment shall be less this third and shall be made within nine days, and there shall be no [waiting] period of one year and one day.

And if no buyer appears, the [inhabitants] of the *anteiglesia* where the property is located shall be required to take the property at the said price, as the close relatives would have had to, but reducing it by said third for the *anteiglesia*, and taking that property for their own to do with as they wish.

But if that relative were a child, a grandchild or great-grandchild of the person who owned the property, they have one year and a day in which they can claim the property, and their right to buy [it] shall not end sooner, and it is understood that the price shall be ascertained according to the other cases spoken of in this law, etcetera.

### 91. That the Exchange [of Property] Cannot Be Undone After One Year Has Passed.

Furthermore they said that they had as *fuero* and of custom that if one man trades his property for the property of another man, and if one of the parties should afterward reclaim [his property] by saying that it was a fraud, he shall not be heard, and the exchange shall be valid if he does not reclaim it within one year.

And if within one year, one party or the other reclaims [his property], then, by order of the *alcalde*, three men shall see which of those properties is better, and if it is found by those three appraisers that one property is worth one-third more than the other property, the fraud shall be undone. And it shall be the choice of the person against whom the claim for property is made [as to whether he will] give the property back to the one who is said to be defrauded or [whether he will] pay the difference, and the exchange shall [then] be valid. But if the difference [in the value of the properties] were less than one-third, the exchange shall remain valid, and he shall not be required to pay any [additional] price at all, etcetera.

### 92. That the Announcements and Noticings [of Property Sales] Shall Be Made Publicly on Sunday during the High Mass.

Furthermore they said that even though announcements and noticings [of property sales] are made in the churches for any kind of movable goods or land that must be sold, as well as for announcements about living allowances and burial expenses, many deceits are perpetrated by sometimes announcing [the sale] before witnesses who keep it secret, and the parties who must respond and have some right to [the property] do not know about [the sale].

Therefore, to eliminate that deception they said that they ordered and mandated that whenever those announcements or noticings had to be made for all of the aforementioned things or any one of them, it was to be done publicly before all the people on Sunday at the time of the high mass, with a ringing of the bell, before the whole town. And that announcement and notice shall be valid. And anything done in any other manner shall not be valid, etcetera.

### 93. Concerning the Sale of a Property Involving Partners.

Furthermore it [sometimes] happens that [a person] wishes to sell, in one of the aforementioned manners, some part of a property that he owns with other partners without dividing [the property], and afterward some of his relatives, having appointed *fiadores* [to guarantee that they will] buy and pay for that part of the property, allege maliciously in order to avoid payment that the seller should divide the property with the other partners before the appraisal is made and payment should be made in the aforementioned manner. But the seller shall not be required to make the said division, except to sell and sign over what he owned with good or strong *fiadores*, according to what the *alcalde* ordered in accordance with the Fuero of Bizkaia.

## 94. Concerning Pledges.

Furthermore they said that they had as *fuero* and of custom that when some person wants to pledge land for payment [of a debt], as well as a house and farm or foundry or mill or any other property, he shall announce his desire to do so on three Sundays in the church [of the area] where that property is located.

And if some relative of those who have the right to buy it wishes to take it as security for a debt, the owner of the property may not pledge it as security to any other. And when such relative wants it, the property shall be appraised by order of the *alcalde* by three good men, and he who wishes to receive the property as security shall give and pay a monetary sum of what the property was appraised for, less one-third, to those who wish to pledge it as security for payment [of a debt].

And if he who receives the pledged property is holding it [and] the owner wishes to sell it, he may not sell it to any other save to that [person] who holds it as security, if he wishes to buy it. And the sale shall be for the price [set by] three good men according to how it is set down above in the article concerning sales.*

And if no relative appears at the announcements, the owner of the property may pledge it as security to whomever he wishes, and for whatever price he wishes. And no relative may demand it from him, afterwards, since [the relative] did not attend the announcements.

And if he should pledge it as security without announcing it in church, the nearest relative or any other [relative], up to those four times removed, may demand the propery of that pledge for payment from those who have it as if it had been sold. And he who had [the property] shall be required to give it to them, receiving [back] what he gave for the pledged property.

And he who receives the pledged property shall have and hold the property and take away all its fruits and rents and harvest without any discount, until he is repaid all that he thus gave and paid. And when the owner of the property wants to reclaim it, he may do so. And the one who received the property as a pledge [for payment] shall be required to give it back, upon receiving that which he had originally given. But if the owner of the property should wish to reclaim it, and the property had born fruit or had been cultivated through some effort, the holder of the pledge shall not be required to return the property to its owner until the day of St. Mary on the following August 15, even if the owner wishes to reclaim it [earlier].

---

* See Article 84.

And if no fruit appears, or if it had not been planted, but the one who held the pledged property had worked and fenced it in, and the owner should wish to reclaim it, then in that case, [once the owner] pays [back] what he received [in pledge], and the cost of the labor and the fencing, [then] the one who holds the pledged estate shall be required to turn it over to him, and this cannot be avoided by saying that he does not want to give it [back to the owner] until the day of St. Mary in August, etcetera.

## 95. Concerning the Sale of Movable Property Pledged as Security.

Furthermore they said that they had as *fuero* and of usage and of custom that whenever some person receives another person's movable property as security for some quantity of *maravedís* until a certain time, or without the time being declared.

Anytime after the end of that period he who holds those pledged items of personal property may go, if he wishes, to the *alcalde de Fuero* or to the *corregidor*, and ask him for an order to sell that pledged property. And the *alcalde* or the *corregidor* shall be required to give the order for him without any fee. In the following manner: [the holder of the property] shall advise the owner or his household in such a way that it will come to his attention that he has received authorization from the *alcalde* to sell the pledged items of movable property, and [ask] if he wishes to redeem [those items by paying the money owed]. Otherwise he shall put them up for sale. And if [the owner] should redeem the property, well and good. If not, from that moment onward, whenever [the holder of the property] wishes, he may take it to the church where he is a parishioner on three consecutive Sundays at the hour of the high mass. And he shall first have it on display. And on the third Sunday he may auction it off to the highest bidder without any penalty. And he shall receive his payment from the *maravedís* that [sale of the property] brings.

And if those pledged items of personal property are worth more than the quantity for which they are held [as security], then the excess shall be turned over to the owner of the property by the third day following, under pain [of a penalty] of double the amount of the excess that those pledged items of personal property were worth. And if by chance the owner of the said pledged items of personal property was not in the district, and was unable to receive the excess, then [the holder of the property] shall be required to publicly place the excess in the hands of a credible man, so that the owner of the pledged items of personal property shall receive any excess that [the sale of his] property brings.

And he shall not be allowed to sell any pledged items in his possession other than in the aforementioned manner.

And if a dispute should arise between [the person] who holds the pledged items and the owner concerning the price set upon the pledged items, then this [price] shall be decided by the one who holds the pledged items, since he possesses them, etcetera.

## 96. Title Concerning Matrimonial Property.

Furthermore they said that they had as *fuero*, usage and of custom in Bizkaia that when a man married a woman and the woman [married] the man, the movable property and real estate of both shall be held equally, and by halves, the property as well as the usufruct, even if at the time that they were married the husband may have had much property and the woman may not have had any property. Or the woman had much and the husband nothing at all.

## 97. Concerning Marriage Gifts.

Furthermore they said that they had as *fuero*, usage and custom that if the husband makes a marriage gift [of property] to the wife, or the wife to the husband, of some item or farm or other pieces of real estate, and if he [or she] should secure the marriage gift by providing *fiadores* to guarantee it, whatever they give each other thusly as a marriage gift shall be valid, even though it consists of all their truncal property.

But the marriage gift that was thus made shall be presented before a notary or before witnesses, who are good men and of good repute.

## 98. Concerning the Same Marriage Gifts.

Furthermore they said that they had as *fuero* and usage and custom that if the property thus given as a marriage gift were [comprised of] two or three houses or more, or of iron foundries or mills or [mill] wheels or any other real estate [located in] different places and *anteiglesias*, the gift shall be presented by naming each item individually in the house where [the giver] resides, and of any other real estate no matter where located. And the marriage gift that was thus made by the husband to the wife, or by the wife to the husband, shall be valid, etcetera.

## 99. Concerning the Same Marriage Gifts.

Furthermore they said that they had as *fuero* and usage and custom and that they established by law that the property of which the husband thus made a gift to the wife, or the wife to the husband, shall become one family holding, by declaring whatever properties and houses and real estate comprise the marriage gift, [and] by the husband physically turning it over to the wife, or the wife to the husband, placing it in the house where the gift was presented, and turning over the house tile and a tree branch and land as a sign of possession of all the property that is thus given as a marriage gift; the wife taking the house from the husband, or the husband [taking it] from the wife, [and] providing *fiadores* who shall have knowledge of that marriage gift. And these *fiadores* shall be residents of the *anteiglesia* in which the house where the gift was presented was located.

And the gift which was presented in this way, [and] all the properties of which it was comprised, shall be valid, even though some other houses or lands or mills or [mill] wheels or endowments should lie outside that *anteiglesia*.

### 100. Concerning the Same Marriage Gifts.

Furthermore they said that they had as *fuero* and usage and custom that the husband may not make a gift of movable property to the wife, nor may the wife to the husband. But if the husband should die, the wife shall have one-half of all movable property with no part of it going to the children they had together, to do with as she wishes. And the same [shall be true for] the husband if the wife should die.

### 101. Concerning the Same Marriage Gifts.

Furthermore they said that they had as usage and of custom that if after the marriage gift was thus made by the husband to the wife or by the wife to the husband, if one should die before the other, and [they] had children together, and afterwards the living spouse should marry again, and if the husband should make some improvements or purchases or [build new] buildings with his second wife, or if the wife [should do so] with her second husband, then everything they bought, improved and acquired within the boundaries of the property where the marriage gift was made shall be for and belong to the children of the first wife or husband to whom that gift was presented, with no part of it going to the second husband or second wife, nor to his or her heirs.

### 102. Concerning Proof of the Marriage Gifts.

Furthermore they said that husbands give marriage gifts to their wives and wives to their husbands at the time they marry. And many times it happens that it is not done in the presence of a notary public. And upon the death of the husband or the wife who thus presented the gift, somebody files a suit against the surviving spouse, or against the heirs, for the property contained in the marriage gift. And so, out of fear and misgiving of what could arise, before dying, the one who dies specifies the marriage gift in the last will so that there will not be any division among the heirs.

But there is a doubt whether this declaration of the husband or wife can prevent injury to the second wife or husband or their heirs. And in order to remove this doubt, they said that they ordered and established by law that if the one who dies, whether it be the husband or the wife, makes it known in his or her will, swearing to God and to the Holy Gospels on his or her soul, that the marriage gift was presented [either by] the husband to the wife or the wife to the husband, then this declaration shall be valid and shall be taken as final proof.

And if the one who dies does not make this declaration, and some lawsuit over [the properties] should arise between the person to whom the properties were given as a marriage gift and the heirs, with other persons, then the surviving spouse may give proof of what was presented as a marriage gift by providing two eyewitnesses of good reputation who were present when the marriage gift was given and with two other credible witnesses. And the surviving spouse who claims the marriage gift was made, shall swear to this in the church designated for oath taking in the area where the marriage gift property was located, [and] then the property in question shall belong to the person or persons whom they say it belongs to by reason of the marriage gift, free and exempted [from encumbrances].

### 103. Title Concerning Inheritances and Bequests.

Furthermore they said that they had as a *fuero*, usage and custom that when the husband and wife are thus married and bound by marriage gifts, and have children together, these children shall inherit the property which comprised the marriage gifts, and not any other children. Even though the husband or wife may have other child heirs [because] the husband married another woman after the death of the first wife to whom he gave the marriage gift. Or the wife [married] another man after the death of the first husband. But the husband and the wife, both together or each acting individually, may give their half to whichever son, or daughter, or sons, or daughters that they had together and so desired.

### 104. Concerning the Same Matter.

Furthermore they said that they had as *fuero*, usage and custom that whenever any woman was married under the law and with the blessing of the Holy Church, [and that woman] was bound by a marriage gift and left legitimate children by her husband from whom she

received the marriage gift, then those children, or whomever she choos-
es from among them, shall inherit the property that was given as a marriage gift to their mother, the usufruct as well as the physical property.
And regarding that which belonged to his wife, the father shall have
none of that property nor the usufruct of it, even if the heirs are in the
father's custody. And what they said about the man pertains to the
woman as well if the husband should die.

## 105. That They May Give and Ordain All Property to One Child by Leaving the Others a Tree.[*]

Furthermore they said that they had as *fuero*, usage and custom
that any man or woman who had legitimate children by a legitimate
marriage may give, in life as well as at the moment of death, all his or
her movable property and immovable real estate to one of his or her
sons or daughters, by giving and leaving some quantity of land, small or
large, to the other sons or daughters, even though they are of legitimate
marriage.

And if he or she had no children, the same applies to the grandchildren.

And if there were no legitimate children or grandchildren from a
legitimate marriage, in this same way he or she may give and leave his
or her movable and truncal property to the illegitimate children that he
had by an unmarried woman or she [by] a man.

However, children by a concubine may not inherit with the children
of a legitimate marriage, unless the father or the mother leaves or gives
them something out of recognition, either movable or truncal property.

And if he or she had no legitimate or illegitimate children, and there
were children that the married man had by some woman while the legitimate wife lived, or the married woman [had] by some man while the
legitimate husband lived, or [there were] other bastards such as children
born of incest, engendered in a harmful union, they may not inherit any
of the father's immovable property, unless [the child's birth] were legitimized by the Lord King. But the father may give them whatever he
wishes of his movable property, and the same goes for the mother, even
if [the children] are not legitimate.

---

[*] The concept regards the testator's capacity to essentially pass on all heritable land
to a single heir(ess) providing his or her siblings with a patch of land only capable of growing a single tree.

## 106. Intestate Heirs.

Furthermore they said that they had as *fuero* and custom that if some man or woman should die without making a will or bequest, and should leave legitimate children, those children shall inherit all their property.

And if they had no children [living], the grandchildren [should inherit].

And if they had no grandchildren, the closest relatives of the [blood] line from which the property originates [shall inherit].

And if the dead person had property which he or she had inherited from his or her father, the father's closest relatives shall have that property with no part of it [going to] the relatives of the mother's side, even if they be closer [relatives]. And the same holds true for the property inherited from the mother, the relatives shall have it. And this is understood for truncal real estate, but with movable property, all the relatives on the father's side and the mother's [side] should inherit equally.

And even if there were more siblings and relatives on the father's side than the mother's, or if there were more on the mother's side than the father's, the other half of the said property is given by the person who died intestate, unless during his lifetime he had made some gift or donation or bequest of those properties or goods to one of those relatives, or to an outsider.

## 107. Title Concerning Bequests, Gifts and Inheritances.

Furthermore they said that they had as *fuero* and usage and custom, and they established by law, that if some man or woman should have many houses and foundries and mills and [mill] wheels and other properties, and the owner of those houses and foundries and mills and [mill] wheels and properties should wish to give or bequest them to his or her child or sell or give them away to any other person.

He must present that property, along with six strong *fiadores* of the bequest, by marking the boundaries around the house where he or she lives, and naming and declaring individually each of the houses and foundries and mills and [mill] wheels which he or she is giving away, and [the person] to whom he or she is giving it. And that bequest shall be valid whether some or all of the houses and foundries and mills and [mill] wheels and other properties are outside of the *anteiglesia* where the bequest was made, or whether they are in the same *anteiglesia*. And the same shall hold true, where real estate is concerned, for items that the father [gives] to the child, or siblings [give] to siblings, or any people whomsoever give to each other.

### 108. Concerning the Same Matter.

Furthermore they said that it happens at times that some person or persons give a house or farm to their children or to some other persons, bequesting it them in the aforementioned manner. And they include all the real estate that was within the boundaries from one place with another without declaring each property individually.

And in such a case they said that they established by law and *fuero* that all the real estate within the declared boundaries possessed by the [person] making the bequest shall be understood to have been given [away], as well as the property that the bequest dealt with specifically, and [the bequest] shall be valid as if each property were named individually, unless the bequestor makes an exception of something, or if some foundry or mill or [mill] wheel should lie within those boundaries, and be named and declared individually.

### 109. Concerning Bequests for Dowries.

Furthermore when some people arrange marriages or engagements for their sons or daughters by oral agreement, the father and mother or relatives of those who are marrying should and do bequest to them some house or foundry or other property. And after they are married or betrothed, [the relatives] give or bequest the house or houses or properties that they first gave [to the marrying child] to other children or to other people, [something] which is done against the better interests of those to whom it was first given.

For that reason they said that they established and ordered that whenever a marriage was contracted, and bequests of properties are made to those who are getting married or engaged, the owner of those properties and bequests may not afterwards give them away to anyone else.

And to that end, at the time when a donor makes his or her bequests, he or she must provide four honest and propertied *fiadores* who guarantee that [in future] he or she will give and sign over, and provide [then] four strong *fiadores* guaranteeing the bequest to those who were engaged or married. And those *fiadores* shall be required to guarantee with strong *fiadores* the bequest of that property for a year and a day from the day the bequest was made.

And if it should happen that the person who bequested that property does not wish to give and hand it over to whom he or she bequested it, and the *fiadores* become involved in lawsuits over [the properties], they shall not be released [from their obligations] whether the suit is brief or lengthy. But if the *fiadores* are not sued within a year and a day, or involved in a lawsuit, then from that time onward those *fiadores* shall not be obligated, but rather shall be released.

And this shall hold true for real estate, because for movable property [it] shall always be up to those who bequested [it] to give that which they bequested, whether they provide *fiadores* or not.

## 110. Concerning the Bequests of Movable Property.

Furthermore they said that when someone bequests some house or farm with all the movable property and real estate that pertains to it to his son or daughter or some other heir, there is some doubt concerning whether the general giving of movable property is valid or not.

And in order to remove this doubt they said that they ordered and established that the general bequest of a house and farm and real estate shall be valid. But the bequest of movable property shall not be valid unless they give it by naming and declaring each item individually.

But in a general bequest where livestock and monies are not individually named, it shall be assumed that the [items of movable] property that the Old Law of Bizkaia calls *urde urdaondo e açia etondo,*[*] which includes the breeding stock of pigs that were at the house, and the grain stored in the house, the wheat as well as the millet, and barley that had been harvested that year, have been bequested. But this does not include the grain that was brought in from outside [the property], nor [does it include] the sides of bacon, no matter how many there might be, except those which had already been cut, and a cider barrel that has been tapped, a chest in which baked bread is stored, and the cauldron which is used every day and some tablecloths and spades, hoes, axes and common things for working the land that there might be in the house, and any bed or bedding that there might be in the house.

## 111. Concerning the Bequest [of] Movable Property.

Furthermore they said that they had as *fuero* that any man or woman who had movable property, whether cows or pigs or beasts or any other livestock, wool and linen clothing, gold or silver, or any other movable property, may give and bequest all that property or part of it to any person or persons that he or she may wish, whether they be strangers or relatives, or do what he or she wishes with it or even keep

---

[*] *urde urdaondo e açia etondo*: "pigs and neutered pigs and everything"; *urde* is Basque for "pig"; *urdaondo* is Basque for "pig neutered after giving birth"; *e açia etondo* appears to be a phonetic rendition of the Spanish *y asi en todo*, "and all, and everything."

it, not bequesting it even if there are legitimate children or other heirs, descendants, forebears or distant [relatives]. But paying debts that he or she might owe from the movable property, neither selling nor giving away the real estate that [he or she] might have.

## 112. Concerning Real Estate Bought and Acquired During One's Lifetime.

Furthermore they said that up until now in Bizkaia they had as usage and custom that all real estate that a person bought was possessed during his or her lifetime as movable property so that [he or she] could do with it as he or she wished and give it away like other movable property which they said was harmful to the inheriting legitimate children.

Consequently they said that they ordered and established as law that all land or property and real estate that was purchased shall be held as real estate and not as movable property. And that real estate may not be given away or bequested to strangers or anyone except the heir or heirs who by right should have and inherit their property as in the case of any other real estate that one might have, etcetera.

## 113. Concerning Gifts Made During One's Life to One Who Dies Before the Donor.

Furthermore they said that many give what is theirs to their children while they are alive and the children have to support them during their life and take care of the burial at death and, [when] the giving is done in this manner, it often happens that the child or children, or to whomever the gift was made, die before the parent, leaving no legitimate children or other descendants.

In such a case they said that they ordered and established by law that if the son or daughter who received the bequest should die before [the person] who made the bequest, and leave no inheriting descendant, then the inheritance of the person who died shall be returned to the parent or the other [person] who made the bequest, even if up until now it was the usage and customary to do differently. But the father or mother who made the bequest may not sell or give that property away to strangers, even though it is returned, but may only avail himself or herself of the usufruct during his or her lifetime, and [then] give [the property] to whichever of the heirs he or she so desires.

## 114. No Bequest of Real Estate Shall Be Made to a Stranger When There Are Heirs and Descendants, etcetera.

Furthermore they said that they had as *fuero* and custom that no man or woman may make a bequest of any truncal real estate that he or she might have to a stranger when he or she has inheriting descendants or close relatives descended from a common ancestor, with the exception of movable property with which he or she may do as he or she wishes. And if there is no personal property, then he or she may give no more than one-fifth of real estate to the church, and no more, etcetera.

## 115. Concerning Sepulchers.

Furthermore they ordered and established that when someone had an ancestral mansion and house and had a tomb in the church where that person is a parishioner. And that person bequests the ancestral mansion and house to some son or daughter, not mentioning the tombs in his or her last will or at the time of the bequest, then, in that case, all the heirs shall hold the tomb or tombs in common.

But the person to whom he or she leaves the house or family home and who has the benefit of the right of being entombed at the head of such sepulcher, shall be responsible for the upkeep of that tomb. But at the time that he or she bequests or gives those tombs to one of his or her heirs, he or she may give [them] to any child or children that he or she wishes, in the same manner in which he or she could give any of his or her other real estate. But if the other heirs and siblings of the person to whom the tombs were given have no other tomb, the person to whom it is given may not prevent them or their children from being buried in one of the tombs, and he or she shall choose one of the tombs he or she was given and say that it is his or hers, etcetera.

## 116. That Whoever Mistreats His or Her Father, Mother or Bequestor Shall Lose the House and Property that Was Left Him or Her, etcetera.

Furthermore they established and ordered that if the son or daughter to whom property was given by the father or mother in the aforementioned manner should injure the father or mother who had given them the property by laying hands in anger upon them, this being verified by good witnesses of good reputation, then that ingrate shall lose the property that was given and bequested to him or her, if a case is filed and the charges are proven to be true within one year and a day.

And if within a year and a day [the injured parent] should not file and prove [the charges], or if after [the son or daughter] does the injury [the parent] should speak to him or her or eat or drink with him or her at the same table, then from that time on the parent may not file suit, nor will the son or daughter lose the property or inheritance that he or she had or was given.

But if the father or the mother file suit because of some ingratitude or injury [other than laying hands in anger upon them] that he or she says that [the son or daughter] did to him or her, [the parent] may not for that reason disinherit [the son or daughter] regarding property that [the parent] had given him or her, and the bequest that was made shall be valid, etcetera.

### 117. Title Concerning the Earnings of the Husband and the Wife, etcetera.

Furthermore they said that they always had as usage and custom and *fuero* that whenever a man marries a woman or a woman marries a man under the law and with the blessing, as mandated by the Holy Mother Church, then all movable property and real estate that the husband and wife have shall belong to both and be shared equally, even if the husband had much property and the wife had little or the wife [had] much and the husband little. And they thus ordered and mandated that it should be so according to what the usage and custom has traditionally been and as contained in this law, etcetera.

### 118. The Wife Is Not Responsible for the Husband's Crimes, Nor Is Her Property.

Furthermore they ordered by law and by *fuero* that [neither] the wife nor her property may be held for any crime of murder or robbery or larceny or other wrongdoing that the husband may commit. Even if she had knowledge of that crime, because the wife may not go against the will of her husband.

But if she took part in that crime or committed some other crime, she shall suffer the penalty of the perpetrator both corporally and in property.

And [neither] the husband nor his property shall be held for [any] crime that the wife commits, unless he knew about that crime before she committed it. And if he knew about it and did not prevent the wife [from committing it], it is just that he receive the same punishment as the wife because he consented to the crime that she committed. And they thus ordered it so by law and by *fuero*, etcetera.

### 119. That the Wife Is Not Responsible for the Debts of the Husband if She Does Not Enter into the Obligation and Contract with Him, etcetera.

Furthermore it often happens that men incur debts and obligations without the knowledge of their wives, and later the creditors of those obligations file suit against the wives and their property for [payment of] those debts that their husbands incurred. Because of which they are dispossessed and they lose their property. Which was a very grave injury and fraud against women.

For that reason they ordered and established by Fuero and by law that neither the wife nor her property may be held for payment of any debts that the husband might incur without her, even if the wife knew of them, unless she consented to the obligation or debt in person, and with her husband's permission. This is so even if the creditors claim and demonstrate that the monies [involved] were converted into the community property of the husband and the wife.

And what goes for debts shall also apply to the guarantees that the husband gives, etcetera.

## 120. If the Husband's Property Is Sold for Debts, He Shall Be Left Nothing of the Wife's [Property] Except the Usufruct While He Is Alive, etcetera.

Furthermore they ordered and established that if the husband's property is sold [to pay] a debt or guarantee that he incurred. And if the husband should want to share equally in the wife's remaining property, he may not do so, nor may he have any part of that property which belongs to her. But he may maintain himself and his wife with the usufruct of that property during his lifetime, and after his death all of that property which belongs to her shall be completely hers to do with as she wishes, with no part of [it going to] the husband and his heirs, etcetera.

## 121. Title Concerning Improvements on the Truncal Property of the Other.

Furthermore it sometimes happens that the husband and wife together make some improvements and [build] buildings on, or make purchases of property for, hereditary land and estates belonging to the husband, or on land or the hereditary estate belonging to the wife. There applies the right of purchase by kinship of the husband's hereditary property or [the right to build by means of] ownership, without any part [of it going to] the wife, [or her relatives], or [the same situation holds true for] the wife's [hereditary property] without any part [going to] the husband's [side]. And [it sometimes happens that] the husband or the wife, or both of them, die without having any children together, and among their heirs, or between the surviving partner and the heirs of the deceased, there arise questions, debates and lawsuits over [the ownership of the improvements or additions that were made].

And, for that reason, in order to avoid the lawsuits and questions that can arise in such a case, they said that they had as *fuero* and of custom, and that they ordered and established that if those improvements were made on land or on the estate that comes from the husband's side [of the family], and if the right to purchase [the property on which] the husband or wife made [improvements together] should belong to the [family of the] husband, then, in that case, should the husband and wife die, the husband's heirs shall pay the wife's heirs half of the fair price of those improvements and purchases, and by thus paying for [them], all of those improvements and purchases shall belong to the husband's heirs.

And if those improvements and purchases were made on [property] that came from the mother's side of the family, those improvements and purchases shall belong to her heirs in the aforementioned manner, [after] paying the said price to the husband's heirs.

And if the wife should die and leave the husband living, all of that property shall belong to the husband [after] paying the wife's heirs the aforementioned sum.

If those improvements and purchases were made on property that came from the husband's side of the family, and if the husband should die and leave the wife living, the wife may have and hold half of that property during her lifetime, even though it came from the husband's side of the family, and after her death that property shall be divided among the husband's heirs and the wife's [heirs] according to how it was aforementioned.

And this shall be true for the property, improvements and purchases that they made on either the husband's [property] or the wife's, and in that way jointly between the husband and the wife and their heirs.

## 122. The Husband May Not Sell Real Estate of Which the Wife Owns Half.

Furthermore some men were often in the habit of selling real estate without the wife's knowledge, through which [transactions] wives receive an injury.

And wishing to remedy [this situation], they said that they establish and have established that the husband may not sell or give away any real estate that belonged half to the wife without the wife's consent, and if he does so [the transaction] is not valid, even if that property came from the husband's side of the family, because it would do great harm to the wife and is unlawful.

123. **That the Husband and the Wife Shall Each Pay Half the Debts Incurred by Both.**

Furthermore they said that sometimes the husband and wife are both committed to pay or do something for some other person, but before they make the payment the husband dies and leaves the wife [living], or the wife dies and leaves the husband living, or they both die. And the holder of the obligation attaches the husband's property or that of his heirs, letting the wife's [property] alone, or [confiscates] the wife's [property], letting the husband's alone.

In that case they established that if the creditor of that obligation should receive payment by selling the property of one [spouse], then the other and his or her heirs shall be required to pay his or her half of what the creditor should receive, along with the [legal] costs, to the person to whom the property was sold,* for it is not lawful that the property of one [spouse] should suffer for the debts [incurred by] both, and the [property] of the other spouse should remain free and clear.

124. **Title Concerning That the Children Shall Pay Half of the Debts That the Father or Mother Owes from Their Half [of the Property].**

Furthermore they said that they had as a custom, and they established by law, that should the husband die and leave the wife living, or should the wife die and leave the husband living, [and] they had children together, then those children and the living father or mother shall have all the movable property, [and] they shall pay and be in charge of paying all debts that the husband and wife had. And the children of the dead person [shall pay] half, and the living father or mother [shall pay] the other half.

125. **Title Concerning Wills and Bequests and Which Ones Shall Be Valid or Not.**

They said that they had as *fuero* and of custom formerly that if the husband, in sickness or in health, and the wife should make a will and bequests by mutual agreement and together, then that will and [those] bequests contained therein are valid.

And neither the husband after the wife's death nor the wife after the husband's death may revoke [them] if the other spouse had died within the year and a day.

---

* We assume that, in return, the family receives half of the previously sold property back from the buyer.

And if both should be alive after one year and a day, then either of them may revoke [them] and make a [new] will and bequests as he or she so desires. And consequently, they said that they affirmed [and] established by Fuero and by law the said usage and custom, which would be valid from this time forward.

### 126. Title Concerning the One-Fifth of the Property That Goes to the Soul [Church].

Furthermore they said that they had as a usage and custom that a man or woman who had no inheriting offspring could not leave any immovable property that they had as an inheritance to anyone else except to closest relatives from the line from which the inheritance originated. But that they may each do what they wish with movable property.

Which [custom] they understood should be amended, and amending it they said that they ordered and established that any man or woman who had no such inheriting offspring and no movable property could bequest and give away one-fifth of his or her real estate to the church, if he or she lacked movable property. But if he or she had movable property that amounted [in value] to one-fifth of that real estate, then he or she could not bequest or give away the said immovable property, except to his or her heirs. It may be given to whichever of the close relatives that he or she desires, as long as the other close relatives are provided with some part of the real estate, as much or as little as [the donor] wishes. And he or she may do whatever he or she wishes with movable property, etcetera.

### 127. Title Concerning a Will Made by Proxy, etcetera.

Furthermore it often happens that some men or women are not able to arrange their wills and bequests or, although they are able, they cannot or do not wish to declare their last will in order to make their testaments and establish heirs. And they give the authority to other relatives and friends, and husbands [give their proxy] to the wives and wives to the husbands, so that after their death [those people] may make bequests and a will in their place, in order to give away and distribute and divide all their personal property and real estate among their heirs as they wished and thought best. And it is doubtful whether that proxy and that which was bequeathed by virtue of it, after the death of the testator, is valid or not.

And wanting to be rid of this doubt, they said that they ordered and established that whenever some men or women give such authority to someone, whether the husband [gives it] to the wife or the wife to the husband, all that which is done and ordered and bequested by those who were given such authority shall be valid as if the testator had done so and so ordered while alive, etcetera.

## 128. Title Concerning the Witnesses of Wills.

Furthermore this land of Bizkaia being mountainous, and neighbors and dwellers therein living in places [which are] separate and distant from each other, [and] they cannot have as many witnesses as they want in such mountainous places when they want to make their wills at the time of their death, [nor can they have] a notary before whom they may make it. Because of which those [people] who are bequeathed something by those testators cannot prove [the validity of] that will by letter nor with five witnesses.

And so that there would be no doubt in that [matter], nor should those to whom something was bequested by that will and bequest lose it, they said that they ordered and established that [if] any man or woman in those mountainous places who made their will and bequests in the presence of two good men and a woman who are of good reputation, who are present as witnesses at the request of the testator, and these witnesses swear an oath in some church where the *alcalde* orders [it done], and declare under oath that they were present at the time that the said dying person made his or her will and bequests, and they declare what was ordered and bequested, then that which the three witnesses declare shall be valid and shall be accepted as a will.

And the *alcalde* before whom the witnesses are brought shall receive this oath. And if the *alcalde* will not or cannot receive the oath in the church, he shall order [the oath] sworn in the presence of a credible man whom the *alcalde* shall name, and if the witnesses do not wish to go before the *alcalde*, or cannot go before the one who is supposed to approve [their testimony], then he shall ask the *alcalde* and the *alcalde* shall insist that those witnesses appear before him at the appointed times under pain of the penalties that he may impose on them, and they shall be required to give that testimony even though they say that they do not know anything about the deed and that they cannot swear the oath. And whoever brings those witnesses shall be required to pay the *alcalde*'s fee for the hearing. And if the testator of such will were to make it in a populated place where he could have more witnesses, he shall do so before five witnesses if they are available, three men and two women, or all men, of good reputation.

And the will and bequest made in any manner described above shall be valid as if it were made before a notary public.

And if the will is made before a public notary, there shall be three witnesses of good reputation [present], and they shall be male, etcetera.

## 129. Title Concerning the Divisions [of Property].

If the husband and the wife having children in common acquired some property or goods, before having children, and either the husband or the wife, the father or the mother survives, then that property acquired before the births of children shall be held in common before any divisions are made, and half of [that property or those goods] shall be divided with the children, etcetera.

## 130. The Child Who Wishes to Share in the Gains Shall Share in the Debts, etcetera.

Furthermore if the surviving father or mother should make some [financial] gains before dividing [the property of the deceased] with the children, and incurred some debts as well as gains, and those children wish to benefit from the improvement, they shall be required to pay half of those debts. And it shall be the children's choice to either pay half those debts, and receive half those gains, or to give up the gains and not pay the debts, etcetera.

## 131. Title Concerning the Guardianship of Minor Children.

Since, until now, they formerly had as an ancient usage and custom, and they established by law that when some man or woman in their will left executors and guardians for their children or heirs who were less than fourteen years old, and those testamentary guardians wished to accept the post of the guardianship and administration [of the will], they were required to go before the *alcalde de Fuero* within thirty days following [their appointment] and provide propertied *fiadores* with no legal disqualifications from their jurisdiction. And the *alcalde*, upon receiving an oath and guarantee, may appoint [that person] to the guardianship according to the law. And from that time forward those guardians may take the minors and their property into their charge and carry out the office of guardian, and not in any other manner.

But the husband may not appoint the wife, nor may the wife appoint the husband, as testamentary guardian of the children.

And if testamentary guardians do not appear before the *alcalde* or swear the oath within the said thirty days, from that moment on the closest relatives of those minor children, one from the father's side [of the family and] another from the mother's side, shall be guardians and administrators of those minor children and their property, by swearing the said oath before the *alcalde*, and by being appointed guardians by him, and in no other manner.

And those guardians shall make a public inventory of the property and goods that they received within thirty days, under pain of the loss [of their position] and of [paying] the damages and costs that the minor children should receive, etcetera.

### 132. If Some Guardian or Caretaker Should Die, the Others Who Remain Living Shall Take His Place.

Furthermore if two or three or more guardians were appointed and one or some of them should die, the one or ones who remain alive shall be guardians and shall have the minor children and their property in their charge. And the heirs of the deceased guardian or guardians shall be required to make an accounting to those left alive of all the real estate and personal property that the deceased guardian(s) received and had charge of, just as they would have owed [an accounting] to the minors when they came of age, etcetera.

### 133. [The Child Who Is] Older Than Fourteen Years May Choose a Guardian.

Furthermore they said that they had as usage and of custom and established by *fuero* that anyone younger than twenty-five years and older than fourteen years could take whomever he or she wished for his or her guardians, regardless of the fact that other relatives of the minor might want to be guardians, etcetera.

### 134. That Justice Compels the Closest Relatives to Be Guardians or Caretakers.

Furthermore if [neither] the testamentary guardians nor the closest relatives wish to be guardians of those minors, the *alcalde* being asked [to do so] by those minors, or by their father or by their mother or by other relatives, may force the closest relatives to take the position of guardian or caretaker, [and] they will be required to fulfill [that duty] as they were so ordered by the *alcalde*, under pain of the penalties which he might place upon them, etcetera.

### 135. The Minor Attaining Eighteen Years of Age May Leave the Care of Guardians.

Furthermore regardless of the fact that, according to law, the guardians of minor children must have charge of them and their property until they reach the age of twenty-five. Since some of those under twenty-five and older than fourteen years of age are as competent and diligent, and of such a mind and conduct, as others who are older than twenty-five.

For that reason they ordered and established that any man or woman eighteen years of age might appear before the *alcalde de Fuero*, and ask that guardians be removed from power, and ask for a full accounting of his or her property. Then the *alcalde* shall gather information as to the truth of whether that minor is a person of such understanding, manner and conduct that he or she can manage, guard, put in order and administrate himself or herself and his or her real estate and movable property without those guardians. And if the *alcalde* should find that he should do [as the minor has requested], he may remove the minor and his or her property from the charge of the guardians and order that they give a full accounting of all his or her property, its fruits and income, within a time set by the *alcalde*. And those guardians shall be required to do so and comply without any excuses, etcetera.

### 136. Concerning the Salary and Compensation for the Guardians.

Furthermore it is not fair that such guardians of minor children should work, guard, manage and administer the minors and their property without recompense for their work.

For that reason they ordered and established that guardians of minor children should receive reward for their work from the property of the minor children under the guidance of good men, according to what was reasonably discerned and ordered by the *alcalde de Fuero*, taking into consideration and having respect for the property, administration and labor, etcetera.

### 137. How Parents Who Have Given Their Farm to the Children on Condition That They Support Them Must Ask for Their Living Allowance upon the Death of the Children, etcetera.

Furthermore it often happens that the father or mother gives some truncal real estate and property to one of their children upon his or her marriage, or in some other way, reserving [a right to] their living allowance and burial expenses. And afterwards the child who received such property dies before the father and mother. And the dead child left children. And after the death of the child [to whom the property was given], the father and the mother of the deceased, in order to cheat their grandchildren, the children of the deceased, give the property first given [to the deceased] to some other child, announcing in church who [i.e. the new heir(ess)] will provide their living allowance and burial expenses since the grandchildren are minors and [will not] wish to take charge of supporting them because of being minors. And for this reason they wish to give that which they had first given [to the deceased] to another child, either because the child is closer [to them] than the grandchild or because they are moved to [do so] by their own will.

And because it is not fair that the parents who have thus given away their property should have their living allowance reduced, or that the minor children should lose their right [to their inheritance] because of their minor status, they ordered and established that if the child should die before the father or the mother who gave [him or her] his or her property, and children of [the deceased] remain [living], then the father or mother who thus gave up their property may, if they wish, ask for their living allowance from the guardians of those minor children before the *alcalde de Fuero*, [and the *alcalde*] shall make the guardians and caretakers provide the living allowance from the property of the minor children.

And if those guardians and caretakers who by law should be constrained [to do so], should not wish to provide that living allowance, those who asked for the allowance shall announce [it] in church on three Sundays, and if those guardians or caretakers or other relatives of the minor children should come forth and provide *fiadores* [to guarantee that they will] give the customary living allowance, the grandparents of those minors shall be required to accept their living allowance from those [people] who wish to give it in the name of the minor children.

And if neither the minors nor their guardians nor their caretakers nor anyone else comes forth on their behalf, then after those announcements the grandparents who made the announcements shall go before the *alcalde de Fuero* and ask his permission to do whatever they wish with their property. And the *alcalde* shall choose an appraiser in the name of the minor children, and the grandparents [shall choose] another for themselves, and one appraiser [shall be chosen] in common between them [and the *alcalde*] shall order those three appraisers to examine that property and [its] fruits and income, and [determine] whether they are maliciously asking for that living allowance or [asking] out of necessity, because they cannot support [themselves] on that property. And if those three good men, or two of them, one of whom is the intermediary, find that the living allowance was maliciously requested, and that those who requested it could support themselves from their property and its fruits and income, then they may not give it to another child, nor to any other person, to the detriment of their minor grandchildren. And if it is found that they ask for it out of necessity, being unable to support themselves on that property, in that case the grandparents who request the living allowance may give [the property] to whichever of the other children or heirs they wish, and what they thus give shall be valid, regardless of the fact that they had first given and bequested [it] thusly. And it remains to the minor children to recover any losses from their guardians and caretakers if they receive some injury through their neglect.

And if the grandfather died and the grandmother lived, or the grandmother died and the grandfather lived, the one who survived may ask for his living allowance from the half of the property [belonging to] the deceased, leaving the grandchildren without the responsibility of any living allowance for the surviving grandparent, even if they are summoned in the aforementioned manner.

### 138. Title Concerning Crimes and Punishments.

First they said that they ordered and established that any person by himself could enter and pass freely and without penalty through any property owned or held by another, even if that property is fenced in or its boundaries marked.

But if someone enters with a cart or with a shod beast, and the property were fenced in or its boundaries marked, then [that person] shall pay 48 *maravedís* in old money as a fine for each time that he enters thusly. And this also holds true if he should pass through with a cart or with a shod beast against the prohibition of the owner of the property.

And if a solitary man enters someone else's property and does some damage, he shall pay double the damages to the owner of that property, etcetera.

### 139. [Concerning] He Who Enters Another Person's Property While the Owner Is Present, etcetera.

Furthermore any person who enters another person's property while the owner is present, and the owner of the property appoints a *fiador* in his place [to forbid] him from entering the property, and he enters against [the owner's] will, then he shall pay 48 *maravedís* in old money as a fine to the owner for each time that he enters [the property].

And if there were a lot [of people] who entered [the property], each one shall pay the above fine.

And if the owner of the estate at the time that they entered did not have a *fiador* to send them away, then he [himself] shall demand that they do not enter his property. And if [they] enter against his will, then they shall pay the aforementioned fine, even if [the owner] does not appoint a *fiador*, etcetera.

### 140. Those Who Take Oxen and Yoke Them Against the Will of Their Owner.

Furthermore many dare to take other people's oxen from the pasture without the permission of the owner and yoke them up to perform labor with them, and sometimes the oxen are lost and sometimes not.

And because it is not fair that anyone should take or work with what belongs to another without the owner's permission, they ordered that any person or persons who thus take someone else's oxen and yoke them up without the owner's permission shall pay 48 *maravedís* in old money as a fine for each time that he yokes up each ox that he takes in said manner. And twice as many [*maravedís*] for unyoking them.*

And if one or more of those oxen should be lost in any way between the time they were thus taken and the time the owner has them in his charge, then the person or persons who took the oxen from the pasture shall be required to pay the owner of the lost ox or oxen double their value in addition to the aforementioned fines, once it is proven by witnesses of good reputation how he took them. And if it cannot be proven, then the defendant shall be required to swear an oath in a church designated for the swearing of oaths, that neither he nor any other [person] under his orders took or yoked those oxen as they charged him with doing.

And a suit may be filed over this within the year in which the oxen were taken and yoked, and not after, etcetera.

### 141. Concerning Those Who Take Other People's Oxen, Even If They Do Not Yoke Them.

Furthermore if [a person] should take some other oxen with those [oxen mentioned in Article 140] and afterwards they are lost, that same fine shall apply even if he did not put yokes upon them.

But if [the owner] expels from the pastures one or more yearling bulls belonging to outsiders, or from the pastures those oxen or any other livestock belonging to outsiders, then he who turned them out shall not incur any fine, even if they were lost because he turned them out, etcetera.

### 142. Concerning Pigs That Grow Fat in Another Person's Woodland.

Furthermore some heirs have hereditary shares in woodlands and boundaried pasturage with acorns. And they bring pigs in from outside

---

* That is, for taking the yoke off of oxen that had been yoked by their owner.

to be fattened up on said holdings for a price paid to them by the owners of the pigs, and sometimes those pigs pass from said holdings onto others, and the other landowner or landowners onto whose patrimonial lands those pigs wander corral them, and they do not want to give back the pigs of the [person] who was supposed to fatten them up [to anyone] except the principal owner.

In that case they ordered that whenever pigs were taken in the aforementioned manner, if the landowner who took the pigs to his patrimonial land to fatten [them] up wishes and would like to pay the penalty and fine incurred [by the pigs], one *maravedí* in old money for each pig that was found on another's fenced-in land during the day and two *maravedís* during the night, then they shall be required to give the pigs to the person paid to fatten them up, even though the principal owner does not [come forth to] demand them. And if those pigs enter another person's property by day or by night and do damage, [and] the person who brought the pigs in to be fattened provides a *fiador* [to guarantee that he will] comply with his obligation concerning that damage, then [the pigs] will not be kept from him by the injured party once the *fiador* is provided, under penalty of 48 *maravedís* in old money, each *fiador* guaranteeing his portion, etcetera.

### 143. Concerning the Cutting of Fernlands.

Furthermore some *prestameros* or *merinos*, or their men are accustomed to going through the land at the time of cutting the fernlands, saying that up until the feast day of San Cebrian,* he who cuts the ferns shall incur a fine, and [because of this] officials are bribed.

And wanting to resolve the matter, they ordered that no *prestamero* or *merino*, or any of their men, shall dare to prohibit anyone from cutting ferns on his own property, or on communal lands that anyone is tenanting from the first day of the month of September onward, nor [may they dare] to take or ask for any fine. And [a person] may cut, sell and protect [his tract] without [incurring] any fine.

### 144. That One May Buy Cattle from Asturias and from Outside Bizkaia for Resale, etcetera.

Furthermore many in the Countship of Bizkaia are accustomed to bringing in oxen and cows from Asturias and other places, and because of such outside cattle, there arises much harm to the cattle of the land.

---

* Probably San Sipriano, or St.Cyprian, whose feast day is September 16.

And, consequently, they ordered and established that no person from the said Countship should bring in any cattle for resale from outside, unless some person or persons would like to bring in and buy [cattle] individually for his household, and not for resale. And if some person or persons should bring in cattle from outside to sell, then no person or persons shall dare to buy them, except for the provisioning of his household and not to resell.

And someone or somebodies who shall go against the above shall lose all the cattle that he or they thus brought in and bought beyond that which he or they brought in and bought for his or their own household or households. Of that which was thus taken from him or them, one-third shall be for the *anteiglesia* where they reside, and one-third for the accusing party, and the other third for the *prestamero* or *merino* of that *merindad* who files the first complaint.

But any public butcher or butchers may bring in cattle from any place for slaughter and sale in the butcher shops without [incurring] any fine, [but] not for resale, unless one butcher [sells] to another, etcetera.

### 145. Fines for Livestock That Enter Another Person's Property by Day or by Night, etcetera.

Furthermore many [people] who have livestock [such as] horses and mules and asses and cows and pigs and sheep and goats do great damage with their livestock to other people's property, in wheat fields as well as in vineyards and apple orchards and seed beds and gardens and other grainfields used for fodder, because of poor vigilance of such livestock.

Consequently, they ordered and established that whoever had animals or livestock should keep them in such a way that they cause no damage.

And if they should do damage to another person's property by entering [there] by day or by night, then [the owner of the livestock] shall pay one *quarta** of wheat for the damage that was done if [the livestock] should enter by day. And if [the damage] were [done] in a millet field, [he shall pay] one *quarta* of millet. And if [the livestock] were to enter a barley field, [the owner should pay] one *quarta* of barley, and so on by this same formula, [if it should enter] any other grainfields, and if it should enter an apple orchard or a vineyard then [the owner of the livestock] shall pay one *maravedí* for each pig, and the same for sheep.

---

* *Quarta* (*cuarta*) = (in Asturias and Galicia) a unit of dry measure, one-fourth of a *ferrado* (3 to 4 liters); *ferrado* = land measure of between 4 and 6 *ares* (1/100 of a hectare); corn measure between 13 and 16 liters.

And he shall pay three *maravedís* for each head of goats or other live-stock, in addition to [paying] double the damage that was done to the vineyard, the apple orchard or the other aforementioned places, at the price set by three good men.

And if that livestock did the damage at night, then [its owner] shall pay the aforementioned fines twice over, or provide valuable items of movable property as security for payment, or he who received the damage shall corral the livestock and shall not be required to give it back until the [owners of the livestock] make payment to him or give him the said items of property as security.

And if the owner of the property cannot corral the livestock and [the animals] flee from him, then in that case, by swearing that the live-stock did the damage to his [property] or that he found it on his land, the owner of the land shall be believed. And there shall be no lawsuit over this, and [the owner of the livestock] shall then give him that live-stock, or those items of property [as security], under pain of a fine of 110 *maravedís*.

But if, before the damage is done, the owner of the livestock should advise the owner of the land that his property is open, or that he does not have a good fence, in that case the owner of the property shall be required to close it [off] under the eye of three good men. And if he does not close it off, and the livestock should enter and cause damage, then the owner of the livestock shall pay [only] the damages, and shall not incur any other fine. And if he advises [the owner of the land] after the damage is done, he shall pay the first damages along with the above-named fines, and the owner of the land shall close off his proper-ty in the manner described above. And if he does not close it off and receives some [more] damage, the owner of the livestock shall pay the price of those damages with no other fine. And if the owner of the prop-erty [still] does not close it off after having been advised, and once again receives damage, the owner of the livestock shall not be required to pay any damages. But if one person who has livestock should advise the owner of the land and livestock belonging to another [person] who had not advised [the property owner] should do some damage or should enter his property, then [the latter owner of livestock] shall pay in the aforementioned manner. And all this applies to residents of the *villa* with respect to outsiders, and to outsiders with respect to residents.

And since the said livestock causes more damage in vineyards than on any other property, it is understood that [the owner of the livestock] shall pay a fine of four *maravedís* for each head of cattle, horses or pigs for each occurrence, beyond the damages stated above, and in like man-ner [for] livestock that enters a seed bed, etcetera.

## 146. Concerning Those Who Sow on Communal Lands, etcetera.

Furthermore if someone encloses and makes an enclosure and seeding on communal woodland and some livestock damages it, let [the encloser] repair [the damage] at his will, and the owner of the livestock shall not be required to pay any damages or any other fines, etcetera.

## 147. Concerning Nets and Fish Traps, etcetera.

Furthermore any *hidalgo* may place a gill net from the [tidal] bar to the sea. But if he places it in fresh water, then the owner of the nearest property may take [the nets], even if they are fish traps or other things for fishing, without penalty.

## 148. Title Concerning the Planting of Trees and Their Fruits, etcetera.

First of all they said that in many places in the said Land of Bizkaia there are two or more houses which have their sites where everyone has a communal right. And some resident occasionally plants trees in such places, in order to have for himself the usufruct of those trees and orchards which were thus planted, without the other shareholders in the property [receiving any usufruct]. Which was damaging to the other residents of those places who have a share.

Consequently they said that they had as *fuero* and they ordered and established that nobody or somebodies should dare to cut down those trees and orchards which had been thus planted, nor [should they dare] to tip or shake the trees in order to knock down and gather the fruit, even if the planters should wish to do so. And whoever shall shake and knock down the fruit of those trees by climbing up the tree with a pole shall pay 48 *maravedís* in old money as a fine to the other shareholders in the commons. And the fruit that falls to the ground by itself shall be shared by all of them, and each one may gather as much as he can.

And the planters may not prevent [this] by saying that they planted it, since they did so on land common to all. And whoever shall fall under the aforementioned penalty shall be required to pay the fine within thirty days after he is advised [of it]. And if he is not advised of it within thirty days from the day on which he incurred the fine, from that time on he shall not be required to pay it, nor to answer for [his actions].

But if all the shareholders, or the majority of them, after advising the others should agree to knock down and gather such fruits from the trees in the planted areas, it shall be and be understood that these are the fruits and trees that were planted in the commons and on communal lands.

### 149. Concerning Those Who Plant on Undivided Properties That They Have.

Furthermore it happens that two or three or more partners hold some property together without dividing it, and some of those shareholders plant apple trees on that undivided property or on part of it, without the other shareholders and without informing them.

In that case they ordered and established by law, that if someone should plant apple trees on property held in common and without the permission of the other shareholders, and within a year and a day the other shareholders oppose [the planting] and want to pay the cost of it, they shall all own it jointly according to [how they stand to] inherit the property.

And if a year and a day should pass and they do not oppose [the planting of those trees], then from that time on, even if the other shareholders want to pay the costs [of the planting] and have a share in it, the planter, by giving [them] another property in another location equivalent to the planted [property] that is part of that same patrimony, shall own that which he planted, without the participation of the other shareholders.

And if by chance he did not have or could not give another such property that was from said patrimony from which came [the land] that he planted as aforementioned, then in that case the planter shall be required to care for and manage those apple trees. And once they are grown, he shall pay half the fruit that God provides on them, for as long as the apple trees shall last, to each shareholder according to [the manner in which] they inherited the land.

And after the apple trees are spent, they shall hold the land in common according to how they [held it] before the apple trees were planted. And this is understood for other trees as well, etcetera.

### 150. Concerning [the Person] Who Plants Apple Trees on Another Person's Property.

Furthermore if some [person] should plant apple trees on another person's property without permission from the owner, [who] within five years appoints a *fiador* to request that he leave his property, the planter shall be required to give [the trees] to him, [once] the owner pays him the price placed on the trees by three good men. And if the owner of the property does not want to pay the appraised amount, then the planter may uproot and move the apple trees to wherever he wishes without [incurring] any penalty, and the property shall remain with its owner. And this shall be the choice of the owner of the property [to buy the trees or have them moved], but the planter may not be required to uproot the apple trees until the following months of January and February, because [to do so before] would harm the apple trees.

But if the owner of the property does not oppose the planter within five years, [then] once [the trees] are planted, the planter shall work and hoe and fertilize and care for that apple orchard. And once [the trees] are grown, the planter and the owner of the property shall share equally the fruit of the apple orchard.

For as long as two-thirds of the apple trees shall last, the planter shall be required to hoe over the earth of the orchard twice a year, and to fertilize every three years, for the first twelve years. And after twelve years are passed, every five to five years after that. And if he does not work the land every year, then the first year that he does not work the land, all the fruit produced that year shall belong to the owner of the property. And if he does not work the land the second year, then the property and all the apple trees shall belong to the owner, with no part going to the planter.

But [even if the land is] worked [the way it should be], when two-thirds of the apple trees no longer bear fruit, the owner of the property shall enter [the orchard], and the planter shall have to vacate and leave it to its owner. And he shall not be required to work the orchard after leaving, but he shall still take half the fruit of the apple trees which remain, etcetera.

**151. That the Owner of the Property May Enter [the Orchard] and Take Half the Fruit That Falls to the Ground at Any Time, etcetera.**

Furthermore let it be known that until now it has been the usage and custom in Bizkaia that the planters of such apple orchards would not allow the owner of the property to enter the orchard and pick up and take away his half of the fruit that fell by itself to the ground until the feast day of Santa Cruz.* Which was a great damage and detrimental to the owners of the property.

Therefore they ordered and established that the owner of that property may pick up and take away one of every two ripe apples beginning on the day on which the apple trees bear fruit and continuing, irrespective of the above-mentioned custom. And the planter shall not dare to either pick up or take away any apples from that orchard in large baskets, or [small] baskets, or large sacks, or any other container, without

---

* September 14th.

the knowledge of the owner of that property, under pain of paying the owner twice [the value of] that which he took in that manner.

### 152. That He Who Plants on the Property and Land of Another Shall Lose That Which He Planted, and It Shall Belong to the Owner of the Property, etcetera.

Furthermore let it be known that many [individuals] dare to plant walnut trees, as well as chestnut trees and ash trees and fruit trees and other trees, on other people's property without permission from the owner of it in order to thus charge the owner rental [for the improvements to the property].

And so that those daring [persons] may not profit from their deceit, they ordered and established that if a person plants fruit or trees on the property of another, then he shall lose all that he thus planted, and all of it shall belong to the owner of the property, with no part of it going to the planter. But this law may not contradict the aforementioned other law that speaks about the planter of apple trees.

### 153. Concerning Those Who Plant Close to Other People's Property, etcetera.

Furthermore [they] let it be known that many disputes and lawsuits arise over trees that are planted near the property of another, saying that according to the *fuero* and custom of Bizkaia that the owners of those trees must cut them back and remove them from the proximity of other people's property that is [used] to grow wheat, in the following manner: the oak [must be removed to a distance of ] twelve *brazas*,* the ash to twelve *brazas*, the chestnut to eight *brazas*, the walnut tree to six *brazas*, the apple tree to one and a half *brazas*, and the pear trees, medlars, fig trees, peach trees and other small fruit trees to one and a half *brazas*.

They said that this was the *fuero* and custom of Bizkaia, and declaring the said *fuero* and custom of Bizkaia, they established and ordered that if the owner of those trees were ordered by the owner of the property to cut down and uproot those trees, then he shall be required to cut them down or uproot those trees.

But if the trees were so old that the petitioner's ancestors had not demanded [that they be cut down] and the planters of those trees were

---

* *Braza*: unit of linear measurement equal to 5.46 feet or 1.6718 meters. Hence, the distances which must be maintained between one person's trees and another person's trees and another person's property are: 65.52 feet for oak trees and ash trees; 43.68 feet for chestnut trees; 32.76 feet for walnut trees; and 8.19 feet for apple trees, pear trees and other fruit trees.

dead, [then] they may not have those [trees] cut down, unless it is done to clear a space of five paces distant from the property which [the tree] is damaging.

But if some tree should be located on some plot of land [used] to grow wheat, and the owner of that plot of land is incurring damages because of that tree, and the owner of the tree is receiving little profit from the tree, [then] in that case the parties [involved] shall go before the *alcalde*, and the *alcalde* shall order them to appoint three good men who shall examine the damage done to the property. And if the three good men find that the tree is doing no harm and should remain, then the owner [of the tree] shall not be required to cut it down. And if they find it is doing harm, and the tree is producing little profit, then [the owner] shall cut it or prune it in the manner ordered by those three good men, and [their decision] shall be valid, etcetera.

## 154. Title Concerning Building.

First of all, let it be known that the common lands and commons of Bizkaia belong to the Lord and the *hidalgos*. And some people cast *bidigazas** in the rivers and streams and pass through those common lands and put up *abeurreas*** there so that they may put some dam at the location of the *bidigaza* for the iron foundry, mill or mill wheel which they planned to build in the location of the *abeurreas*. They did this very secretly in order to appropriate that property for themselves, having secretly thrown that *bidigaza* in the water [and left it there] for a year and a day so that no one knew about it.

Therefore they said that in such cases they had as *fuero* and usage and custom and they ordered that if any person publicly casts a *bidigaza* or raises *abeurreas* for a year and a day, and notifies the *anteiglesia* in which that property is located, and no one contradicts [that claim] within a year and a day, after that time that person may build the dam and foundry or mill or mill wheel without any opposition, as if [it were] on his own property. And if he does not publicly announce the *bidigaza* in church, or if someone from the *anteiglesia* opposes [him], he may not put up the building.

---

* *Bidigaza/bedigaza* (Basque: *bidegaza*): object cast into the water at a certain place to indicate the intention of building a dam or ditch there to divert water for use in an iron foundry or mill.

** *Abeurreas/abeuras*: object placed [raised] on public land in Bizkaia for the purpose of declaring one's intention of obtaining the right to build there.

And he who wins the [right to the] water in the aforementioned manner with *bidigaza* and *abeurreas* shall be required to begin and carry out his building within one full year after winning the [right to the] water, and [may] continue his work if he wishes. And if within the year and a day he does not wish to build, any other person from that *anteiglesia* may do so without opposition from the one who thus won [the right to] the water or from anyone else, if he first begins building after the year and a day have passed. And if he who wins the [right to the] water should build, he may not win [the right to build] or have another building or any construction in another location on common land [during] that year. [But] he may do so on his own [land], etcetera.

### 155. Concerning Those Who Have *Bidigazas*, on Property Belonging to Shareholders, etcetera.

Furthermore it happens that [when] a property belongs to many shareholders, some of them want to build an iron foundry and mill or mill wheel or other building. And that person or persons post their *abeurreas* and cast *bidigazas*…in the channel from which they must take the water without the other partners [having knowledge of it or giving consent], and arguments arise over that.

Therefore in order to rid men of lawsuits and differences and contentions, they said that they had as *fuero* and of custom and they established by law that if the person who wants to build casts the *bidigaza* or raises the *abeurreas* for a year and a day, and the other shareholders do not oppose [him], then after the year and a day have passed, even if the shareholders should say that they now want to participate, he may build without any opposition from the other shareholders, by paying the other shareholders money amounting to twice the price of the part that they inherited, the price of the land of the inheritance being determined by three good men.

But if they block him within a year and a day, and the shareholders who block him appoint *fiadores*, each shareholder who so objected shall have his share in that building and project according to [how much of the] land he inherits, and [the owner] of the ground of the place where the foundry or mill wheel or mill would be located shall have the other half.

And for owning part of the property between the dam and the ancestral property where the building will be, over which must pass the locks and barriers so that the water from the dam may reach [the building]…[the shareholder] shall have no part of that building nor may he forbid the passage of water over his property, once [the builder] pays the owner of that property double the price set upon it by three appraisers.

And, if by chance, the land upon which that building or dam was built belonged to the Lord or the Church, then the Lord or the Church shall have this same right with other people [shareholders], but as far as the price is concerned, he who constructs the building shall be required to pay double [the value of] the property in the form of another property to the Lord or the Church.

## 156. Concerning the Same Matter.

Furthermore it may be that some of those who construct the afore-mentioned buildings are shareholders in the [building of the] dam, but not in the ground where the iron foundry or mill wheel or mill will be located, and it may be that they are shareholders in the ground [where] the foundry or mill [are located] and not in the dam. And there may be doubt as to whether the shareholder in the ancestral property where the iron foundry or mill will be located may compel the shareholders in the property where the waterway will be located [to participate in its construction], and [whether] the shareholders in the waterway may compel the shareholders of the property on which they are constructing the building [to participate in its construction].

And in order to eliminate this doubt, they said that they had as *fuero* and usage and custom and they ordered by law that if the owners of the ground on which that building will be located should wish to compel those who have a share in the property where the waterway will be [to participate in its construction], then they may compel them to do their share of the building.

But the owners of the property [containing] the dam may not com-pel those [who own] the property [on which] the house [is located]. And if the shareholders of the property and dam, being required [to partici-pate], should not wish to do so, then the owner of the ancestral proper-ty [on which is built] the foundry or mill may carry out his construction, even though those [who own] the waterway are opposed, saying that they do not want to build it nor consent to the building, etcetera.

## 157. Concerning Those Who Build Iron Foundries to the Detriment of the Aforementioned.

Furthermore many [new] iron foundries, mill wheels and mills are built in Bizkaia, to the detriment of others which were built previously, in such a way that many of the foundries, mill wheels and mills which were built first are unable to forge iron or grind [grain] because of the damage [done] by the water stoppage, over which there arise many law-suits and debates.

And consequently, in order to eliminate these doubts and debates, they said that they had as *fuero* and usage and custom and they established by law that whoever builds a new foundry or mill or mill wheel close by another [foundry or mill] shall build it in such a manner that the water shall flow freely, and not be blocked, so that it shall neither obstruct nor impede the first foundry, wheel or mill with the dam, [and] thus the new edifice shall be built below the first foundry or wheel or mill.

And they shall build it in such a manner that it provides a space of three *jemes** of running water, and if it does not provide this amount, then the owner of the upper foundry or mill shall be required to lower its dam so that the water shall flow in the amount of three *jemes* from the discharge of the upper foundry, wheel or mill, [and what] remains of the water shall be for the lower dam. These *jemes* shall be according [to the measurements] of a common [normal] man.

## 158. Concerning the Flow through the Floodgate When There Is Little Water.

Furthermore many times it happens [that] many of the foundries and waterwheels and mills cease founding and milling because of a lack of water.

In that case they said that they had as *fuero* and usage and custom and they established by law that whenever there is a lack of water the owners of the foundries and mills and waterwheels may put floodgates in the channels where the water runs in the following manner: one floodgate for each foundry or waterwheel or mill. But whoever shall put such a floodgate in place shall leave a space of at least four fingers above it where the water passes [over] so that another waterwheel or mill or foundry, which might be located below [the first], may carry out its operations freely. And [this distance of] four fingers [above] the floodgate, if it belongs to a foundry, shall not be above the floodgate of the waterwheel for the hammer, but rather above the floodgate of the waterwheel for the bellows. And the same shall apply to the [floodgates erected] by the mills. And this law shall apply if it is proven that the upper foundry or waterwheel or mill was built after the lower [foundry, mill or waterwheel]. But if it was built first, then they may close the entire floodgate.

---

* *Jeme* (also *xeme* and *geme*): distance between the tip of the thumb and the tip of the forefinger.

159. Concerning the Validity of *Abeurreas* or *Bidigazas* [Which Are] Secretly Placed, and If Not the Punishment of Whomever Removed Them.

Furthermore they said that they had as *fuero* and usage and custom that when someone wished to place *abeurreas* or *bidigazas* for the purpose of gaining [the right to erect] some building, they sometimes did so maliciously and posted them secretly, [and] in that case [the law] shall be maintained according to the aforementioned manner, and in no other manner, whether dealing with foundries or waterwheels or mills or with any other new buildings. And after the *abeurreas* are posted, and the *bidigaza* is posted and made public in the *anteiglesia*, if it was posted on communal land, no one shall dare to touch or remove either the *abeurreas* or the *bidigaza* without an *alcalde's* order, under penalty of 1,100 *maravedís* for each offense, [and the fine shall be paid] to the person who posted the *abeurreas* and *bidigazas*, and five cows [shall go] to the Lord on a first offense. For a second offense, [the perpetrator] shall be legally put to death. And if by chance a person should post *abeurreas* and *bidigazas* not on communal land but on another person's property as if it were his own, then that person shall incur this same penalty.

160. Concerning Foundry Buildings and Mills and Waterwheels That Have Fallen into Ruin and Disrepair, etcetera.

Furthermore it often happens that some people have on their property some foundry or waterwheel or mill which later falls to ruin by reason of the fact that they do not forge or mill [anything there] for a long time, nor does that place have the appearance of the foundry or waterwheel or mill which was there originally. And after [the building] has fallen to ruin, and much time has passed, some person or persons build foundries or waterwheels or mills above or below where the first foundry or waterwheel or mill [was located], [and in doing so] stop the flow of water. And afterward it sometimes happens that the owner or owners of that property where the original foundry or mill or waterwheel was located build, or wish to build, a foundry or waterwheel or mill, and doubt arises over who has the water rights, [the owners of] the building which was built while the original was in ruins or the owner of the original structure who now wishes to rebuild.

And in order to eliminate this doubt, they said that they had as *fuero* and usage and custom and ordered that if some building on a person's property, such as a foundry or waterwheel or mill, should fall into ruin in any manner for any amount of time, and afterward some other person constructs a building upstream or downstream, [that person] shall do so in a way that will not be detrimental to the owner of the original building. And if he does build it in a detrimental manner, and afterward the owner of that property constructs a building on the location where the original [building] was located, he may do so without opposition from the [owners of the] other buildings [which were] built later upstream or downstream. And that building shall have the measure of three *jemes* of water in its discharge below the headboard as is customary in Bizkaia [see Article 157], etcetera.

### 161. That Building Materials May Pass Through Another Person's Property If Reparations Are Paid.

Furthermore they said that they had as *fuero*, usage and custom that if someone had to build a simple house or a fortified house and, in order to do so, it was necessary to transport wood or stone or wooden beams of an apple press across another person's property, that person may do so by paying the owner of the property any damages, set by good men, if there were no reasonable route for transport available without entering the other person's property.

### 162. Concerning the Denunciation of New Buildings.

Furthermore they said that they had as *fuero*, usage and custom that any *hidalgo* may build any kind of fortified house or simple house on his property in Bizkaia without any opposition. But if someone appoints a *fiador* and denounces the new building, then they shall go before the *alcalde* and shall order the possessor to produce a *fiador* before his *alcalde*. If the person who wishes to build possesses the property for a year and a day, and provides *fiadores* [to guarantee that he will] demolish the building [if necessary], he may build the structure without any delay and without waiting for a period of the 90 days. And this by order of a judge and in no other manner. And this applies to *hidalgos*, and no *villano* [townsman] or *labrador* enjoys this privilege, etcetera.

### 163. Title Concerning Lawsuits and Responses and the Appointment of *Fiadores* Whereby Litigation Begins.

First they said that they had as *fuero* and usage and custom that whenever someone has a claim or wants to sue for something other than heritable land, then the claimant shall take items of movable property as security from the defendant,[*] and he may make him provide *fiadores*

---

[*] Written as the *demandador* in the text but should be *demandado*.

[to assure that he will] comply with the law. And that *fiador* shall cast lots [to determine] when and before which *alcalde de Fuero* the parties will appear, the one to make his case and the other to defend [himself]. And if some person wishes to sue another for some heritable real estate, the claimant shall appoint a *fiador* to guarantee that he will comply with the law, regarding that which he claims, and the defendant must provide within nine days his own *fiador* guaranteeing compliance with the law. And after the *fiadores* are thus appointed, the *fiadores* of both parties shall cast lots [to determine] before which of the said *alcaldes* the parties will appear in the aforementioned manner. And these *fiadores* shall be those [persons] who have livestock as security to ensure that one party complies with that which is decided for the other party according to the Fuero of Bizkaia, etcetera.

## 164. That If the *Alcalde* Should So Order, Second *Fiadores* Shall Be Appointed, etcetera.

Furthermore they said that they had as *fuero* and usage and custom that after the parties [in a suit] have provided *fiadores* and drawn lots, they shall appear before the *alcalde* chosen by lot, and the *alcalde* may order one or both parties to provide other stronger *fiadores*, as *fiadores*, to follow through and comply with the law to simply [guarantee] the complete fulfillment of it. And after both parties or one of them provide second *fiadores* by order of the *alcalde*, then the first *fiadores* shall be relieved of their obligation as guarantors, unless they were selected once again, etcetera.

## 165. That If the Claimant Fails to Pursue [The Case Within] One Year and a Day, the *Fiador* of the Claim Shall Be Free of the Guarantee.

Furthermore it happens that [once] the *fiador* or *fiadores* have been appointed on both sides to guarantee fulfillment of obligation before the *alcaldes de Fuero*, and the claimant fails to pursue the case for such a long time that the *fiador* does not remember the obligation, or even if he does, [the claimant] fails to pursue his case for so long that the *fiador* should be allowed to withdraw from the obligation of *fiador* for the defendant, [and in such case] it is not fair that the *fiador* should be held responsible.

Consequently they said that they had as *fuero* and ordered by law that if any person receives a *fiador* or *fiadores* concerning a lawsuit or lawsuits and fails to pursue his case within a year and a day, then from that time on the *fiador* shall not be required to respond to any matter concerning that suit, unless it was a case pending before the *alcaldes de Fuero* continuing [beyond a year and a day] before either the [*alcaldes de Fuero*] or the *corregidor*, or before either one of them, or a decision was handed down.

**166. That the Case Goes to Court over the Head of the *Fiador* before He Could Draw Lots [for the Alcalde], Then the *Fiador* Is Valid and Shall Compel the Party to Comply, etcetera.**

Furthermore it often happens that, concerning the *fiador* or *fiadores* appointed by each of the parties in the aforementioned manner, the parties go before some *alcaldes* and receive a judgment in a case without the *alcaldes* having been drawn by lot by the *fiadores*. And afterwards one of the parties says, maliciously and in order to prolong the case, that he did not accept the decision, [since] the *fiador* that he had chosen [did not] draw lots, nor was a time set [for the case]. And that the decision is not valid. Because of which, the lawsuits are prolonged and the parties are exhausted by expenses.

Consequently they said that in such a case they had as *fuero* and established by law in order to avoid wrongdoing, that if the parties went before an *alcalde* or *alcaldes* and received a decision, then the *fiador* shall be required to make the party who chose him comply with that decision, and neither the party nor the *fiador* may be excused from complying with [the decision], even if the parties should appear before and receive a decision from the *alcalde* without the *fiador* drawing lots or the *alcalde* summoning [them].

**167. That *Fiador* Who Does Not Wish to Draw Lots for the *Alcalde* Shall Not Be a Valid *Fiador*.**

Furthermore if someone promises another person [that he will provide] a *fiador* over some lawsuit, and the other person in turn appoints another *fiador* or *fiadores* [because] one of the parties is suing the other, then when the *fiadores* of both parties are present, those *fiadores* and one party and the other shall draw lots and set a time to appear before the *alcaldes de Fuero*, and the *fiador* of one party or the other who provides what securities he has, or that he provides the guarantees does not wish to draw lots immediately, nor appoint a time for his party to appear before the *alcaldes de Fuero* and without delay.

In such a case they said that they had as *fuero* and established by law that the *fiador* or *fiadores* who do not wish to draw lots shall not be valid [*fiadores*], nor shall they be had as *fiadores*, nor may they be of use to the person who presented them as a *fiador*. And this shall be true in those cases that have not yet begun. However [once the] *fiadores* have drawn lots, and the case has already begun and lots have been cast by *fiadores*, [then] the appointment of the *fiador* shall be valid, and the *fiador* shall be required, [under pain of losing that which he posted as] security, to make the party continue with the case and comply with that [obligation] because he was chosen as a *fiador*.

### 168. That Whoever Wishes to Sue Another for Personal Property Shall Seize the Other Person's Goods.

Furthermore they said that they had as *fuero* and usage and custom that whenever any person wanted to file suit against others, whether the suit involves truncal real estate or movable property, the claimant shall seize some of the movable property of that person whom he wishes to sue.

And after the movable property is taken, [he shall] make known how he took the items of security from him.

And if the person whose goods were seized went with a *fiador* and presents him as [guarantee that he will] fulfill his obligation as set by the *alcaldes de Fuero*, [then] the goods must be returned to him. And if they are not returned and the goods are damaged, he shall pay [the owner of the property] double the damages plus 48 *maravedís* in old money for each *fiador* that he provided. And if the party does not believe [that they are *fiadores*], then by swearing in a church designated for the swearing of oaths that they are *fiadores*, whatever the *fiadores* said in their oath shall be valid.

And if the person whose property is seized approaches the person who is taking it, and asks him to wait for him, and says that he will bring a *fiador* [whose guarantee shall take the place of] his property, and gives something that was before him [as security] and goes to the field where [the seizer] places the property, then while he is bringing the *fiador*, [the seizer of goods] shall not carry the property any further from that house, and he [the owner] shall have two hours in which to bring forward this *fiador*. And if he does not appear before [the seizer of goods] within two hours with the *fiador*, then [the person who is taking them] shall continue taking his goods until he reaches the limits of the district. And [the person taking the goods] shall be required to hold them for that night and the following day before he leaves [the district], and if [the person who owns the goods] does not return to him with a *fiador*, then he shall take the property to his house. And if the owner of the goods does not return to him with a *fiador* by the third day, then after that time he may sell the property on the following Sunday in the church where its owner is a parishioner, and the *maravedís* that [it] was worth [when sold] shall be held [by the seller] as security for the debt until the [debtor's] obligation is fulfilled.

And if he should realize that he does not have the equivalent [of the debt], then he shall return in the aforementioned manner for other goods, so that he shall have the equivalent [value] of his demand. However he may not go for more goods until the first [batch that was seized] is sold in the stated manner. And if [the owner of the movable property] comes forth to provide a *fiador*, as he should at the second or third seizures of goods, then once he has appointed a *fiador*, the seizer of them shall return to him the amount of money [he received] from all the other property that he sold, once he accepts the *fiador*. And this shall be understood in those matters which have not yet been decided.

And if the owner of that property does not appear with his *fiador* within thirty days after the public sale of it, then the [money received for the] seized or auctioned goods shall remain with the person who took it from that time onward as payment of, and compensation for, the debt he was collecting, in a case where afterwards he appoints a *fiador* against other seizures of goods.

If by chance the lawsuit is over real property that belongs to the plaintiff, and if they do not want to go to [seize his] movable property, and the plaintiff appoints a *fiador* to the person who has the property so that he will release what is his or comply with his obligation, and the defendant does not in turn appoint another *fiador*, then anytime after the following day, whenever he wishes, [the plaintiff] may go with another *fiador* up to three times, and if the defendant does not respond with a *fiador* of his own within nine days following [the appointment of] the third *fiador*, then after that time the plaintiff may go before any of the *alcaldes de Fuero* and ask and complain that [the defendant] is on his property by force [against the wishes of] *fiadores*, not wanting to comply with his obligations. And the *alcalde* shall be required to give an order to the *prestamero* or *merino* to remove the defendant from the property and put the plaintiff in possession of it, once [the plaintiff] shows before the *alcalde* that he appointed *fiadores*. And once the plaintiff is put [in possession] and the one who was removed sues the other who is now in possession, the one who is in possession shall be required to comply in this same manner. But still it is understood that the plaintiff shall be required to advise the other person that he once again give him property or a *fiador* [who will assure that he will] fulfill his obligation to the [plaintiff] concerning the debt. And being advised in the above manner, if [the defendant] does not wish to give him goods, [then] the plaintiff may take property as stated above.

And no plaintiff shall take any goods without first giving the aforementioned warning, under penalty of [having to give] 48 *maravedís* in old money to the owner of the goods, and five cows to the Lord. And if the person taking the goods, without providing a *fiador*, approaches the defendant and takes the property by force, then he shall pay another 48 *maravedís* in old money to the other party and five cows to the Lord, etcetera.

169. **That No Exceptions May Be Raised [over the *Alcalde*'s Order] to Appoint *Fiadores* to Follow Through and Comply in a Suit and Claim, Regarding Property, Nor May the Case Continue [Indefinitely].**

Furthermore until now in Bizkaia it was the usage and custom that when parties go before the *alcalde* regarding any civil suits, the plaintiff asks the *alcalde* to order that the heritable property or item of real estate being litigated be held in guarantee, and be covered by the appointment of *fiadores* each to the other [to guarantee] pursuit and compliance of the law concerning the property, according to the *fuero* of the land. And the defendant raises dilatory, and other types of, exceptions so that those *fiadores* should not be appointed to comply with and follow the law in the matter of that property. And the *alcalde* orders that each party entrusts the other with two *fiadores* [who will guarantee that they will] follow through and comply with the law. And [the parties involved] appeal the order [to provide these *fiadores*] before another *alcalde*, and thus [they go] from *alcalde* to *alcalde*, prolonging the case until they have returned [to appear again] before that *alcalde* before whom the case was begun. And even if at first they were acting on a single exception, later they made another, and then another, in such a way that suits were appearing before five *alcaldes*, from one *alcalde* to another, over each objection, for lack of a plea [by the defendant], and for that reason the suits never end.

They said that they found that this *fuero*, usage and custom was a failure and needed to be amended, and they said that they established as *fuero* and law that when the plaintiff and the defendant appear before the *alcalde*, chosen by lot, on account of some real estate, and either of the parties asks that the property be covered by the appointment of *fiadores* to comply with the law, and the *alcalde* before whom the case was begun then orders the same with each [party providing a] *fiador*, according to the *Fuero* of Bizkaia. Then the parties shall be required to do so and comply [with the *alcalde*'s order]. And neither of the parties shall be able to raise any exception for this reason, nor shall the *alcalde* entertain [any exception], since according to the *Fuero* of Bizkaia, until they have first provided *fiadores* in the above manner to cover that property, no process or judicial order that is carried out, nor any judgment that is handed down, shall be valid, even if it were to the liking of both parties. And if one of the parties should appeal the *alcalde*'s order before another *alcalde*, or before the *veedor*, he shall not be granted any appeal or recourse. And the *alcalde* may impose a fine of 36 *maravedís* in old money [on] each of the parties [involved], and said fine shall apply to the obedient party as well.

170. **How the Plaintiff and Defendant Must Make Requests and Responses Orally and Not in Writing.**

Furthermore they said that they had as *fuero*, usage and custom, and they established by law that when the parties appoint *fiadores* to cover the property [and guarantee that they will] follow through and comply with the law, and the parties appear before the *alcalde*, the plaintiff shall make his demand not in writing, but orally, in the manner which suits him, either before a notary or before witnesses. And if the defendant should then wish to respond, he shall respond orally, and not in writing, and if he should not wish to respond then, and requests a time within which to comply, [the *alcalde*] shall give him a period of nine days so that he may respond to that suit properly, stating any exceptions or defenses that he had on the ninth day. And moreover the parties shall be required to appear before the *alcalde*. And each of the parties shall declare everything he wishes to say and explain, orally, with no other extensions of time. And neither of the parties shall explain in writing, nor will the *alcalde* accept any written document. And if any of the parties should bring forth any written document, the *alcalde* shall take the document and tear it up so that it may not be read. And he shall make the parties conclude [the matter] then without any other extensions of time, and he shall conclude [the matter] with them. And he shall then hand down his judgment if he so wishes at that time, except in those instances which are mentioned later in this Fuero.

171. **That If the Plaintiff Has Movable Property That May Be Seized, He Shall Not Be Required to Appoint a *Fiador* [at the Request of] the Defendant Nor to Respond to a Cross-Action Suit.**

Furthermore they said that it sometimes happened that when the parties appeared before the *alcalde* chosen by the drawing of lots, and the plaintiff states his case, the defendant maliciously asks the *alcalde* to order the plaintiff to provide a *fiador* [to guarantee that he will] comply with his obligations under the law, or he files a cross-action suit [against the plaintiff], saying that for such a period of time he need not respond to the suit which the plaintiff has filed against him, and because of this, many suits are prolonged and turned around.

In such cases they said that they had as *fuero*, and established by law, that if the plaintiff is a person who has movable property that can be seized, he shall not be required to provide a *fiador* [at the request of] the defendant, nor shall the plaintiff be required to respond to the cross-action suit that the defendant files against him, but the *alcalde* shall make him [the plaintiff] provide a *fiador* [to guarantee that he will] fulfill his obligation [once] his property is seized, if it suits him [the *alcalde*] to do so. But if the plaintiff has no movable property which can be seized, or if he is not a very powerful man, the plaintiff shall be required to provide a *fiador* [to guarantee that he will] comply with the law before the *alcalde*. And this *fiador* shall be from the same *anteiglesia* as the defendant. And if they are unable [to provide a *fiador*] in that *anteiglesia*, with an oath that one cannot be found, then the second *anteiglesia* shall provide one. And if there is no one in that *anteiglesia* [to serve as *fiador*], then let him be from the *merindad* where the property is located. And until a *fiador* is provided, the defendant shall not be required to respond to the suit against him, etcetera.

172. **That the Ninth Day Assigned by the *Alcalde* Each of the Parties Shall Say What He Has to Say, and the Defendant Shall Respond to the Principal Claim of the Plaintiff, etcetera.**

Furthermore sometimes the defendants raise exceptions before responding to the principal claim, and because of that exception, they go from *alcalde* to *alcalde*, and from appeal to appeal. And [only] after the suit over the exception that they are litigating dies, whether the exception was accepted by the *alcaldes* or not, do the defendants respond to the principal demand, and for this reason, the suits are prolonged.

Therefore they said that they ordered and established that on the ninth day, which was assigned by the *alcalde*, each of the parties shall speak and state all that they wish to say and declare, according to what is contained in the above law. And the defendant may not avoid responding to the principal demand. And if he should raise some objection before responding to the principal demand, and [thereby] should not respond, and it is decided by one of the *alcaldes* or by the *veedor*, or either one of them, through a final judgment, that the exception should not be accepted, then in that case the defendant shall be assumed to have confessed to the principal claim, and shall not be heard concerning that claim. But, concerning the judgment that the *alcalde* hands down regarding this question, either party that feels aggrieved may appeal that judgment and appear before another *alcalde*. And thusly from *alcalde* to *alcalde*, and afterward before the *veedor*, until the case is ended by a final decision, etcetera.

### 173. That a Clergyman Who Files Suit Against a Layman Before a Secular *Alcalde* Has the Same Legal Status Before the Law in a Cross-Action Suit.

Furthermore they said that sometimes a clergyman will file a claim against a layman over some property, and the clergy have many properties in the land of noblemen which fall under secular jurisdiction. And cross-action suits are filed by some laymen against the clergy before the secular judges. And the clergymen want the suits they have filed against the laymen to be judged by secular judges. But they ask that the suits filed against them by the laymen be transferred to ecclesiastic judges, [and] because of this, justice is denied to the laymen.

In that case they said that they had as *fuero* and custom and they established by law that whenever a clergyman files a claim against a layman before secular judges, whether over movable property or real estate, and the layman files a cross-action suit against the clergyman plaintiff, then in such a case the clergyman shall be required to respond to the layman before the secular judge with whom he filed his claim. And if he asks transfer before ecclesiastic judges, and does not wish to respond to the layman and comply with the law in such case before the secular judge, then [the judge] shall not accept nor hear that clergyman in the suit he filed in order that justice may be equal, etcetera.

### 174. Concerning the Fine That Must Be Paid by the Defendant Who Does Not Respond at the Time Assigned by the *Alcalde*.

Furthermore they said that they had as *fuero* and they established by law that when the defendant does not appear at the time the *alcalde* appointed for him, and the *fiador* or *fiadores* had assigned him [a time] in the presence of the *alcalde* who was chosen by lot, he shall be required to pay the plaintiff 12 *maravedís* for each offense, and the plaintiff shall make him pay the 12 *maravedís* by putting the *fiador*'s movable property in an enclosure if he so wishes. And if the defendant should not receive a hearing, then that same [defendant] shall pay the plaintiff another 12 *maravedís*, and he shall make him pay them by putting the *fiador*'s property in an enclosure if he wishes. And if he so wishes, he [the plaintiff] shall not respond to the suit until [the defendant] pays him the fine, etcetera.

175. **That When Appealing Before Another *Alcalde*, No New Reasons May Be Stated and No New Exception May Be Raised, Only the Same Ones as Before.**

Furthermore they said that they had as *fuero* and custom, and that they established by law, that when the plaintiff files his case and responses, or the defendant [states] his exceptions and defenses before the *alcalde* who first hears the case, and the parties appeal whatever judgment the *alcalde* hands down before any other *alcalde*, or before the *veedor*. And one of the parties wishes to add to, or delete from, the claim or exceptions or defenses or responses [when appearing] before any of the other *alcaldes*, [his changes] shall not be accepted, and suits shall be decided by hearing the same reasons that were stated before the first *alcalde*, and based upon which [the] *alcalde* handed down a judgment.

But if before the *veedor* one of the parties requests that the *alcaldes* [who heard the case] appear before the *veedor*, in that meeting each of the parties may add [to his declaration], in the following manner: the plaintiff [may add to] his claim and responses, and the defendant [may add to] his exceptions and defenses in such a way that each of the parties may have equal rights both in stating the claim and posing the defense, even though one of the parties, through ignorance and error, may have [originally] committed errors of omission to his own detriment. But if, before that *alcalde*, one of the parties should make some confession, that confession shall be valid, even if it is harmful [to the party who made it], for it is not right that a confession made in court be invalidated or revoked, even if the party says that he made it in error or in ignorance.

176. **Concerning Those Who Give Over Livestock to a Shared Arrangement.**

Furthermore it often happens that some people give over some livestock, such as cows or pigs or goats or sheep or other livestock to be held in common so that [others] will have them and raise them in their homes. And after a while, ignoring their consciences, they [the latter] deny that they took that which they received to care for or on a half share basis, and [deny] that [they] are not theirs. And they [can] do this because according to the Fuero of Bizkaia for the possessor [of livestock], his *alcalde* is his *fiador*, and afterward his oath is valid, and there is no way to prove [otherwise].

In that case, they said that they had as a *fuero* and of custom and they established by law that any person or persons who give over such livestock to be held in common, in the aforementioned manner, shall receive *fiadores* from the guardian [of the livestock], and he shall accept [the *fiadores* who will guarantee] that he shall be informed about the said livestock and their products and offspring, [and] shall be given an accounting with payment [for the products and offspring]. And these *fiadores* that were thus appointed shall serve for the entire time until the livestock, offspring and products [therefrom] shall be given [back to the owner], unless those *fiadores* were appointed [to serve for a] definite limited time. And after the said *fiadores* are thus appointed, [if] the one who took the livestock should deny that he received it in the manner described above, and it should be proved against him with the *fiadores*, he shall be required to turn over double the [original number of] livestock and products [there from], and offspring, if none of them belonged to him. And if some did belong to him, he shall lose [those] because he committed robbery and denied [that he had taken in another person's livestock].

### 177. Title Concerning Temporal Limitations [Regarding Property Ownership] and the Ways of Those Limitations.

First they said that in Bizkaia until now they had had as *fuero* and usage and custom that if someone possessed some house and farm or other heritable landed property for a year and a day without opposition, then the possessor [of that property] shall appoint a *fiador* to his *alcalde* and, once the *fiador* is confirmed, [the possessor] may swear, orally, with two vouching credible persons [present], that the property was his with no part of it belonging to any demanding party, and [that] his father or mother left him [the property] verbally, or by means of a bill of sale or exchange, or trade. And once this oath has been sworn, then those who have possessed [the property] for a year and a day shall own the property in dispute, even though they neither possessed nor demonstrated [any] other title.

Furthermore they had as *fuero*, usage and of custom that even though someone possessed some house and farm or heritable property or foundries or mills or any other truncal real estate for a year and a day, and for twenty and thirty and forty and fifty and sixty and a hundred years or more, if some other person should claim that property, then there shall be no temporal limitation concerning [ownership of] the property, nor may one avoid swearing the oath before credible persons vouching over that property. And many lawsuits and debates have arisen and continued over this custom.

And wanting to rectify and eliminate doubts and lawsuits and debates that could arise over this, they said that they ordered and established by law that if anyone possessed as their own any house or houses or any other heritable properties for a year and a day without any opposition from any claimant, the status of the property in question being evident and unchallenged by possible claimants, then, for the person who possesses the thing [in question], a *fiador* [who appears before] the *alcalde* concerning that possession shall be valid. But although that *fiador* shall be a valid means for [the owner] to show possession for a year and a day, the [possession of that] property shall not be validated through the oath, with vouching credible persons, unless it is shown that [the owner] had and possessed the property for a year and a day with a proper title [as mentioned above] and in good faith. But if the possessor [of the property] shows the proper title by which he owns it, then it shall belong to him without swearing an oath.

Otherwise if the possessor of that house or property or other goods should possess it for two years, and if there is no title, then the *fiador* shall be a valid *fiador* [before] his *alcalde*, and by swearing the oath with the vouching credible persons [present], the property shall belong to [the one who possessed it for two years].

And the person who must swear this oath with vouching credible persons shall do so in a church designated for oath taking according to, and at the time appointed by, the *alcalde*'s order. And the two vouching credible persons shall be property holders with no legal disqualifications and residents of the *anteiglesia* where the property concerned in the lawsuit is located. And if these vouching credible persons do not exist, or cannot be found in that *anteiglesia* or district where the case is filed against the defendant, the person who is to swear the oath shall inform the plaintiff three days before he is to swear the oath that the vouching credible persons cannot be found in that *anteiglesia* or within its district. And if he wishes, the plaintiff may receive the oath of the defendant to the effect that he could not find [any vouching credible persons], and once this oath is sworn [the defendant] shall have nine days in which to bring vouching credible persons from the second *anteiglesia* [to hear the oath] concerning the principal case. And these nine days shall run from the day that he swears that no vouching credible persons can be found in the first *anteiglesia*. And within this time period of nine days, [the defendant] shall swear the said oath with the vouching credible persons of the second *anteiglesia* [present]. And if he cannot find any in the second *anteiglesia* within nine days, he shall inform the [other] party three days before they are supposed to swear [the oath] that there are no vouching credible persons to be found in the second *anteiglesia*. And he shall swear that none could be found if the other party wishes to receive [such an oath] from him. And, on the ninth day, after that [the defendant] shall swear the said oath with vouching credible persons who are residents of the third *anteiglesia*. And if there are no [vouching credible persons] to be found in the third *anteiglesia*, he shall inform the [other] party three days before he is supposed to swear [the oath], and [once he] swears that he could not find them in the third *anteiglesia*, if the plaintiff will receive [that oath], on the ninth day following that [day] before noon he shall swear the principal oath with vouching credible persons. And he shall bring the vouching credible persons from any place he can find them within the *merindad* where the property is located. And he who is thus to swear the oath shall do so within the church designated for taking oaths accordingly as the *alcalde* orders, and when the party leaves the church after swearing the oath, the vouching credible persons shall say outside the door of the church that, upon their souls, they have borne true witness. And [once] the said oath is sworn with vouching credible persons in the aforementioned manner, then the property over which the case is to be heard shall guarantee the proceedings. And if the said oath is not sworn, and cannot be sworn, with the vouching credible persons in the aforementioned manner, then [the possessor] shall turn over the property to the person demanding it, according to the order of the *alcalde*, and according to the *fuero* and custom of Bizkaia, etcetera.

### 178. How Time Is Limited for Any Action or Claim on Truncal Real Estate or Movable Property.

Furthermore because there is no prescription in Bizkaia for the passage of time, after long periods [some people] file claims against their opponents over real estate, as well as over movable property, and concerning gives and takes, and debts and obligations, both personal and those pertaining to property and [over] inheritances. And the defendants cannot show payment of those debts or pledges or obligations, nor do they know where that property is or where they got it from, either because the persons they inherited from as well as the strong *fiadores* of the bequest are dead, or because the letters of payment or contracts that they had are lost, or because of other reasons. And because they cannot show payment nor swear an oath with vouching credible persons in the manner contained in the above law, many lose their rights and are divested of their property, and they pay many debts of which they knew nothing, from pledges as well as in other ways.

For that reason they said that they ordered and established by *fuero* and law that [when] any man or woman takes action or [files a] claim against movable property, real estate or inherited property that another person has had in his posession for ten years without any opposition,

then he who possesses that property or real estate or inherited property, the status of the property in question being evident and unchallenged
by possible claimants, [in the presence] of the claimant shall swear by
himself without vouching credible persons [that all obligations have
been met], and shall not be required [to do] more, and that property,
whether it be houses or farms or foundries or mills or mill wheels or
other heritable properties shall belong to him, even if the claimant is a
brother or sister or cousin or some other relative of the defendant, and
is of [legal] age. And if after ten years and up to twenty years no claim
is made against the property, the property holder shall not be required
to swear any oath or respond to any claim.

And concerning movable property and debts and pledges, whether
there was an obligation or any other actions regarding real estate or
movable property of any kind, if the claimant does not file a claim or
lay seizure to the debtor or his property or make him go to court within ten years, then from that time onward, the defendant* shall not be
required to respond to that claim.

And so that through this law the claimants will not lose their rights
to file claims against property and claims and inheritances and debts
that were not filed during the ten-year time period [immediately preceding the approbation of this law], they may file their actions and claims
during the next five years. And after that time, they cannot file claims
against defendants. And [the cases filed concerning] the items that are
claimed after the ten years have passed, but which are claimed within
the aforementioned five years, shall be decided according to that which
is contained in this law.

## 179. When the Defendant or Claimant Shall Be Required to Appoint a Fiador.

Furthermore any person who is the holder of personal property for
a year and a day with title and in good faith shall provide a *fiador* before
the *alcalde* for the holdings that he had, and the plaintiff must pursue
the case with his *fiador*. But if there were a case among siblings over
some inheritance, it shall be pursued through *fiadores* appointed by one
side, the other and another, and it shall be decided according to what
has been declared in the above law. But if the claimant were a minor
when the defendant took possession, the passage of time shall not prejudice the damage done to that minor.

---

* Manuscript reads *demandador* (claimant), but this must be in error.

180. **That Person Who Needs to File a Claim Against a Principal Debtor or His *Fiadores* Shall File within Ten Years, and the *Fiadores* Who Paid [the Debt] for the Principal Debtor [Shall Also File within Ten Years].**

Furthermore in Bizkaia men are accustomed to making pledges to each other concerning debts or seizures, and the *fiadores* [in such cases] are sued by the claimants, and the *fiadores* then sue the principal debtors or their heirs to remove themselves from that pledge, or other *fiadores* come forward maliciously after a great length of time passes, because they are under oath to the [aforementioned] *fiadores*, for which reason many lawsuits arise, and many [people] even pay [debts] that they do not owe.

Consequently they said that they ordered and established that anyone who had a claim against those *fiadores* and principal debtors, whether they were alive or dead, may file that claim within ten years. And if they do not file a claim within ten years, then from that time on, neither the *fiadores*, their heirs, nor the principal debtor shall be required to respond to any claim that was filed for that reason.

181. **Debts of the Deceased Shall Not Be Paid Unless They Are Declared in a Will or Public Document or by *Fiadores*.**

Furthermore it happens that after the death of a father or mother, the children and heirs [of] the deceased are sued by others [who] say that the deceased owed them some amount [of money or property], and those children and heirs know nothing [about that debt], and because of this, many lawsuits and debates and questions arise.

Consequently they said that they ordered and established that if that debt did not appear in the will of the deceased, or [if it was not declared] in some public document or by landowning and credible *fiadores*, with property-holding *fiadores* with no legal disqualifications, that the deceased debtor had given the claimant [some pledge regarding payment of debts], then the deceased debtor's heirs shall not be required to pay that debt, but only to swear in their church designated for oath taking that they know nothing about that debt, or if [its existence] is certain.

And if the children and heirs of the deceased who were being sued were minors, even if they have guardians or caretakers, neither they nor their guardians shall be required to answer for those debts and claims until they are of legal age, and if the minors do not desire it, they do not have to respond to the claimant until they are of age even if, in the passage of time, [the claimant is unable] to file suit within the required ten years.

But if [the debt] appears in a will, or in a public document, or [is declared] by *fiadores*, the defendants cannot avoid responding, even though they are minors, and no other proof shall have a place, for that is the *fuero* and custom of Bizkaia.

### 182. Title Concerning Debts and Obligations and Payments and Discharging of Debts, Which Ones Shall Be Valid or Not, and the Nature of Them, etcetera.

Furthermore they said that they had as *fuero*, usage and custom and they established that any *hidalgo* of the Land of Bizkaia may pledge himself and his movable property and real estate, in part or in full, for the payment of debts. But having movable property or truncal real estate, he may not be taken into custody. And that which [applies to] the *hidalgos* shall [apply] to other persons, male or female, who are [at least] twenty-five years old. But the debtor shall be required to provide *fiadores* [to guarantee that he will] produce that property at the time of the public sale at auction.

### 183. [Concerning] Those [Heirs] Who Incur Debts [When] They Are Obliged to Support Their Parents by Means of the Properties That They Have Indebted or Pledged.

Furthermore it often happens in the Tierra Llana of Bizkaia that fathers and mothers give children or other heirs upon [the occasion of] their wedding some houses and farms and other property from their [own] marriage and property holdings, retaining [that needed to ensure] their [the donors'] maintenance and burial expenses. And some of them bequest those properties [to be passed on] after their days [are ended]. And some [hand over] half [the property] at the hour of the bequest and the other half after their days [are ended]. And others give the property entirely over at the hour of the bequest. And afterwards those children and heirs to whom that gift and bequest is made, in any of the aforementioned manners, incur debts and obligations themselves and upon their property, and their creditors seize and sell that bequested property for [payment of the] debt [incurred] by the children or heirs.

[And] they said that that was done to the great detriment of the givers [of the bequest], and it was a wrongful thing that the father or mother should be deprived of their property while alive, nor should they receive support from a stranger, being able to support themselves from their property.

For that reason they said that they had as *fuero* and usage and custom and they established by law that whenever either the father or the mother gives and bequests his or her house and farm to one or more of their children, or to any other heir in any of the aforementioned manners, then the property thus given and bequested may not be sold or given away [to pay] for any debt or obligation that the child or any other heir might incur, nor [may any] part of that [property be sold] during the lifetime of the father and the mother who thus gave and bequested it, nor during the lifetime of either one of them should one of them die. But the creditors may have and collect what is owed them if the debtor has other property of his or her own or after the death of the father and of the mother, etcetera.

### 184. No Obligation That the Father or Mother Makes to the Children, or the Children to the Parents, before [the Children] Marry Shall Be Valid, etcetera.

Furthermore many times it happens that people give and bequest houses or properties to a son or sons or daughters upon [the occasion of their] wedding or in some other manner. And after that wedding, it seems at times that the parent, before [making] that bequest, was under an obligation to that child or to another child that he or she had, or the child was under obligation to the parent, to give some quantity [of money] or to do something. And they do this deceitfully for two reasons: the first [reason], in order to marry a son or daughter to the son or daughter of an honorable man, or because of the many properties they [his or her parents] will give him or her upon his or her wedding, and afterward, because the parent may collect some quantity [of money or property] in payment of that pledge, a quantity that the woman was bringing to the marriage, to give to other children that [the parent] may have, to the detriment of the woman who thus married the son. The second [reason is] because if the parent owes some quantities [of money] to other persons, and creditors sue the parent, the son can take those properties from the parent by reason of the obligation [the parent made to give the property to the child], saying that [this obligation] is older.

And since it is not right that those deceitful purposes should exist, they said that in those cases they had as *fuero* and custom and established by law that no obligation that the father or mother or one of them should make to the son, or the son to the father or mother, shall be valid, if those obligations be [made] before the wedding [of the children], since they are not people who can obligate themselves to each other. And that which applies to the sons shall apply to the daughters, etcetera.

185. **The Person Who Demands [Payment of] a Satisfied Debt Shall Pay Twice the Amount [of the Debt] as a Punishment to the Defendant.**

Furthermore they said that once some debtors pay their debts to creditors who hold letters [of obligation] against those debtors and their property, those creditors, after receiving payment, wrongfully demand that those debtors turn over property, either for other debts or for pledges. And [they said] that it was not right that the person who did that should not be punished.

Consequently they said that they had as *fuero* and established as law that if some person should demand [payment for], or have seized property as payment of, satisfied debts or letters, and if the debtors can provide clear proof of the payments, then the claimant shall be required to pay the defendant double the amount that he was demanding or for which he confiscated [the other's property]. [Proof of payment] for letters of obligation [shall consist of] a letter of payment or the word of five property-owning witnesses of good reputation. And [proof of payment] for *fiadores* who sue for [payment of] pledges, or for the principals represented by those *fiadores*, [shall consist of] two *fiadores* who are knowledgeable about the payment.

186. **How the Man from a *Villa* May Demand [Payment of] Debts or Obligations before His *Alcaldes de Fuero* and against Those from the Tierra Llana, etcetera.**

Furthermore some *villa*s take *hidalgos* into custody by order of the *alcaldes* of said *villa* for debts that they owe when they [the *hidalgos*] had no such obligations, saying that they [the *hidalgos*] came into that *villa* as debtors, and thereby unduly saddling them [the *hidalgos*] with expenses.

In such a case, they said that they had as *fuero* and usage and custom that no person from the Tierra Llana of Bizkaia shall file any claim before the *alcalde* of said *villa*, providing a *fiador* to comply with the law before his *alcaldes*, unless [he] himself made an obligation concerning [that matter]. And if after a *fiador* is appointed they do not release him, or they do not transfer his case to his *alcaldes*, then all of the [people] of the Tierra Llana of Bizkaia and the Encartaciones shall be required to support [that *hidalgo*] and speak up for him. And the same [shall hold true for] the resident of the *villa*. A *fiador* [appearing before] the *alcalde* shall be valid [for him], if the *prestamero* or the *merino* arrest him in the Tierra Llana in the aforementioned manner, etcetera.

187. Title Concerning the Proof of Bequests and Their Oaths.

They said that they had as *fuero*, usage and custom that whenever someone has to prove with strong *fiadores* of a bequest how some house or farm or other property was sold or given or bequested or willed to him, he shall be required to demonstrate and prove it in this way.

If the house or farm or foundry or mill wheel or mill or mountain pasturage (*sel*) over which the case is being litigated is claimed in its entirety, [the holder of the property] shall be required to demonstrate how it was bequested with six landed and credible *fiadores* of the bequest of good reputation who have no legal disqualifications and are residents of the *anteiglesia* where that property is located. And if the claim was made for half of the house or farm or foundry or mill or mill wheel or *sel* or any other property, or for less than half, then three *fiadores* of the bequest shall [be required to] prove [how it was bequested].

And if those *fiadores* of the bequest were not [all] residents of the *anteiglesia*, then two-thirds shall be from the *anteiglesia* and the other third from the second *anteiglesia*. And he who had need of them shall be required to bring these six *fiadores* of the bequest before the *alcalde de Fuero*, and if he should wish to bring more [*fiadores*] of the bequest, then he may do so. And let the plaintiff and defendant and those *fiadores* go [to] the house or foundry or mill or *sel* or property regarding which the case is being heard, and having measured the boundaries around it, those *fiadores* of the bequest shall appoint two *fiadores* to swear to that which the *fiador* of the oath has to say. And [once] the *fiadores* [are] thus appointed, let the parties [involved] and the *fiadores* of the bequest go to the church designated for oath taking from [the area] where that house or property is located at the time assigned to them by the *alcalde*. And have those *fiadores* swear in that church, accordingly as the *alcalde* ordered. And if one of the *fiadores* should be unable to swear the oath, then he shall pay 48 *maravedís* in old money to the plaintiff. And the defendant shall provide another *fiador* to replace that one. And this [newly] appointed *fiador* shall be from among those appointed by the *fiador* of the oath. And if another *fiador* were not to swear the oath in that same manner, [he shall] pay the above-named fine [of 48 *maravedís* and be replaced] in such a way that six *fiadores* of the bequest shall swear [to the matter] concerning the house or farm or foundry or mill or mill wheel or *sel*. And those that are required [in order to prove a bequest of] half of the house or foundry or mill or mill wheel or *sel* shall [number] three *fiadores* of the bequest. And those that are required [in order to prove a bequest of] less than half [of the property] shall [number] two *fiadores* and no fewer. But if the defendant wishes to provide more *fiadores*, he may bring them from [the group of] those who serve as *fiador* for swearing about that property. But if the six *fiadores* of the bequest were not [all still] living, then [at least] four of them should be living and the other two [*fiadores* should be] sons or sons-in-law of the dead *fiadores*. And [if three *fiadores* are required and all are not living, then] of the three *fiadores*, two [should be] alive and one [*fiador* should be] the son or son-in-law of the dead man. And of the two *fiadores*, one [should be] alive and the other [should be] the son of the dead man. And as soon as those *fiadores* have sworn in the aforementioned manner, then he who brought them to the *anteiglesia* shall swear that he truly did bring the ones who swore the oath [to that place to do so].

And [once] the said bequest is proven in the aforementioned manner, it shall be accepted as proven, and the house and property over which the lawsuit was filed shall belong to the defendant. And if it is proven with some of the *fiadores*, but not all of them, [the bequest] shall not be valid, and the property shall be ceded to the plaintiff. And if that bequest appeared in a public document, [written] by a notary of good reputation [in the presence] of three good witnesses, there shall be no swearing by the *fiadores* against it, etcetera.

## 188. Concerning Those Who Do and Do Not Go to Swear [Their Oaths] at the Appointed Time, etcetera.

Furthermore they said that they had as *fuero* and custom [that] whenever anyone had a lawsuit with another over any complaint that existed between them, [and that case was heard] before the *veedor* or before the *alcaldes* or before any one of them, and one party was supposed to swear an oath in his church designated for oath taking concerning the judgment handed down.

And on that day on which [that party] was to swear his oath, [if] it happened that [he] did not go to swear the oath, feeling that it was not necessary. And [if the person] who was to receive the oath went to keep his appointment, then that person's contention shall be considered proven.

And if the one who was supposed to swear the oath went to the church, and the person who was to receive the oath was not there, then his oath will be accepted as sworn even if he doesn't take it, and his intention [to swear the oath] will be accepted as proven, as if he had sworn the oath.

And if by chance both parties [involved in the case] should each bring their good man, but the good man [appointed] in common should fail to go [to the church] because of [something done by] one of the parties, then whoever caused the good man in common to fail to go [to the church] shall lose any legal right he had in that case, and the other [party] shall [be considered to] have proven his contention as described above [in the case of the party who fails to appear at the church]. And if, by chance, both parties shall be in agreement in a case where the good man in common does not go [to the church designated for the swearing of oaths, to attend] the giving and receiving of the oath, then if the oath is sworn [in that good man's absence], it shall be valid.

And matters being thus, it shall be as follows: that in a case where it is usual to appoint a *fiador* [to guarantee] the swearing of the oath, neither of the parties shall be required to appoint that *fiador*, but only [to appoint] the *fiador* [who guarantees] to pay the fine of 48 *maravedís* in old money, if the oath cannot be sworn.

And if it should happen that both parties, or members of each party, go with force to the church to give and receive the oath on the appointed day, and the *fieles* who should receive the oath refuse to receive both parties or one of them for appearing armed, he who so appears shall lose his right in that claim, and the other party shall prevail. But if both parties appear with force, the *fiel* will appoint another time for the oath taking.

### 189. Those Who Must Swear the Oath Should First Go See and Mark the Boundaries of the Property or Item, etcetera.

Furthermore before the oath is sworn, the person who is to swear the oath and the person who is to receive it shall go over the property in contention and shall mark the boundaries around it, before swearing the oath with good *fiadores* of the bequest, [and] he who is to receive the oath [shall confirm the boundaries] for he who is to give the oath so that there shall be no more lawsuits over that [property] in question once the oath is sworn and accepted. And in this way the person who is supposed to swear the oath shall provide two *fiadores* to the one who is to receive the oath in order to [guarantee that he will] relinquish and no longer make any claim on that [property], if the oath is not sworn or [if] he does not want to swear the oath. And if the lawsuit were over movable property, then let that quantity [of goods] be placed in neutral hands before any oath is sworn, and no oath need be sworn until [this is done]. And all the oaths that must be sworn in those [oath taking] churches concerning any matter whatsoever must be sworn before noon and not afterward.

## 190. Title Concerning Proxies.

First they said that in some *villas* of the Countship of Bizkaia they had ordinances [which said] that no resident may select as a representative or proxy any resident of the Tierra Llana, nor may any resident of the Tierra Llana select a representative or proxy from residents of any *villa* of the Countship. That ordinance is in effect under penalty of a fine of 600 *maravedís*, half of which [shall go] to the judge before whom they acted as [someone's] representative or proxy, and the other half [shall go] to the party against whom they acted as [someone's] proxy or representative. But an individual may file a suit with no penalty whatsoever [as long as it is not done by proxy]. But if any of the *villas* wishes to remove that ordinance, then in that case one may select a proxy or representative or act as an attorney for any resident of that *villa* with no penalty whatsoever.

## 191. In What Way the Clergy May Represent Lawsuits, etcetera.

Furthermore they said that they had as *fuero*, usage and custom that no cleric may act as legal representative for any person in any lawsuit [that is heard] before either the *veedor* or any of the *alcaldes de Fuero*, unless it were a case dealing with the Church or with clerics [and] their consorts or for one's father or mother or for minor orphans or for widows and poor people. And the *alcalde* or *veedor* before whom [the cleric] appears will not accept him as a representative or lawyer, except in the above-mentioned cases, and [only] if the party whom he is defending is present. But if the party he is defending is present, then he may litigate. And since no cleric may be compelled by secular judges, anyone who hands over his representation to a cleric shall pay a fine of 600 *maravedís* to the other party. And if the one who thus granted said obligation [representation] were the defendant, his case shall not be heard, and he shall pay the fine, etcetera.

## 192. Any Lawyer Named by a Party As His Spokesman Shall Be Heard [As If He Were] the Party Himself.

Furthermore they said that they had as *fuero*, usage and custom that whenever parties involved in any civil case provide each other with *fiadores* [to guarantee that they will] comply with the law or follow through and comply with the law, and either of the parties names [those *fiadores*] as his spokesman, or lawyers, or representatives in the suit, [then those *fiadores*] shall be accepted by the parties during the trial and outside of it, both on the part of the claimant and on the part of the defendant. Any or all proceedings carried out by them and sentences received by them shall be valid, as if the case were pursued and handled and a decision received by the princpal parties, even though they had no other representation whatsoever. And they found the said *fuero* and usage and custom to be good, and thus they established and ordered it [to be in effect], etcetera.

### 193. What to Do When Someone Rejects a Representative or Lawyer.

Furthermore if by chance one party or another says before the *alcaldes* that one of the spokesmen is not who he was supposed to be, and if a question should arise over it, [then] by producing the *fiadores* before whom they were appointed as lawyers, they shall be validated. And the other party shall be held in contempt in that case, once its [worth] is demonstrated with *fiadores*.

### 194. Title Concerning How a Person Cannot Be Accused Again of a Crime of Which He Was Acquitted Beneath the Tree [of Gernika].

They said that it sometimes happens after the death of a man that he leaves minor children, and some relatives of the deceased file a complaint over the death, and after the complaint has been filed, an investigation made and [people] have been summoned to appear under the tree of Gernika, and those summoned and accused [who] have presented themselves before the judge are sometimes acquitted, either fraudulently or lawfully, by the decision of a competent judge. And after the accused is acquitted of the charge for which he was summoned, the person who first filed the accusation and lawsuit, or some other relative of the deceased, ignores the investigation, saying that it was done deceptively or fraudulently or [the dismissal] is the result of a bribe received by the first accuser, and [the person] files another lawsuit over the same matter. [And] many questions and debates arise over this.

In such cases they said that they had as *fuero*, usage and custom and they established by law that whenever anyone filed a lawsuit because of the death of his sibling or cousin or any other relative, and a person or persons are summoned [to appear] under the tree [of Gernika], and present themselves, and are acquitted of the charge by the decision of a competent judge, then after the decision is handed down, no other relative of the deceased may file a suit nor accuse any acquitted person of the crime for which he was summoned [and acquitted], unless the minor children of the deceased wish to file a suit at the time they inherit, [which they may do] by proving how the first person who filed charges received [a bribe] from the accused. And in that case the child of the deceased may file a lawsuit and pursue the death of his father. But if it is found that, in the first lawsuit and prosecution, there was no fraud or deceit, and [the accused] was acquitted by the judge, then the child of the deceased may not file suit again, nor may anyone else, for it is not right that a man be tried twice for the same crime.

### 195. Concerning the Abolition [of Charges] and the Pardoning of Crimes and Murders.

Furthermore they said that they had as *fuero* and usage and custom that if, through legal action over someone's death, some people were summoned and the initiator of the legal action should grant [pardon to] or acquit one [of the accused] without the authority of a judge. And he still wishes to charge the others after they have been summoned, [he may not do so except in the circumstance described below]. For after having pardoned one of those [people] who seem to be the principal murderers, they may not charge the others, and they should be acquitted of that crime. But if through the investigation [that individual] does not appear as guilty as the others, then in that case the others should not be excused [by the pardoning of one individual], if they deserve some punishment.

### 196. Title [Concerning] How Much Time a Judge Has in Which to Pronounce Sentence or Deliver a Decision and the Fees That Are Required [If He Fails to Meet His Time Limit].

First they said that when a case is concluded before the *veedor*, he sometimes postpones the orders of payment in such a way that the litigants accrue many costs.

And therefore, in such a case, they said that they had as a *fuero*, usage and custom and they established that once a lawsuit brought before the *veedor* has been concluded by [him] and the parties involved, if one or both parties should request it, either in a civil or criminal suit, then [the *veedor*] shall be required to hand down a decision. If it is an interim decision, [it must be handed down] during the following ten days, and if it is a final decision within twenty days. And if the *veedor* does not hand down his decision or decisions within these time limits, he shall be required to pay the costs and damages that each of the parties incurs, unless he can show legitimate cause for not having made his announcement. And all of Bizkaia shall make the *veedor* pay those costs and damages, because no other judge can compel him [to do anything]. But if the party [whose fees he was supposed to pay] should wish to prosecute the *veedor*, he may do so.

## 197. The Fees That [the *Alcaldes de Fuero*] Should Receive.

Furthermore they said that they had as *fuero* and usage and custom that when the *alcaldes de Fuero* have to gather *a locue* (*loque, loare*) or in a meeting of the *alcaldes* concerning civil suits in order to hand down their decisions, they shall receive the following fees for carrying out the duties of their office:

First of all, 2,000 *maravedís* in salary from the Lord for each one every year.

Item, when the *alcaldes* gather *a locue*, which is a meeting of the *alcaldes* from each case, with or without the *veedor*, to decide cases of each *locue*, then for each decision that they hand down that they give in each case, each shall receive 30 *maravedís*, and this shall apply [only] to final decisions, not to interim hearings.

Item, for ordering that a division of property be made, the *alcalde* shall receive 24 *maravedís*. But if the parties [involved] wish to compromise, they may do so without any order of the judge by appointing two *fiadores*, each to one another. And the decision made by the arbitrators shall be valid as if it were handed down by a judge.

Item, when some people have lawsuits and questions, and [the *alcaldes*] put the parties in the hands of arbitrators to give authority to [the arbitration], [the *alcalde* shall receive] another 24 *maravedís*.

Item, for establishing guardians for minors and presenting their decree, [he shall receive] 24 *maravedís*.

Item, for ordering the seizure and auction of property of someone because of debt, [the *alcalde* shall receive] another 24 *maravedís*, but he shall receive no fee for ordering the sale of clothing that one person has [taken] from another, unless it appears to be the [sort of] debt where he may order such a sale carried out.

And none of those *alcaldes* shall dare to take or receive more [money] than outlined above, nor [shall they receive money] for any other reason, under pain of falling into the same category as those judges who take bribes not to uphold the law, unless the *veedor* orders that the *alcaldes* receive the [extra] fee for some legitimate reason, which shall be investigated by the *veedor*, and [the *veedor*] shall be in charge if someone wishes to prosecute one or more of the said *alcaldes* because of such a thing [as taking a bribe or more money than they should].

Furthermore it sometimes happens that by order of the *alcalde*, or by virtue of some letter of obligation, the property of a person in debt to many people is seized and sold. And when that property is sold at auction, not only the person at whose request the seizure of property was made, but other creditors who hold notes against that debtor and his property, also appear before the *alcalde*. And [sometimes] when those other letters [of obligation] are presented after the auction, the *alcaldes* request [payment] from the parties involved of 24 *maravedís* for each letter of obligation that was presented before them, even though they had not ordered the seizure of property based on those letters, because [they had not seen them before and thus] they could not do so.

Therefore in such cases they said that they had as *fuero* and usage and custom in Bizkaia, and they ordered by law, that no *alcalde* shall ask for or receive or order, nor dare to order or receive, [payment of] such fees for any letter of obligation which is presented before him in the aforementioned manner [after the seizure and auction of property], but [shall only be paid for] that single letter which initiated the seizure of property, and he shall receive only that which is due him for giving such an order, under pain of the aforementioned penalty.

### 198. Concerning the Fee for Traveling on a Road.

Because it is the law of the Hermandad that no one may take or levy any tax or fee for [the use of] any road, nor may they ask for anything [in exchange] for traveling on such common road, or for infringing beyond its boundaries if it is not closed off, unless some cart or beast of burden is passing by, under pain of a fine of eleven hundred *maravedís* for the Hermandad and the other half for the accuser. But if some road had to be repaired, and the place or *anteiglesia* repaired it, then [the people from that place] should go to the *Corregidor* of Bizkaia, and once he has seen what they have spent [on the repairs], he may give two people permission to demand and receive a certain amount from foot traffic on the road as it passes by there, until [they have] recovered what they spent. And that these [two] persons shall be good [people] and of good reputation.

### 199. That *Alcaldes* Shall Not Hand Down Any Judgement That Contradicts the Fuero of Bizkaia.

Item, if [any] *alcalde de Fuero* should judge or order or hand down any decisions that contradict the chapters [articles] and *fueros* of Bizkaia, which are written down in this book, whether [the decision] is appealed and comes before the *locue*, or in any other manner, then [the *alcalde* that handed down that illegal decision] shall pay eleven hundred *maravedís* to the Hermandad for each offense, and [shall also pay] the costs to the party [involved in the case], who shall be believed upon swearing an oath. And if the *alcalde* [who has been] fined [in this manner] wishes to appeal and plead, saying that he wishes to justify his decision, then he shall be required to appeal before the *veedor*, and not before anyone else, and [he must] follow through and present [his case] by the third day. And after that time he will not be heard, and the [imposed fines] shall be paid.

### 200. Concerning Alliances and Illegal Monopolies.

Furthermore [they said] that alliances and illegal monopolies among any municipalities or persons from the Villas, the Tierra Llana and the Encartaciones shall be ended and shall not be maintained from this time onward, nor shall they be formed anew. And those who do the contrary shall pay ten thousand *maravedís* if it were between municipalities. And [if such an illegal agreement is made] between individual persons, each one [shall pay] eleven hundred *maravedís* to the Hermandad. And this shall be an Hermandad matter. And the accuser shall receive one-third of this fine.

### 201. Fines Against the *Alcalde de Fuero* and [the *Alcalde*] *de Hermandad* Should They Accept Bribes or Extra Fees.

Furthermore if the *alcaldes de Fuero* and [*alcaldes* de] *Hermandad* should demand any bribes or too many fees, above and beyond the fines [imposed by] law, then they shall return twice the amount that they thus received to the party from whom they received it and [shall also pay] eleven hundred *maravedís* to the Hermandad. And this [shall hold true] whether [the *alcalde*] receives it himself or through a go-between, under whatever pretext or reason there might be. And the *veedor* shall be the judge of this. And the *veedor* shall carry out an investigation every year among the *alcaldes* [to determine whether] they are receiving bribes or extra fees or not. And in a case where the *veedor* cannot remedy the aforementioned, then the Assembly shall interfere in the matter.

### 202. That the *Alcalde* Who Hands Down a Bad Decision Shall Be Sentenced [to Pay] the Costs [of the Case].

Furthermore if the *alcalde de Fuero* were [to have a case] appealed, and he who presides over the appeal should find that [the *alcalde*] decided badly [in the case] and should revoke his decision, then [the *alcalde*] shall be sentenced [to pay] the costs incurred by the party [against whom the bad decision was handed down].

### 203. That House or Farm Bequeathed to a Priest May Not Be Left to His Son or Daughter, etcetera.

Furthermore we order that if a priest is given, bequeathed or donated a house or farm and lands or heritable property by his father or mother, or by either of them, then the said priest shall have and hold those [properties] for his whole life and shall receive their fruits and income. And after his death he may not give or bequeath it to any son or daughter that he had, and the property shall return to the closest living relatives from the family line [from which the property came]. But if that priest had necessity and such severe need during his life that he could not maintain himself without selling that property, then he may sell it to another person according to the *fuero*, and in no other manner, nor under any other pretext or exquisite excuses, etcetera.

## 204. Title Concerning the Fees Notaries Should Receive.

First they said that they had as *fuero*, usage and custom that no notary shall receive more than 4 *maravedís* for carrying out any duty at the request of or by order of the *alcalde*.

Item, [the notary shall receive] 12 *maravedís* for a seizure [of property] up to a league* [away] and another [12] from its sale at auction. And if it were farther away than one league, [he shall receive another 12 *maravedís*] and another 2 *maravedís* in old money for each page of the proceedings which pass through his hands, when they are given over, signed on each of the eight sides of a folded *quarto* of paper, each side containing sixteen lines and each line containing seven or eight words, and no fewer than that.

Item, [the notary shall receive] 4 *maravedís* for each signed document which is presented before the judge.

Item, [the notary shall receive] 10 *maravedís* for a letter of obligation regardless of its amount. And [he shall receive] another 10 *maravedís* for a letter of proxy.

Item, [the notary shall receive] 6 *maravedís* for a testimony and 2 more *maravedís* for each page it contained.

Item, [he shall receive] 50 *maravedís* for a letter of guardianship.

Item, [he shall receive] another 50 for a letter of compromise.

Item, [he shall receive] 12 *maravedís* for an open letter of sale that is not part of a bequest. And for that which was part of a bequest, 24 *maravedís* if it contained no other conditions except the open sale.

Item, [he shall receive] 12 *maravedís* for a lease.

Item, [the notary shall receive] 12 *maravedís* for each signed sentence handed down by the *alcalde*, and more for the writing of it.

---

* League: a unit of distance that varies from country to country and time to time. In English-speaking countries today, a league is about three miles. In Spain, it is 20,000 feet or about 5,572 meters (closer to four miles).

Item, [he shall receive] 6 *maravedís* for [writing down] any order from the *alcalde*.

Item, for a lawsuit heard before the *alcalde de Hermandad*, 12 *maravedís*. And for the presentation of the testimony of each witness in a criminal case, [the notary shall receive] 4 *maravedís*. And for its publication, [he shall receive] 2 *maravedís*.

Item, for the presentation of the person who was summoned beneath the tree of Gernika in a criminal case, [he shall receive] 12 *maravedís*. But he must deliver it signed. And if many people were summoned in a case, and they presented themselves in a group, then they all shall pay 36 *maravedís*, and they shall all be included under one signature. And if each one wishes to give testimony, then each one shall pay 12 *maravedís* for each signature [of each person testifying].

Item, [the notary shall be paid] 12 *maravedís* for recording the sentence handed down at the summonses and 4 *maravedís* for each leaf.

Item, [he shall receive] 12 *maravedís* for a closed presentation concerning a criminal case.

Item, a judge shall determine [what the notary shall receive] for all other documents that he must prepare.

## 205. Title Concerning Appeals.

First they said that there was no appeal, nor should there be any appeal, for criminal or civil cases which were implemented in the Tierras Llanas before the *veedor*, or before the *alcaldes*, nor [was there any appeal] for a sentence or sentences handed down by them in those cases, [and there shall be no appeal] outside the Seigniory of Bizkaia, [or] before the said Lord of Bizkaia, except for [cases occurring in] the Merindad of Durango, which does have the right to appeal to the Lord of Bizkaia, and before no other official of his. For which reason they said that their *fuero* is of *alvedrío*, and that any sentence or sentences handed down by such *veedor* or *alcalde* according to the *fuero* of *alvedrío* and usage and custom of Bizkaia could be commonly revoked by anyone outside the Seigniory of Bizkaia, because the Lord or his officials cannot be [well] informed about the said Fuero of the Land, being outside of the said Seigniory.

Hence they said that they had as *Fuero* and usage and custom that if a lawsuit begins before the *alcaldes* of the Tierras Llanas of Bizkaia, and one of the *alcaldes* hands down a sentence in that lawsuit, then the party who feels aggrieved by that sentence should appeal before another *alcalde*. And [he may do so] in that way from *alcalde* to *alcalde* [up to four *alcaldes*]. And afterward [may appeal] before the *veedor*. And if the *veedor* is not in the territory, [the aggrieved party] may appeal the sentence of the fourth *alcalde* before a fifth [*alcalde*] with the Assembly of Bizkaia. And then the *prestamero* may call an Assembly, and shall hold a meeting or Assembly of Bizkaia in the accustomed place. And that fifth *alcalde* shall come to agreement with the Bizkaians, and hand down his sentence. And if the party wishes to appeal that sentence, then he may present himself and his appeal before the *veedor* after that [official] returns to the territory. And if by chance the *veedor* were in the territory, then the aggrieved party should appeal before him without calling into session the General Assembly of Bizkaia, because to do so incurs great expenses for the assemblies, so the aggrieved party may appeal from the fourth to the fifth *alcalde* [instead]. And that the sentence of the fifth *alcalde* may be appealed by the aggrieved to the *veedor*. And there shall be no appeal or supplication over the sentence handed down by the *veedor* except in a lawsuit before the King, as Lord of Bizkaia.

And the aggrieved party may bring suit against the said *veedor* [before] said Lord of Bizkaia wherever he may be. And the Lord of Bizkaia should order the *veedor* to appear before him, whether the sentence were handed down in a criminal case or in a civil one. And once he appears, or refuses to appear, the Lord should assign a commissary judge to hear the case. And so that the Fuero of the Land will be upheld, the Lord of Bizkaia, or that person to whom he assigned the case, shall hear evidence from the parties [whether] the *veedor* is present or not, [and] the Lord, or that person appointed by him, shall order information taken for the Bizkaians gathered together in the General Assembly. And if it seems likely that said information would best be gathered in each of the *anteiglesias* of the Tierras Llanas of Bizkaia, let it be so. And if according to the information that he receives, it is found that the said *veedor* judged [the case in question] well, and according to the fuero and custom of Bizkaia, the decision shall stand, and the parties [who appealed] shall be condemned [to pay] the fines imposed by that *veedor*. And if it is found that he judged [the case in question] badly, then the *veedor* shall be condemned in the party's [appealed] case, and he shall be made to pay the costs from his own property. And this shall hold true also if the *veedor* was not in the Land, and someone should file suit against the sentence handed down by the last [fifth] *alcalde*, and should file suit with the said Lord King, as Lord of Bizkaia.

**206. That If the *Alcaldes* Should Judge [a Case] Badly and Not in Accordance with the Law, What Should Be Done Against Them.**

Furthermore if one or more of the *alcaldes de Fuero* of Bizkaia should hand down a judgement that contradicts the laws in any part of this Codex and Fuero, and the party against whom the sentence was handed down wishes to file suit against that *alcalde*, or *alcaldes*, he may file suit with the *veedor* who was in Bizkaia on the Lord's behalf. And if the *veedor* were outside the Countship, then [the party] may file suit when he returns. And if the *veedor* before whom the decision was appealed should find that that *alcalde*, or those *alcaldes*, had judged [the case] in a manner they should not have, they shall be required to pay to the party against whom the [wrongful] decision was handed down all the damages that he incurred as a result of the judgement. Moreover if the person against whom the decision was handed down should appeal before the *veedor*, and the *veedor* should revoke the decision handed down by the *alcaldes*, or by one of them, and the *alcaldes* are condemned [to pay] the costs and damages [incurred] by the party. Then the sentence handed down by the *veedor* concerning the decision of those *alcaldes* shall be final, and there shall be no appeal before the Lord.

But if the party against whom the *veedor* passes judgement should wish to file suit with the Lord against the *veedor*, he may do so. But he may not appeal before the Lord, or before any other, in either a criminal case or a civil case, unless the aggrieved party prefers that there be a review before the Assembly of Bizkaia, instead of a suit against the *veedor*, so that Bizkaia might appoint deputies (*diputados*) who are familiar with the deed, and who shall hear the case along with the *veedor*: but the *alcaldes* who handed down the first sentence may not take part in that review. And if in the course of that review it is found that the sentence is unjust and aggrieved, then the judges shall be condemned [to pay] the costs that the party incurred while pursuing the case or [provide] just compensation. And if it should happen that the *veedor* does not agree with the advice that those *diputados* received from legalists or informed men, then in that case the *diputados* shall pronounce and declare their verdict as one body, with all of Bizkaia in the *veedor*'s place, and that [decision] shall be valid and final.

207. **Lawsuits of the Residents of the Villas Can Be and Should Be Appealed Like Those of the [Residents of the] Tierra Llana and in the Lands of Noblemen, and Not to the Royal Court.**

Furthermore [the situation described in this article] happens in lawsuits [heard] before the *alcaldes de Fuero* of Bizkaia, as well as [in those heard] before the *veedor*, [in cases] between residents of some *villa*, as well as between residents of the *villa* and outsiders, [in cases] over noble properties in jurisdiction of the *alcaldes* and *veedor* of the Tierra Llana, and [in matters] of any kind of giving and taking. And the residents of the Villas appeal the sentence, or sentences, that those *alcaldes* and the *veedor* hand down before the court [of the King], saying that they have [the right to] appeal according to their *fuero*, [and] that they do not want to follow the Fuero of the Tierra Llana, even if the properties [in question] fall within that jurisdiction. [And] many lawsuits, questions and debates arise over this [situation].

And in that case they said that they had as *fuero* and usage and custom that there be no appeal [to the Royal Court] of the sentences handed down by the *alcaldes de Fuero* of Bizkaia or the *veedor*, dealing with lands or properties of Tierra Llana, whether the lawsuits be between [two] residents of the same *villa* or between an outsider and a resident of a *villa*. And that all should occur according to, and in the manner described in, the aforementioned laws which speak of appeals. And if someone should [try to] appeal, that appeal shall not be granted. And if he were injured by the decision, and he brought a letter from the Lord King asking that the appeal be granted or an inhibition [imposed], then that letter or letters from the King or Lord shall be obeyed but not complied with. And the person who brought them shall pay for each instance [of bringing forth such a letter] a fine of ten thousand *maravedís*, half to the Hermandad and one-quarter for the accuser and the other quarter for the *prestamero*. And until he pays the said fine of ten thousand *maravedís* the appeal [process] shall be discontinued, and they shall detain him and hold him prisoner [for] the *prestamero*. And if some costs and damages and lawsuits should arise against the *alcalde* or the *veedor* or the *prestamero* or the party who was summoned because of [the appeal], then all of Bizkaia shall take up the case and speak out and pay all the costs and damages that arise to each one of the judges, as well as to the party concerned. And if [that person] brings another letter concerning that [case], then any person or persons of that Countship may kill that person without any penalty, as one who violates the law [of the Land]. And all of Bizkaia shall give the killer of that person 2,500 *maravedís*, and Bizkaia shall assume all responsibility that arises over the case, whether lawsuits or fines or any other matter whatsoever, etcetera.

## 208. Title Concerning Those Who Abandon Census-Encumbered Farms and Go to Live on Noble Lands.

Furthermore they said that the said Lord King, as Lord of Bizkaia, had taxed, assessed and imposed upon the *labradores* of Bizkaia, and those *labradores* who were living in the aforementioned census-encumbered farms go to inhabit and live on the lands of the nobility, [and they do so] with ill-intent in order not to pay that which befell them in the tax list of the Lord of Bizkaia, and in order not to pay as much as they should, those census-encumbered farms are abandoned by the people who live on them. And from [a distance] they harvest the fruits, revenue and crops of the census-encumbered farms. And where they should have paid the entire tax imposed on census-encumbered farms, they do not pay [their share of the common tax assessment]. And the responsibility for that which they do not pay falls to the [remaining] *labradores*. For that reason *labradores* who flee because they cannot pay [and] desert the census-encumbered farms in such a manner that, if this is often tolerated, where the *labradores* have to pay one hundred thousand *maravedís* in old money to the Lord of Bizkaia, soon they will not be able to pay him anything. And what [is] worse [is] that the *labrador* will not be distinguished from the *hidalgo* after he lives for a long time on the *hidalgo's* property.

They ordered that those *labradores* who have passed to the lands of nobles, or sons or grandsons who lived on that census-encumbered farm, shall be required by the *prestamero* or *merino* of the *merindad* to leave the [*hidalgo's*] property and return within six months to inhabit the census-encumbered farm where was raised after the day the order is given. And if by chance [said *labrador*] did not so reinhabit the census-encumbered farm where he or his father or grandfather were raised within that six months, then the *prestamero* or *merino* shall take him into physical custody and shall make him provide landed and credible *fiadores* [to guarantee] that he will inhabit the said census-encumbered farm and keep it inhabited and pay the tax that was imposed on him. And if he does not leave that house which he had on the nobleman's property, and does not return to the census-encumbered farm before the six months are up, then the *prestamero* or the *merino* shall tear [that house] down at the cost of the *labrador* and shall take the wood and roof tiles from the nobleman's property and return it to the census-encumbered property. And if the *prestamero* or the *merino* stand in contempt, and do not wish to comply, then the *veedor* shall comply with the surrounding regions and shall ask if it please his Lord to so order and give and confirm as *fuero* [all the aforementioned].

## 209. Concerning Those Same *Labradores*.

Furthermore they said that since those *labradores* and their children and grandchildren [sometimes participate in] truces and [deal with] rebellious men, and it is not known which are *hidalgos* and which are *labradores* [and] children and grandchildren of *labradores*, a great disservice is done to the Lord of Bizkaia and an injury to the *hidalgos*.

And they said that they had as *fuero* and usage and custom that no *labrador* or child or grandchild of a *labrador*, even if they be residents on a noble's land, shall enter into truces with any *hidalgo*, nor may he ally himself with or fight with any *hidalgo*, nor may the *hidalgo* do so with the *labrador*. But if he were an *hidalgo*, even if he should dwell on a working farm, he may enter into and disentangle himself from truces and ally himself with and fight with [anyone he wishes], as long as one and the other is an *hidalgo*. And if the *labrador* or the child or grand-child of a *labrador* should enter into truces, then each one [of them] who is required to do so by the *prestamero* or the *merino* shall disen-tangle himself from [the truces]. And if he does not, the *prestamero* or *merino* may take him into custody and hold him prisoner, until he extracts himself from those truces. And for having such audacity, he shall give the Lord five cows.

And furthermore, if the *hidalgo* should challenge or fight a *labrador*, then each one ordered to do so by the *veedor* shall be required to withdraw from the challenge, under pain of penalties imposed [by the *veedor*].

Furthermore they said that [the aforementioned] is regulated by the laws of the Codex of Bizkaia, and that the laws contained in that Codex shall be maintained.

### 210. Title Concerning Roads and Paths and Cart Paths, and How They Should Be.

First they said that no one shall dare transport a plow, except by way of the royal road, and not by [crossing] any property belonging to another. And if he does pass over [that property], then he shall pay 48 *maravedís* to the owner of the property and the five cows to the King for each infraction, inasmuch as they said that they had that as *fuero* and of custom.

Furthermore, concerning the royal roads, they should be 12 feet wide and curves in the road should measure 20 feet across.

### 211. Concerning Blockage and Narrowing of Roads.

Furthermore many persons dare to block and narrow the royal roads and other open roads, planting trees or fencing [them] in with hedges or putting up other obstructions, in order to appropriate for themselves the land where the roads are [located] by concealing [the roads]. That [action] causes great disservice to the King and great harm to the Land and to decent travelers and the public.

For that reason, they ordered that no one shall dare to plant trees or put hedges or fence in or obstruct the roads, and if someone should put up [such obstructions], then any planter from the said Countship [who dares to do this] shall be required to uproot and cut down the trees and fruit trees and remove the obstruction from the road within 30 days from the day he was ordered to do so. And if he has not done so within 30 days, he shall pay a fine of 48 *maravedís* in old money to the *anteiglesia* in which the road is located. And those of the *anteiglesia*, once they are ordered to do so by the *prestamero* or *merino*, shall be required to uproot and cut down the trees and remove the obstruction within another 30 days. And if the *anteiglesia* were negligent, and did not thusly open the road and remove the obstructions after being ordered to as aforementioned, then from that moment on any person of the Countship may take [the matter] to the *prestamero*, if he is available, or if not to the *merino*, to get that road cleaned up and unblocked at the *anteiglesia*'s expense, and the aforementioned 48 *maravedís* shall [in that case] go to the person who takes [the matter] to the *prestamero* or *merino*, and not to the *anteiglesia*.

Furthermore, they said that the *prestamero* or *merino*, whether someone complains or not, may remove the obstructions from the roads, and keep the fine, etcetera.

## 212. Concerning the Roads from the Ports to the Iron Foundries.

Furthermore it is necessary that the roads that exist in the ports and [those] that go from the ports to the iron foundries be wider, because when carts go from the port to the iron foundries and from the foundries to the ports, if they move onto the road, they [must] be able to pass each other at one place or another without any obstruction.

For that reason, they said that they had as *fuero*, and they ordered that all those roads from the ports to the foundries and from the foundries to the ports over which the carts pass, shall be four and a half *brazadas* wide. And if on those roads there were some narrower places or the roads, no matter how often they repaired them, were such that loaded carts could not pass through the narrow places or over the bad roads, then by order of the *alcalde*, three good men shall examine those roads to see if they are four and a half *brazadas* wide or to see if the bad roads can be repaired. And if those three good men, being under oath, should find that the roads are narrower [than they should be], or that the roads cannot be repaired for a reasonable cost, then in that case the owner of the property or properties adjacent to those roads shall be required to provide roads [from his own land], and [the property shall be] examined by the three good men, [but] first those who want the road shall pay the owner of the property double the price set on the property by the three good men. And if they find that those roads are four and a half *brazas* wide, and the carts are able to travel on them or the roads can be repaired, then in that case the owner of the [adjacent] properties shall not be required to give up his property for a road if he does not wish to do so, nor shall he be compelled to do so.

### 213. Title Concerning the Maintenance of Iron Foundries and Their Scales and Veins of Ore.

First they said that in Bizkaia the King derives great service from the iron foundries, and the inhabitants [derive] great benefit from them, and it is necessary for the iron foundries to maintain [forested] mountains for the making of charcoal for the founding of the iron.

And in order to do that they had as *fuero* and usage and custom, and they ordered that if the owners of the iron foundries should claim [as] their own a pasture or boundary-marked property belonging to others which contained a [forested] mountain, those [from whom] they claim it shall not be compelled nor required to give up their own [property] if they do not so wish. But [they] may give other mountains instead which belong to the community that are communal lands, if [the trees there] had been cut one or more times before in order to maintain the foundry. [And] they shall be required to give up those communal lands at the price [set by] three good men, according to the going price in the region for a similar mountain. But no other [person] may acquire [property] in the manner described above other than the owners of the iron foundries, and [they may do so only] at this price. And if by chance any other should buy that [forested] mountain, the heritable property holders associated with that communal land having sold it, then the buyer of that mountain shall be required to give and pay the owner or owners, of the iron foundries the aforementioned price [set by] three good men, according to what was stated above. And if any owner or owners of the iron foundries should buy those mountains, and if one or more other owners of that iron foundry or other foundries should demand their share [of the forest on that mountain], then that buyer shall be able to share, paying the price that it cost [the original buyers], because they maintain in common some foundries as well as others.

### 214. Concerning the Ore.

Furthermore they said that many people buy ore on the road from cart drivers or muleteers, and they unload it and put up scales in some places in order to resell the ore that they bought in that manner, [a practice] which was detrimental to the Lord of Bizkaia and to the iron foundries of the said Countship and to the iron workers in them.

Consequently, in such a case, they said that they had as *fuero*, usage and custom that no person shall dare to buy any ore from any cart driver or muleteer, nor shall they do any unloading or set up a scale in any location whatsoever for the selling and reselling of ore, except at the iron foundries. And whoever does the contrary and goes against this law shall pay a fine of 600 *maravedís* for each instance proven [against him], and if it was found [that he had done this], he shall lose the ore that he bought in that manner, half to [go to] the Lord of Bizkaia and the other half to the accuser. But if a person or persons should wish to take ore from the vein and unload it where they wish, they may do so without any penalty whenever they wish. But no scale shall be set up except in one or more of the iron foundries, under pain of the aforementioned penalty.

### 215. Concerning the Iron Foundry Scales.

Furthermore they said that the quintal of refined weight of iron worked in the iron foundries of Bizkaia is equal to 144 pounds,[*] each pound [consisting] of 16 ounces, and in some foundries they are accustomed to having lighter weights, and, in the places where the iron is weighed to determine taxes, heavier ones. [And] many debates and differences arise over that [situation].

Consequently they said they had as *fuero*, usage and custom and they ordered that each one should have those weights and quintals for weighing iron in his iron foundry, and the functionaries in the weighing places [and the weights should be] accurate and true, and neither less nor more than 144 pounds to each quintal and 16 ounces to each pound. And whoever should do the contrary, and it be proven that they did so, shall pay a fine of 600 *maravedís* for each instance, half to the Lord of Bizkaia and the other half to the accuser. But if the owners of the iron foundries should wish to have heavier weights to measure iron, they may have them, and they shall incur no penalty for it, etcetera.

### 216. Title Concerning the Patronages of the Churches and Their Fees, and to Whom They Belong and By Whom They Should Be Judged.

First they said that half of all the churches in the Tierras Llanas of Bizkaia belong to the said Lord of Bizkaia and the other half to the *hidalgos*. Concerning the ownership of these churches, they said that they are uncertain because they do not hold [them] by consent of the Pope, and in those cases where they do have them by consent of past Holy Fathers, no papal bull whatever appeared concerning the [matter]. For that reason, they humbly beg the King, as Lord of Bizkaia, and ask

---

[*] Subsequently, a quintal was 46 kilograms or 100 pounds; a metric quintal is 100 kilograms or 217 pounds.

him if he would be so kind as to send letters of supplication to the Pope, asking if he wishes to make a gift to the King and Lord of Bizkaia and to his Bizkaian subjects so that they may have and take advantage of [the churches] and the revenue from them, according to [the manner in which] they have held them and made use of them until now, and [asking him if] he wishes to issue a papal bull concerning this matter, since the Christians won all of this land from the Moors, and the King is at war with the Moors, on sea as well as on land.

### 217. [Concerning the Same].

Furthermore they said that the patronages of the churches of the Tierra Llana of Bizkaia were always held and are [still] held [by] the *hidalgos*, some belonging to the Lord of Bizkaia and others possessing a common heritable patrimony. And they held them in this manner as *fuero*, usage and custom. And some clergymen or laymen daringly acquire and bring letters, with false documents, from the Pope or from some other bishop, so that the churches will be given to them, to the detriment of the Lord of Bizkaia and the *hidalgos* and patrons of those churches.

And in that case they said that those churches and the patronages of those [churches] shall be held by the Lord, as well as by the *hidalgos* possessing a heritable patrimony, according to the form and in the manner which they [now] hold them and have held them in times past, by said Lord King as by those property holders. And if some person or persons, either clergymen or laymen, should bring an illegal letter into the Countship from any jurisdiction in any manner contrary [to the established law] and should read it in the said Countship, [then] that letter shall not be obeyed or complied with, because such they have as *fuero* and usage and custom that the shareholders of [the patronages] of such churches may demand and have their inheritances according to the manner in which it has been usage and custom until now in Bizkaia.

### 218. [Without Title].

Furthermore they said that formerly it was the usage and accustomed in Bizkaia that the *alcaldes de Fuero* or the *veedor* should take charge of the lawsuits that arose over the churches, those concerning the inheritances that the *hidalgos* had in them, as well as those [lawsuits] over the maintenance of the clergy. Furthermore as well concerning the tombs and burials and tithes, and all other properties and goods that belong to the churches.

And for some time now because of the divisions that have occurred in Bizkaia, the archpriests and Bizkaian vicars who have been newly [appointed in] the said Countship, with the support of *parientes mayores* (senior band leaders), have usurped jurisdiction beyond that which the law grants them, [and] have interfered with, and [still] interfere with, the judging of questions concerning the churches and their property. And furthermore in fact they took charge of other cases between the *escuderos* (noblemen) and laymen of the Countship in greater numbers than was customary to in times past. From which [situation there arose] two kinds of disservice to the King and Lord of Bizkaia and damage to those of the Countship: one [disservice], the jurisdiction of the Lord King and his judges was being given away to others, [and] the other [ignored that] in the said Countship, in the legal cases the regimen of [canon and civil] law is not followed, nor are there proofs, nor in the judgements are the solemnities and subtleties of [canon and civil] law safeguarded. And the said *alcaldes* and *veedor* judged those cases according to the unwritten *fuero* of *alvedrío* and their usages and customs, without the appearance of a [civil law] trial. And the said archpriests, without maintaining this order, judge the lawsuits according to the form of [canon and civil] law, from which there arose much damage and many expenses for the inhabitants of said Countship.

And wanting to be rid of those damages and costs, and wanting [order] to be maintained without the King's command and involvement, they said that they ordered that no person from the Countship shall cite or summon to a court of law any other layman from that Countship before any of the archpriests or vicars, nor before any other ecclesiastic judge over any civil or criminal case, unless [it be] over a crime of heresy, or over the rescinding of an excommunication, or over some robbery or theft that was done in the church or violence [committed] to the church, or over some crime of incest committed by someone who is married or living with a concubine in order to extricate himself from a sinful state, if that [sin] falls within the fourth degree [of kinship], or over a marriage, or over some case which by right or usage or custom those secular judges should not or could not judge, or over some sacrilege, or over any other ecclesiastic crime, or over any case or cases which pertain [to the church] by right, or in any of the foregoing.

And in the event that it be brought before the court or cited because of those aforementioned reasons or one of them, and a lay person of any station in life who goes against the aforementioned law in any manner was summoned or cited, or pressing a lawsuit against any person before any or all of the said archpriests or vicars or before any other ecclesiastic judge, or [if any person] within the Countship should acquire a letter from the bishop or from another vicar or ecclesiastic judge [from a jurisdiction] outside the Countship in order to [deal with] the aforementioned matters, or any other [matters whatsoever] which, according to the law, the judges of the said Lord King are able and capable of handling, [then the person who does try to take such a case before the ecclesiastic judges] shall pay eleven hundred *maravedís* for a first offense, and for a second offense the fine shall be doubled, and for a third [offense] all his real property shall be laid waste and destroyed, and his houses [shall be] burned, and the land shall remain scorched for his heirs. And if [that person had no real property [worth] up to the amount of 100 *florins*, then he shall be exiled from Bizkaia for five years, and the property that he did have shall be lost as aforementioned. And if by chance, after being exiled, [that person] should enter Bizkaia during that five-year period, then the judges of Bizkaia may seize him and kill him. And the same shall hold true if by chance, either before or after the judges have thus seized him, another person or persons from Bizkaia should run into the exiled person within the [boundaries of] the Countship, [in which case] that [person or persons] may kill [the exile] as [they would any] enemy of Bizkaia. And of the aforementioned fines, one-third of the amount shall go to the King, and another third shall go to the person [who was] summoned and cited, and another third for the accuser.

## 219. Concerning the Entrance of the Bishop and His Vicars into Bizkaia.

Furthermore they said that since ancient times they had as *fuero* and usage and custom that neither the bishop nor his vicars, nor any other may enter the Countship [of Bizkaia], if [the purpose of their visit was to enable] Bizkaians from Bizkaia to publish [the bishop's] illegal letters against the *escuderos* and good men of the Countship. Because of the many disagreements and scandals that have occurred up until now in the Countship, some *parientes mayores* and lineages, in order to do their deeds and take revenge on their enemies, brought vicars of the bishop and [ecclesiastic] *procuradores fiscales* (fiscal prosecutors) into the Countship and published [the bishop's] letters. And [they said] how they experienced [the situation] personally and have seen [it] and lived through [it] and it was proven in the said Countship that those vicars, through their judgement and handling of lawsuits and trials, constituted usurpation of the jurisdiction of our Lord the King and that of his judges. And furthermore [there have occurred] deviations from the *fueros* and usages and customs of Bizkaia, [and there has been] furthermore a besmirchment of the *hidalgos* and inhabitants of [Bizkaia], [in the form of] the prosecutor looking for pretexts to take bribes and money in those trials and lawsuits, this being the final conclusion of the said vicar. Furthermore the prosecutor is not responsible for the care of the lives or the souls of *escuderos* and *hidalgos* and good men of the Countship.

And because many times the noble *escuderos* and good men of said Countship see the damage and evil done to the residents of said Countship that arises from that prosecutor's [actions] and those letters and require that the senior band leaders do not support those vicars and the fiscal prosecutors.

And because up until now they had not put this into effect, they ordered, in maintaining the said Old Fuero, that no person or persons from any walk of life or estate, [who are] residents in the said Countship, shall be required to bring in or support any vicar or vicars or prosecutor or prosecutors or do favors for the bishop, nor [shall they be requested] to do favors for or help any vicar or vicars or prosecutor or prosecutors who might be brought in or other commissary judges who came or might come or who wish to come to reside in said Countship. And any person or persons who do the contrary shall be seen as violators of the *fueros* of Bizkaia, and they shall lose all their property. And the *escuderos* of the said Countship of Bizkaia and the judges shall be required to take their [property] and destroy it at their expense. And once this destruction is done and the said cost [of it is] recovered, if some property remains, then that property shall belong to the Lord. And the bare ground shall belong to the heir. However, if some person or persons should wish to resist that destruction or deaths or lawsuits arise over it, then Bizkaia shall be required to assume and take upon itself the matter, at the expense of those people who resisted, and Bizkaia shall carry out and sustain, at its own cost, the reduction of the resisters' property. And if by chance it were verified or decided that the above be decided and carried out and executed, then all the aforementioned [Bizkaians] shall be required to go to the execution [of that decision]. And if by chance someone were in contempt, then they shall carry out this same [destruction and] seizure of property [against him] that they carried out against the violator of the said *fuero*. And the execution of the first seizure [of property] of the said violator of the said *fuero* shall not be cancelled by the other.

And furthermore, if some person or persons should do a favor for vicars or prosecutors or commissaries or presenters of letters from the said bishop, and [that person or persons] were killed or wounded by one of the Bizkaians for being violators of said *fuero*, the [murderers or attackers] shall suffer no penalty, nor may the judges or justices arrest them or order them arrested or hold any investigation [into the matter]. And if they do so, then [the actions of the judges and justices] shall not be valid.

## 220. Concerning the Payment of Ecclesiastical Tithes.

Furthermore all Christian people of the Catholic faith are required to pay tithes to the churches for those things which are tithed. And some men or women, not respecting their consciences, do not tithe entirely in the manner they should, nor do they pay the tithes due the patrons of the church in the manner that they should. And afterward those patrons file suit against the tithers, saying that they are not tithing as they should, over which [situation] there used to arise many debates and lawsuits between the patrons of the churches and the tithers.

And in that case they said that they had as *fuero* and usage and custom that any tither who has to pay tithes on anything whatsoever shall be required to give one in ten things to the church where the tithes are owed or to that patron who should have them, with no deceit or fraud whatsoever. But if the patron who should receive tithes learns that the tithepayer is not tithing as he should, then he may file a lawsuit against him before the *alcalde de Fuero*. And if the quantity being asked of him were 100 *maravedís* or more, the tithepayer shall be required to swear that he tithed properly, according to the manner in which he was ordered to [tithe] by the *alcalde*, in his church designated for the taking of oaths. And if it were less [than 100 *maravedís*], the *alcalde* may receive the oath over the sign of the cross, according to the manner described by law. And if he should swear that he tithed properly, he shall be acquitted of the charges. And if he does not swear, [then] the one who owes shall pay that which it is understood that he did not pay. And if he does not wish to swear in that case in which he is charged, [then] he may swear the oath that he was required to swear in the church before a credible man who was chosen by both parties [involved in the case]. And because men have to pay tithes on many things at different times, and [because] it is not fair that the tithers should swear an oath for each item that is demanded of them at each time.

Therefore they ordered that if the patron, or whoever was to receive those tithes, should wish to file suit against those tithers, he may do so [only] once a year and [then only] for the tithe [owed] for that year and no more, nor [may he sue] in the current year for tithes [not paid in] the past year, etcetera.

## 221. That Censures May Not Be Read in Cases of [Robberies of] Fruits and Orchards, and Other Such Minor Matters.

Furthermore many [clergymen] are accustomed to reading letters of excommunication over various types of robberies, especially in cases of fruit trees and apple orchards, and [trespassing] on other landed properties and fruit orchards, and in livestock cases and many other things, which they said was understood to be a disservice to God and a usurpation of secular justice and a great danger to the souls.

Consequently they said that they ordered that no one shall dare to read any letter of excommunication at all in cases of [robbery of] fruit from orchards or because of trespassing or for any other similar reasons. But [they said] that if clergymen should wish to request an investigation by the officials of the *anteiglesia*, then they may do so and file suit against whomever did the damage. And whoever shall read the letter of excommunication shall pay a fine of 600 *maravedís* for each offense, half to the *anteiglesia* where [the letter] was read and the other half for the maintenance of such a church. But if in cases other than those mentioned above, as in cases of cutting firewood or trees, an investigation had been previously made by secular judges and no malefactor was found, then any [clergyman] may read letters of excommunication, with no penalty whatsoever, etcetera.

### 222. Title Concerning How and Where and in What Manner They Might Hunt.

They said that the *hidalgos* are accustomed to hunt for boar and deer on their mountain lands and territories. And [sometimes] after the boar or deer is flushed, it moves to other places and other mountains, and the *hidalgos* chase after the boar or deer onto lands and into the jurisdictions of other *hidalgos*, and questions and debates arise among men over this.

And in such a case they said that they had as *fuero*, usage and custom and they ordered by law that when an *hidalgo* flushes a boar or deer on his land or in his jurisdiction where he is accustomed to hunting, and that boar or deer enters the land or jurisdiction of another *hidalgo*, [then the first *hidalgo*] may go after the boar or deer as far as he can and hunt down and kill it. [And] no one shall disturb him, nor is anyone allowed to disturb or resist him by saying that those mountains and lands do not belong to him, under penalties established in the law. And if some person or persons should kill the boar or deer that another [person] is hunting, and if afterward the origial hunter of the boar should arrive any time before noon the next day, then the person who killed the boar or deer shall be required to give it to the person who flushed it and tracked it, under the aforementioned penalty. But if some *hidalgo* should flush a boar or deer in the jurisdiction of another *hidalgo* where he does not usually hunt and some other person should kill it, then [that person] may kill it and have it for himself, without any penalty whatsoever. And if some doubt should arise over this, the question shall be decided according to royal law by the *veedor* of Bizkaia.

### 223. Title Concerning How Bizkaians Must Come to the Aid of an *Hidalgo* if the Council from a *Villa* Should Arrest Him.

Furthermore they said that councils and *villas* of this Countship of Bizkaia forceably sieze the property and cut down the trees and do many other unjust things to *hidalgos* and the residents of the Tierra Llana, in fact and against the law, in such a way that they [the *hidalgos*] are the recipients of many damages and injuries.

Consequently they said that they order and ordered that if some *villa* or *villas* of the said Countship should rise up against some residents or inhabitants of the Tierra Llana, and they should make seizures or do injustices or take prisoners, and the recipient of this damage or dishonor should appeal to the Hermandad, then all the residents and inhabitants of the Tierra Llana of the said Countship shall be required to speak up for the injured party or on behalf of the person pleading his case or the arrested party, and [they shall be required] to correct that which was done to [the person] by the *villa*. And if it were found that the person who appealed [to the Hermandad] were guilty, and that those of the *villa* had just cause, then [that person] shall pay all the costs and damages that [both] those of the Tierra Llana of Bizkaia and those of the *villa* incurred, and moreover [he shall pay the] maintenance of Bizkaia [the fees normally incurred during such an action]. This [amount] shall be determined by the *veedor* of Bizkaia, etcetera.

\* \* \*

And after this, under the tree of Gernika where the General Assembly of Bizkaia was usually held, on the 21st day of the month of July, in the aforementioned year of the birth of Our Lord Jesus Christ, 1452.

Assembled in that place were the said Doctor Pero González de Santo Domingo, *corregidor* and *veedor* for our Lord the King in Bizkaia and the Encartaciones, and Fortún Sáenz de Villela, and Íñigo Martínez de Suasti, Íñigo Sáenz de Ibárgüen and Pero Martínez de Albiz, *alcaldes de Fuero* of Bizkaia for our Lord the King, and Ochoa Sáenz de Gorostiaga, *alcalde de Fuero* for Diego López de Anunzibay [who is] *alcalde de Fuero* for our Lord the King, and Ochoa Sáenz de Guinea, *logarteniente* of the *prestamero* in Bizkaia for Juan Urtado de Mendoza, the high *prestamero* for the Lord King, and Rui Martínez de

Albiz, *merino* of the Merindad of Busturia, and many other *escuderos* and *fijosdalgos* and *omes buenos* (good men) of Bizkaia.

And they said [that the men listed below] were gathered under the tree of Gernika and in the General Assembly of the Bizkaians, according to [the manner in which] all Bizkaians were generally accustomed to meet, the five horns [having been] sounded, as confirmed by the *sayón* Martín de Berroia, who had the five horns sounded according to custom, by order of the *prestamero* who was present, especially there being [in attendance] the said *corregidor* and above-named *alcaldes*, and [also] Joan Sáenz de Mezeta, Joan García de Yarza, Gonzalo de Aranzibia, Gonzalo Ibáñez de Marquina, Rodrigo Martínez de Aranzibia, Ochoa López de Urquiza, Martín Ruiz de Albiz, Juan Ruiz de Adoriaga, Joan Hortiz de Lecoya, Martín Ibánnez de Garaunaga, Martín Sáenz de Mundaca, Pero Martínez de Albiz, Lope González de Aguero, Ochoa Urtiz de Susunaga, Pero Ibáñez de Salazar, Martín de Asúa, Diego de Asúa, Pero Ruiz de Aguirre, Pedro de Garay, Martín de Mendieta, Pero de Uriarte, and Sancho Martínez de Goiri, a notary, and Joan Sáenz de Tornotegui, and Sancho del Castillo. And many other *escuderos* and *fijosdalgo* and *omes buenos* of the said Countship of Bizkaia, in the presence of myself, Fortún Iñiguez de Ibargüen, a notary, and the witnesses noted below.

The aforementioned [having been] selected to organize said laws and *fueros* and customs and exemptions and liberties of the said Countship of Bizkaia, they stated in said Assembly that insofar as the said *alcaldes* and *escuderos* and *hidalgos*, being in General Assembly, in the place of Idoibalzaga, had given to the said aforementioned selected persons the power to declare and organize the laws and *fuero* and rights and usages and customs that they had as *alvedrío* and exemptions and liberties. Regarding which they have ordered or declared or made me, the said notary, write down under oath and they were received by the said *corregidor*, according and in the manner and form that they best could and understood as is [stated] in the said book and *fuero*, written above.

Furthermore all of the aforementioned selected persons stated to the said *corregidor* and to all the men [assembled], *prestamero* and *merinos* and noble *escuderos* (*escuderos fijosdalgo*) and good men, that were in the said General Assembly, that they examine and evaluate the said laws and *fuero* and rights, usages and customs and exemptions and liberties that they had found and organized and established and had written down. And that which they found to be just, they confirm; and where they so understood that they amend.

And later the said Lord Doctor [*Corregidor*] said that if it was understood that there should be amendments in one or other parts of it, and before it be viewed and examined, then he did not wish to participate [in that process]. And he departed and left the said Assembly.

And having thus departed the said *corregidor*, afterwards the said *alcaldes* and *merinos*, noble *escuderos* and *omes Buenos* in the said Assembly ordered me, the said notary, to read out the aforementioned laws and *fueros* and rights and exemptions and liberties and usages and customs and ordinances and rules made and organized by the said aforenamed knowledgeable persons selected by the Bizkaians. Because once [the text] were read aloud it would be evident that which they should do and examine in it.

And later I, the aforementioned notary, read aloud the aforementioned Fuero and the laws and ordinances and rules contained in it, each chapter [article] in itself publicly in the said Assembly.

And once the said aforementioned laws and *fuero* and rights and usages and customs were read aloud and examined and accepted, all of the *fijosdalgo* and *escuderos* and good men, as well as the said *alcaldes*, as private persons, all of one voice and accord and council said that they held to be good and just the rights [stated in] the said *fuero* and usages and customs and laws and exemptions and liberties [redacted by] the aforementioned said selected persons, and by each one of them. And therefore they have had and wish to have from now on as their *fuero* of laws, and wished to use as it [*fuero*] and as laws all those contained within it, and each one of them. And they asked of said Lord King, as Lord of Bizkaia, the favor that he be pleased to confirm the said *Fuero* and the laws contained in it, and regard them as legal *Fuero*, according to which they would [be able] to maintain themselves and live and know how to judge [matters].

And furthermore they gave the order to the said *alcaldes*, as well as to the *prestameros* and *merinos*, and to any and all other persons of the Countship, that from this day forward, and even before the time when these laws and Fuero are confirmed by His Highness the King, they shall make use of these laws and they shall judge and administer any civil or criminal suits, and any other major or minor cases of any nature by the said Fuero and the laws contained in it. And they may be judged and administered by the laws of the aforementioned Fuero, and not by any other law or custom whatsoever, in the cases which may be decided by it. And no person of the said Countship shall dare to move or act against it, nor against any part of it, under pain of the penalties contained in the established laws of the aforementioned Fuero.

And all the Bizkaians themselves, and all their personal property and real estate, both in their possession and that which they may possess, shall be obligated to relieve and protest and shield from any damage said *alcaldes* or any other persons might incur for applying said Fuero as the law in litigations, before being confirmed by the said Lord King. Concerning the above, all the aforementioned *escuderos* and *fijosdalgo* and good men who were in the General Assembly shouted, in one voice and of one accord, "it is right" (*vala*).

And they ordered me, the notary, to give over the Fuero and all the aforementioned, and each item in it for witnessed signature.

Witnesses who were present for all the aforementioned [were] Martín Ruiz de Albiz, son of Martín Ruiz de Albiz, and Fernán Martínez de Albiz, and Fortún García de Arteaga, and Juan Perez de Arteaga, his brother, and Martín Ruiz de Aranzibia, and Juan Sáenz de Asúa, and Juan de Ibargüen, a notary, and others.

# Bibliography

Adams, John. 1856. *The Works of John Adams: Second President of the United States*/with a life of the author, notes and illustrations by his grandson Charles Francis Adams. Vol. 4. Boston: Little, Brown.

Aizpún Tuero, Rafael. 1945. El pacto sucesorio en el Derecho civil navarro, *Anuario de Derecho Aragonés* 2:159–186.

Altuna, Jesús. 1998. Las investigaciones prehistóricas en el País Vasco, *Revista Internacional de los Estudios Vascos* 43(2):481–514.

Alonso Romero, María Paz. 1985. Aproximación al estudio de las penas pecuniarias en Castilla (siglos XIII–XVIII), *Anuario de Historia del Derecho Español* 55:9–94.

Altamira, Rafael. 1981. *Historia de la propiedad comunal*. Madrid: Instituto de Estudios de Administración Local.

Angulo Laguna, Diego. 1983. *Derecho privado de Vizcaya*. Madrid: Hijos de Reus.

Aquí comienza el reinado del rey Don Fernando. In Rosell, Cayetano (ed.), *Crónicas de los reyes de Castilla: desde Don Alfonso el Sabio hasta los católicos Don Fernando y Doña Isabel / Colección ordenada por...* Chapter XV. 1953. Biblioteca de autores españoles, 66, volume 1. Madrid: Atlas. Pp. 150–159.

Arco, Miguel Ángel del. 1957. Contribución al estudio de la historia de la pena de muerte, *Anuario de Derecho Penal* 10:9–39.

Areitio y Mendiolea, Darío de. 1928. *Algunos pueblos de Castilla que tenían el Fuero de Vizcaya*. Donostia/San Sebastian: Imprenta de la Diputación de Guipúzcoa.

———. 1977. Las ediciones del Fuero de Vizcaya. In Areitio Mendiolea, Darío de (ed.), *El Fuero, privilegios, franquezas y libertades del M. N. y M. L. Señorío de Vizcaya*. Bilbo/Bilbao: Publicaciones de la Excma. Diputación de Vizcaya. Pp. LXXI–XCI.

———. 1985. Derecho civil de Vizcaya. In Pellisé Prats, Buenaventura (ed.), *Nueva Enciclopedia Jurídica Seix*. Barcelona: Seix. Pp. 307–349.

Arocena, Ignacio. 1969. Los banderizos vascos, *Boletín de la Real Sociedad Bascongada de los Amigos del País* 25:275–312.

———. 1981. Linajes, bandos y villas. In Caro Baroja, Julio (ed.), *Historia general del País Vasco*. Volume 5. Bilbo/Bilbao: La Gran Enciclopedia Vasca.. Pp. 9–124.

Astuy, José. 1909. *Fuero de Vizcaya acordado en la Junta de 2 de junio de 1452 dentro de la Iglesia de Santa María la Antigua de Guernica por los alcaldes de Fuero y los diputados en la Junta General de Idoibalzaga*. Bilbo/Bilbao: Imprenta y Librería de José de Astuy.

Aznar Gil, Federico R. 1989. *La institución matrimonial en la Hispania cristiana bajomedieval (1215–1563)*. Salamanca: Universidad Pontificia.

Baker, John Hamilton. 2000. *An Introduction to English Legal History*. (4th ed.), London: Butterworth.

Balparda, Gregorio de. 1903. *El Fuero de Vizcaya en lo civil*. Bilbo/Bilbao: Imprenta de la Casa de Misericordia.

———. 1924–1945. *Historia crítica de Vizcaya y de sus fueros*. (3 vols.). Madrid-Bilbo/Bilbao: Artes de la Ilustración. [Reprint. (2 vols.). 1974. Bilbo/Bilbao: Caja de Ahorros Municipal de Bilbao].

———. 1929. *Discurso de apertura de curso... de 1929. Del hidalgo al ciudadano*. Bilbo/Bilbao: Santa Casa de Misericordia.

———. 1932. Las Hermandades de Vizcaya y su organización provincial, *Anuario de Historia del Derecho Español* 9:190–199.

———. 1999. *El sentido liberal del Fuero de Vizcaya*. Bilbo/Bilbao: Sociedad "El Sitio".

Banús, José Luis. 1975. Los banderizos. Una interpretación étnica y sociopolítica. In Diputación Provincial de Vizcaya, Junta de Cultura and Real Sociedad Bascongada de los Amigos del País (eds.), *La sociedad vasca rural y urbana en el marco de la crisis de los siglos XIV y XV*. Bilbo/Bilbao: Diputación Provincial de Vizcaya. Pp. 65–81.

Barrero García, Ana María and María Luz Alonso Martín. 1989. *Textos de Derecho local español en la Edad Media. Catálogo de Fueros y Costums Municipales*. Madrid: Consejo Superior de Investigaciones Científicas, Instituto de Ciencias Jurídicas.

Basas Fernández, Manuel. 1972. Importancia de las villas en la estructura histórica del Señorío de Vizcaya. In Real Sociedad Bascongada de los Amigos del País and Diputación Provincial de Vizcaya (eds.),

*Edad Media y Señoríos: el Señorío de Vizcaya.* Bilbo/Bilbao: Diputación Provincial de Vizcaya. Pp. 93–122.

Basterra, Mario de. 1894. *Vizcaya minera. Su historia, legislación foral y derecho vigente.* Bilbo/Bilbao: Imprenta de la Casa de Misericordia.

Beneyto, Juan. 1932. Notas sobre el origen de los usos comunales, *Anuario de Historia del Derecho Español* 9:33–102.

———. 1948. *Manual de Historia del Derecho español.* Zaragoza: Librería General.

Beristáin, Antonio and María Ángeles Larrea, Rafael María Mieza. 1980. *Fuentes de Derecho Penal Vasco (Siglos XI–XVI), recogidas por...* Bilbo/Bilbao: La Gran Enciclopedia Vasca.

Bermejo Castrillo, Manuel A. 1997. Evolución del proceso penal en el ordenamiento español. El ejemplo de la prueba. In Johannes-Michael Scholz and Tamar Herzog (eds.), *Observation and communication: The Construction of realities in the Hispanic World.* Studien zur Europäischen Rechtsgeschichte. Veröffentlichungen des Max-Plank-Instituts für Europäische Rechtsgeschichte. Frankfurt am Main: Klostermann. Pp. 563–605.

———. 2001. Transferencias patrimoniales entre los cónyuges en el Derecho medieval español. In Iglesia Duarte, José Ignacio de la (ed.), *La familia en la Edad Media. XI Semana de Estudios Medievales.* Logroño: Instituto de Estudios Riojanos. Pp. 93–150.

Bidagor, Ramón. 1933. *La iglesia propia en España. Estudio histórico-canónico.* Rome: Analecta Gregoriana, IV.

Bilbao, Jon. 1982. Sobre la leyenda de Jaun Zuria, primer Señor de Vizcaya. In Real Sociedad Bascongada de los Amigos del País (ed.), *Amigos del País, hoy: trabajos de ingresos presentados por los Amigos de Número de la Real Sociedad Bascongada de los Amigos del País... años 1981 y 1982.* Bilbo/Bilbao: Comisión de Vizcaya de la Real Sociedad Bascongada de los Amigos del País. Pp. 235–263.

*Bizkaiko Foru Legeria/Legislación foral de Bizkaia.* 1991. Bilbo/Bilbao: Bizkaiko Foru Aldundia/Diputación Foral de Bizkaia.

Boza Vargas, Juan. 1898. *El Fuero de Baylío.* Fregenal de la Sierra: Imprenta de Indalecio Blanco.

Braga da Cruz, Guilherme. 1941. *O direito de troncalidade e o regime jurídico do património familiar.* Volume I. Braga: Livraria Cruz.

————. 1979. A posse de ano e dia no Direito hispánico medieval. In *Obras esparsas*. Volume I. Coimbra: Universidade de Coimbra. Pp. 259–286.

Brenan Sesma, Ingrid. 1996. La tutela de menores. Transformación de una potestad familiar. In *Homenaje al profesor Alfonso García-Gallo*. Volume 2–II. Madrid: Universidad Complutense. Pp. 211–236.

Cabral de Moncada, Luis. 1925. O duelo na vida do direito, *Anuario de Historia del Derecho español* 2:213–232.

————. 1926–1928. A posse de "ano e dia" e a prescriçao aquisitiva nos costumes municipais portugueses, *Boletim da Facultade de Direito de Coimbra* 10:121–149.

Caenegem, Raoul Charles van. 1928. *The Birth of the English Common Law,* (2nd ed.), Cambridge: Cambridge University Press.

————. 1963. Les Îles Britanniques. In Gilissen, John (ed.), *Introduction bibliographique à l'histoire du droit et à l'ethnologie juridique*, c/5, Bruxelles: Editoriel de l'Université de Bruxelles.

Cannata, Carlo Augusto. 1996. *Historia de la ciencia jurídica europea,* [Spanish translation by Laura Gutiérrez-Masson]. Madrid: Tecnos.

Cárdenas, Francisco de. 1884. Ensayo histórico sobre la dote, arras y donaciones esponsalicias desde los orígenes de la legislación española hasta nuestros días. In *Estudios jurídicos*. Volume II. Madrid: Establecimiento Tipográfico de P. Núñez. Pp. 5–62.

Carle, María del Carmen. 1980. Apuntes sobre el matrimonio en la Edad Media española, *Cuadernos de Historia del Derecho* 63–64:115–177

Caro Baroja, Julio. 1942. Observaciones sobre la hipótesis del vasco-iberismo, considerada desde el punto de vista histórico, *Emerita* 10:236–286; 11:1–59.

————. 1943. *Los pueblos del norte de la Península ibérica (Análisis histórico cultural)*. Madrid: Consejo Superior de Investigaciones Científicas, Instituto Bernardino de Sahagún, Patronato Menéndez Pelayo, Museo Etnológico. [(2nd ed.). 1973. Donostia/San Sebastian: Txertoa].

————. 1956. *Linajes y bandos: a propósito de la nueva edición de "Las Bienandanza e fortunas"*. Bilbo/Bilbao: Diputación Provincial de Vizcaya.

————. 1980. *Los vascos*. (7th ed.). Madrid: Istmo.

————. 1981. Las escrituras referentes a Vizcaya y el Duranguesado del siglo XI. Su contenido social y económico. In Caro Baroja, Julio (ed.), *Historia general del País Vasco*. Volume V. Bilbo/Bilbao-Donostia/San Sebastian: La Gran Enciclopedia Vasca. Pp. 243–293.

Carreras Candi, Francisco (ed.), 1911–1925. *Geografía general del País vasco-navarro*. 6 vols.. Barcelona: Editorial Alberto Martín.

Celaya Ibarra, Adrián. 1965. *Vizcaya y su Fuero Civil*. Pamplona: Aranzadi.

———. 1966. El régimen de bienes en el matrimonio vizcaíno, *Estudios de Deusto* 27:9–41.

———. 1970. Las declaraciones de derechos y el Fuero de Vizcaya. In Martín de Retana, José María (ed.), *La Gran Enciclopedia Vasca*. Volume 4. Bilbo/Bilbao: La Gran Enciclopedia Vasca. Pp. 569–588.

———. 1972. El testamento por comisario, *Anuario de Derecho Civil*, III (julio-septiembre):735–782.

———. 1975a. El Derecho privado de Vizcaya en la concepción del Fuero de 1452. In Bizkaia. Diputación Provincial. Junta de Cultura and Real Sociedad Bascongada de los Amigos del País (eds.), *La Sociedad vasca rural y urbana en el marco de la crisis de los siglos XIV y XV*. Bilbo/Bilbao: Diputación Foral de Vizcaya. Pp. 313–321.

———. 1975b. *El Fuero de Vizcaya*. Bilbo/Bilbao: Caja de Ahorros Vizcaína.

———. 1975c. La troncalidad en Vizcaya, *Anuario de Derecho Foral* 1:357–379.

———. 1976. Introducción. In Celaya Ibarra, Adrián (ed.), *El Fuero nuevo de Vizcaya*. Durango: Leopoldo Zugaza.

———. 1984. *Derecho Foral y Autonómico Vasco. I. Derecho Foral*. Bilbo/Bilbao: Universidad de Deusto.

———. 1986. El sistema familiar y sucesorio de Vizcaya en el marco del Derecho medieval. In Eusko-Ikaskuntza/Sociedad de Estudios Vascos (ed.), *Vizcaya en la Edad Media*: *Congreso de Estudios Históricos* (1984, Bilbo/Bilbao). Donostia/San Sebastian: Sociedad de Estudios Vascos. Pp. 147–163.

———. 1991. Reflexión final. In Churruca, Juan and María González (eds.), *Jornadas Internacionales sobre instituciones civiles vascas* (1991, Bilbo/Bilbao). Bilbo/Bilbao: Universidad de Deusto. Pp. 342–347.

———. 1993. *Derecho civil vasco*. Bilbo/Bilbao: Universidad de Deusto.

———. 1996. Los estudios acerca del Derecho civil de Vizcaya. In Tamayo Salaberría, Virginia (ed.), *Jornadas sobre el estado de la cuestión del Derecho Histórico de Euskal Herria* (1993, Donostia/San Sebastian). Donostia/San Sebastian: Instituto Vasco de Administración Pública. Pp. 123–134.

Cerdá Ruiz-Funes, Joaquín. 1962. En torno a la pesquisa y al procedimiento inquisitivo en el Derecho castellano-leonés de la Edad Media, *Anuario de Historia del Derecho español* 32:483–517.

Cerro y Sánchez Herrera, Eduardo. 1974. *Investigación sobre el Fuero de Baylío.* Madrid: Revista de Derecho Privado.

Chalbaud y Errazquin, Luis. 1898. *La troncalidad en el Fuero de Bizcaya: sucesión troncal, llamamiento en las transmisiones onerosas.* Bilbo/Bilbao: Tip. de Sebastián de Amorrortu.

Champeaux, E. 1933. Jus sanguinis, trois façons de calculer la parenté au Moyen Âge, *Revue d'Histoire de Droit Français et Étranger,* 12: 241–290.

Cillán Apalategui, Antonio. 1959. *La comunidad de pastos de Guipúzcoa.* Donostia/San Sebastian: Diputación Provincial de Guipúzcoa.

*Colección documental del Archivo General del Señorío de Vizcaya.* 1986. Colección Fuentes documentales medievales del País Vasco, 9. Donostia/San Sebastian: Eusko-Ikaskuntza/Sociedad de Estudios Vascos.

Collantes de Terán de la Hera, María José. 1969. El delito de adulterio en el derecho general de Castilla, *Anuario de Historia del Derecho* 66:201–228.

———. 1997. *El régimen económico del matrimonio en el Derecho territorial castellano.* Valencia: Tirant lo Blanch.

Comisión Especial de Codificación de Vizcaya. 1902. *Actas de las sesiones celebradas por la Comisión Especial de Codificación de Vizcaya.* Bilbo/Bilbao: Comisión Provincial.

Conde de Barcelos. 1856. Livro dos Linhagens. In Herculano, Alexandre (ed.), *Monumenta Portugaliae Historica,* Scriptores I. Lisbon: Academia das Ciencias. Pp. 230–390.

Coronas González, Santos M. 1995. Notas sobre las leyes fundamentales del Antiguo Régimen, *Anuario de Historia del Derecho español* 65:127–218.

———. 1996. Estudio preliminar. In Coronas González, Santos M. (ed.), *El Libro de las leyes del siglo XVIII.* Madrid: Boletín Oficial del Estado, Centro de Estudios Constitucionales. Pp. 9–39.

Craddock, Jerry R. 1981. La cronología de las obras legislativas de Alfonso X el Sabio, *Anuario de Historia del Derecho españo* 51:365–418.

Crónica del rey Don Juan, primero de Castilla, Chapter XI. In Rosell, Cayetano (ed.), *Crónicas de los reyes de Castilla: desde Don Alfonso el Sabio hasta los católicos Don Fernando y Doña Isabel/ Colección ordenada por...* 1953. Biblioteca de autores españoles, 68. Volume 2. Madrid: Atlas. Pp. 138–140.

Díaz Palos, Fernando. 1954. *Bibliografía española de Derecho penal.* Barcelona: Consejo Superior de Investigaciones Científicas. Instituto de Derecho Comparado.

Díez de Salazar Fernández, Luis Miguel. 1988. El Derecho y las Instituciones públicas en Euskalerría en la Baja Edad Media (Balance o aproximación a las recientes aportaciones). In Gobierno Vasco. Servicio Central de Publicaciones (ed.), *II Congreso Mundial Vasco. Congreso de Historia de Euskal Herria, II. Instituciones, economía y sociedad (siglos VIII–XV)* (1987, Bilbo/Bilbao). Donostia/San Sebastian: Gobierno Vasco. Servicio Central de Publicaciones. Pp. 9–46.

Du Boys, Albert. 1872. *Historia del Derecho penal de España... para servir de continuación a la Historia del Derecho penal de los pueblos modernos, del mismo autor.* [Spanish translation, annotated and extended by J. Vicente y Caravantes]. Madrid.

Duker, William F. 1980. *Constitutional History of Habeas Corpus.* Westport (Conn.): Greenwood Press.

Echegaray, Carmelo de. 1895. *Las Provincias vascongadas a finales de la Edad Media. Ensayo histórico.* I. Donostia/San Sebastian: F. Jornet. [Facsimile edition. 1984. Echévarri: Amigos del Libro Vasco].

—————. 1922. *La casa de Juntas de Guernica.* Barcelona: Imprenta Viuda de Luis Tasso.

Echegaray y Corta, Bonifacio de. 1923. La vida civil y mercantil de los vascos a través de las instituciones jurídicas, *Revista Internacional de los Estudios Vascos* 13:173–336, 582–613; 14:27–60.

—————. 1950. *Derecho foral privado.* Donostia/San Sebastian: Biblioteca Vascongada de los Amigos del País.

—————. 1952. Origen de la voz Vizcaya, *Boletín de la Real Sociedad Bascongada de los Amigos del País* 8:323–343.

*El Fuero nuevo de Vizcaya.* 1976. Celaya Ibarra, Adrián (ed.). Durango: Leopoldo Zugaza.

*El Fuero, priuilegios, franquezas y libertades de los caualleros hijos dalgo del Señorío de Vizcaya, confirmados por el Rey do[n] Felipe*

*II... y por el Emperador y Reyes sus predecesores.* 1575. Medina del Campo: Francisco del Canto.

*El Fuero, privilegios, franquezas y libertades de los cavalleros hijos dalgo del Señorío de Vizcaya confirmados por el Rey D. Felipe III Nuestro Señor y por los Señores Reyes sus predecesores.* 1643. Bilbo/Bilbao: Pedro de Huydobro.

*El Fuero, privilegios, franquezas y libertades de los cavalleros hijos dalgo de el muy noble y muy leal Señorío de Vizcaya confirmados por el rey D. Carlos tercero nro. Señor y por los señores reyes sus predecesores.* 1762. Bilbo/Bilbao: Antonio de Egusquiza.

*El Fuero, privilegios, franquezas y libertades del M. N. y M. L. Señorío de Vizcaya [con una introducción de Darío de Areitio].* 1950. Bilbo/Bilbao: Junta de Cultura de la Diputación de Vizcaya. [Reedition 1977. Bilbo/Bilbao: Diputación Provincial de Vizcaya].

Elías de Tejada, Francisco. 1963. *El Señorío de Vizcaya (hasta 1812).* Madrid: Minotauro.

Enríquez Fernández, Javier and Concepción Hidalgo de Cisneros Amestoy, Araceli Lorente Ruigómez, Adela Martínez Lahidalga. 1994. *Fuentes jurídicas medievales del Señorío de Vizcaya. Fueros de las Encartaciones, de la Merindad de Durango y de las Ferrerías.* Colección Fuentes documentales medievales del País Vasco, 51. Donostia/San Sebastian: Eusko-Ikaskuntza/Sociedad de Estudios Vascos.

Enríquez Fernández, Javier, and María José Sarriegui. 1986. *La Colegiata de Santa María de Cenarruza, 1353–1515.* Colección Fuentes documentales medievales del País Vasco, 10. Donostia/San Sebastian: Eusko-Ikaskuntza/Sociedad de Estudios Vascos.

Esjaverría, José María de. 1914. El apartamiento en el Fuero y en la Compilación del Derecho civil de Vizcaya, *Estudios de Deusto* VII (14):471–581.

Etxebarría Mirones, Jesús and Txomin. 1994. *Orígenes históricos de las Encartaciones. Siglos X–XIII, toponimia, onomástica y lengua propia.* Bilbo/Bilbao.

Fabre, Laurent. 1930. *Les successions testamentaires et ab intestat en pays de droit écrit.* Toulouse: H. Cléder.

Fairén Guillén, Víctor. 1946. El Fuero del Señorío de Vizcaya en lo civil durante los siglos XVIII y XIX, *Revista General de Legislación y Jurisprudencia* 179:300–329.

Fernández Espinar, Ramón. 2001. Las injurias en el derecho histórico español (anterior a la codificación penal). In Zugaldia Espinar, José Miguel and Eduardo Roca Roca (ed.), *Los Derechos humanos. Libro homenaje al Excmo. Sr. D. Luis Portero García.* Granada: Universidad de Granada). Pp. 167–190.

Fonsar Belloch, Enrique. 1995. La disolubilidad del matrimonio en la legislación de las Españas medievales, *Revista de la Facultad de Derecho de la Universidad Complutense de Madrid* 85:23–68.

Font Rius, José María. 1954. La ordenación paccionada del régimen matrimonial de bienes en el Derecho medieval hispánico, *Anales de la Academia Matritense de Notariado* 8:189–244.

———. 1967. *La recepción del Derecho Romano en la Península Ibérica durante la Edad Media.* Recueils de memoires et travaux publiés pas la Société d'Histoire du Droit et des Institucions du Pays de Droit écrit, VI: 85–104.

*Fueros, privilegios, franquezas y libertades del M. N. y M. L. Señorío de Vizcaya. (Introducción de Fermín Herrán).* 1865. Bilbo/Bilbao: Juan E. Delmas.

*Fueros, privilegios, franquezas y libertades del M. N. y M. L. Señorío de Vizcaya (Introducción de Fermín Herrán).* 1897. Bilbo/Bilbao: Imprenta de la Biblioteca Bascongada.

*Fueros, franquezas, libertades, buenos usos, y costumbres, del Muy Noble y Muy Leal, Señorío de Vizcaya, confirmados por el rey don Phelipe Quinto, Nuestro Señor, y por los reyes sus predecesores.* [1704?]. Bilbo/Bilbao: Antonio de Zafra. [Facsimile edition. 1981. Bilbo/Bilbao: Imprenta Artigraf].

*Fueros, privilegios, franquezas y libertades del M. N. y M. L. Señorío de Vizcaya.* 1898. Bilbo/Bilbao: Imprenta Provincial.

*Fueros, privilegios, franquezas y libertades del M. N. y M. L. Señorío de Vizcaya: confirmados por el rey nuestro señor don Carlos III (que Dios guarde) y sus gloriosos predecesores.* 178?. Reprint. Bilbo/Bilbao: Viuda de Antonio Egúsquiza.

Gacto Fernández, Enrique. 1969. *La filiación no legítima en el Derecho histórico español.* Seville: Anales de la Universidad Hispalense.

———. 1971. La filiación ilegítima en la Historia del Derecho español, *Anuario de Historia del Derecho español* 41:899–944.

———. 1990. Aproximación a la historia del Derecho penal español. In Clavero, Bartolomé and Paolo Grossi and Francisco Tomás y

Valiente (eds.), *Hispania: entre derechos propios y nacionales, Quaderni Fiorentini* (Milano) 34–35: 501–530.

Galán Lorda, Mercedes and Amparo Zubiri Jaurrieta. 2002. La trascendencia social de los denominados "faceros", Un caso en la Merindad de Estella. In Erro Gasca, Carmen and Iñigo Mugueta Moreno (eds.), *Grupos sociales en Navarra. Relaciones y derechos a lo largo de la Historia.* Actas del V Congreso de Historia de Navarra I (5°. 2002, Pamplona) Pamplona: Eunate. Pp. 417–424; 459–469.

Galíndez Suárez, Jesús de. 1934. *La Legislación penal de Vizcaya. Trabajo presentado en la cátedra de Derecho Penal de la Universidad de Madrid. Con la transcripción como apéndices del Quaderno penal de 1342 y del Quaderno de Hermandad de 1394.* Bilbo/Bilbao: Gráficas Verdes Achirica.

———. 1947. *El Derecho vasco.* Buenos Aires: Ekin.

Galicia Aizpurua, Gorka H. 2002. *Legítima y troncalidad: la sucesión forzosa en el derecho de Bizkaia.* Madrid: Marcial Pons.

Gámez Montalvo, María Francisca. 1998. *Régimen jurídico de la mujer en la familia castellana medieval.* Granada: Comares.

Gárate, Justo. 1951. Evolución del concepto territorial de Vizcaya, *Boletín de la Real Sociedad Bascongada de Amigos del País* 7: 527–530.

García de Cortázar, José Ángel. 1966. *Vizcaya en el siglo XV. Aspectos económicos y sociales.* Bilbo/Bilbao: Ediciones de la Caja de Ahorros Vizcaína.

———. 1977. Los estudios de tema medieval vascongado: un balance de las aportaciones de los últimos años, *Saioak* 1:181–201.

———. 1978. Ordenamientos jurídicos y estructura social del Señorío de Vizcaya. In Estudios Universitarios y Técnicos de Guipúzcoa (ed.) *Historia del pueblo vasco.* Volume I. Donostia/San Sebastian: Erein. Pp. 223–267.

———. 1986. La sociedad vizcaína altomedieval: de los sistemas de parentesco de base ganadera a la diversificación y jerarquización sociales de base territorial. In Eusko-Ikaskuntza/Sociedad de Estudios Vascos (ed.), *Congreso de Estudios Históricos. Vizcaya en la Edad Media* (1984, Bilbo/Bilbao). Donostia/San Sebastian: Sociedad de Estudios Vascos. Pp. 63–81.

———. 1988. Poblamiento y organización social del espacio vasco en la Edad Media. In Gobierno Vasco. Servicio Central de Publicaciones (ed.), *II Congreso Mundial Vasco. Congreso de Historia de Euskal*

*Herria, II. Instituciones, economía y sociedad (siglos VIII–XV)* (1987, Bilbo/Bilbao). Donostia/San Sebastian: Gobierno Vasco. Servicio Central de Publicaciones. Pp. 421–443.

García de Cortázar, José Ángel and Beatriz Arízaga Bolumburu, María Luz Ríos Rodríguez and Isabel del Val Valdivielso. 1985. *Bizcaya en la Edad Media. Evolución demográfica, económica, social y política de la comunidad vizcaína medieval.* (4 vols.). Donostia/San Sebastian: Haranburu.

García de Salazar, Lope. 1914. *Crónica de las siete casas de Vizcaya y Castilla, escrita por Lope García de Salazar, año 1454.* [Edited by Juan Carlos Guerra]. Madrid: Rivadeneira.

———. 1967. *Libro de Las bienandanzas e fortunas: códice del siglo XV.* [Prologue, notes and indexes by A. Rodríguez Herrero]. 4 vols. Bilbo/Bilbao: Diputación de Vizcaya.

García de Valdeavellano, Luis. 1947. El apellido. Notas sobre el procedimiento *in fraganti* en el Derecho español medieval, *Cuadernos de Historia de España* 7:67–105.

———. 1977a. Bienes muebles e inmuebles en el Derecho español medieval. In *Estudios medievales de Derecho privado.* Seville: Servicio de Publicaciones de la Universidad de Sevilla. Pp. 3–19.

———. 1977b. La limitación de la acción reinvindicatoria de los bienes inmuebles en el Derecho medieval español. In *Ibidem.* Pp. 21–60.

———. 1977c. La comunidad patrimonial de la familia en el Derecho español medieval. In *Ibidem.* Pp. 295–321.

———. 1977d. La cuota de libre disposición en el derecho hereditario de León y Castilla en la Alta Edad media. Notas y documentos. In *Ibidem.* Pp. 323–363.

———. 1977e. Sobre la prenda inmobiliaria en el Derecho español medieval. In *Ibidem.* Pp. 364–396.

García Gallo, Alfonso. 1950. *Curso de Historia del Derecho Español,* (5th ed. revised). Madrid.

———. 1951–1952. El libro de las leyes de Alfonso X el Sabio. Del Espéculo a las Partidas, *Anuario de Historia del Derecho español* 21–22: 345–528.

———. 1959. Bienes propios y derecho de propiedad en la Alta Edad Media española, *Anuario de Historia del Derecho español* 29: 351–387.

———. 1966. L'evolution de la condition de la femme en Droit espagnol, en *Annales de la Faculté de Droit de Toulouse* 14:73–96. [1982. La condición jurídica de la mujer (estudio presentado en las Jornadas franco-españolas de Barcelona en 1966). In *Estudios de Historia de Derecho Privado*. Sevilla: Servicio de Publicaciones de la Universidad de Sevilla. Pp. 145–166].

——. 1977. Del testamento romano al medieval, Las líneas de evolución en España, *Anuario de Historia del Derecho español* 47: 425–497.

——. 1980. El pactismo en el reino de Castilla y su proyección en América. In Legaz Lacambra et alii (eds.), *El Pactismo en la Historia de España. Instituto de España, Cátedra Francisco de Vitoria*. Madrid: Instituto de España. Pp. 143–168.

——. 1982a. El problema de la sucesión *mortis causa* en la Alta Edad Media española. In *Estudios de Historia del Derecho Privado*. Sevilla: Servicio de Publicaciones de la Universidad de Sevilla. Pp. 251–271.

——. 1982b. *Manual de Historia del Derecho español*, I. *El origen y la evolución del Derecho* (9th ed., revised). Madrid.

——. 1984. La obra legislativa de Alfonso X. Hechos e hipótesis, *Anuario de Historia del Derecho español* 54:97–161.

——. 1986a. El régimen público del Señorío de Vizcaya en la Edad Media, In Eusko-Ikaskuntza/Sociedad de Estudios Vascos (ed.), *Congreso de Estudios Históricos. Vizcaya en la Edad Media* (1984, Bilbo/Bilbao). Donostia/San Sebastian: Sociedad de Estudios Vascos. Pp. 83–98.

——. 1986b. La labor legislativa de Alfonso X el Sabio. In Pérez Martín, Antonio (ed.), *España y Europa. Un pasado jurídico común*. Murcia: Universidad de Murcia. Pp. 275–599.

——. 1997. *Atlas histórico-jurídico*. México: Instituto de Investigaciones Jurídicas, Universidad Autónoma de México.

García González, Juan. 1962. Traición y alevosía en la Alta Edad Media, *Anuario de Historia del Derecho español* 32:323–345.

García Marín, José María. 1980. La legítima defensa hasta fines de la Edad Media, *Anuario de Historia del Derecho español* 50:413–438.

García Royo, Luis. 1952. *La Foralidad civil de las Provincias vascongadas con directrices para Navarra, Aragón, Cataluña, Galicia y Baleares: filosofía del irracionalismo en el derecho*. (3 vols.). Vitoria: Editorial S. Católica.

Gaudemet, Jean. 1963. *Les communautés familiales*. Paris: Marcel Rivière.

————. 1987. *Le mariage en Occident. Les moeurs et le Droit.* Paris: Editorial du Cerf.

Gibert, Rafael. 1957–1958. La paz del camino en el derecho medieval español, *Anuario de Historia del Derecho español* 27–28:831–851.

————. 1973. Fueros de francos en la Hispania medieval (comunicación de 1968), *Revista de la Facultad de Derecho de la Universidad Complutense de Madrid* XVII–48:473–500.

Gilissen, John. 1979. *Introduction historique au Droit: esquisse d'une histoire universelle du droit: les sources du droit depuis le 13 siècle: éléments d'histoire du droit privé.* Brussels: Bruylant.

Giesey, Ralph E. 1968. *If not, not, The Oath of the Aragonese and the Legendary Laws of Sobrarbe.* Princeton, New Jersey: Princeton University Press.

Gómez Jiménez de Cisneros, Juan. 1948. *Algunos tipos de delitos recogidos en nuestra legislación histórica desde el Fuero Juzgo hasta las recopilaciones.* Murcia: Publicaciones de la Universidad.

Gómez Rivero, Ricardo. 1979. *El pase foral en Guipúzcoa en el siglo XVIII.* Donostia/San Sebastian: Diputación Provincial.

González Alonso, Benjamín. 1971. Los delitos patrimoniales en el derecho pirenaico local y territorial, *Anuario de Historia del Derecho español* 41:237–334.

————. 1996. Consideraciones sobre la historia del Derecho de Castilla (c. 800–1356). In Barrios García, Ángel and Gregorio del Ser Quijano (eds.), *El Fuero Viejo de Castilla.* Valladolid: Consejería de Educación y Cultura. Pp. 13–70.

Gutiérrez Fernández, Benito. 1866. *Examen histórico del derecho penal.* Madrid: Antonio Peñuelas.

Hespanha, Antonio M. 1987. Da 'Iustitia' a 'disciplina'. Textos, poder e política penal no Antigo Regime, *Anuario de Historia del Derecho español* 57:493–570.

Hidalgo de Cisneros, Concepción and Elena Largacha Rubio, Araceli Lorente Ruigómez and Adela Martínez Lahidalga. 1986. *Fuentes jurídicas medievales del Señorío de Vizcaya. Cuadernos legales, Capítulos de la Hermandad y Fuero Viejo (1342–1506).* Colec. Fuentes documentales medievales del País Vasco, 8. Donostia/San Sebastian: Eusko-Ikaskuntza/Sociedad de Estudios Vascos.

Hinojosa Naveros, Eduardo. 1955a. La condición civil de la mujer en el Derecho español antiguo y moderno. In García Gallo, Alfonso (ed.), *Obras completas*. Volume II. Madrid: Instituto Nacional de Estudios Jurídicos. Pp. 343–385.

———. 1955b. El elemento germánico en el Derecho español, (memoria presentada en el Congreso histórico de Berlin de 1908). In *Ibidem*. Pp. 405–470.

Iglesia Ferreirós, Aquilino. 1969. La crisis de la noción de fidelidad en la obra de Diego de San Pedro, *Anuario de Historia del Derecho español* 39:707–723.

———. 1971a. *Historia de la traición. La traición regia en León y Castilla*. Santiago: Universidad de Santiago de Compostela.

———. 1971b. Las Cortes de Zamora de 1274 y los casos de Corte, *Anuario de Historia del Derecho español* 41:945–971.

———. 1974. Uniones matrimoniales y afines en el Derecho Histórico español, *Revista de Derecho Notarial* 85–86:71–107.

———. 1986. La labor legislativa de Alfonso X el Sabio. In Pérez Martín, Antonio (ed.), *España y Europa. Un pasado jurídico común*. Murcia: Universidad de Murcia. Pp. 275–599.

———. 1988. Individuo y familia. Una historia del Derecho privado español. In Artola, Miguel (ed.), *Enciclopedia de Historia de España, I. Economía. Sociedad*. Madrid: Alianza Editorial. Pp. 433–536.

Isábal, Marceliano. [1915?]. Derecho civil de Vizcaya. In Mouton y Ocampo, Luis (ed.), *Enciclopedia Jurídica Española*. Volume XI. Barcelona: Francisco Seix. Pp. 37–43.

———. Fueros de Vizcaya. [1915?]. In *Ibidem*, XVI. Pp. 831–834.

Iturriza y Zabala, Juan Ramón de. 1967. *Historia General de Vizcaya y Epítome de las Encartaciones*. (2 vols). Bilbo/Bilbao: Librería Arturo.

Jado y Ventades, Rodrigo. 1900. *Derecho civil de Vizcaya. Comentarios a las leyes del Fuero de Vizcaya con la jurisprudencia del Tribunal Supremo de Justicia y de la Dirección de los Registros civiles, de la propiedad y del notariado, precedidos de un estudio acerca del territorio en que rigen esas leyes*. Bilbo/Bilbao: Casa de Misericordia de Bilbao. [2nd ed. 1923. Bilbo/Bilbao].

Juaristi, Jon. 1980. *La leyenda de Jaun Zuria*. Colec. Temas vizcaínos, 62. Bilbo/Bilbao: Caja de Ahorros.

Labayru y Goicoechea, Estanislao J. 1895–1903. *Historia General del Señorío de Bizcaya*. Bilbo/Bilbao: Librería de Victoriano Suárez. (6 vols.). [Facsimile edition. 1968. Bilbo/Bilbao: La Gran Enciclopedia Vasca].

Lacarra, José María. 1972a. El Señorío de Vizcaya y el Reino de Navarra en el siglo XII. In Real Sociedad Bascongada de los Amigos del País and Diputación Provincial de Vizcaya (eds.), *Edad Media y Señoríos: el Señorío de Vizcaya*. Bilbo/Bilbao: Diputación Provincial de Vizcaya. Pp. 37–50.

———. 1972b. *El juramento de los Reyes de Navarra (1234–1328)*. Madrid: Real Academia de la Historia.

Lacruz Berdejo, José Luis. 1959–1960. Una cuestión de derecho histórico en temas de retracto gentilicio, *Anuario de Derecho Aragonés* 10: 7–22.

Lafourcade, Maïte. 1992. Droit successoral et droit matrimonial en Pays Basque sous l'Ancien Régime. In *Le Droit de famille en Europe. Son evolution depuis l'antiquité à nos jours*. Strasbourg: Presses Universitaires de Strasbourg. Pp. 517–529.

Lalinde Abadía, Jesús. 1961. La problemática histórica del heredamiento, *Anuario de Historia del Derecho español* 31:195–233.

———. 1962. La propiedad en el Derecho medieval español. In Salvá, Rafael (ed.), *VI Congreso del Instituto de Derecho Comparado* (Hamburg, 1962). Barcelona: Instituto de Derecho Comparado. Pp. 7–22.

———. 1966. La creación del derecho entre los españoles, *Anuario de Historia del Derecho español* 36:301–377.

———. 1969. Las instituciones de la Corona de Aragón en el siglo XIV. In Congreso de Historia de la Corona de Aragón (8th. 1967, Valencia) (ed.), *VIII Congreso de Historia de la Corona de Aragón. II.* Valencia: Caja de Ahorros. Pp. 9–52.

———. 1972. El sistema normativo valenciano, *Anuario de Historia del Derecho español* 52:307–330.

———. 1974. *Derecho histórico español*. Barcelona: Ariel.

———. 1975a. Apuntes sobre las ideologías en el Derecho histórico español, *Anuario de Historia del Derecho español* 45:123–157.

———. 1975b. Las libertades aragonesas, *Revista Zaragoza* 39–40: 89–118.

———. 1978a. *Iniciación histórica al Derecho español*. (2[th] ed.), Barcelona: Ariel.

———. 1978b. Los parlamentos y demás instituciones representativas en la Corona de Aragón desde Alfonso el Magnánimo a Fernando el

Católico. In Congreso de Historia de la Corona de Aragón (9th. 1973, Napoli) (ed.), *IX Congreso de Historia de la Corona de Aragón*. Volume I. Naples: Societá Napolitana di Storia Patria. Pp. 103–179.

———. 1978c. Notas sobre el papel de las fuerzas políticas y sociales en el desarrollo de los sistemas iushistóricos españoles, *Anuario de Historia del Derecho español* 48:249–268.

———. 1979. El ordenamiento interno de la Corona de Aragón bajo Jaime I. In Congreso de Historia de la Corona de Aragón (10th. 1976, Zaragoza) (ed.), *X Congreso de Historia de la Corona de Aragón*. Zaragoza: Institución Fernando el Católico. Pp. 169–211.

———. 1980. El pactismo en los reinos de Aragón y Valencia, In Legaz Lacambra et alii (eds.), *El pactismo en la Historia de España*. Madrid: Instituto de España. Pp. 113–139.

———. 1985. *Los Fueros de Aragón*. (4th ed.), Zaragoza: Librería General.

———. 1986. El sistema normativo vizcaíno. In Eusko-Ikaskuntza/Sociedad de Estudios Vascos (ed.), *Congreso de Estudios Históricos. Vizcaya en la Edad Media* (1984, Bilbo/Bilbao). Donostia/San Sebastian: Sociedad de Estudios Vascos. Pp. 115–145.

*Las Siete Partidas del sabio rey don Alonso el Nono... nuevamente glosadas... por Gregorio López*. 1587. Valladolid: Diego Fernández de Cordoua. [Facsimile edition. 1974. Madrid: Boletín Oficial del Estado].

Lasala Navarro, Gregorio. 1951. La cárcel en Castilla durante la Edad Media, *Revista de la Escuela de Estudios Penitenciarios*, 80: 61–67.

Lecanda y Mendieta, Manuel de. 1889. *Memoria sobre las instituciones civiles que deben quedar vigentes en las Provincias Vascongadas: escritas con arreglo a lo dispuestos en el RD de 2 de febrero de 1880*. Madrid: Imprenta del Ministerio de Gracia y Justicia.

———. 1888. *Legislación foral de España. Derecho civil vigente en Vizcaya. Precedido de la memoria sobre las instituciones civiles de aquel país*. Madrid: Establecimiento tipográfico de Pedro Núñez.

Lemaire, André, 1928. Les origines de la communauté de biens entre epoux dans le droit coutumier français, *Revue Historique de Droit Français et Étranger* 7:584–643.

Letinier, Rosine. 2001. Aproximación histórica a los derechos sucesorios de los ascendientes, *Anuario de Historia del Derecho español* 71: 371–394.

Liñán y Eguizábal, José de. 1897. *La Jura de los Fueros por los Señores de Vizcaya, su trascendencia histórica y social.* Bilbo/Bilbao: Imprenta de la Propaganda.

López Amo Marín, Ángel. 1956. El Derecho penal español en la Baja Edad Media, *Anuario de Historia del Derecho español* 26:337–367.

López-Cordón, María Victoria. 1994. Esponsales, dote y gananciales en los pleitos castellanos: las alegaciones jurídicas. In Sholz, Johannes Michael (ed.), *Fallstudien zur spanischen und portugueisischen Justiz, 15. bis 20. Jahrhundert.* (Rechtsprechung. Materialien und Studien. Veröffentlichungen des Max-Plank-Instituts für Europäische Rechtsgeschichte, 8). Frankfurt am Main: Klostermann. Pp. 33–58

Lopez Nevot, José Antonio A. 1998. *La aportación marital en la historia del derecho castellano.* Almeria: Universidad de Almería.

López Ortiz, José. 1942–1943. El proceso en los reinos cristianos de nuestra Reconquista antes de la recepción romano-canónica, *Anuario de Historia del Derecho español* 14:184–226.

*Los Fueros de Vizcaya.* 1869. Mexico: I. Escalante y Cª.

Luiz-Gálvez, Estrella. 1990. *Statut socio-juridique de la femme en Espagne au XVIe. siécle. Une étude sur le mariage chrétien faite d'après l'Epitome de matrimonio de Diego de Covarrubias y Leyva (Droit Canon). La legislation royale et les moralistes.* Paris: Didier Erudition.

Luján de Saavedra, Mateo (pseudonym of Juan Martí). La Segunda Parte de la Vida de Guzmán de Alfarache. (caps. VIII–XI). In Valbuena Prat, Angel. 1946. *La novela picaresca española.* Madrid: M. Aguilar. Pp. 580–702.

Machado Bandeira de Mello, Lydio. 1961. *O direito penal hispano-luso medieval,* Belo Horizonte.

Madariaga, Ramón de. 1932. *El Derecho foral de Vizcaya en relación con la organización familiar.* Bilbo/Bilbao: Tipografía del Norte.

Madrid del Cacho, Manuel. 1963. *El Fuero de Baylío: un enclave foral en el Derecho de Castilla.* Córdoba: Tipografía Artística.

Maldonado y Fernández del Torco, José. 1944. *Herencias en favor del alma en Derecho español.* Madrid: Revista de Derecho privado.

Mañaricúa, Andrés Eliseo de. 1950. *Santa María de Begoña en la historia espiritual de Vizcaya.* Bilbo/Bilbao: La Editorial Vizcaína.

———. 1971. *Historiografía de Vizcaya [desde Lope García de Salazar hasta Labayru].* Bilbo/Bilbao: La Gran Enciclopedia Vasca.

———. 1972. Orígenes del Señorío de Vizcaya. In Real Sociedad Bascongada de los Amigos del País and Diputación Provincial de Vizcaya (eds.), *Edad Media y Señoríos: el Señorío de Vizcaya*. Bilbo/Bilbao: Diputación Provincial de Vizcaya. Pp. 13–26.

———. 1984. *Vizcaya, siglos VIII al XI. Los orígenes del Señorío*. Bilbo/Bilbao: Caja de Ahorros Vizcaína.

Maravall, José Antonio. 1986. *Estado moderno y mentalidad social: siglos XV a XVII*. (2th ed.). 2 vols. Madrid: Alianza Editorial.

Marichalar, Amalio and Cayetano Manrique. 1868. *Historia de la legislación y recitaciones del Derecho civil de España. Fueros de Navarra, Vizcaya, Guipúzcoa y Álava*. (2th ed.), Madrid: Imprenta. de Gasset, Loma y Compañía. [Facsimile edition. 1971. Donostia/San Sebastian: Editorial Auñamendi].

Marín Padilla, María Luisa. 1992. *Historia de la sucesión contractual*. Zaragoza: María Luisa Marín.

Martín Osante, Luis Carlos. 1996. *El régimen económico matrimonial en el Derecho vizcaíno. La comunicación foral de bienes*. Madrid: Gobierno Vasco. Departamento de Justicia, Economía, Trabajo y Seguridad Social.

Martín Rodríguez, Jacinto. 1968. Figura histórico-jurídica del Juez Mayor de Vizcaya, *Anuario de Historia del Derecho español* 38: 641–669.

———. 1973. *El honor y la injuria en el Fuero de Vizcaya*. Bilbo/Bilbao: Diputación Provincial de Vizcaya.

Martínez Díez, Gonzalo. 1974. *Alava medieval*. (2 vols). Vitoria: Diputación de Alava.

———. 1975. Poblamiento y Ordenamiento jurídico en el País Vasco. El estatuto jurídico de la población rural y urbana. In Real Sociedad Bascongada de los Amigos del País and Vizcaya. Diputación Provincial. Junta de Cultura (eds.), *Las formas de poblamiento en el Señorío de Vizcaya durante la Edad Media*. Bilbo/Bilbao: Diputación Foral de Vizcaya. Pp. 129–169.

———. 1979. Fueros de La Rioja, *Anuario de Historia del Derecho español* 49:329–474.

———. 1982. *Fueros locales en el territorio de la Provincia de Burgos*. Burgos: Caja de Ahorros Municipal de Burgos.

Martínez Gijón, José. 1957–1958. La comunidad hereditaria y la partición de la herencia en el Derecho medieval español, *Anuario de Historia del Derecho español* 27–28:221–303.

————. 1971. Los sistemas de tutela y administración de los bienes de los menores en el Derecho local de León y Castilla, *Anuario de Historia del Derecho español* 41:9–31.

Martínez Marina, Francisco. 1845. *Ensayo histórico-crítico sobre la legislación y principales cuerpos legales de León y Castilla, especialmente sobre el Código de las Siete Partidas de D. Alonso el Sabio.* (3^th^ ed.). Madrid: Imprenta de la Sociedad Literaria y Tipográfica.

Martínez Pereda, Matías. 1925. El Fuero de Baylío, residuo vigente del Derecho celtibérico. Errores de la doctrina y de la jurisprudencia sobre dicho Fuero, *Revista Crítica de Derecho Inmobiliario* I (1): 213–222, 353–363.

Masferrer Domingo, Aniceto. 2001. *La pena de infamia en el derecho histórico español. Contribución al estudio de la tradición penal europea en el marco del "Ius Commune".* Madrid: Dykinson.

Mendibil, Gontzal (ed.). 1999. *Jose Maria Iparragirre: erro-urratsak = raíz y viento.* Vol. 2. Igorre, Bizkaia: Keinu.

Mendoza Garrido, Juan Miguel. 1999. *Delincuencia y represión en la Castilla bajomedieval (los territorios castellano-manchegos).* Granada: Grupo Editorial Universitario.

Merchán Álvarez, Antonio. 1976. *La tutela de los menores en Castilla desde la época hispano-romana hasta fines del siglo XV.* Seville: Servicio de Publicaciones de la Universidad de Sevilla.

Meijers, Eduard Maurits. 1976. *Le Droit Ligurien de succession en Europe Occidental. I. Les Pays Alpins.* Haarlem: H. D. Tjeenk Willink & Son.

Merêa, Manuel Paulo. 1913. *Evoluçao dos regimes matrimoniais.* (2 vols.). Coimbra: Imprensa da Universidade.

————. 1943. Estudos sobre a historia dos regimes matrimoniais, *Boletim da Facultade de Direito portugues* (Coimbra), 18:71–89, 398–408; 19:74–115.

————. 1947. Notas sobre o poder paternal no Direito hispánico occidental durante os séculos XII e XIII, *Anuario de Historia del Derecho español* 18:15–33.

————. 1952a. O dote nos documentos dos séculos IX–XII (Asturias, Leao, Galiza e Portugal). In *Estudos de Direito Hispânico Medieval.* Volume I. Coimbra: Universidade de Coimbra. Pp. 59–138.

————. 1952b. Sobre a palabra "arras". In *Ibidem*, I. Pp. 139–145.

Michelena, Luis. 1968. Aitonen, aitonen seme "noble hijodalgo", *Boletín de la Real Sociedad Bascongada de los Amigos del País* 4:3–18.

Mier Vélez, Ángel de. 1968. *La buena fe en la prescripción y en la costumbre hasta el siglo XV*. Pamplona: Universidad de Navarra.

Minguijón, Salvador. 1960. El Fuero de Baylío. In Pellisé Prats, Buenaventura (ed.), *Nueva Enciclopedia Jurídica Española*. Volume X. Barcelona: Seix. Pp. 301–303.

Monasterio Aspiri, Itziar. 1994. *Los pactos sucesorios en el Derecho vizcaíno*. Bilbo/Bilbao: Diputación Foral de Bizkaia-Instituto de Estudios Vascos. Sección de Derecho Civil.

Monreal Zia, Gregorio. 1973. El Señorío de Vizcaya, origen, naturaleza jurídica. Estructuras institucionales, *Anuario de Historia del Derecho español* 43:113–206.

———. 1974. *Las instituciones públicas del Señorío de Vizcaya (hasta el siglo XVIII)*. Bilbo/Bilbao: Diputación Provincial de Vizcaya.

———. 1985a. Annotations regarding Basque traditional Political Thought in the Sixteenth Century. In Douglass, William A. et alii (ed.), *Basque Politics: A Case Study in Ethnic Nationalism*. Reno, Nevada: Associated Faculty Press and Basque Studies Program. Pp. 19–51.

———. 1985b. Anotaciones para una edición crítica del Fuero de Vizcaya. In Melena José Luis (ed.), *Symbolae Ludovico Mitxelena Septuagenario Oblatae*. Vitoria: Instituto de Ciencias de la Antigüedad. Universidad del País Vasco. Pp. 1203–1212.

Montanos Ferrín, Enma. 1980. *La familia en la Alta Edad Media española*. Pamplona: Universidad de Navarra.

Montanos Ferrín, Enma and José Sánchez-Arcilla. 1990. *Estudios de historia del derecho criminal*. Madrid: Dykinson.

Morales Payán, Miguel Ángel. 1997. *La configuración legislativa del delito de lesiones en el derecho histórico español*. Madrid: Consejería de Educación y Cultura.

Mouton y Ocampo, Luis. [1915?] a. Fuero de troncalidad. In Mouton y Ocampo, Luis (ed.), *Enciclopedia Jurídica Española*. Volume XVI. Barcelona: Francisco Seix. Pp. 731–737.

———. [1915?] b. Fuero de Eviceo. In *Ibidem*, XVI. Pp. 677–680.

Morange, Jean. 2000. Droits de l'homme et libertés politiques. In *Droit fondamental*. París: Presses Univesitaires de France.

Muñoz García, Tomás. 1847. *Colección de Fueros municipales y cartas pueblas de los reinos de Castilla, León, Corona de Aragón y*

*Navarra*. Madrid: Imprenta de D. José María Alonso. [Facsimile edition. 1972. Madrid: Ediciones Atlas].

Naeff, Werner. 1943. *La idea del Estado en la Edad Moderna*. Madrid: Nueva época.

Nieto, Alejandro. 1964. *Bienes comunales*. Madrid: Revista de Derecho privado.

*Obispados de Álava, Guipúzcoa y Vizcaya hasta la erección de la Diócesis de Vitoria (28 de abril de 1862)*. 1964. Vitoria: Eset.

Olmos Herguedas, Emilio. 2001. La imagen de la familia en los textos normativos castellanos. In Iglesia Duarte, José Ignacio de la (ed.), *La familia en la Edad Media. XI Semana de Estudios Medievales*. Logroño: Instituto de Estudios Riojanos. Pp. 471–788.

Orella, José Luis. 1986. La Hermandad de Vizcaya (1320–1498), In Eusko-Ikaskuntza/Sociedad de Estudios Vascos (ed.), *Congreso de Estudios Históricos. Vizcaya en la Edad Media* (1984, Bilbo/Bilbao). Donostia/San Sebastian: Sociedad de Estudios Vascos. Pp. 165–200.

Orlandis Rovira, José. 1942–1943. La prenda como procedimiento coactivo, *Anuario de Historia del Derecho español* 14:81–183.

———. 1944. La paz de la casa en el derecho español de la Alta Edad Media. In *Ibidem*, 15:107–161.

Ortega Galindo de Salcedo, Julio. 1953. *Ensayo sobre los orígenes y naturaleza de Vizcaya*. Bilbo/Bilbao: El Mensajero del Corazón de Jesús.

———. 1965. *Los Caballeros Corregidores del Señorío de Vizcaya (siglos XVII–XVIII)*. Bilbo/Bilbao: Librería Arturo.

Otazu Llana, Alfonso. 1986. *El "igualitarismo" vasco: mito y realidad*. Donostia/San Sebastian: Txertoa.

Otero Varela, Alfonso. 1955. *Dos estudios histórico-jurídicos: el riepto en el Derecho castellano-leonés: la adopción en el Derecho histórico español*. Madrid. Roma: Suc. de Rivadeneyra.

———. 1956. La patria potestad en el Derecho histórico español, *Anuario de Historia del Derecho español* 26:209–241.

Ourliac, Paul. 1953. Las costumbres del Sudoeste de Francia, *Anuario de Historia del Derecho español* 23: 407–422.

———. 1956. La famille pyrénéenne au moyen âge. In Grand, Roger (ed.), *Recueil d'etudes sociales à la memoire de Frédéric Le Play*. Paris: A. et J. Picard. Pp. 257–263.

————. 1958. Les coutumes meridionales et les fueros. Etude de droit français, *Annales de la Faculté de droit de Toulouse* 6(1):49–55

————. 1966. L'evolution de la condition de la femme en Droit français, *Ibidem*, 14(2):43–71.

Pascual López, Silvia. 2001. *La inviolabilidad de domicilio en el Derecho histórico español*. Madrid: Dykinson.

Pascual y Quintana, Juan Manuel. 1955. La desheredación en el Derecho español. Su desenvolvimiento histórico, *Revista de la Facultad de Derecho de Oviedo* XVI(73):227–343.

Pérez Agote, Alfonso. 1972. El contenido penal del Fuero de Vizcaya de 1452, *Estudios vizcaínos* 6:379–390.

Pérez Bustamante, Rogelio. 1992. La communauté de biens en histoire du droit espagnol. In Ganghofer, Roland (ed.), *Le droit de la famille en Europe. Son évolution de l'Antiquité à nos jours*. Strasbourg: Presses Universitaires de Strasbourg. Pp. 541–554.

Pérez de la Canal, Miguel Ángel. 1956. La pragmática de Juan II, de 8 de febrero de 1427, *Anuario de Historia del Derecho español* 26: 659–668.

Pérez de Urbel, Fray Justo. 1972. Vizcaya y Castilla (800–1000), In Real Sociedad Bascongada de los Amigos del País and Diputación Provincial de Vizcaya (eds.), *Edad Media y Señoríos: el Señorío de Vizcaya*. Bilbo/Bilbao: Diputación Provincial de Vizcaya. Pp. 177–203.

Pérez Martín, Antonio. 1984. El Fuero Real y Murcia, *Anuario de Historia del Derecho español* 54:55–96.

Pérez Martín, Antonio and Johannes-Michael Scholz. 1978. *Legislación y jurisprudencia en la España del Antiguo Régimen*. Valencia: Publicaciones de la Universidad de Valencia.

Pérez Prendes, José Manuel. 1989. *Curso de Historia del Derecho español*. (2 vols.) Madrid: Universidad Complutense.

————. 1999. Sobre la prenda extrajudicial, alevosía y riepto, *Interpretatio. Revista de Historia del Derecho* VII(I):719–724.

Petit, Carlos. 1982. Derecho Común y Derecho castellano. Notas de literatura jurídica para su estudio, *Tijdschrift voor Rechtsgeschiedenis* 50:157–195.

Pissard, Hippolyte. 1910. *Essai sur la connaissance et la preuve de la coutume en justice, dans l'ancien droit français et dans le système romano-canonique*. Paris: A. Rousseau.

Planche, Jean de la. 1925. *La réserve coutumiére dans l'ancien droit français.* Paris: Société Anonyme du Recueil Sirey.

Plaza Salazar, Carlos de la. 1899. *Territorios sometidos al Fuero de Vizcaya en lo civil dentro y fuera del Señorío de aquel nombre.* Bilbo/Bilbao: Andrés P. Cardenal.

Poudret, Jean-François. 1987. Réflexions sur la preuve de la coutume devant les jurisdictions royales françaises, notamment le rôle de l'enquête par turbé, en *Revue Historique du Droit* 65:71–86.

Poumaréde, Jacques. 1972. *Géographie coutumière et mutations socials: les successions dans le Sud-Ouest de la France au Moyen Âge.* Paris: Presses Universitaires de France.

Porras Arboledas, Pedro Andrés. 1998. El Fuero de Viceo como régimen económico especial del matrimonio, *Cuadernos de Historia del Derecho* 5:43–126.

Poza, Andrés de. 1981. Ad Pragmáticas de Toro et Tordesillas, manuscrito inédito del Lic. Poza sobre la nobleza de los vascos. In Martín de Retana, José María (ed.), *La Gran Enciclopedia Vasca.* Volume 14. Bilbo/Bilbao: La Gran Enciclopedia Vasca. Pp. 497–679.

Procter, Evelyn S. 1966. The Judicial Use of Pesquisa (Inquisition) in Leon and Castile, (1157–1369). London: Longsman. [Spanish translation. 1978. *El uso judicial de la pesquisa en León y Castilla (1157–1369).* Granada: Universidad].

Puyol Montero, José María. 1997. La abolición de la pena de horca en España, *Cuadernos de Historia del Derecho* 4:91–140.

Quadra Salcedo, Fernando de la. 1916. *Estudios de Derecho. Fuero de la M. N. y L. Encartaciones.* Bilbo/Bilbao: Casa de Misericordia.

Ramos Loscertales, José María. 1951. La tenencia de año y día en el Derecho aragonés, (1063–1247). Colección. *Acta Salmanticensia*, V(1). Salamanca: Facultad de Filosofía y Letras.

Riaza, Román and Alfonso García Gallo. 1934. *Manual de Historia del Derecho español.* Madrid.

Rivero, Jean and Hugues Moutouh. 2003. *Les libertés publiques.* (9th ed.). Collection Themis. Paris: Presses Universitaires de France.

Roberti, Melchiorre. 1919. *Le origini romano cristiane della comunione dei beni fra coniugi.* Turin: Fratelli Bocca.

Rodríguez Gil, Magdalena. 2000. Consideraciones sobre una antigua polémica: las iglesias propias, *Cuadernos de Historia del Derecho español* 7:247–272.

Rodríguez Mourullo, Gonzalo. 1962. La distinción hurto-robo en el derecho histórico español, *Anuario de Historia del Derecho español* 32:25–111.

Rodríguez Herrero, Ángel. 1972. El Fuero de Vizcaya a través de las Instituciones políticas de la España medieval. In Real Sociedad Bascongada de los Amigos del País and Diputación Provincial de Vizcaya (eds.), *Edad Media y Señoríos: el Señorío de Vizcaya*. Bilbo/Bilbao: Diputación Provincial de Vizcaya. Pp. 141–153.

Roldán Verdejo, Roberto. 1978. *Los delitos contra la vida en los fueros de Castilla y León*. La Laguna: Facultad de Derecho, Universidad de La Laguna.

Rubio Sacristán, José Antonio. 1932. "Donationes post obitum" y "donationes reservato usufructo" en la Alta Edad Media de León y Castilla, *Anuario de Historia del Derecho español* 9:1–32.

Ruiz Funes, Manuel. 1934. Progresión histórica de la pena de muerte en España, *Revista de Derecho Público* 3:193–225

Sáinz de Varanda, Ramón. 1947–1948. El retracto gentilicio, *Anuario de Derecho Aragonés* 4:223–335.

Sainz Guerra, Juan. 1998. Hurtadores, ladrones, descuideros y robadores. In Sainz Guerra, Juan et alii (ed.), *Actas de las III Jornadas de Historia del Derecho. "La aplicación del Derecho a lo largo de la historia"* (1997, Jaen). Jaen: Universidad. Pp. 95–128.

Sánchez, Galo. 1917. Datos jurídicos acerca de la venganza del honor, *Revista de Filología Española* 4:292–299.

———. 1926. Algunas observaciones para la historiografía del Derecho penal. In Cuello Calón, Eugenio (ed.), *Derecho penal. Parte General* Barcelona: Ángel Ortega.

Sánchez Albornoz, Claudio. 1929. Divisiones tribales y administrativas del solar del reino de Asturias en la época romana, *Boletín de la Real Academia de la Historia*, 95: 315–395. [Published also in 1972. *Orígenes de la Nación Española. El Reino de Asturias*. I. Oviedo: Inst. de Estudios Asturianos. Pp. 51–100].

Sánchez Arcilla, José. 1986. Notas para el estudio del homicidio en el derecho histórico español, *Revista de la Facultad de Derecho de la Universidad Complutense de Madrid* 72:513–571.

Sarrablo, Eugenio. 1954. La sucesión en el Fuero de Vizcaya, *Revista de la Facultad de Derecho de la Universidad de Madrid* III(11):325–345.

Sayas Abengoechea, Juan José. 1999. De vascones a romanos para volver a ser vascones, *Revista Internacional para los Estudios Vascos* 44(1):147–184.

Serra Ruiz, Rafael. 1969. *Honor e injuria en el Derecho medieval español*. Murcia: Departamento Historia del Derecho, Universidad de Murcia.

Serrano, Luciano. 1941. *Orígenes del Señorío de Vizcaya en épocas anteriores al siglo XIII*. Bilbo/Bilbao: Junta de Cultura de Vizcaya.

Solano y Polanco, José de. 1918. *Estudios jurídicos del Fuero de Vizcaya*. Bilbo/Bilbao: Diputación de Vizcaya.

Soria Sesé, Lourdes. 2002. Bienes comunales en Navarra y las Provincias vascas (siglos XVI–XVII). In Dios, Salustiano and Javier Infante, Ricardo Robledo and Eugenia Torijano, *Historia de la propiedad en España. Bienes comunales*. Madrid: Colegio de la Propiedad y Mercantiles de España. Pp. 101–137.

S. P. 1883. Apuntes sobre las limitaciones que según Fuero de Vizcaya tiene la facultad de disponer de los bienes raíces de Infanzonado, *Revista General de Legislación y Jurisprudencia* 62:431–441.

Stone, Marilyn. 1990. *Marriage and Friendship in Medieval Spain: Social Relations According to the Fourth Partida of Alfonso X*. New York: P. Lang.

Strayer, Joseph R. 1981. *Sobre los orígenes medievales del Estado moderno*. Barcelona: Ariel.

Suárez Fernández, Luis. 1959. *Navegación y comercio en el Golfo de Vizcaya*. Madrid: Consejo Superior de Investigaciones Científicas.

Schwarz-Lieberman von Walhendorf, Hans Albrecht. 1977. *Introduction à l'esprit et à l'histoire du droit anglais*. Paris: L. G. D. J.

Terrón Albarrán, Manuel and Alberto Muro Castillo. 1977. Origen histórico del Fuero de Baylío. In Asamblea de Extremadura (ed.), *Jornadas sobre el Fuero de Baylío. Anuario de Ciencia Jurídica y Sociología de la Asamblea de Extremadura*. Caceres: Asamblea de Extremadura. Pp. 13–40.

Tomás y Valiente, Francisco. 1982. Introducción, notas y traducción. In Beccaria, Cesare, *De los delitos y de las penas*. Madrid: Aguilar. Pp. IX–XLI.

———. 1988. El pensamiento jurídico. In Artola, Miguel (ed.), *Enciclopedia de Historia de España. III. Pensamiento. Cultura*. Madrid: Alianza. Pp. 327–408.

―――. 1997a. El perdón de la parte ofendida en el Derecho penal castellano (siglos XVI, XVII y XVIII). In *Obras completas*. Volume IV. Madrid: Centro de Estudios Políticos y Constitucionales. Pp. 2885–2933.

―――. 1997b. La tortura en España. In *Ibidem*, I: Pp. 757–912.

Torres López, Manuel. 1928. El origen del sistema de "iglesias propias", *Anuario de Historia del Derecho español* 5:83–217.

―――. 1933. Naturaleza jurídico-penal y procesal del desafío y riepto en León y Castilla, *Ibidem* 10:161–174.

Torres Sanz, David. 1990. Sobre el Estado Moderno en España. In Tamayo Salaberría, Virginia (ed.), *De la Res publica a los Estados Modernos*. Bilbo/Bilbao: Servicio Editorial de la Universidad del País Vasco. Pp. 165–175.

Tovar, Antonio. 1959. *El Euskera y sus parientes*. Madrid: Minotauro.

Ubieto Arteta, Antonio. 1961. *Crónica de Alfonso III*. Valencia: Gráficas Bautista.

―――. 1972. Problemas en torno al Conde Momo de Bizkaia. In Real Sociedad Bascongada de los Amigos del País and Diputación Provincial de Vizcaya (eds.), *Edad Media y Señoríos: el Señorío de Vizcaya*. Bilbo/Bilbao: Diputación Provincial de Vizcaya. Pp. 163–173.

Unamuno, Miguel de. 1925. Prólogo. *Bocetos de un viaje a través del País Vasco*. In Sociedad de Estudios Vascos, *Guillermo de Humboldt y el País Vasco*. Donostia/San Sebastian: Imprenta de la Diputación de Guipúzcoa. Pp. 293–294.

Urena y Smenjaud, Rafael de. 2003. *El Fuero de Cuenca*. {Facsimile edition of that published in 1936 in Madrid by the Real Academia de la Historia}. Cuenca: Servicio de Publicaciones de la Universidad de Castilla-La Mancha.

Uriarte Lebario, Luis María de. 1912. *El Fuero de Ayala*. Madrid: Imprenta de Hijos de M. G. Hernández. [Reprint. 1974. Vitoria: Diputación Foral de Álava].

Val Valdivielso, Isabel del. 1986. La solidaridad familiar en Vizcaya en el siglo XV. Eusko-Ikaskuntza/Sociedad de Estudios Vascos (ed.), *Congreso de Estudios Históricos*. Vizcaya en la Edad Media (1984, Bilbo/Bilbao). Donostia/San Sebastian: Sociedad de Estudios Vascos. Pp. 333–337.

Vicario de la Peña, Nicolás. 1901. *Derecho consuetudinario de Vizcaya*. Madrid: Asilo de Huérfanos del Sagrado Corazón de Jesús.

Wesenberg, Gerhard and Gunter Wesener. 1998. *Historia del Derecho privado en Alemania y en Europa*. Valladolid: Lex Nova.

Wieaker, Franz A. 1995. *History of Private Law in Europe*. Oxford: Clarendon Press.

Wordsworth, William. 1892. *The Complete Poetical Works of William Wordsworth*. Introduction by John Morley. New York: Thomas Y. Crowell and Co.

Zink, Anne. 1993. *L'héritier de la maison. Géographie coutumière du Sud-Ouest de la France sous l'Ancien Régime*. París: Editions de l'Ecole des Hautes Etudes en Sciences Sociales.

# Index

House, as marriage gift, 215
— arrest, 198
— arson of, 187
Huidro text, 144
Humanist, 29
Humboldt, Wilhelm von, 16
Hunting, under the New Law, 146
— rights of *hidalgos*, 290
Hurtado de Mendoça, Juan, 164, 291
Husband, 120
— crimes of, 224
— debts of, 224–225
— marriage gift, 215–216

Ibaizabal River, 23–24
Ibáñez de Aloeta, Pero, 45–46, 48
Ibáñez de Alviz, Pero, 42
Ibáñez de Garaunaga, Martín, 42, 292
Ibáñez de Salazar, Pero, 292
Ibargüen, Juan de, 294
Ibarra, 44
Iberia, 18, 120–121, 134
— Península, 24, 30, 76, 78, 132–133, 150
Identity, political, 73
Idoibalzaga, General Assembly of, 40–42, 78, 292
*Iglesia de patronato see* Patronages
Iglesia Duarte, José Ignacio, 297, 315
*Iglesia propia see* Patronages
Iglesias Ferreirós, Aquilino, 150, 157, 308
*Iglesias juraderas* (church for oath-taking), 83
Illegitimacy, 123
— offspring of clerics, 119
Immovable Property *see* Property, immovable
Impunity, 288
Incest, 98

Income, from pledged property for its owner, 213
Indecency, 105
Indemnification, 103
Individual, 16, 80, 114
Indo-Europeans, 21
*In fraganti*, 88
Infante, Javier, 319
*Infante* (successor to the throne), 85
*Infanzonazgo*, (Noble Land), 61. *See also Hidalgo(s)*
*Infanzones see Hidalgo(s)*
Inheritance, concept of, 126–127
— division of property among close kinsmen, 134, 209, 219, 228
— exclusion of legitimate heirs, 131
— forced succession in Bizkaia, 159
Íñiguez de Ibargüen, Fortún, 41–42, 45, 56, 141, 292
Inquiry *see Pesquisa*
Institute of Basque Studies, 8, 50, 145
Instituto de Estudios Vascos, *see* Institute of Basque Studies
Insults, 102, 184
*Inter vivos* succession, 114, 232–234
Investigation, 192, 199
Iparragirre, José María, 18
Iparralde, 21
Iron foundries *see* Foundries
Iron ore, 81, 98, 177
— buying and selling of, 99, 177
Iruña, 13
Isábal, Marceliano, 160, 308
Isabella, Catholic, 144
Italy, 121
Iturriza y Zabala, Juan Ramón de, 153–155, 308
*Ius commune*, 53
*Ius recadentiae*, 134. *See* Principle of truncality
Izurtza, 96

— milling of grain, 104
— new wheels, 245, 247
Minguijón, Salvador, 158, 314
Minority/majority, age of 18, 105
— and wardship, 126, 231–232
— rights and obligations of minors
  in property once attain majority
  age, 261–263
Miraballes, 24, 85, 155
Miravalles *see* Miraballes
*Miserabiles personae*, 111
Modernity, of Kingdom of Castilla,
  31
— of Old Law, 14–16
— state concept, 150
Momo, 73
*Monasterio see* Patronages
Monasterio Aspiri, Itziar, 50, 158,
  314
Moninho (Munio), 70
Monreal Zia, Gregorio, 149, 151,
  153–155, 314
Montanos Ferrín, Enma, 156–157,
  314
Moors, 14, 40, 43, 59, 71, 97, 146,
  166, 285
— prohibition on their residence in
  Bizkaia, 146
— war with, 97, 166
Morales Payán, Miguel Ángel, 156,
  314
Morange, Jean, 154, 314
Moro, Gonzalo, 7, 35–38, 45, 47,
  50–51, 64, 77, 80, 85, 88, 91, 99,
  101, 105, 139–140, 150–151
Mortgage(s), 116–117
— right of consanguineal kinsmen
  to acquire, 116–117
*Mortis causa*, 114
*Mos Gallicus*, 29
Mourning, 147
Mouton Ocampu, Luis, 158–159,
  308, 314
Moutouh, Hugues, 154, 317

Movable property *see* Property,
  movable
Múgica, Juan Alfonso de, 43
Mugueta Moreno, Iñigo, 303
Mules, and damage to another's
  property, 237
Muleteers, 283
Mungia, 24, 155
Munguía, *see* Mungia
Municipal assembly, 88
Municipal *Fuero*, 31
*Municipios rurales see* Anteiglesia
Muñoz García, Tomás, 150, 314
Murcia, 30
Murélaga, 46
Muro Castillo, Castillo, 158, 319
Mussulmans, 22. *See* Moors
Muxica, Juan Alfonso de, 165

Naeff, Werner, 150, 315
Nafarroa *see* Navarra
National Historical Archive
  (Madrid), 44–45
National Library, 44
Natural Law School, 113
Navarra, 7, 13, 22–23, 55, 60–61, 72,
  75–77, 79, 84, 90, 117, 127–128,
  131–132, 156
— Kingdom of, 22–23, 55, 60–61, 72,
  76, 77, 79, 84, 90, 117, 127–128, 131
— law, 131–132, 156
Navarra, University of, 156
*Nemo ius ignorare censetur*, 39
Nerbioi River, 23–24
Nervión River, 23–24
New Law 48, 57, 63, 137, 141–144
— as revision of Old Law, 142–144
— editions of, 144–145
— inventory of, 145
— reasons for, 141
— redaction of, 142–144
Nieto, Alejandro, 154, 315
*Ninguno non responda sin
  quereloso*, 104